HER Royal Highness seems to be angry

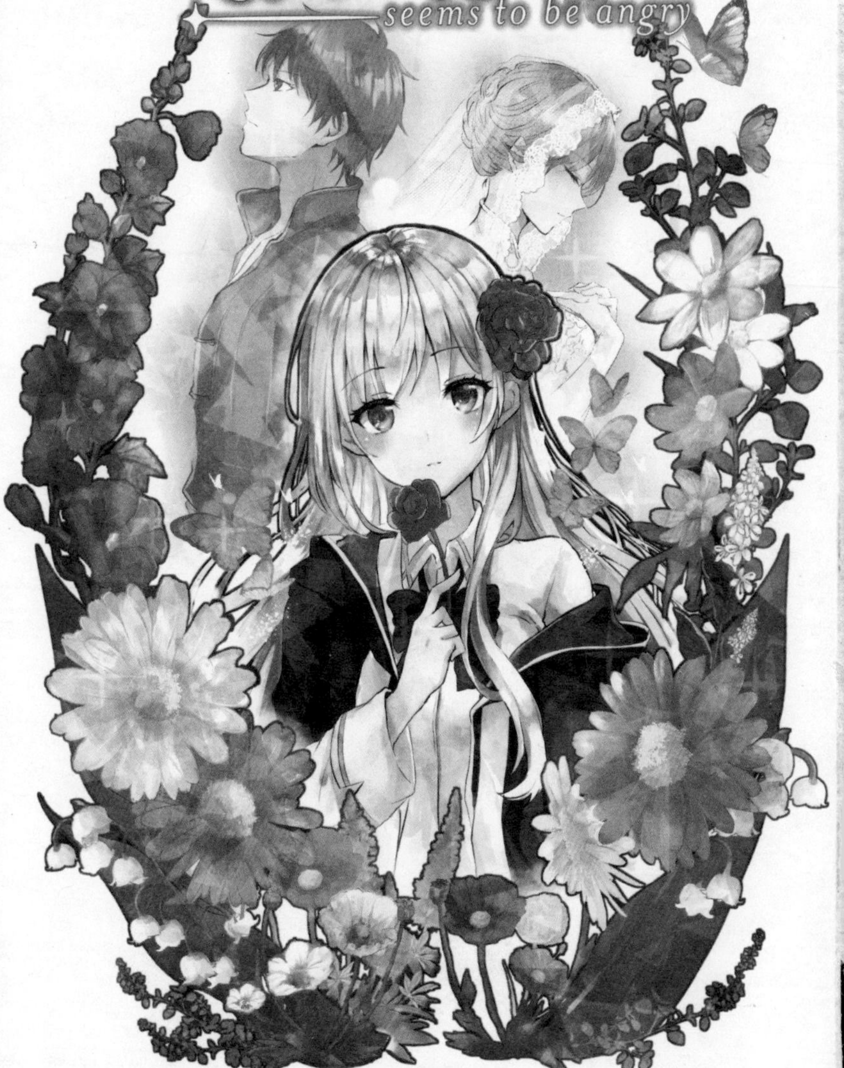

1

tsuba

aracter Design: Mito Nagashiro

CONTENTS

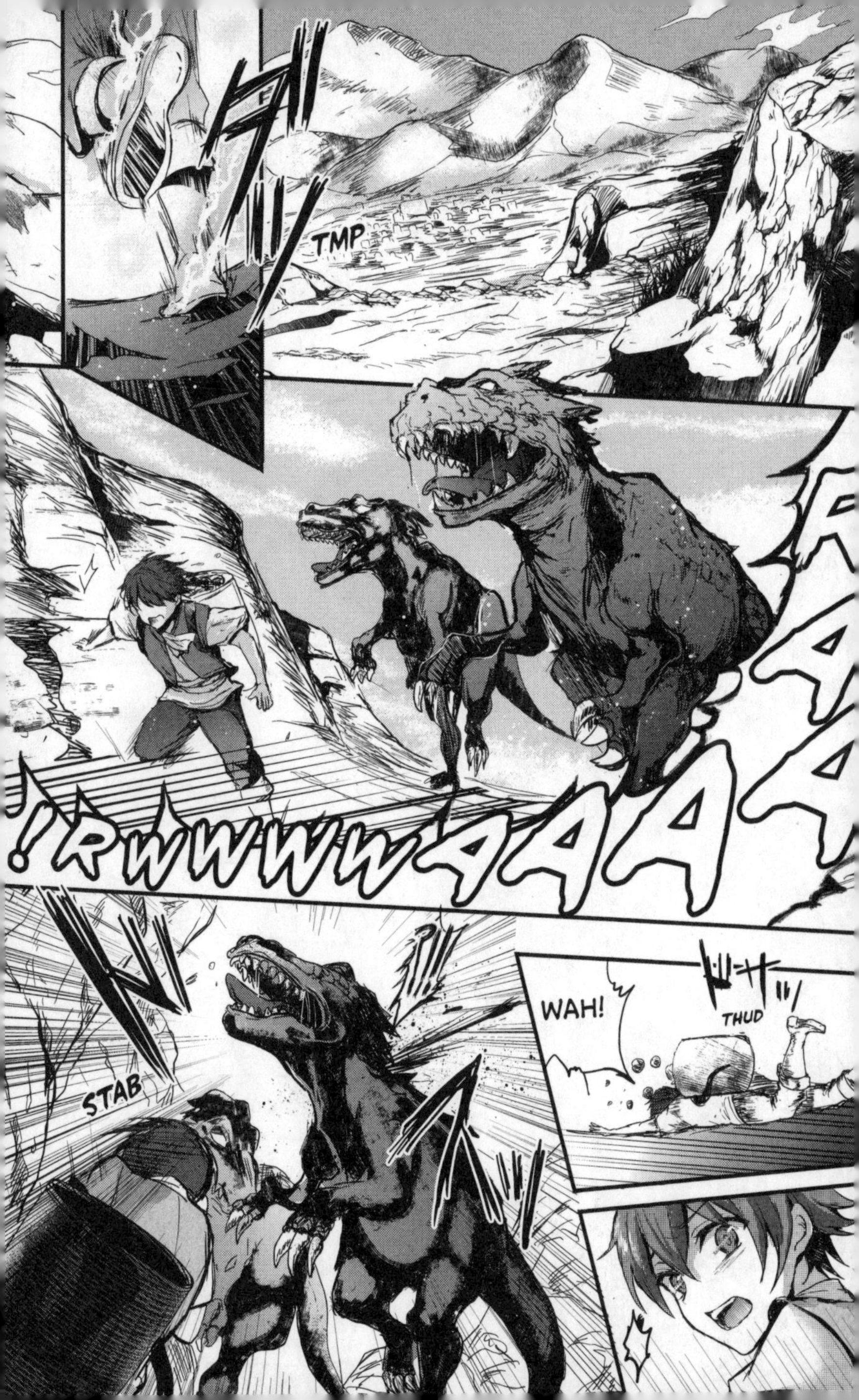
TMP
!RWWWWWAAAA
WAH!
THUD
STAB

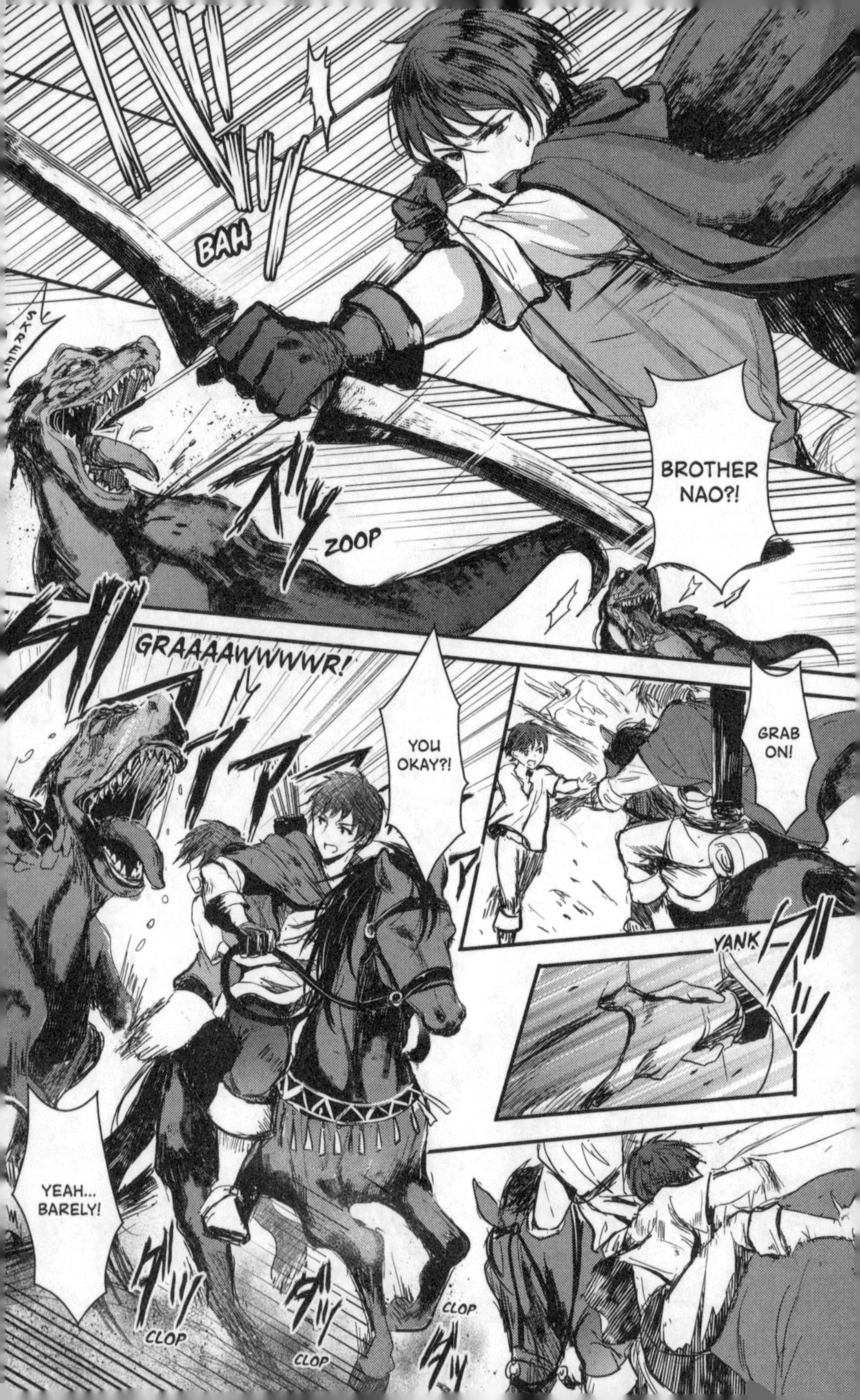
BAH
BROTHER NAO?!
SKREE
ZOOP
GRAB ON!
YANK
CLOP
GRAAAAWWWWR!
YOU OKAY?!
YEAH... BARELY!
CLOP
CLOP

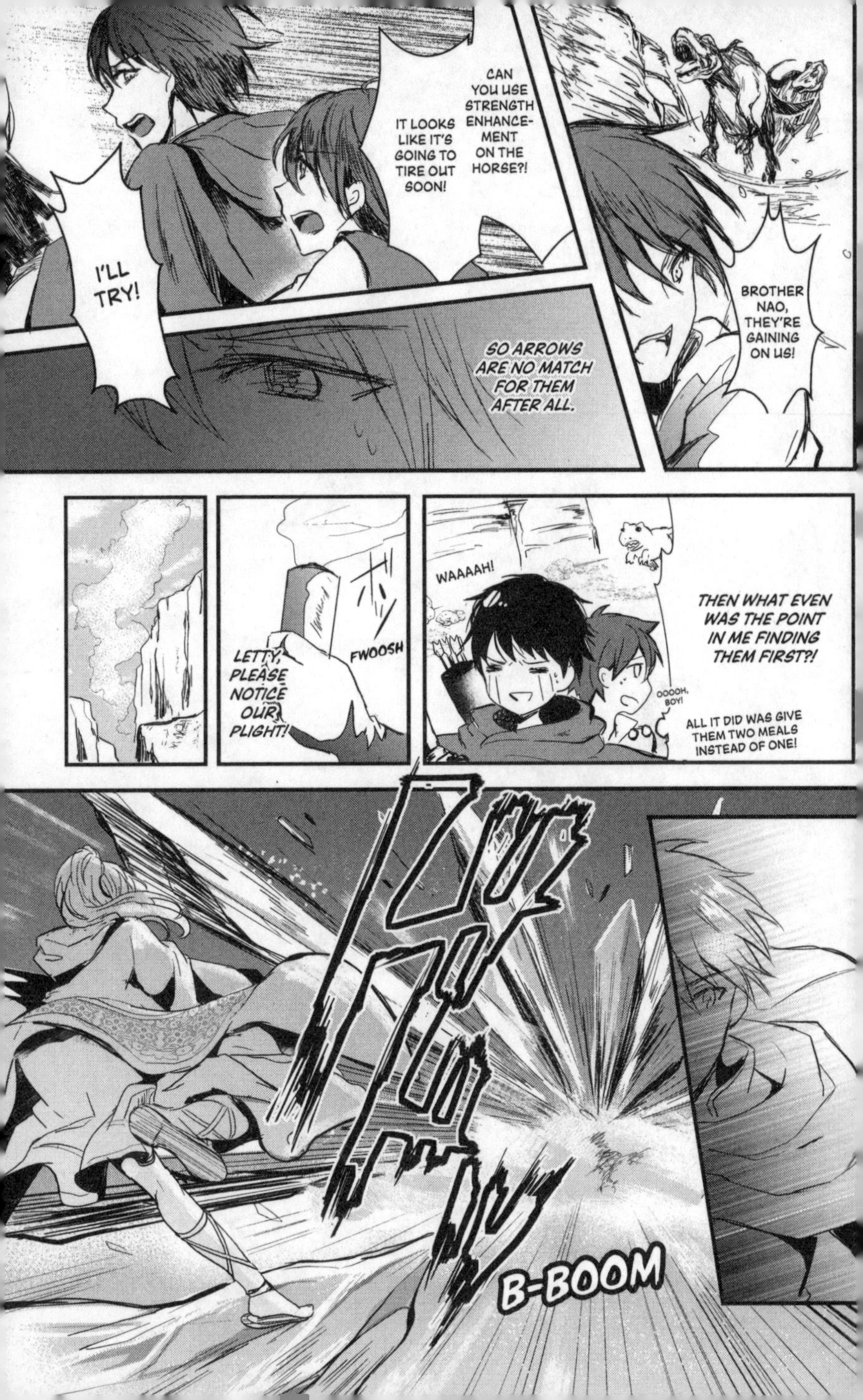
BROTHER NAO, THEY'RE GAINING ON US!
CAN YOU USE STRENGTH ENHANCEMENT ON THE HORSE?!
IT LOOKS LIKE IT'S GOING TO TIRE OUT SOON!
I'LL TRY!
SO ARROWS ARE NO MATCH FOR THEM AFTER ALL.
THEN WHAT EVEN WAS THE POINT IN ME FINDING THEM FIRST?!
WAAAAH!
OOOOH, BOY!
ALL IT DID WAS GIVE THEM TWO MEALS INSTEAD OF ONE!
FWOOSH
LETTY, PLEASE NOTICE OUR PLIGHT!
B-BOOM

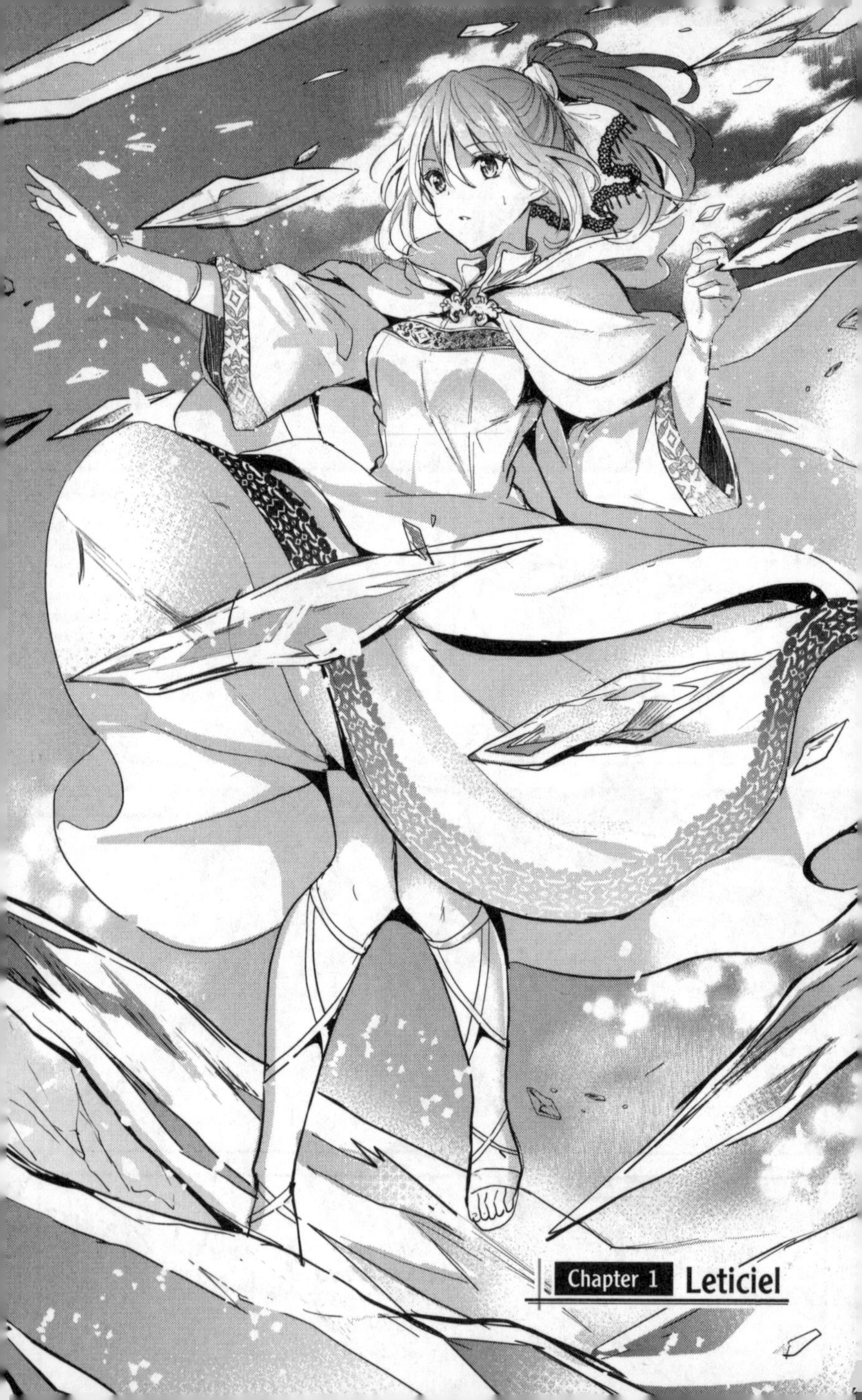

Chapter 1 Leticiel

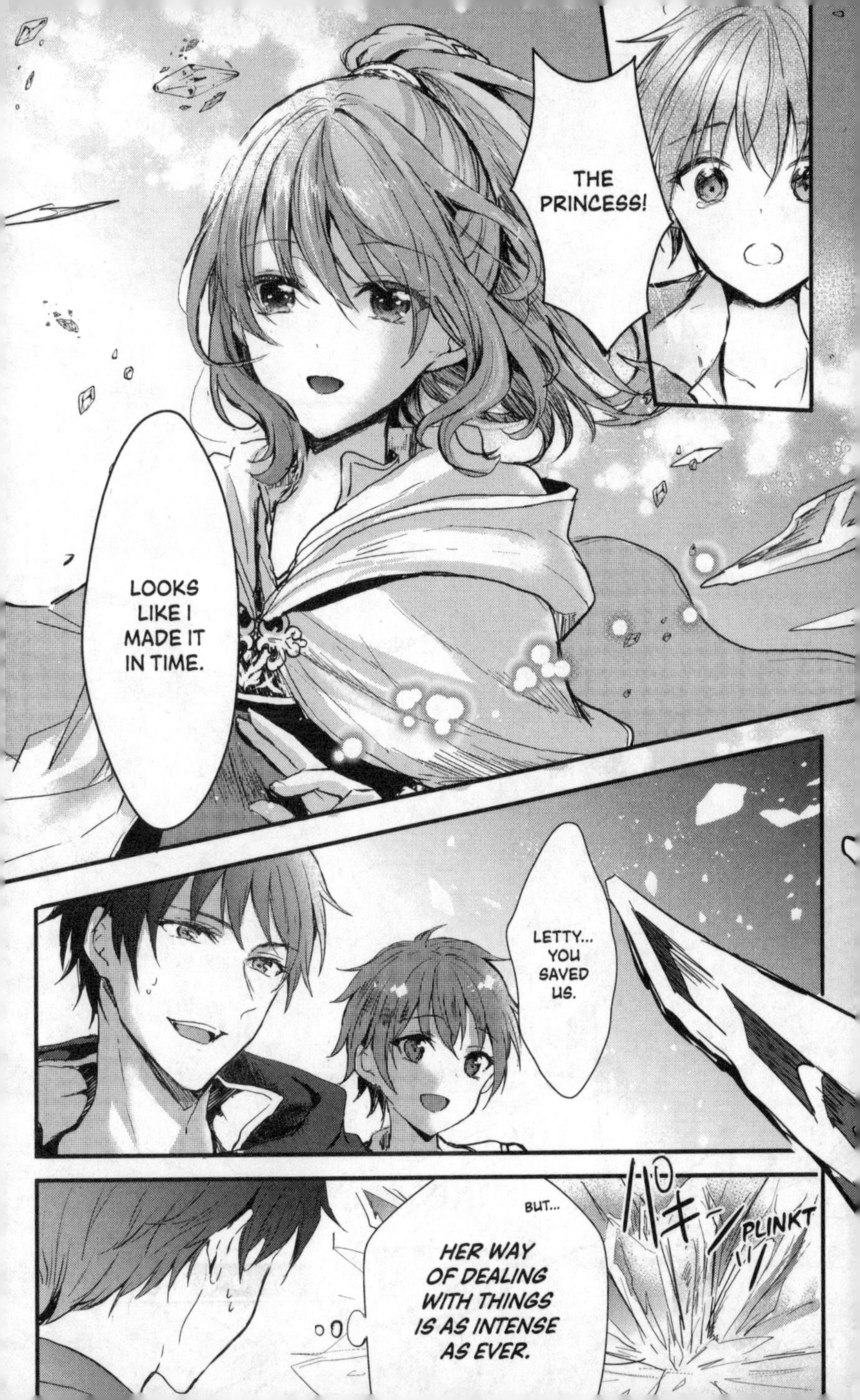
THE PRINCESS!
LOOKS LIKE I MADE IT IN TIME.
LETTY... YOU SAVED US.
PLINKT
BUT...
HER WAY OF DEALING WITH THINGS IS AS INTENSE AS EVER.

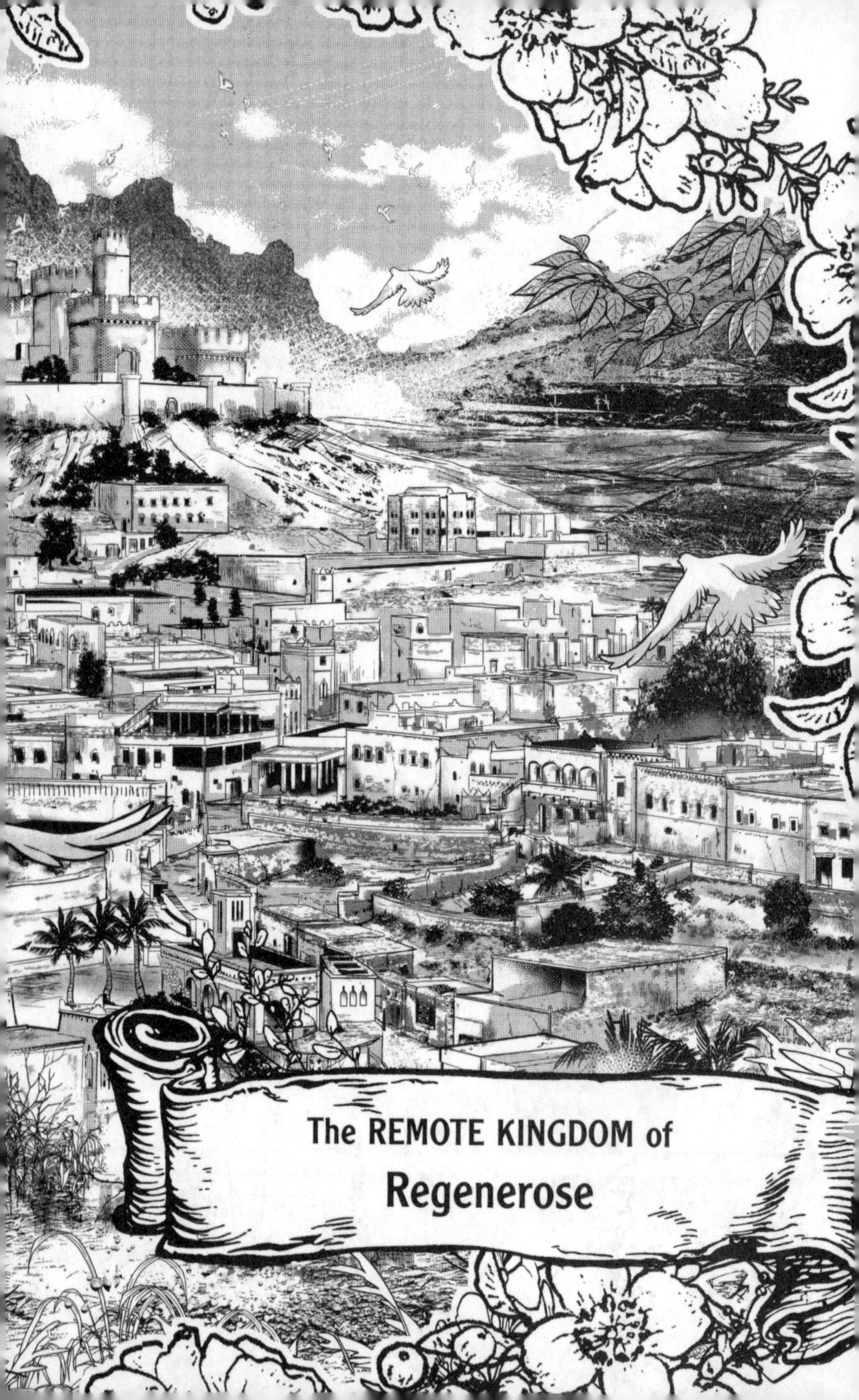
The REMOTE KINGDOM of
Regenerose

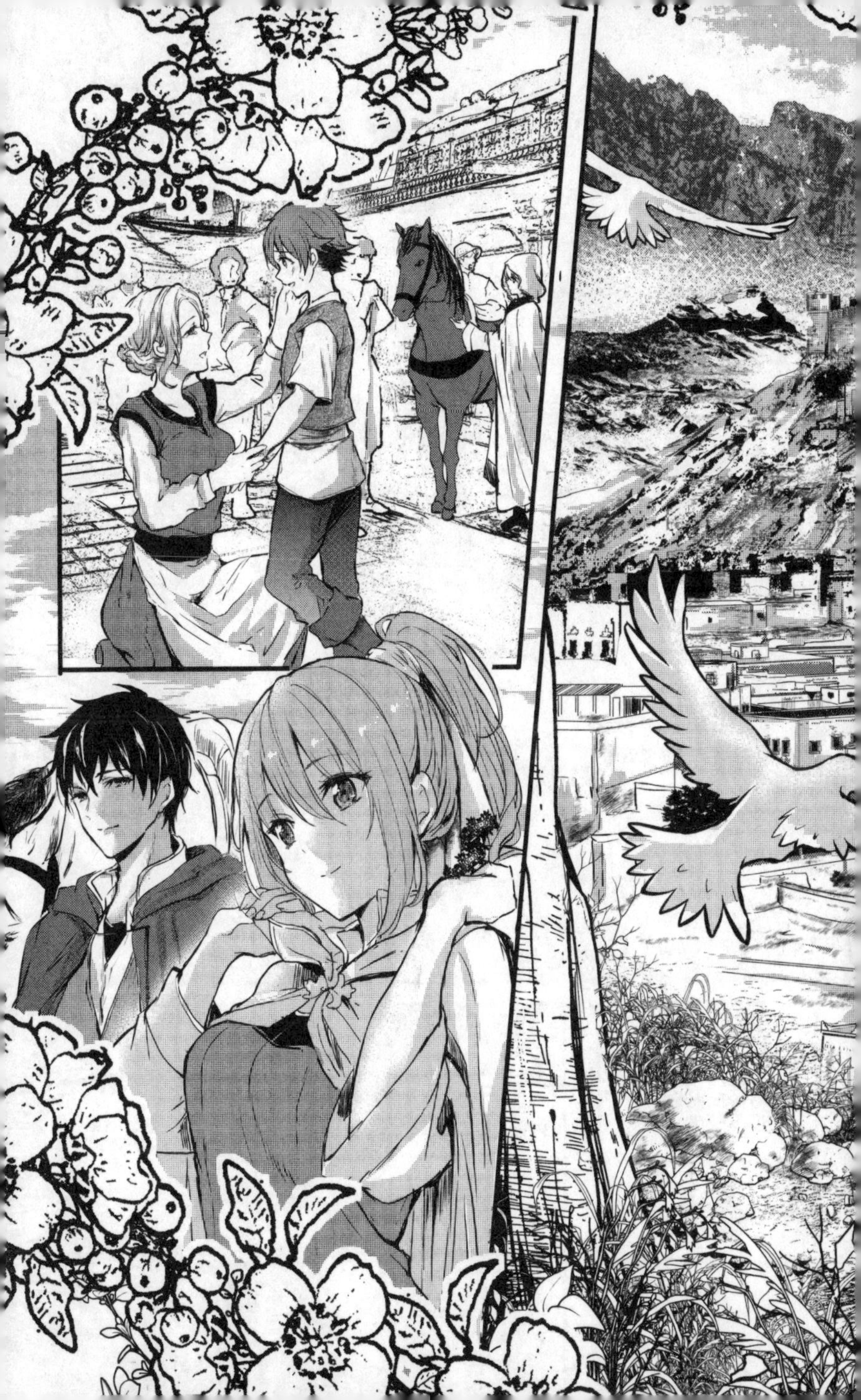

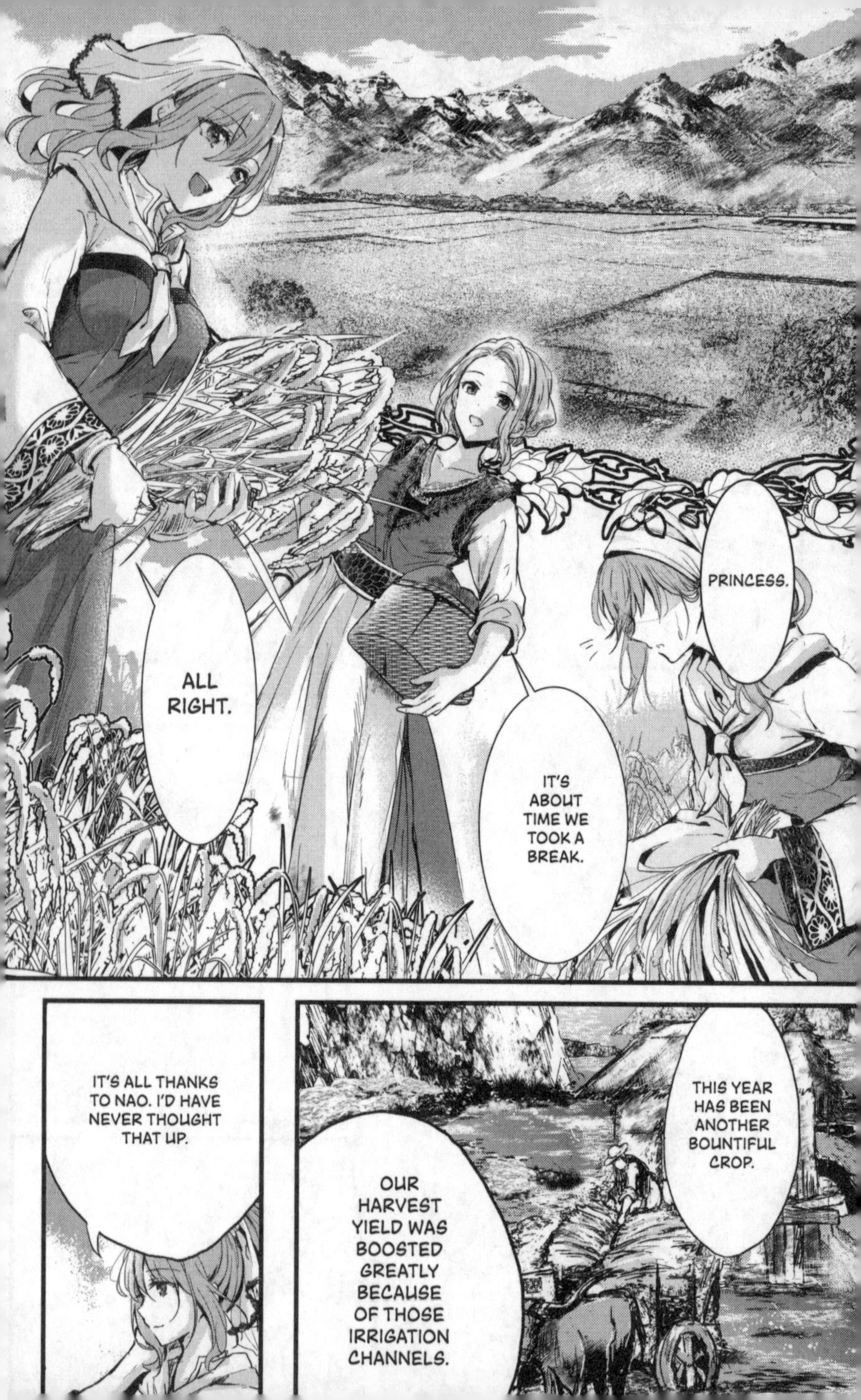
PRINCESS.
IT'S ABOUT TIME WE TOOK A BREAK.
ALL RIGHT.
THIS YEAR HAS BEEN ANOTHER BOUNTIFUL CROP.
OUR HARVEST YIELD WAS BOOSTED GREATLY BECAUSE OF THOSE IRRIGATION CHANNELS.
IT'S ALL THANKS TO NAO. I'D HAVE NEVER THOUGHT THAT UP.

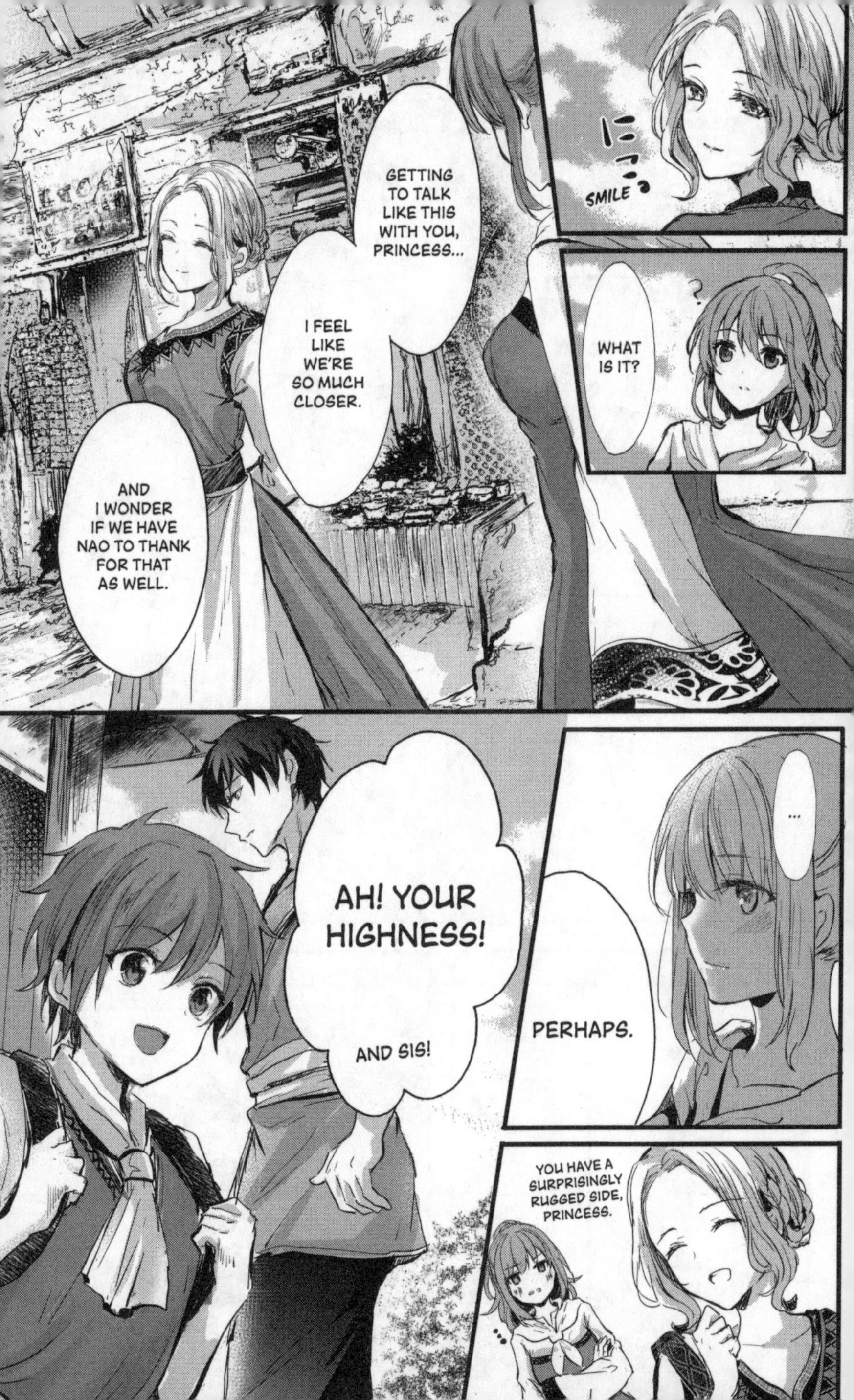
にこっ
SMILE
WHAT IS IT?
GETTING TO TALK LIKE THIS WITH YOU, PRINCESS...
I FEEL LIKE WE'RE SO MUCH CLOSER.
AND I WONDER IF WE HAVE NAO TO THANK FOR THAT AS WELL.
...
PERHAPS.
YOU HAVE A SURPRISINGLY RUGGED SIDE, PRINCESS.
...
AH! YOUR HIGHNESS!
AND SIS!

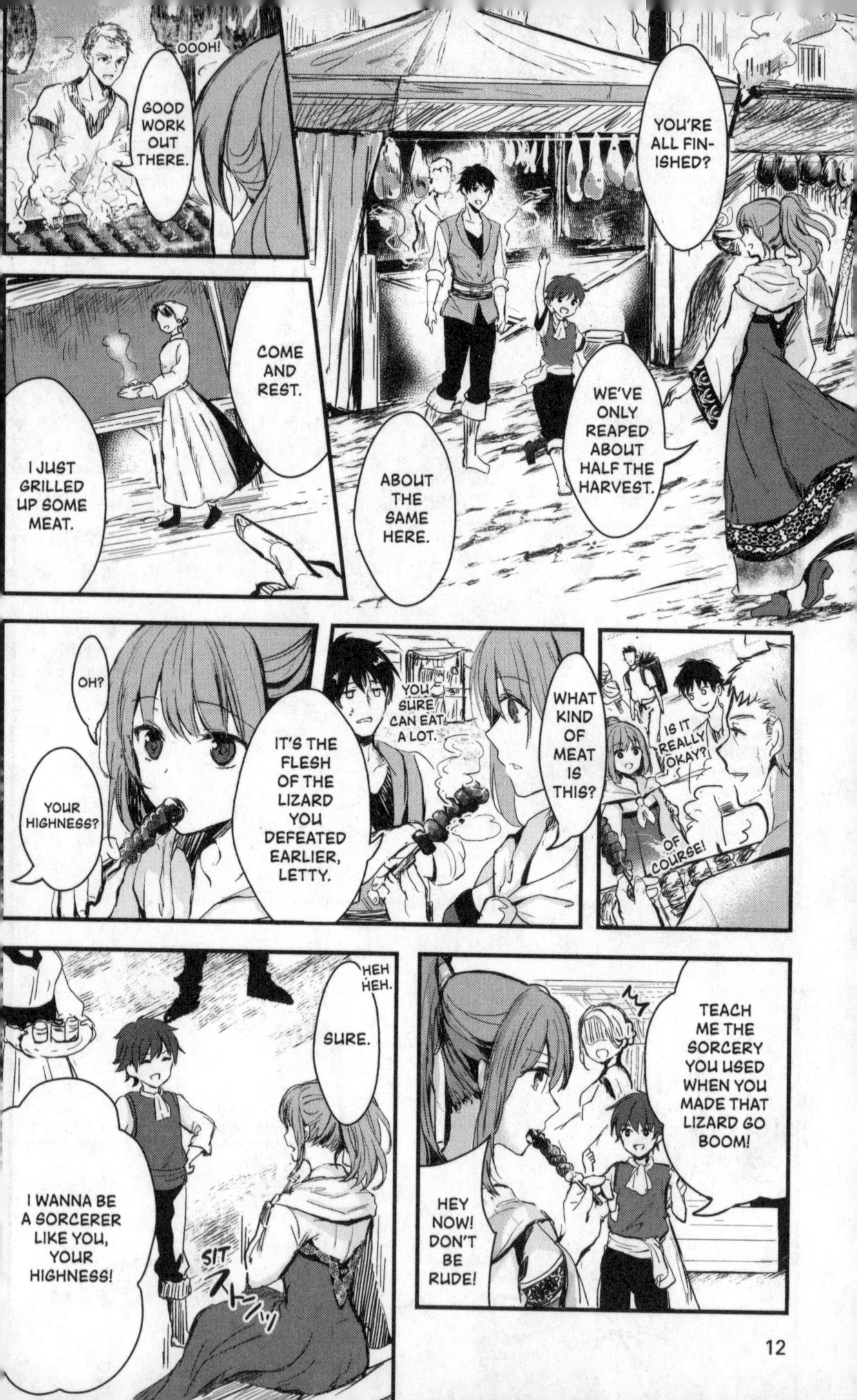

YOU'RE ALL FIN-ISHED?
WE'VE ONLY REAPED ABOUT HALF THE HARVEST.
ABOUT THE SAME HERE.
OOOH!
GOOD WORK OUT THERE.
COME AND REST.
I JUST GRILLED UP SOME MEAT.
IS IT REALLY OKAY?
OF COURSE!
WHAT KIND OF MEAT IS THIS?
IT'S THE FLESH OF THE LIZARD YOU DEFEATED EARLIER, LETTY.
YOU SURE CAN EAT A LOT.
OH?
YOUR HIGHNESS?
TEACH ME THE SORCERY YOU USED WHEN YOU MADE THAT LIZARD GO BOOM!
HEY NOW! DON'T BE RUDE!
HEH HEH.
SURE.
I WANNA BE A SORCERER LIKE YOU, YOUR HIGHNESS!
SIT

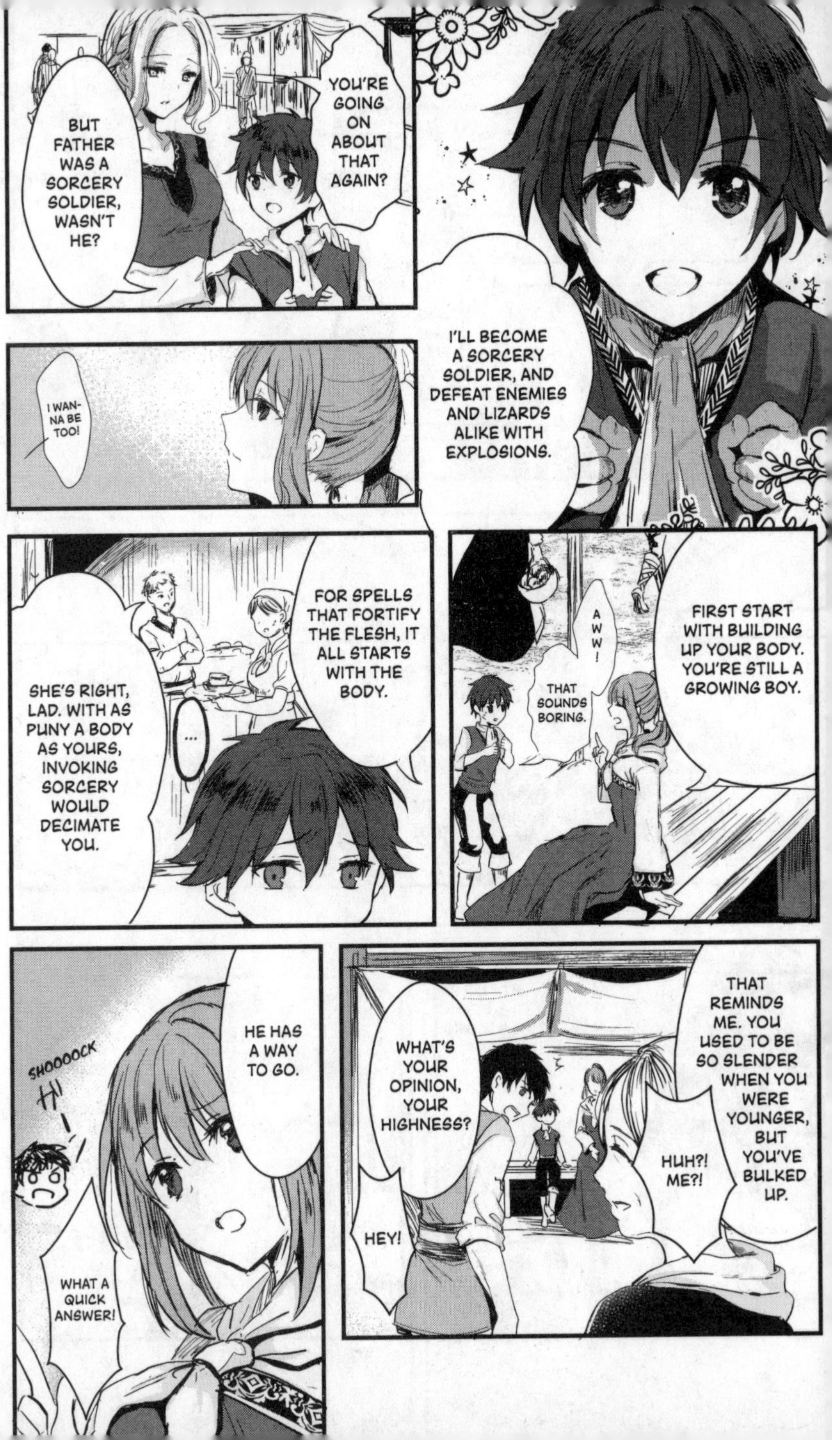
I'LL BECOME A SORCERY SOLDIER, AND DEFEAT ENEMIES AND LIZARDS ALIKE WITH EXPLOSIONS.
YOU'RE GOING ON ABOUT THAT AGAIN?
BUT FATHER WAS A SORCERY SOLDIER, WASN'T HE?
I WAN-NA BE TOO!
FIRST START WITH BUILDING UP YOUR BODY. YOU'RE STILL A GROWING BOY.
AWW!
THAT SOUNDS BORING.
FOR SPELLS THAT FORTIFY THE FLESH, IT ALL STARTS WITH THE BODY.
...
SHE'S RIGHT, LAD. WITH AS PUNY A BODY AS YOURS, INVOKING SORCERY WOULD DECIMATE YOU.
THAT REMINDS ME. YOU USED TO BE SO SLENDER WHEN YOU WERE YOUNGER, BUT YOU'VE BULKED UP.
HUH?! ME?!
WHAT'S YOUR OPINION, YOUR HIGHNESS?
HEY!
HE HAS A WAY TO GO.
SHOOOOCK
WHAT A QUICK ANSWER!

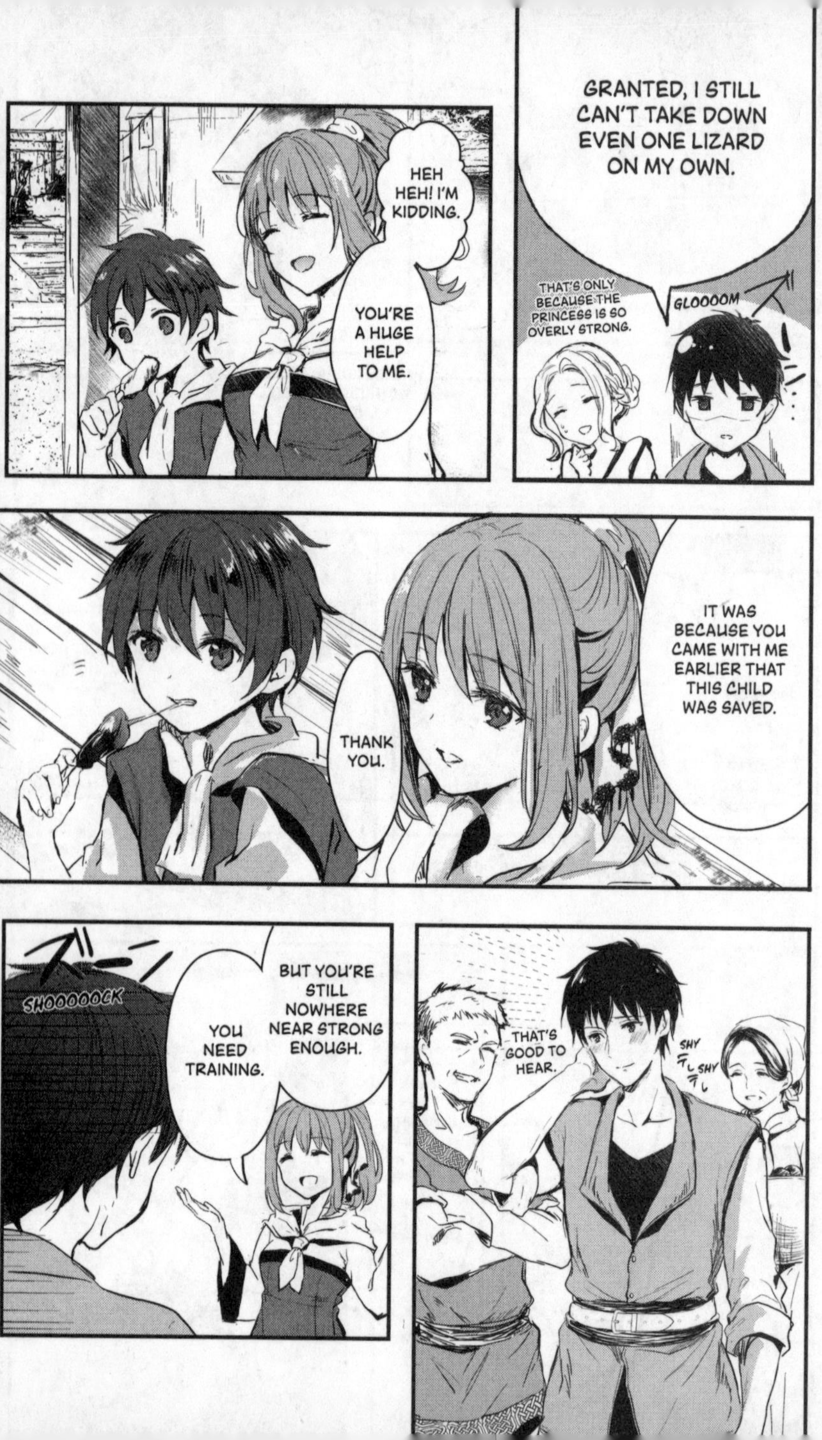
GRANTED, I STILL CAN'T TAKE DOWN EVEN ONE LIZARD ON MY OWN.
GLOOOOM
THAT'S ONLY BECAUSE THE PRINCESS IS SO OVERLY STRONG.
HEH HEH! I'M KIDDING.
YOU'RE A HUGE HELP TO ME.
IT WAS BECAUSE YOU CAME WITH ME EARLIER THAT THIS CHILD WAS SAVED.
THANK YOU.
THAT'S GOOD TO HEAR.
SHY SHY
BUT YOU'RE STILL NOWHERE NEAR STRONG ENOUGH.
YOU NEED TRAINING.
SHOOOOOCK

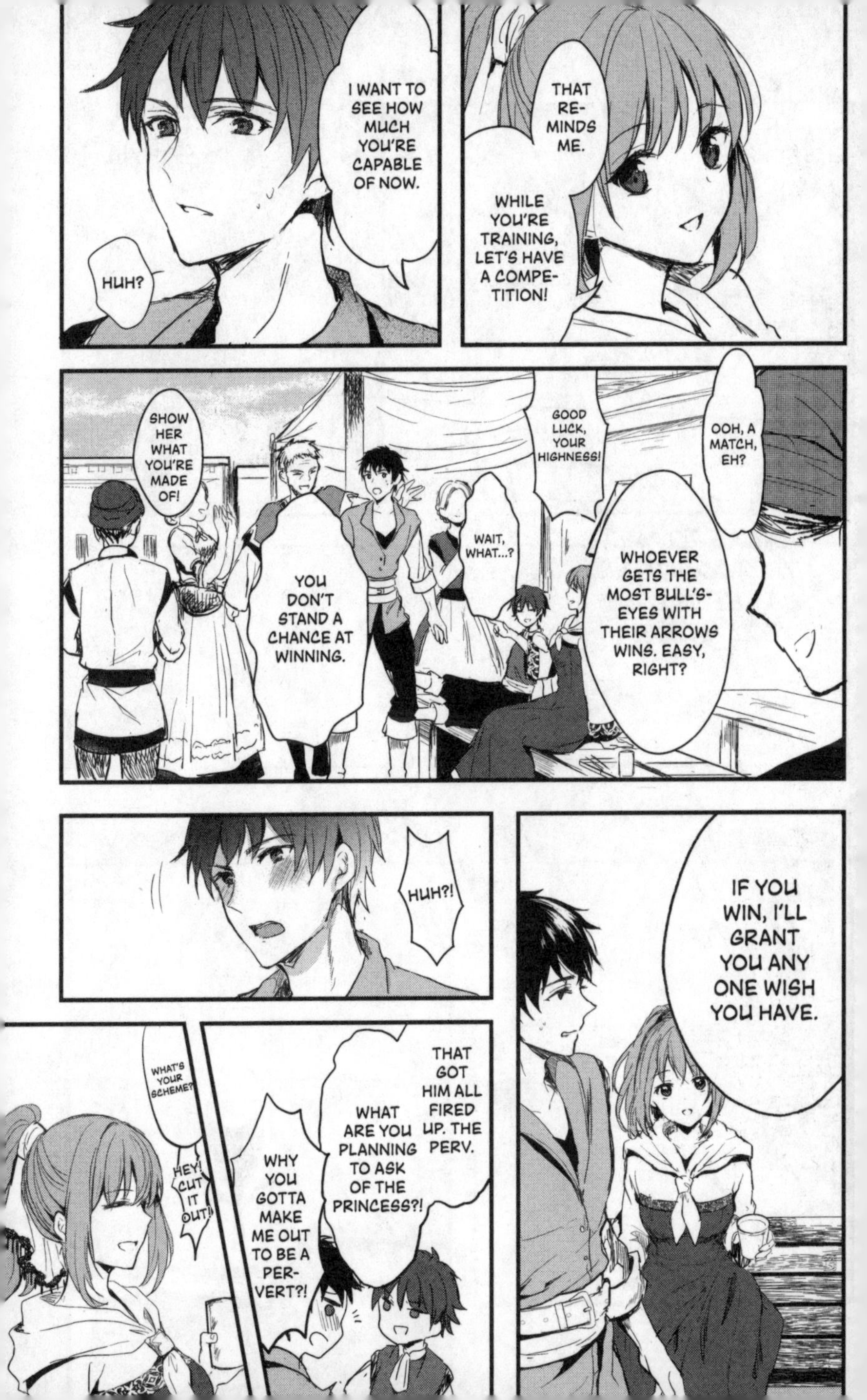
THAT RE- MINDS ME.
WHILE YOU'RE TRAINING, LET'S HAVE A COMPE- TITION!
I WANT TO SEE HOW MUCH YOU'RE CAPABLE OF NOW.
HUH?
OOH, A MATCH, EH?
GOOD LUCK, YOUR HIGHNESS!
WHOEVER GETS THE MOST BULL'S-EYES WITH THEIR ARROWS WINS. EASY, RIGHT?
WAIT, WHAT...?
SHOW HER WHAT YOU'RE MADE OF!
YOU DON'T STAND A CHANCE AT WINNING.
IF YOU WIN, I'LL GRANT YOU ANY ONE WISH YOU HAVE.
HUH?!
THAT GOT HIM ALL FIRED UP. THE PERV.
WHAT ARE YOU PLANNING TO ASK OF THE PRINCESS?!
WHY YOU GOTTA MAKE ME OUT TO BE A PER- VERT?!
WHAT'S YOUR SCHEME?
HEY! CUT IT OUT!

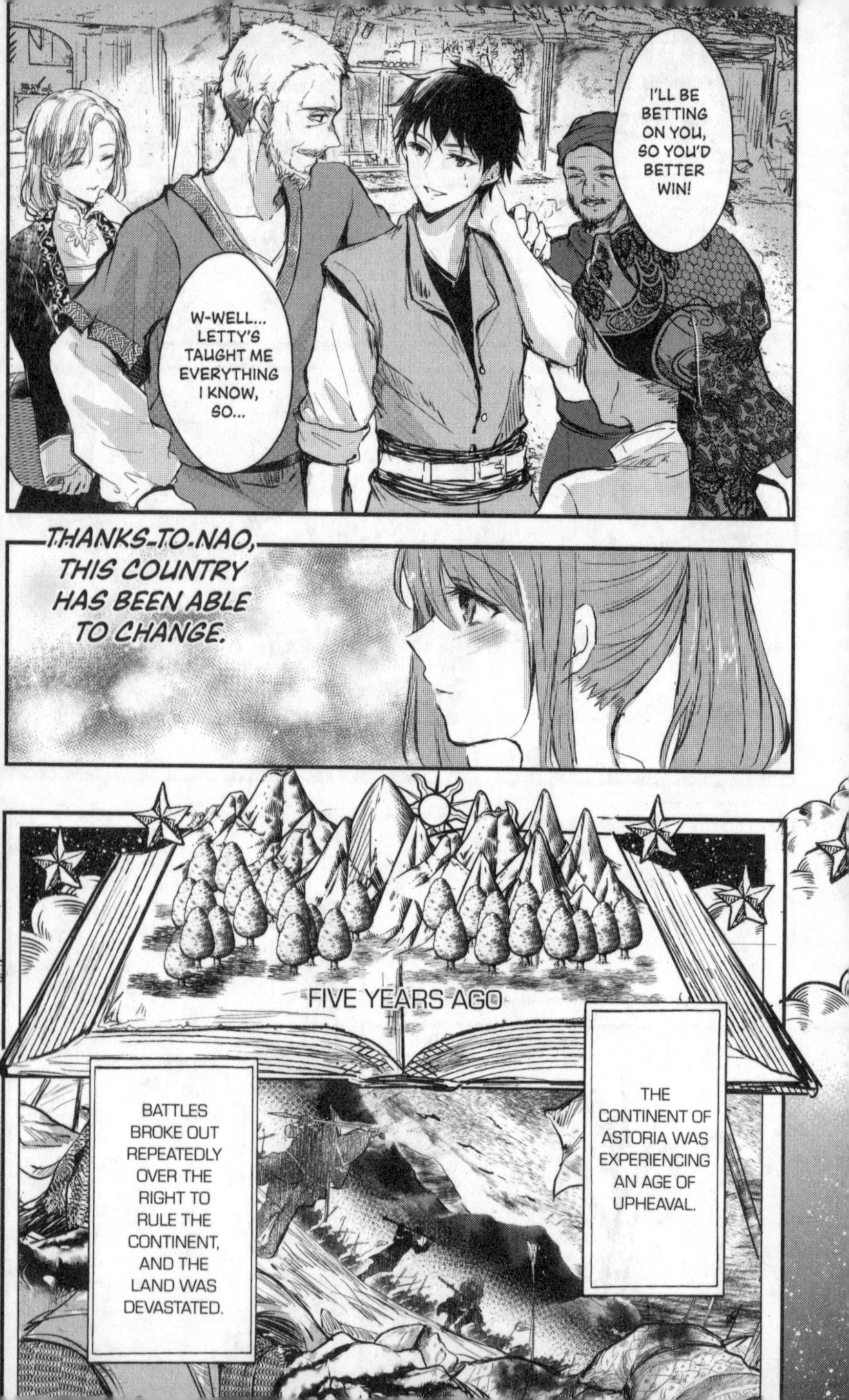
I'LL BE BETTING ON YOU, SO YOU'D BETTER WIN!
W-WELL... LETTY'S TAUGHT ME EVERYTHING I KNOW, SO...
THANKS TO NAO, THIS COUNTRY HAS BEEN ABLE TO CHANGE.
FIVE YEARS AGO
THE CONTINENT OF ASTORIA WAS EXPERIENCING AN AGE OF UPHEAVAL.
BATTLES BROKE OUT REPEATEDLY OVER THE RIGHT TO RULE THE CONTINENT, AND THE LAND WAS DEVASTATED.

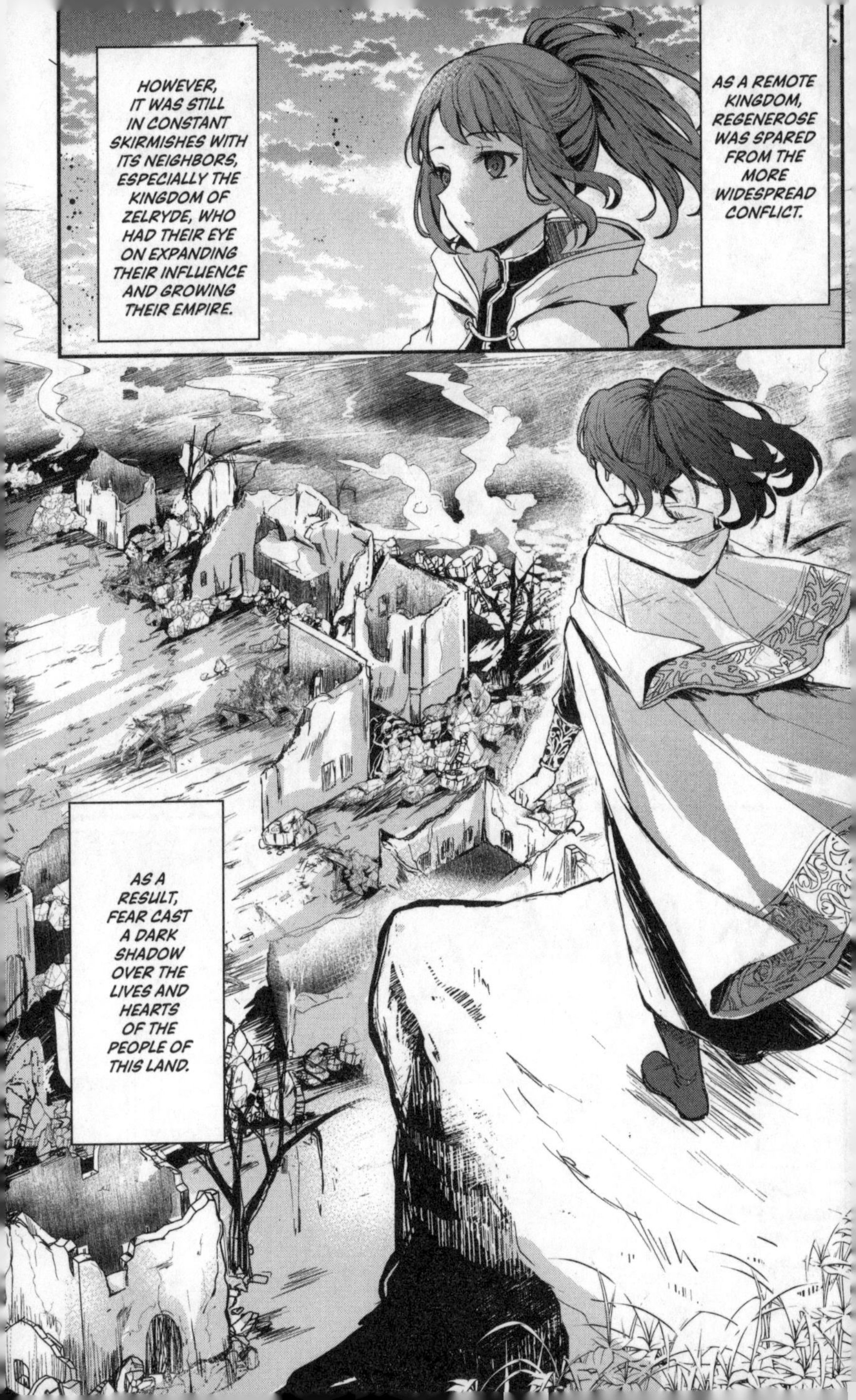
AS A REMOTE KINGDOM, REGENEROSE WAS SPARED FROM THE MORE WIDESPREAD CONFLICT.
HOWEVER, IT WAS STILL IN CONSTANT SKIRMISHES WITH ITS NEIGHBORS, ESPECIALLY THE KINGDOM OF ZELRYDE, WHO HAD THEIR EYE ON EXPANDING THEIR INFLUENCE AND GROWING THEIR EMPIRE.
AS A RESULT, FEAR CAST A DARK SHADOW OVER THE LIVES AND HEARTS OF THE PEOPLE OF THIS LAND.

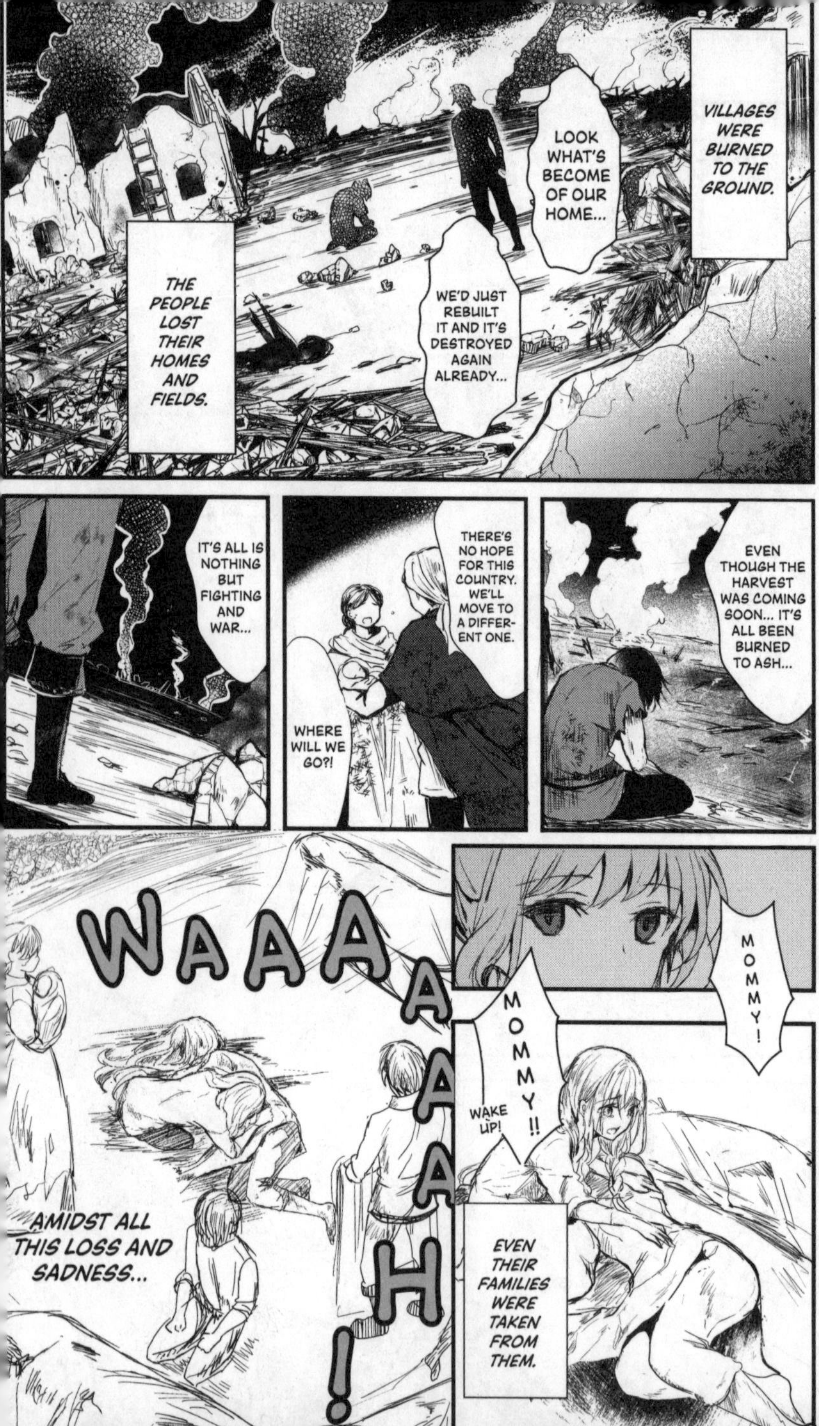
VILLAGES WERE BURNED TO THE GROUND.
LOOK WHAT'S BECOME OF OUR HOME...
WE'D JUST REBUILT IT AND IT'S DESTROYED AGAIN ALREADY...
THE PEOPLE LOST THEIR HOMES AND FIELDS.
EVEN THOUGH THE HARVEST WAS COMING SOON... IT'S ALL BEEN BURNED TO ASH...
THERE'S NO HOPE FOR THIS COUNTRY. WE'LL MOVE TO A DIFFER-ENT ONE.
WHERE WILL WE GO?!
IT'S ALL IS NOTHING BUT FIGHTING AND WAR...
MOMMY!
MOMMY!!
WAKE UP!
EVEN THEIR FAMILIES WERE TAKEN FROM THEM.
WAAAAAAH!
AMIDST ALL THIS LOSS AND SADNESS...

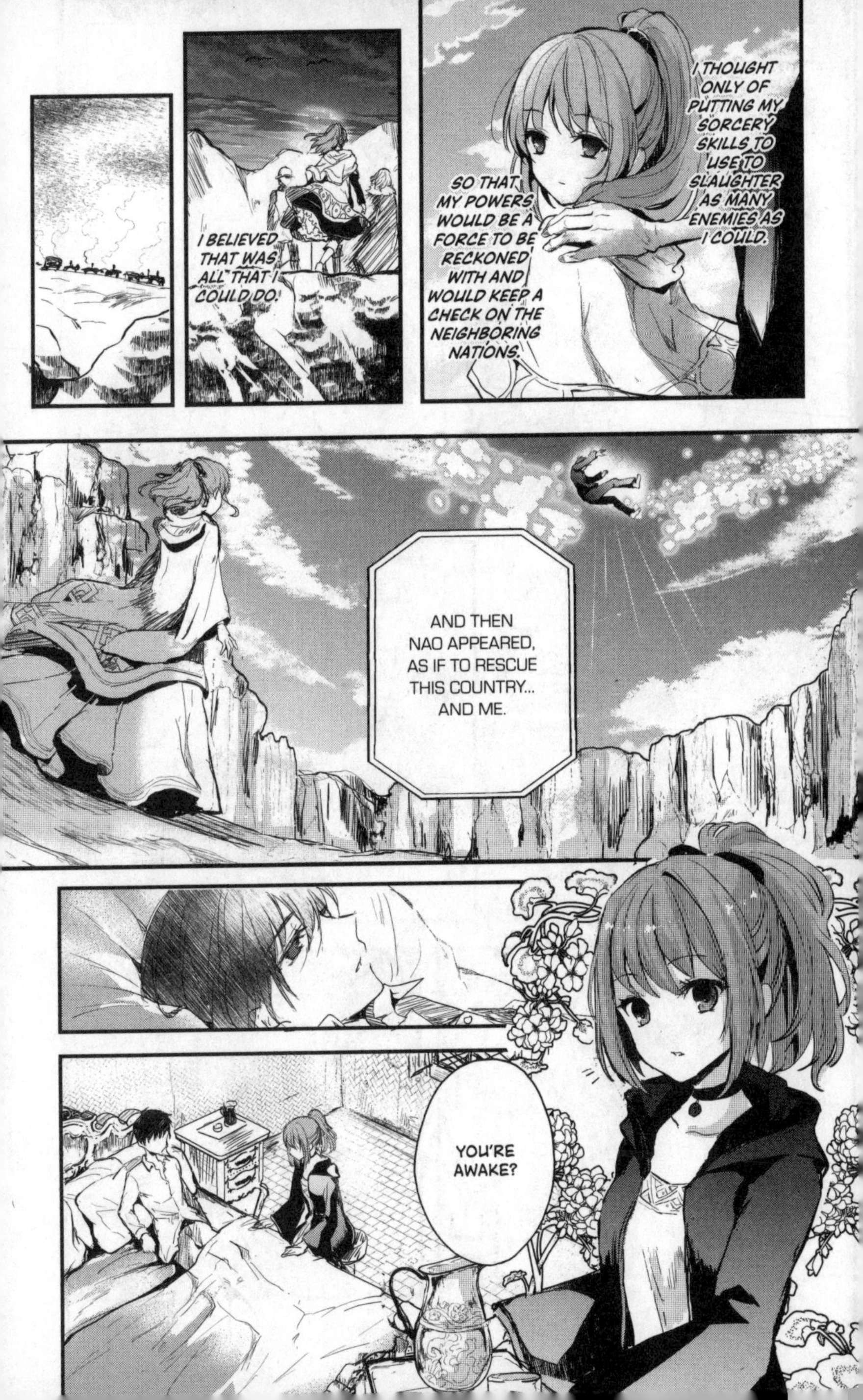
I THOUGHT ONLY OF PUTTING MY SORCERY SKILLS TO USE TO SLAUGHTER AS MANY ENEMIES AS I COULD.
SO THAT MY POWERS WOULD BE A FORCE TO BE RECKONED WITH AND WOULD KEEP A CHECK ON THE NEIGHBORING NATIONS.
I BELIEVED THAT WAS ALL THAT I COULD DO.
AND THEN NAO APPEARED, AS IF TO RESCUE THIS COUNTRY... AND ME.
YOU'RE AWAKE?

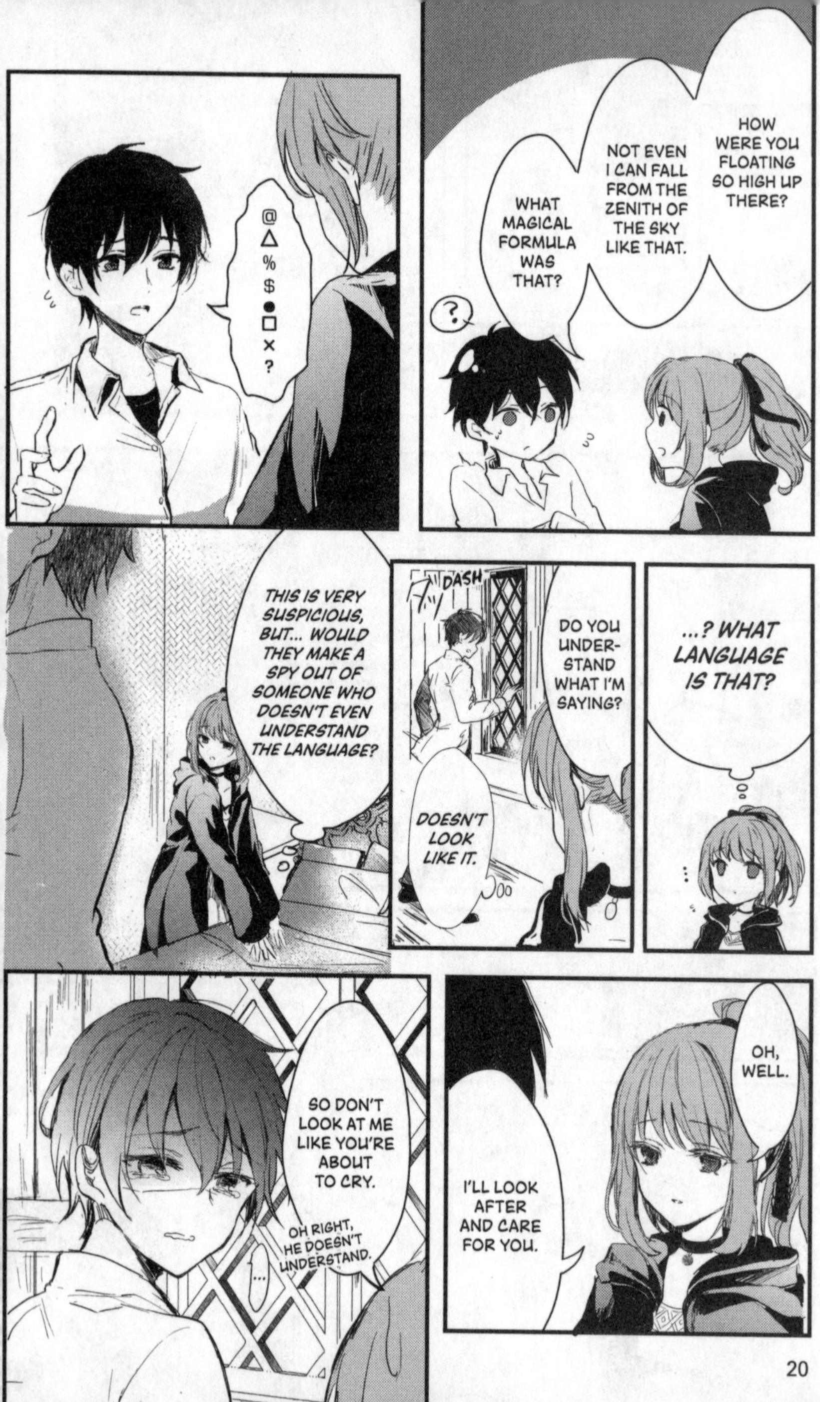
HOW WERE YOU FLOATING SO HIGH UP THERE?
NOT EVEN I CAN FALL FROM THE ZENITH OF THE SKY LIKE THAT.
WHAT MAGICAL FORMULA WAS THAT?
?
@△%$●□×?
...? WHAT LANGUAGE IS THAT?
...
DO YOU UNDER-STAND WHAT I'M SAYING?
DASH
DOESN'T LOOK LIKE IT.
THIS IS VERY SUSPICIOUS, BUT... WOULD THEY MAKE A SPY OUT OF SOMEONE WHO DOESN'T EVEN UNDERSTAND THE LANGUAGE?
OH, WELL.
I'LL LOOK AFTER AND CARE FOR YOU.
SO DON'T LOOK AT ME LIKE YOU'RE ABOUT TO CRY.
OH RIGHT, HE DOESN'T UNDERSTAND.
...

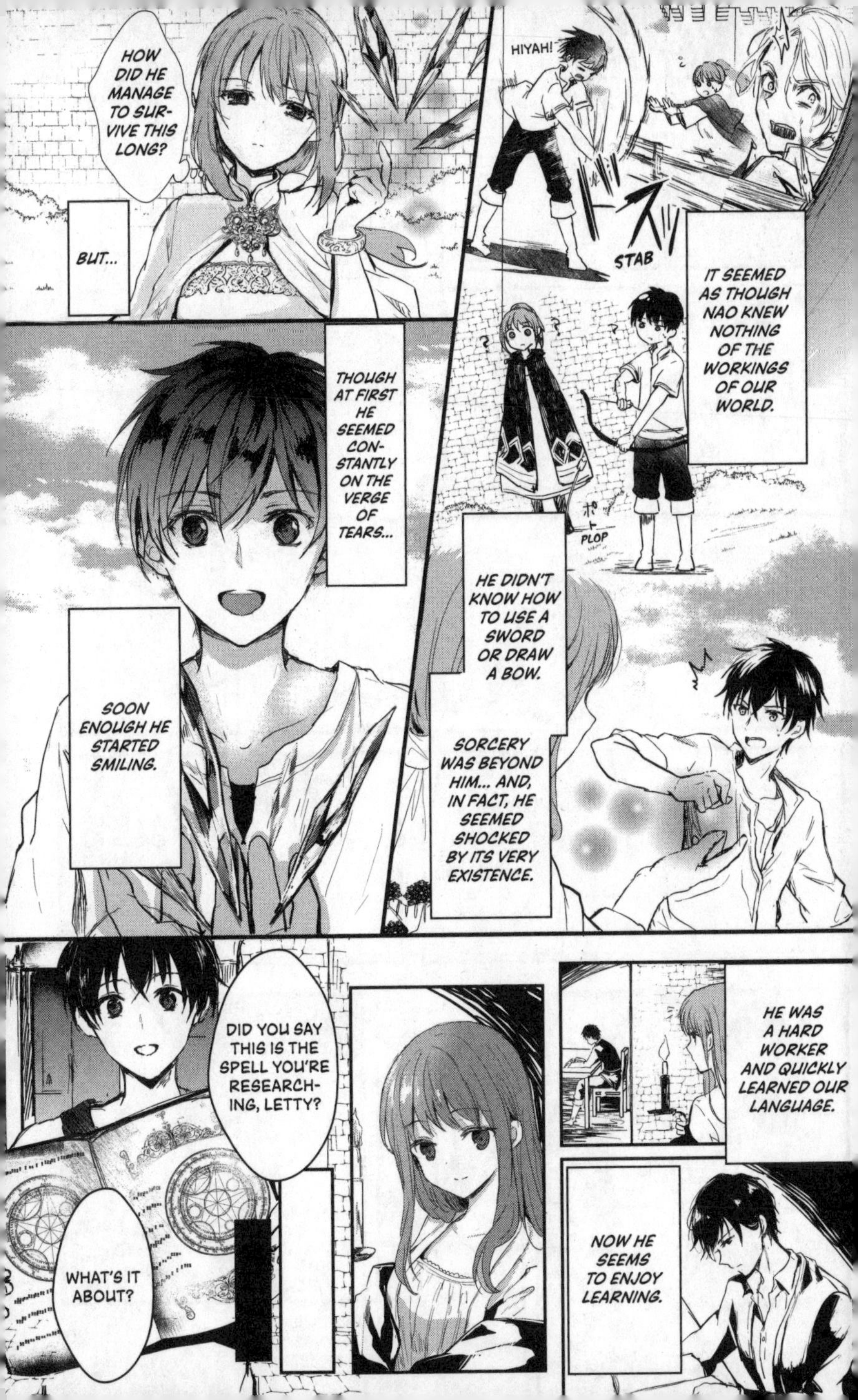
HIYAH!
STAB
HOW DID HE MANAGE TO SURVIVE THIS LONG?
BUT...
IT SEEMED AS THOUGH NAO KNEW NOTHING OF THE WORKINGS OF OUR WORLD.
PLOP
HE DIDN'T KNOW HOW TO USE A SWORD OR DRAW A BOW.
SORCERY WAS BEYOND HIM... AND, IN FACT, HE SEEMED SHOCKED BY ITS VERY EXISTENCE.
THOUGH AT FIRST HE SEEMED CONSTANTLY ON THE VERGE OF TEARS...
SOON ENOUGH HE STARTED SMILING.
HE WAS A HARD WORKER AND QUICKLY LEARNED OUR LANGUAGE.
NOW HE SEEMS TO ENJOY LEARNING.
DID YOU SAY THIS IS THE SPELL YOU'RE RESEARCHING, LETTY?
WHAT'S IT ABOUT?

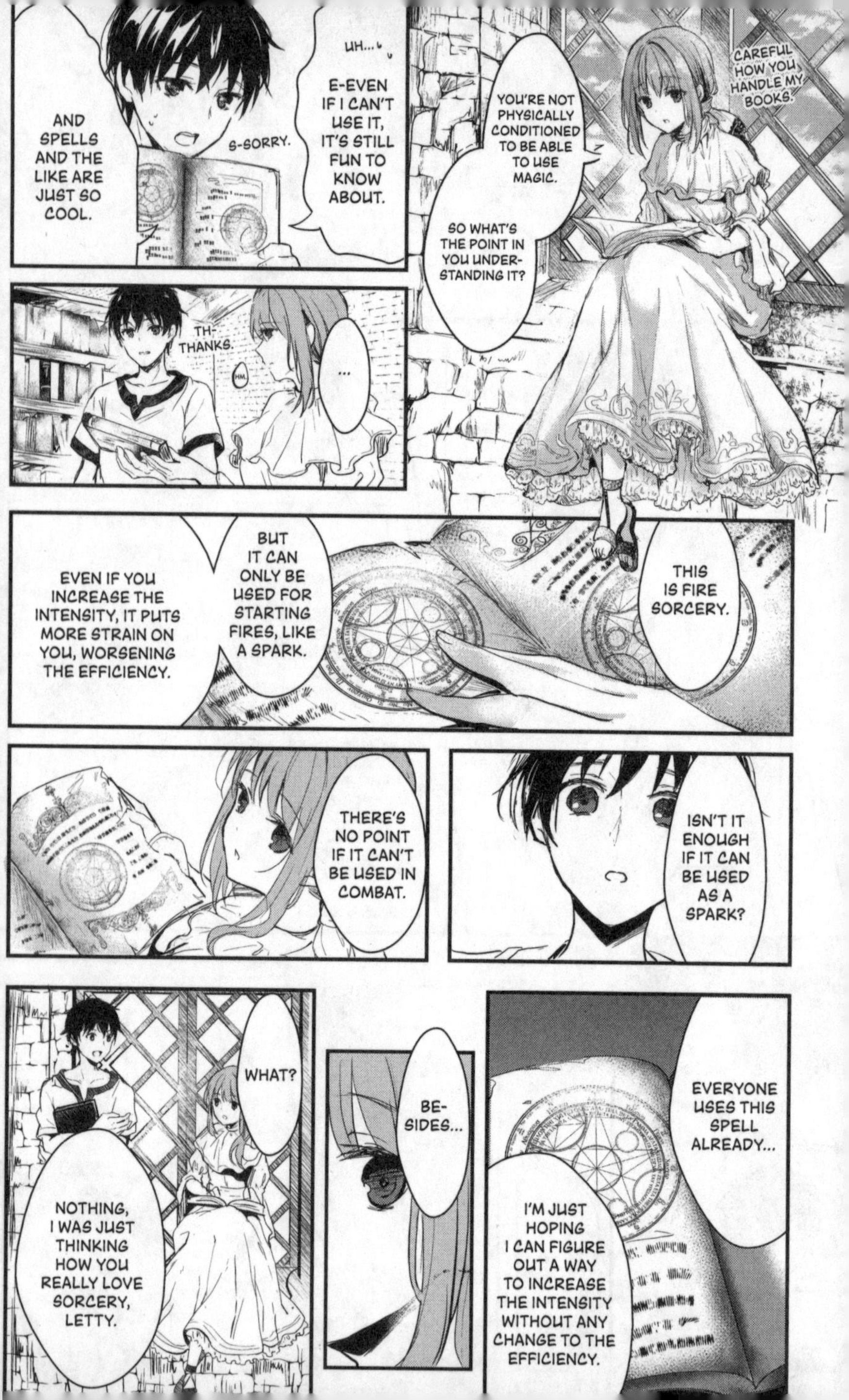

CAREFUL HOW YOU HANDLE MY BOOKS.
YOU'RE NOT PHYSICALLY CONDITIONED TO BE ABLE TO USE MAGIC.
SO WHAT'S THE POINT IN YOU UNDER-STANDING IT?
UH...
E-EVEN IF I CAN'T USE IT, IT'S STILL FUN TO KNOW ABOUT.
S-SORRY.
AND SPELLS AND THE LIKE ARE JUST SO COOL.
...
HM.
TH-THANKS.
THIS IS FIRE SORCERY.
BUT IT CAN ONLY BE USED FOR STARTING FIRES, LIKE A SPARK.
EVEN IF YOU INCREASE THE INTENSITY, IT PUTS MORE STRAIN ON YOU, WORSENING THE EFFICIENCY.
ISN'T IT ENOUGH IF IT CAN BE USED AS A SPARK?
THERE'S NO POINT IF IT CAN'T BE USED IN COMBAT.
EVERYONE USES THIS SPELL ALREADY...
I'M JUST HOPING I CAN FIGURE OUT A WAY TO INCREASE THE INTENSITY WITHOUT ANY CHANGE TO THE EFFICIENCY.
BE-SIDES...
WHAT?
NOTHING, I WAS JUST THINKING HOW YOU REALLY LOVE SORCERY, LETTY.

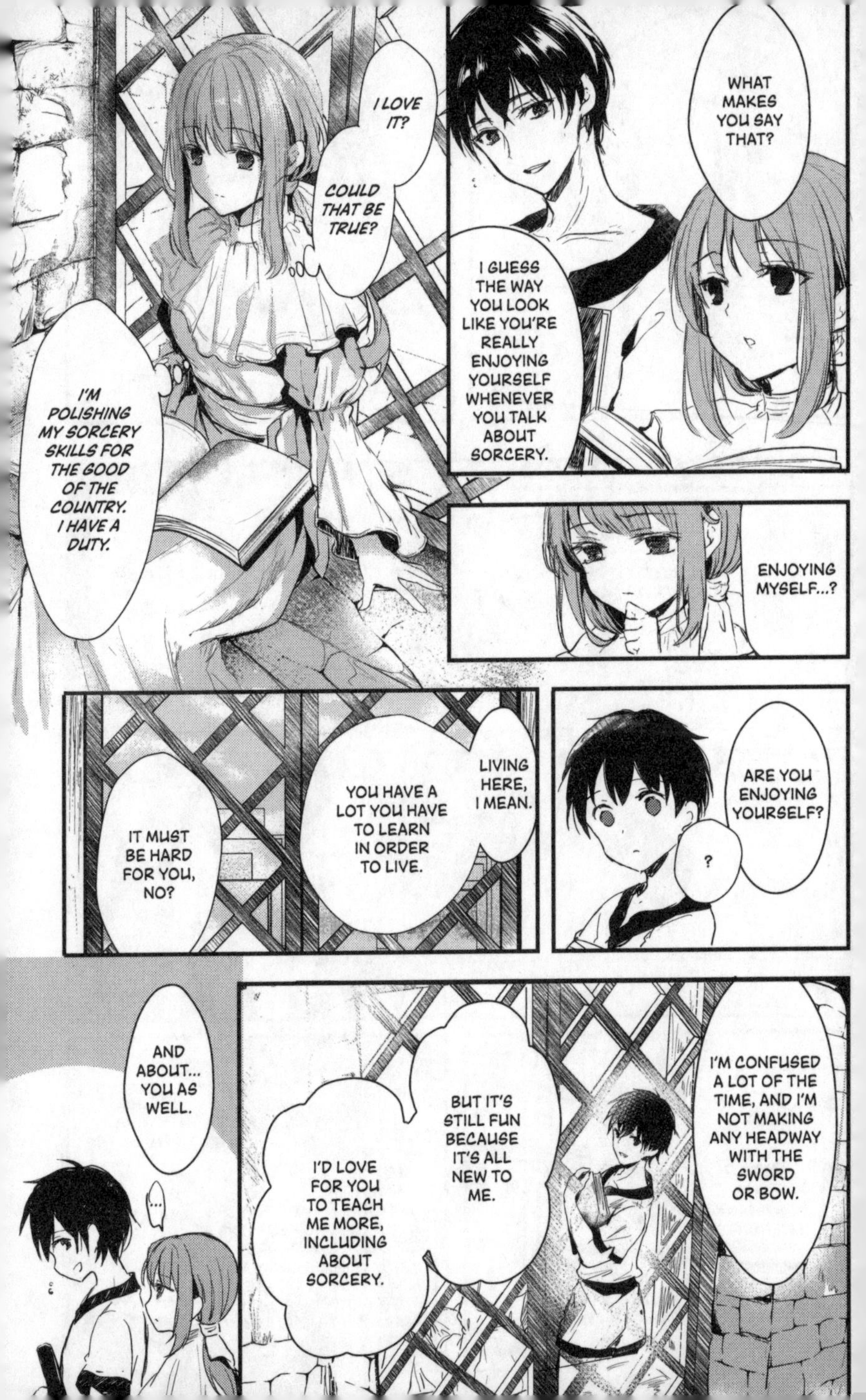
WHAT MAKES YOU SAY THAT?
I GUESS THE WAY YOU LOOK LIKE YOU'RE REALLY ENJOYING YOURSELF WHENEVER YOU TALK ABOUT SORCERY.
ENJOYING MYSELF...?
I LOVE IT?
COULD THAT BE TRUE?
I'M POLISHING MY SORCERY SKILLS FOR THE GOOD OF THE COUNTRY. I HAVE A DUTY.
ARE YOU ENJOYING YOURSELF?
?
LIVING HERE, I MEAN.
YOU HAVE A LOT YOU HAVE TO LEARN IN ORDER TO LIVE.
IT MUST BE HARD FOR YOU, NO?
I'M CONFUSED A LOT OF THE TIME, AND I'M NOT MAKING ANY HEADWAY WITH THE SWORD OR BOW.
BUT IT'S STILL FUN BECAUSE IT'S ALL NEW TO ME.
I'D LOVE FOR YOU TO TEACH ME MORE, INCLUDING ABOUT SORCERY.
AND ABOUT... YOU AS WELL.
...

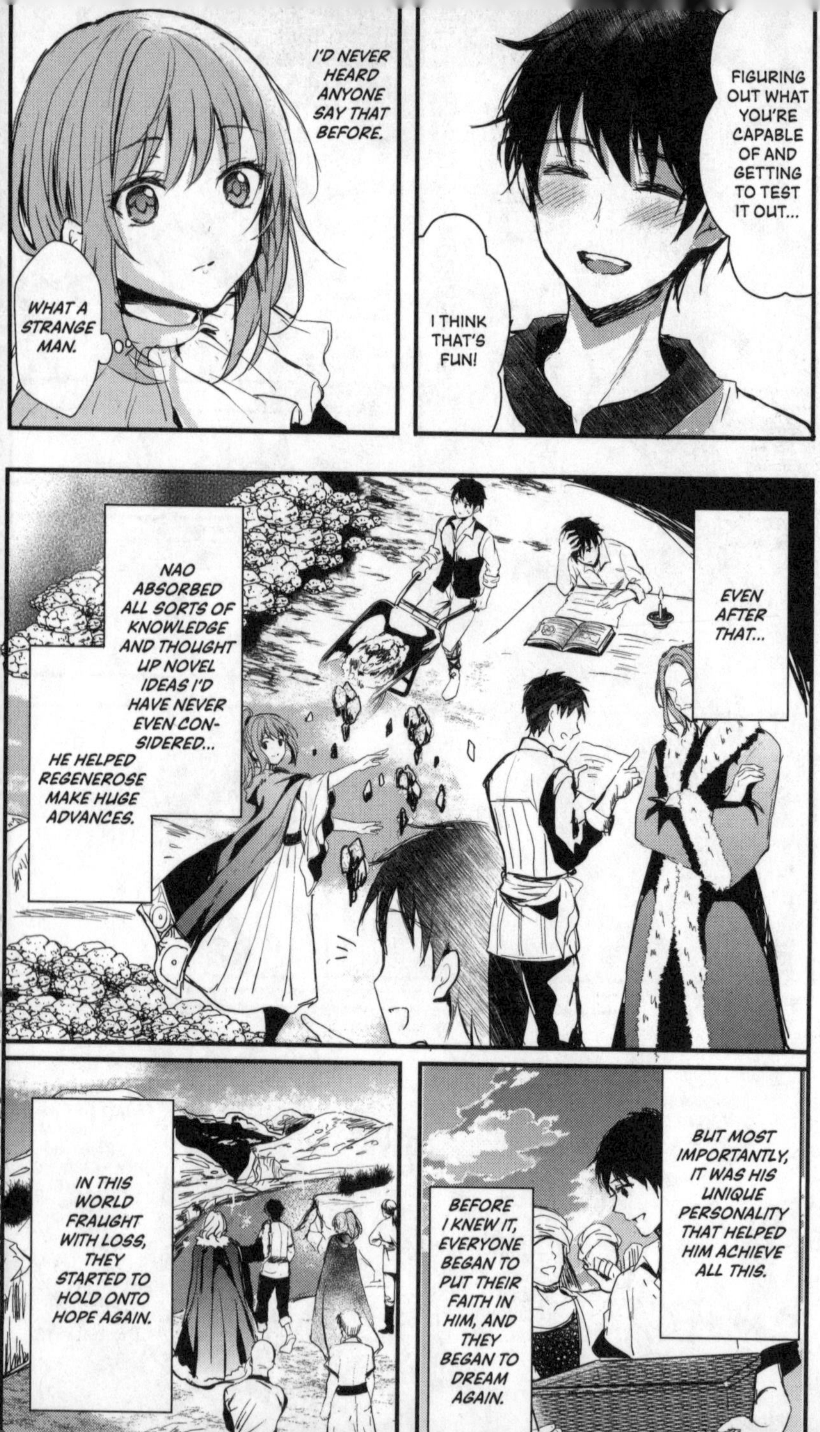
FIGURING OUT WHAT YOU'RE CAPABLE OF AND GETTING TO TEST IT OUT...
I THINK THAT'S FUN!
I'D NEVER HEARD ANYONE SAY THAT BEFORE.
WHAT A STRANGE MAN.
EVEN AFTER THAT...
NAO ABSORBED ALL SORTS OF KNOWLEDGE AND THOUGHT UP NOVEL IDEAS I'D HAVE NEVER EVEN CON-SIDERED...
HE HELPED REGENEROSE MAKE HUGE ADVANCES.
BUT MOST IMPORTANTLY, IT WAS HIS UNIQUE PERSONALITY THAT HELPED HIM ACHIEVE ALL THIS.
BEFORE I KNEW IT, EVERYONE BEGAN TO PUT THEIR FAITH IN HIM, AND THEY BEGAN TO DREAM AGAIN.
IN THIS WORLD FRAUGHT WITH LOSS, THEY STARTED TO HOLD ONTO HOPE AGAIN.

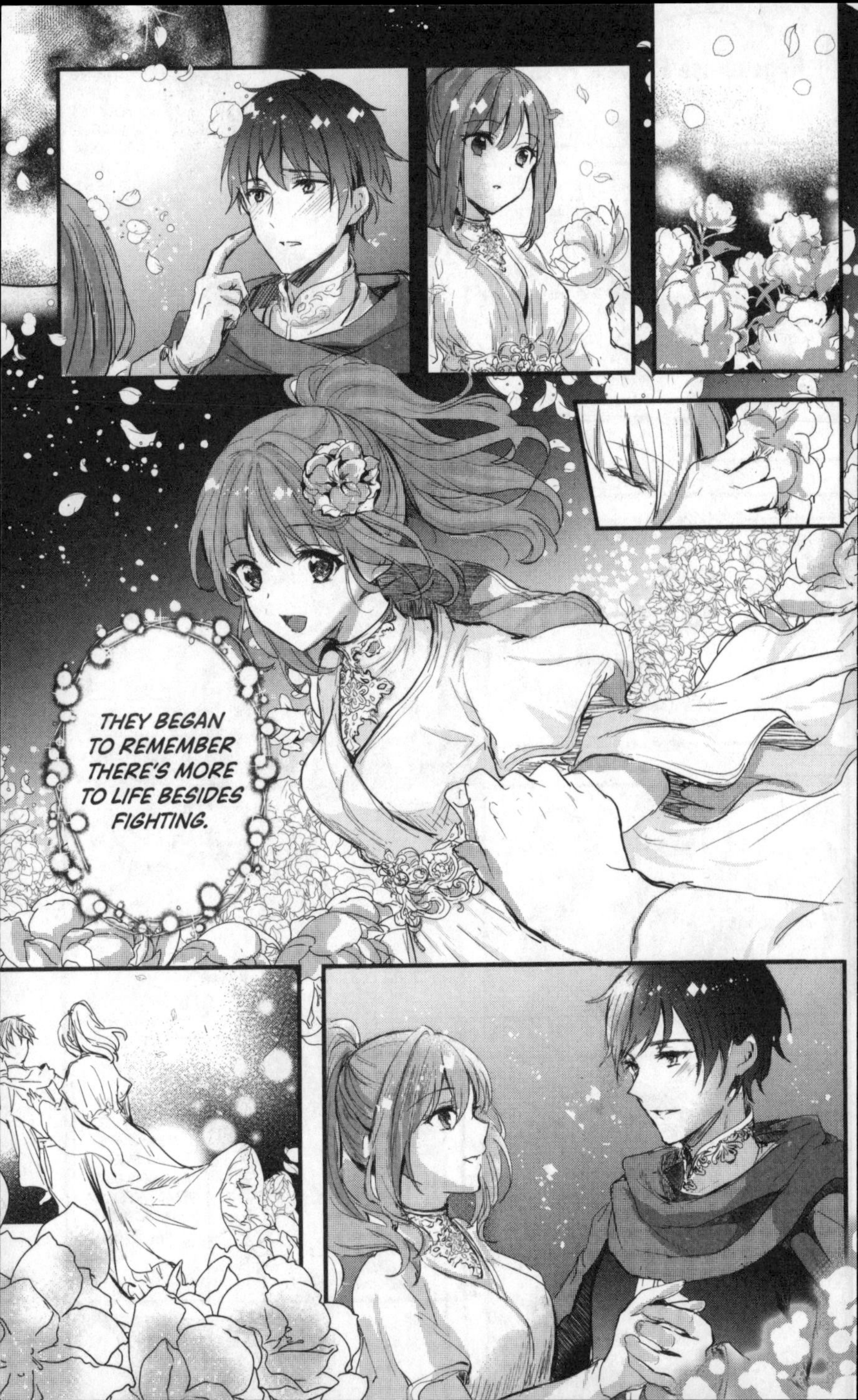
THEY BEGAN TO REMEMBER THERE'S MORE TO LIFE BESIDES FIGHTING.

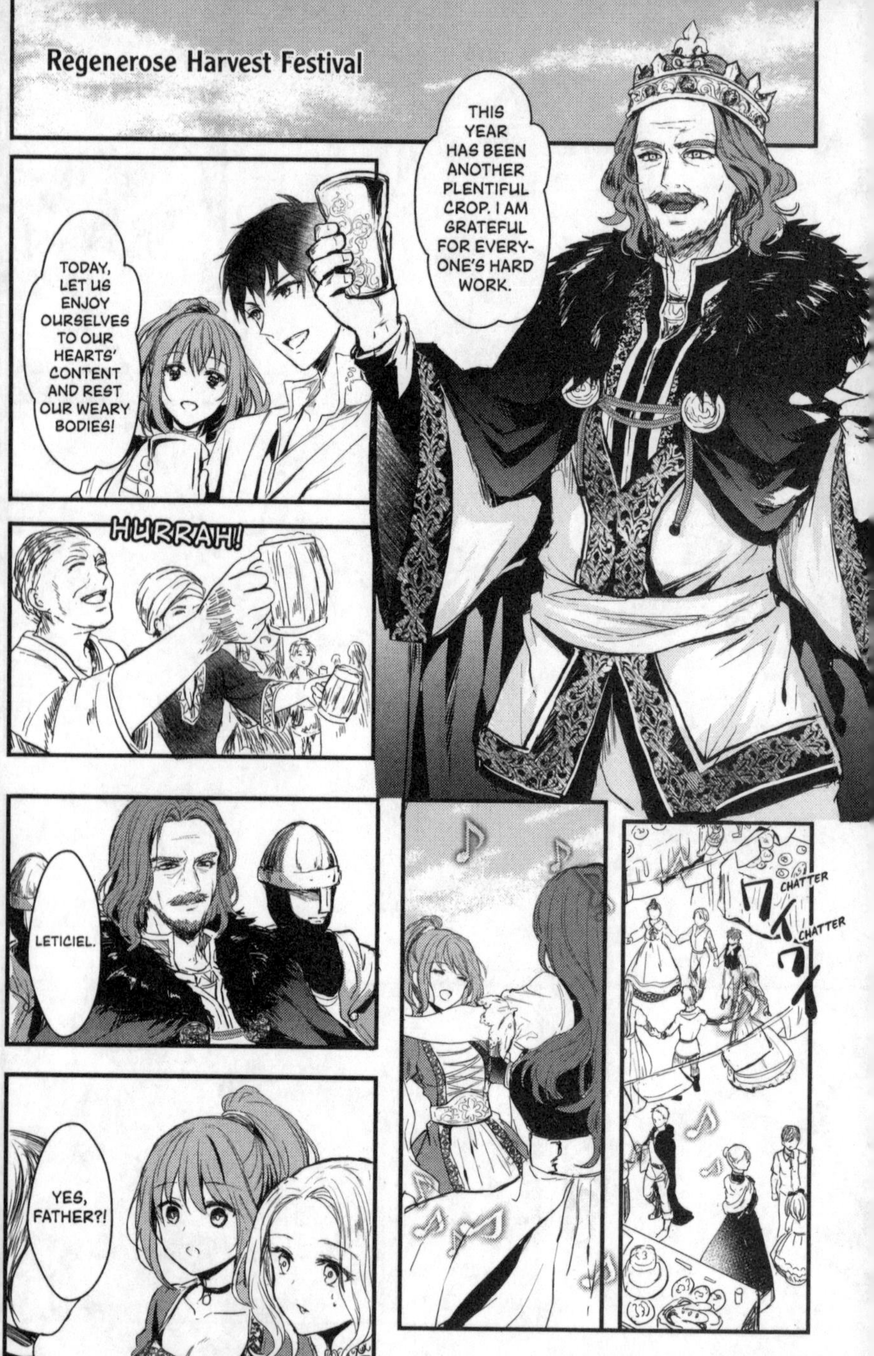
THIS YEAR HAS BEEN ANOTHER PLENTIFUL CROP. I AM GRATEFUL FOR EVERY-ONE'S HARD WORK.
Regenerose Harvest Festival
TODAY, LET US ENJOY OURSELVES TO OUR HEARTS' CONTENT AND REST OUR WEARY BODIES!
HURRAH!
CHATTER
CHATTER
LETICIEL.
YES, FATHER?!

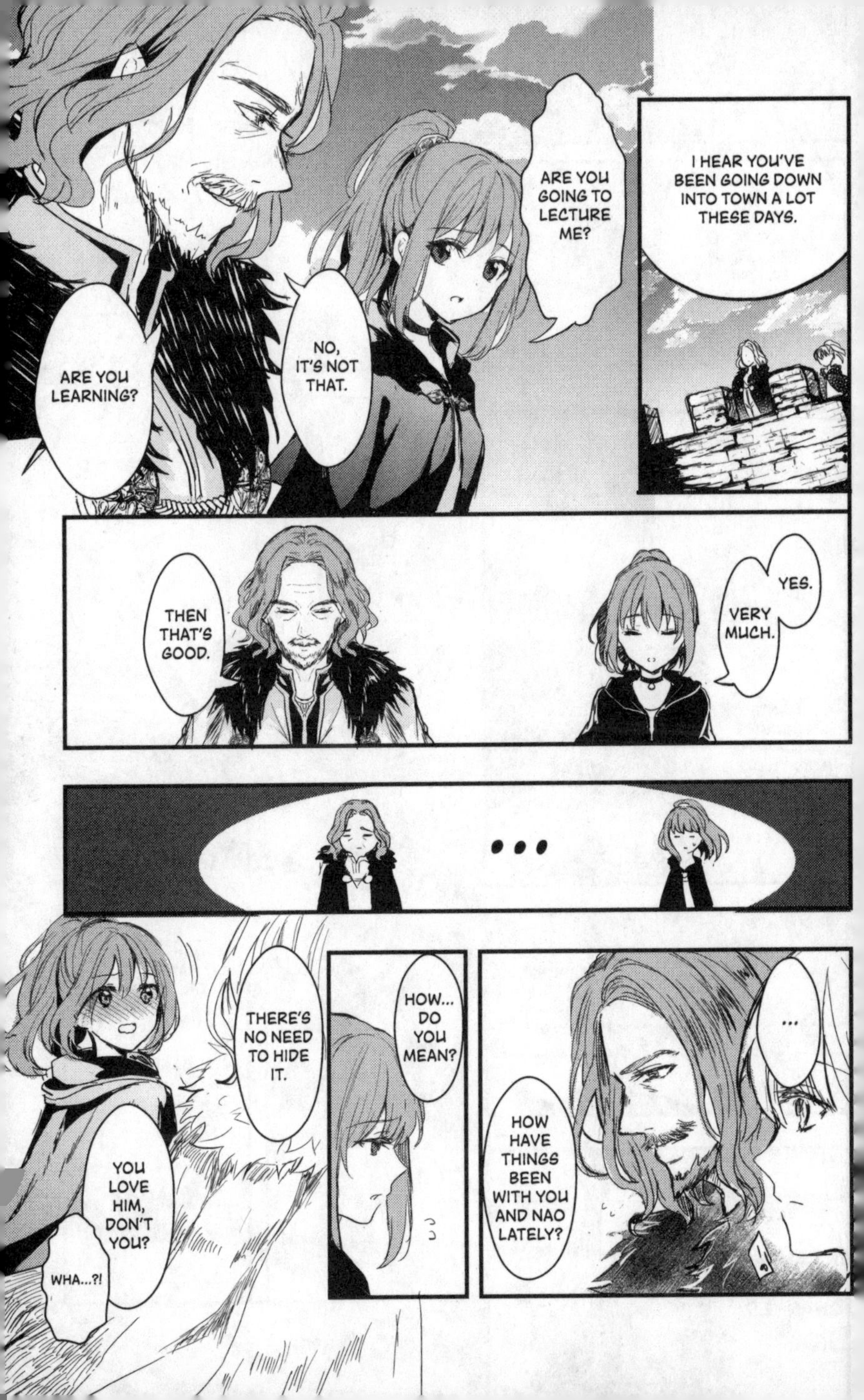
I HEAR YOU'VE BEEN GOING DOWN INTO TOWN A LOT THESE DAYS.
ARE YOU GOING TO LECTURE ME?
NO, IT'S NOT THAT.
ARE YOU LEARNING?
YES.
VERY MUCH.
THEN THAT'S GOOD.
...
...
HOW HAVE THINGS BEEN WITH YOU AND NAO LATELY?
HOW... DO YOU MEAN?
THERE'S NO NEED TO HIDE IT.
YOU LOVE HIM, DON'T YOU?
WHA...?!

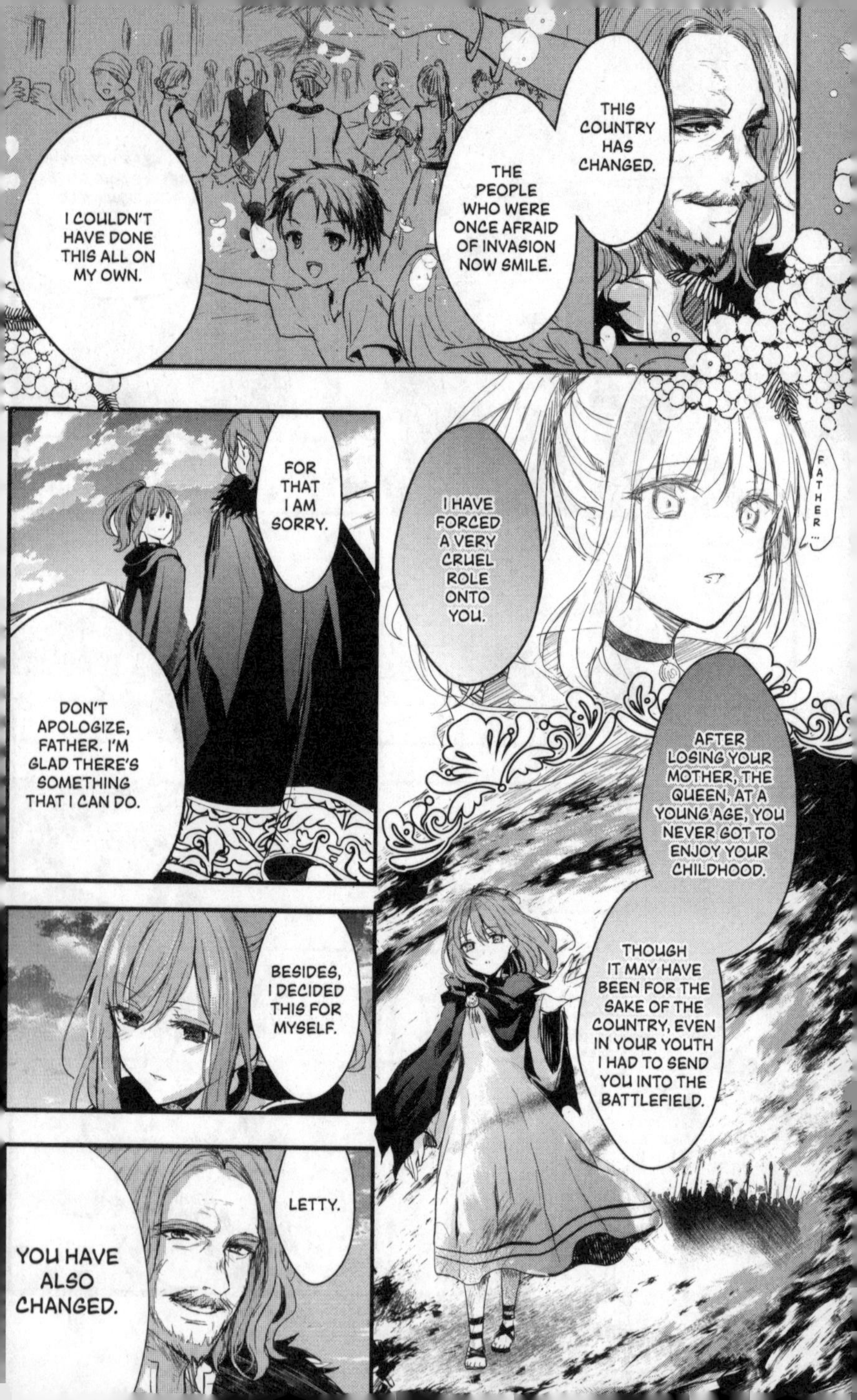
THIS COUNTRY HAS CHANGED.
THE PEOPLE WHO WERE ONCE AFRAID OF INVASION NOW SMILE.
I COULDN'T HAVE DONE THIS ALL ON MY OWN.
FATHER...
I HAVE FORCED A VERY CRUEL ROLE ONTO YOU.
AFTER LOSING YOUR MOTHER, THE QUEEN, AT A YOUNG AGE, YOU NEVER GOT TO ENJOY YOUR CHILDHOOD.
THOUGH IT MAY HAVE BEEN FOR THE SAKE OF THE COUNTRY, EVEN IN YOUR YOUTH I HAD TO SEND YOU INTO THE BATTLEFIELD.
FOR THAT I AM SORRY.
DON'T APOLOGIZE, FATHER. I'M GLAD THERE'S SOMETHING THAT I CAN DO.
BESIDES, I DECIDED THIS FOR MYSELF.
LETTY.
YOU HAVE ALSO CHANGED.

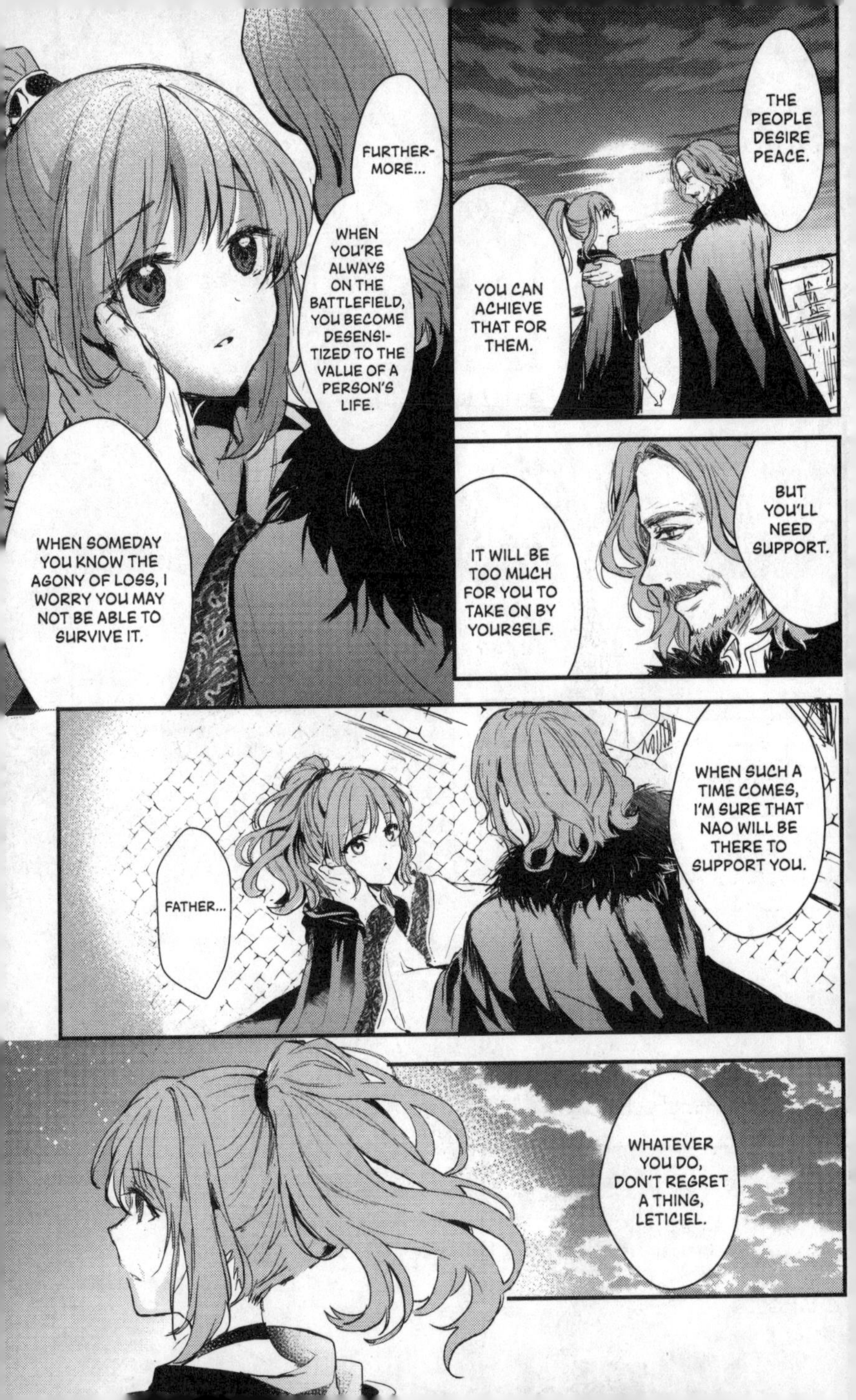
THE PEOPLE DESIRE PEACE.
YOU CAN ACHIEVE THAT FOR THEM.
BUT YOU'LL NEED SUPPORT.
IT WILL BE TOO MUCH FOR YOU TO TAKE ON BY YOURSELF.
FURTHER-MORE...
WHEN YOU'RE ALWAYS ON THE BATTLEFIELD, YOU BECOME DESENSI-TIZED TO THE VALUE OF A PERSON'S LIFE.
WHEN SOMEDAY YOU KNOW THE AGONY OF LOSS, I WORRY YOU MAY NOT BE ABLE TO SURVIVE IT.
WHEN SUCH A TIME COMES, I'M SURE THAT NAO WILL BE THERE TO SUPPORT YOU.
FATHER...
WHATEVER YOU DO, DON'T REGRET A THING, LETICIEL.

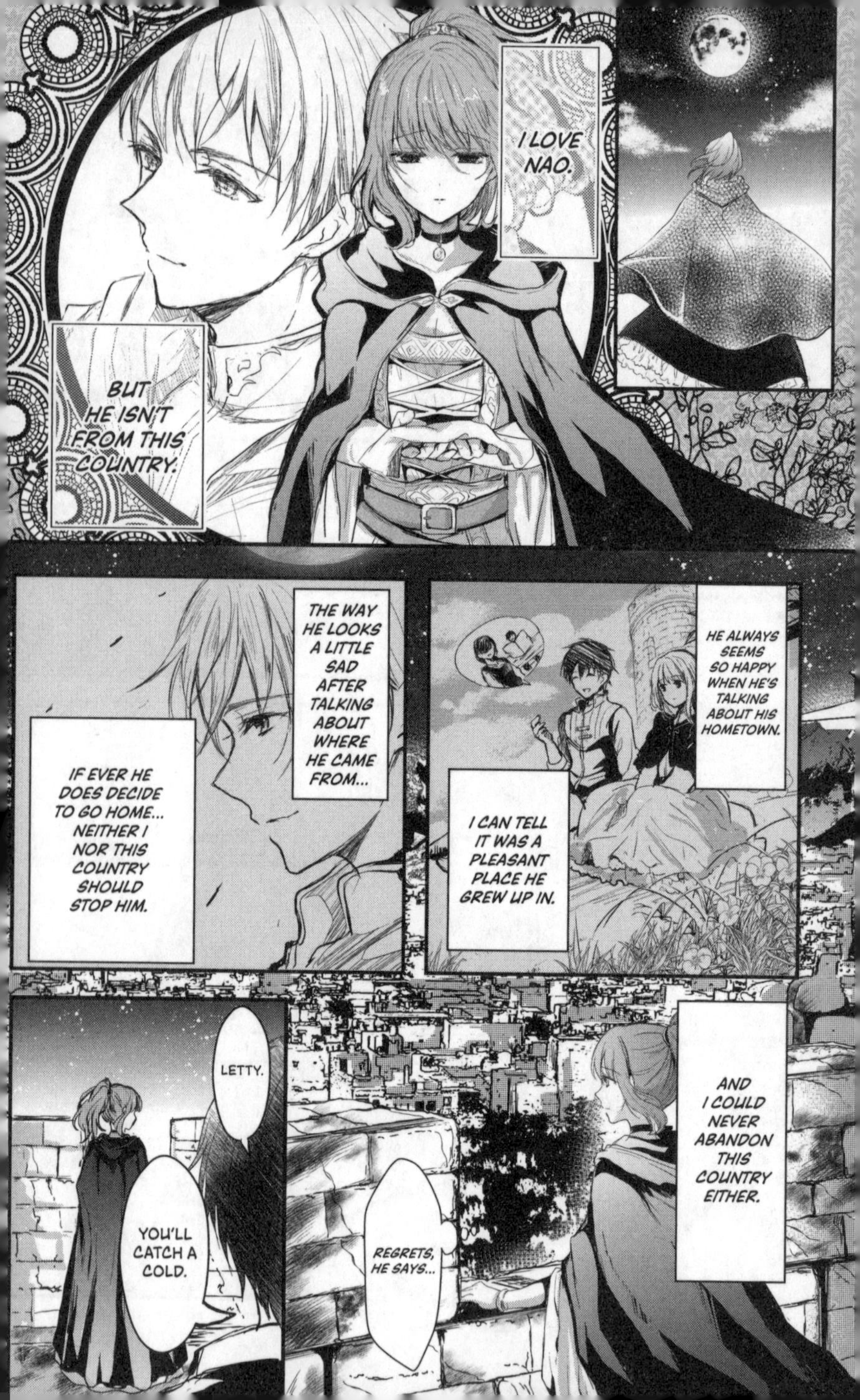
I LOVE NAO.
BUT HE ISN'T FROM THIS COUNTRY.
HE ALWAYS SEEMS SO HAPPY WHEN HE'S TALKING ABOUT HIS HOMETOWN.
I CAN TELL IT WAS A PLEASANT PLACE HE GREW UP IN.
THE WAY HE LOOKS A LITTLE SAD AFTER TALKING ABOUT WHERE HE CAME FROM...
IF EVER HE DOES DECIDE TO GO HOME... NEITHER I NOR THIS COUNTRY SHOULD STOP HIM.
AND I COULD NEVER ABANDON THIS COUNTRY EITHER.
REGRETS, HE SAYS...
LETTY.
YOU'LL CATCH A COLD.

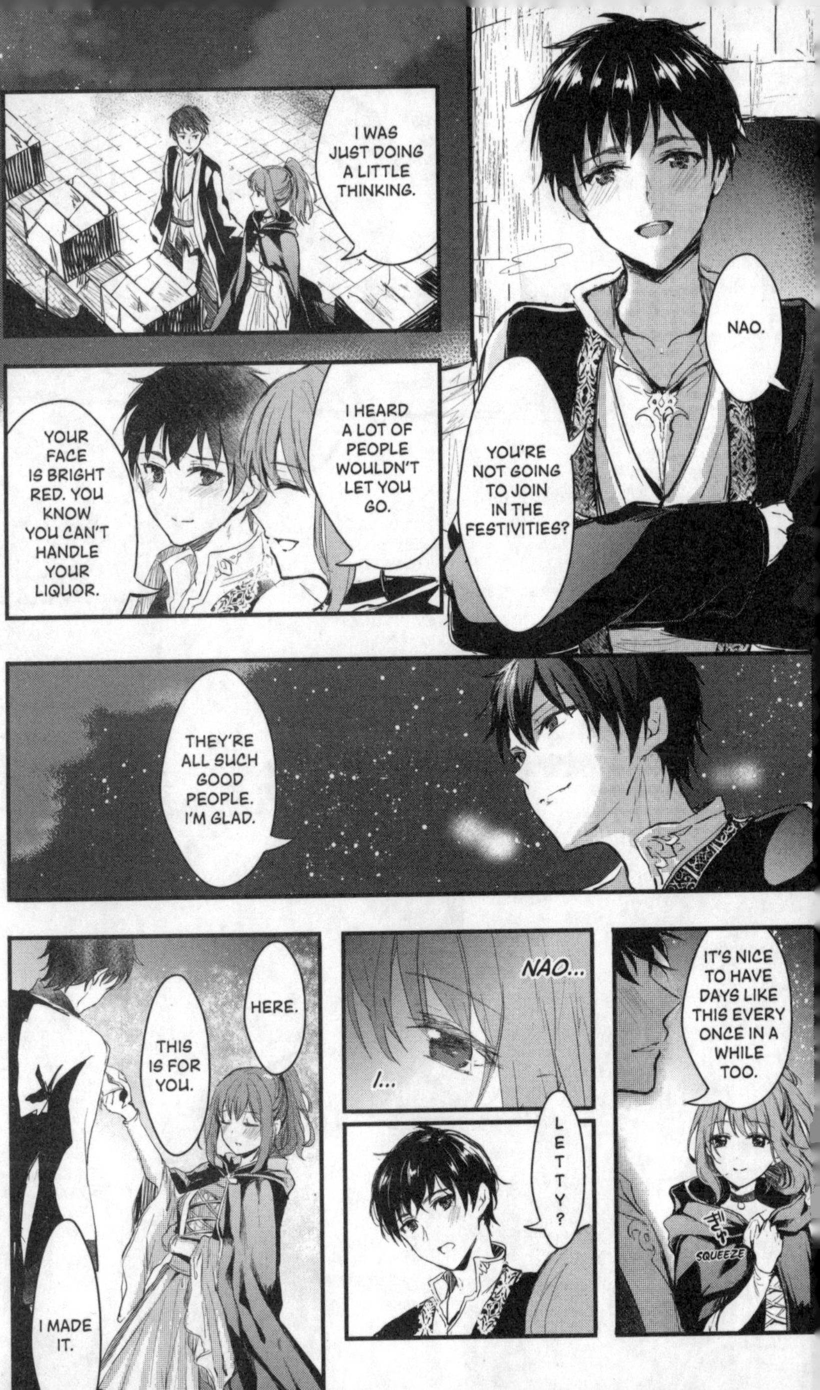
NAO.
YOU'RE NOT GOING TO JOIN IN THE FESTIVITIES?
I WAS JUST DOING A LITTLE THINKING.
I HEARD A LOT OF PEOPLE WOULDN'T LET YOU GO.
YOUR FACE IS BRIGHT RED. YOU KNOW YOU CAN'T HANDLE YOUR LIQUOR.
THEY'RE ALL SUCH GOOD PEOPLE. I'M GLAD.
IT'S NICE TO HAVE DAYS LIKE THIS EVERY ONCE IN A WHILE TOO.
SQUEEZE
NAO...
I...
LETTY?
HERE.
THIS IS FOR YOU.
I MADE IT.

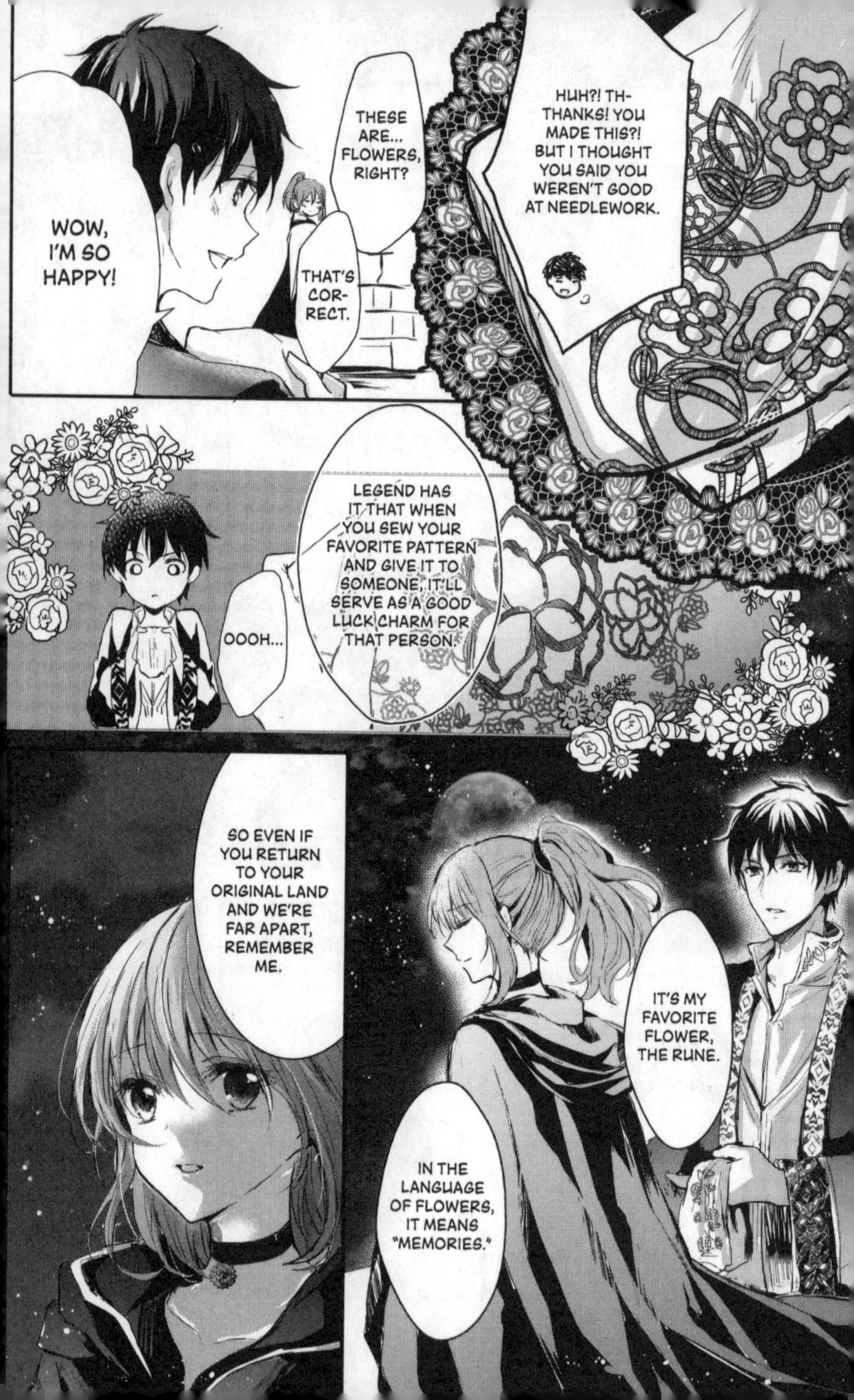
HUH?! TH-THANKS! YOU MADE THIS?! BUT I THOUGHT YOU SAID YOU WEREN'T GOOD AT NEEDLEWORK.
THESE ARE... FLOWERS, RIGHT?
THAT'S COR-RECT.
WOW, I'M SO HAPPY!
LEGEND HAS IT THAT WHEN YOU SEW YOUR FAVORITE PATTERN AND GIVE IT TO SOMEONE, IT'LL SERVE AS A GOOD LUCK CHARM FOR THAT PERSON.
OOOH...
IT'S MY FAVORITE FLOWER, THE RUNE.
IN THE LANGUAGE OF FLOWERS, IT MEANS "MEMORIES."
SO EVEN IF YOU RETURN TO YOUR ORIGINAL LAND AND WE'RE FAR APART, REMEMBER ME.

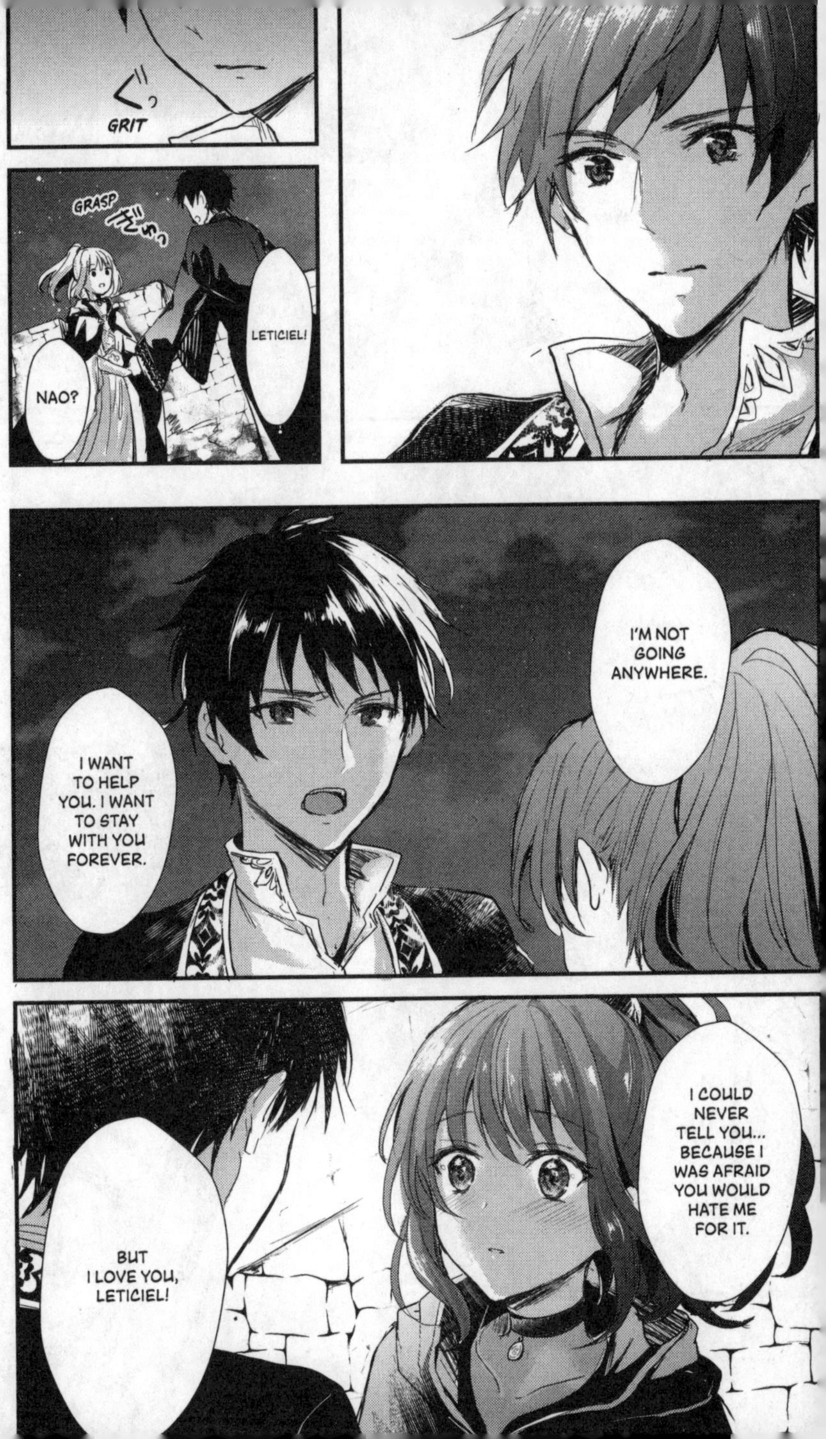
GRIT
GRASP
LETICIEL!
NAO?
I'M NOT GOING ANYWHERE.
I WANT TO HELP YOU. I WANT TO STAY WITH YOU FOREVER.
I COULD NEVER TELL YOU... BECAUSE I WAS AFRAID YOU WOULD HATE ME FOR IT.
BUT I LOVE YOU, LETICIEL!

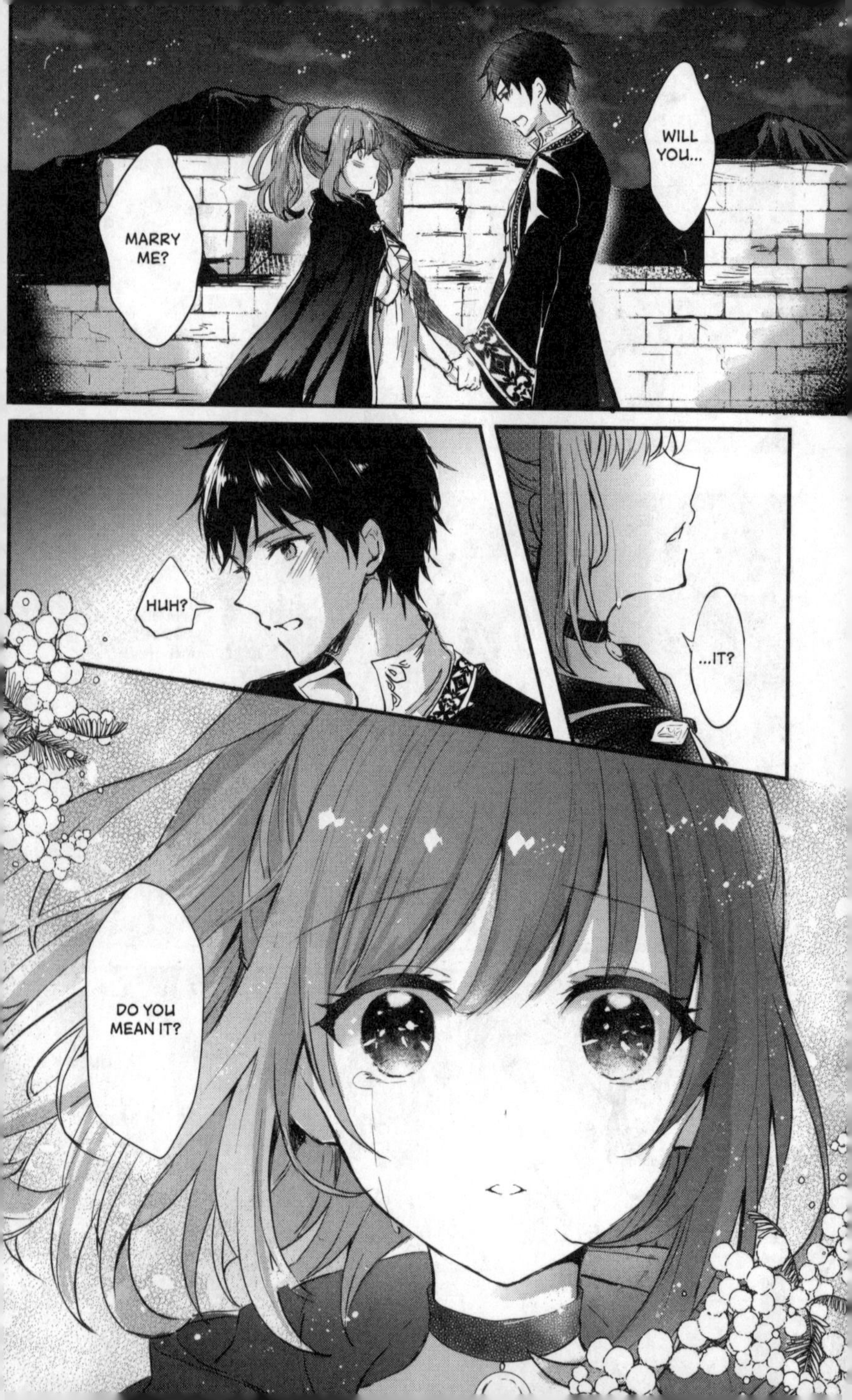
WILL YOU...
MARRY ME?
...IT?
HUH?
DO YOU MEAN IT?

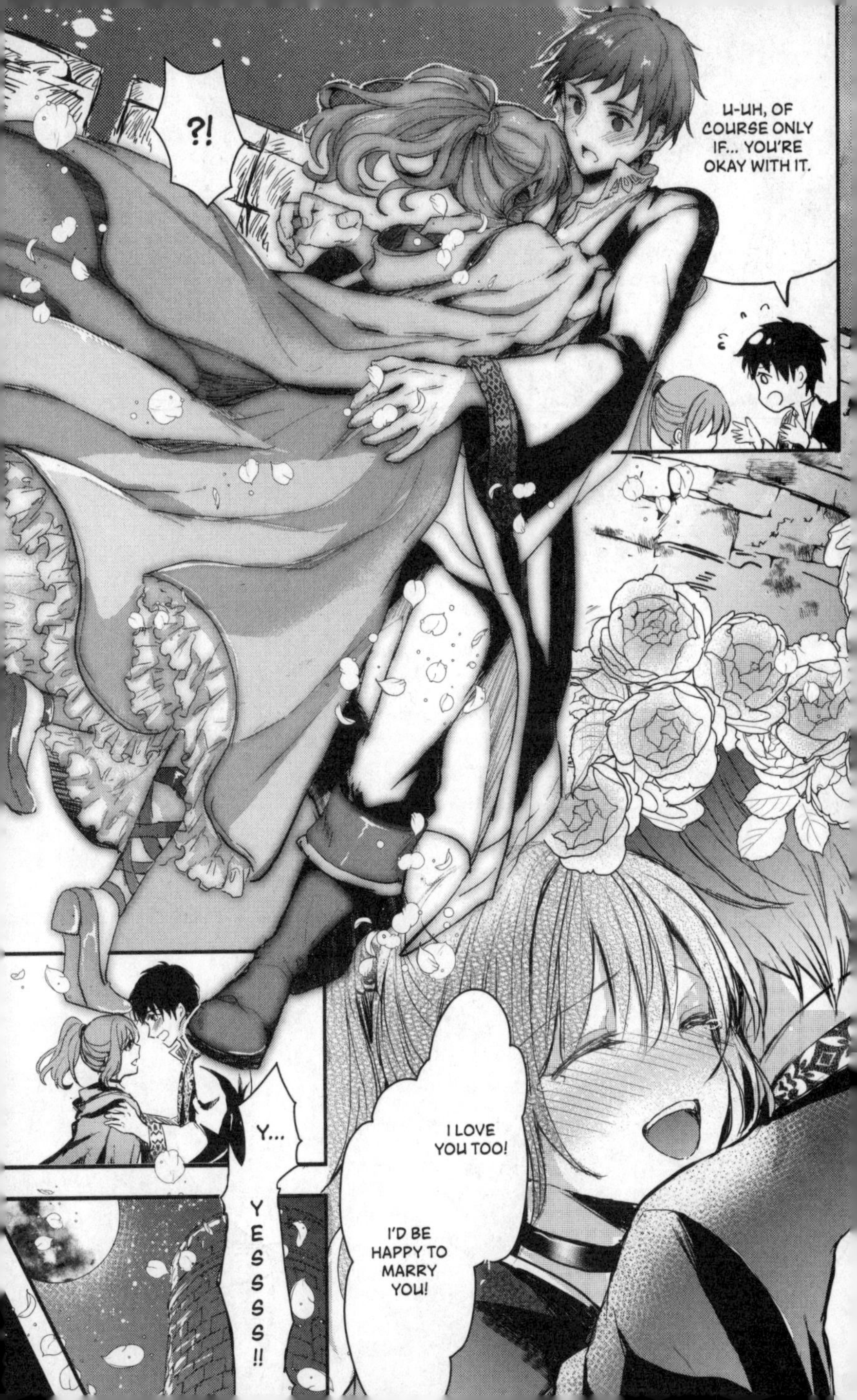
U-UH, OF COURSE ONLY IF... YOU'RE OKAY WITH IT.
?!
I LOVE YOU TOO!
I'D BE HAPPY TO MARRY YOU!
Y...
YESSSS!!

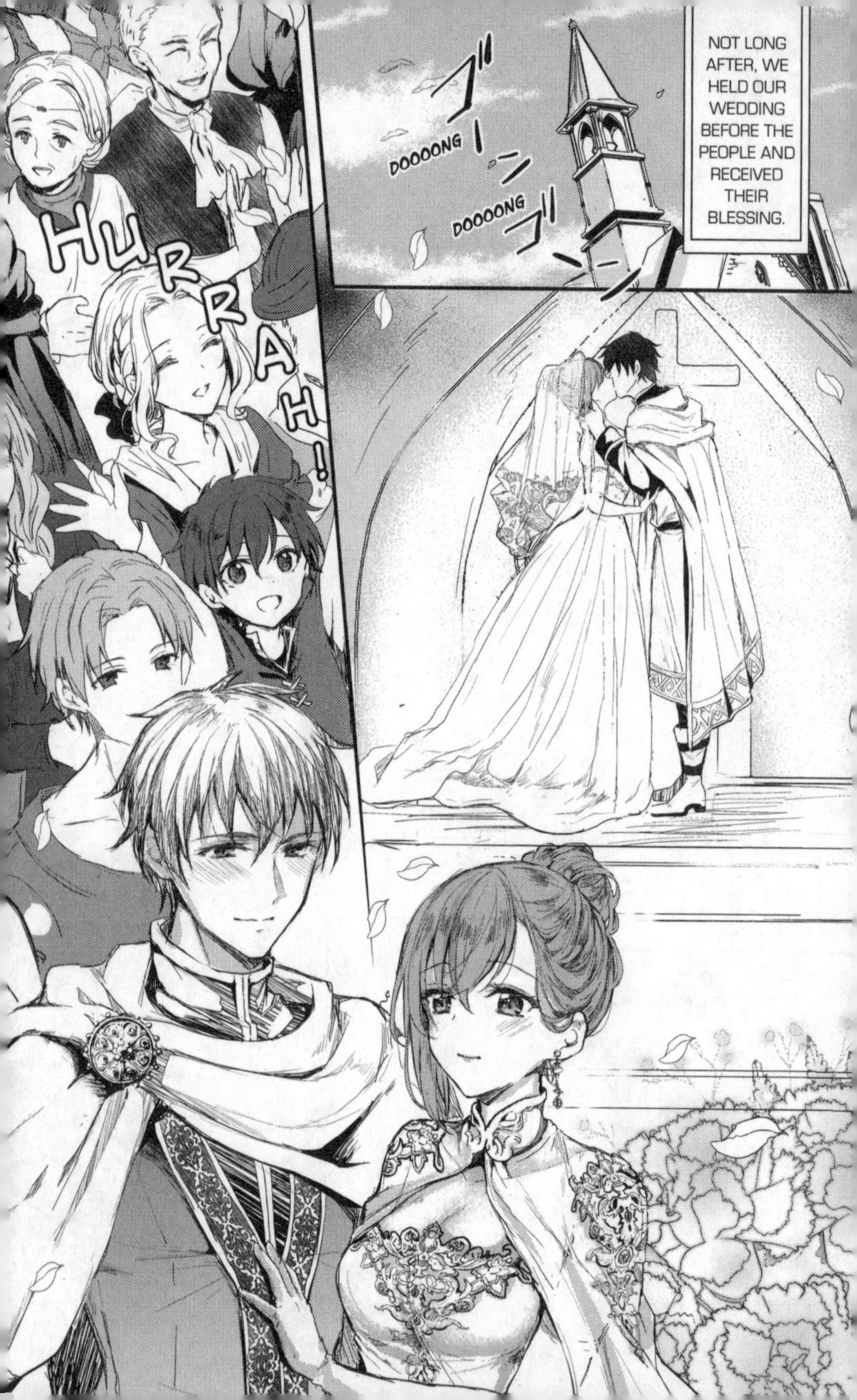
NOT LONG AFTER, WE HELD OUR WEDDING BEFORE THE PEOPLE AND RECEIVED THEIR BLESSING.
DOOOONG
DOOOONG
HURRAH!

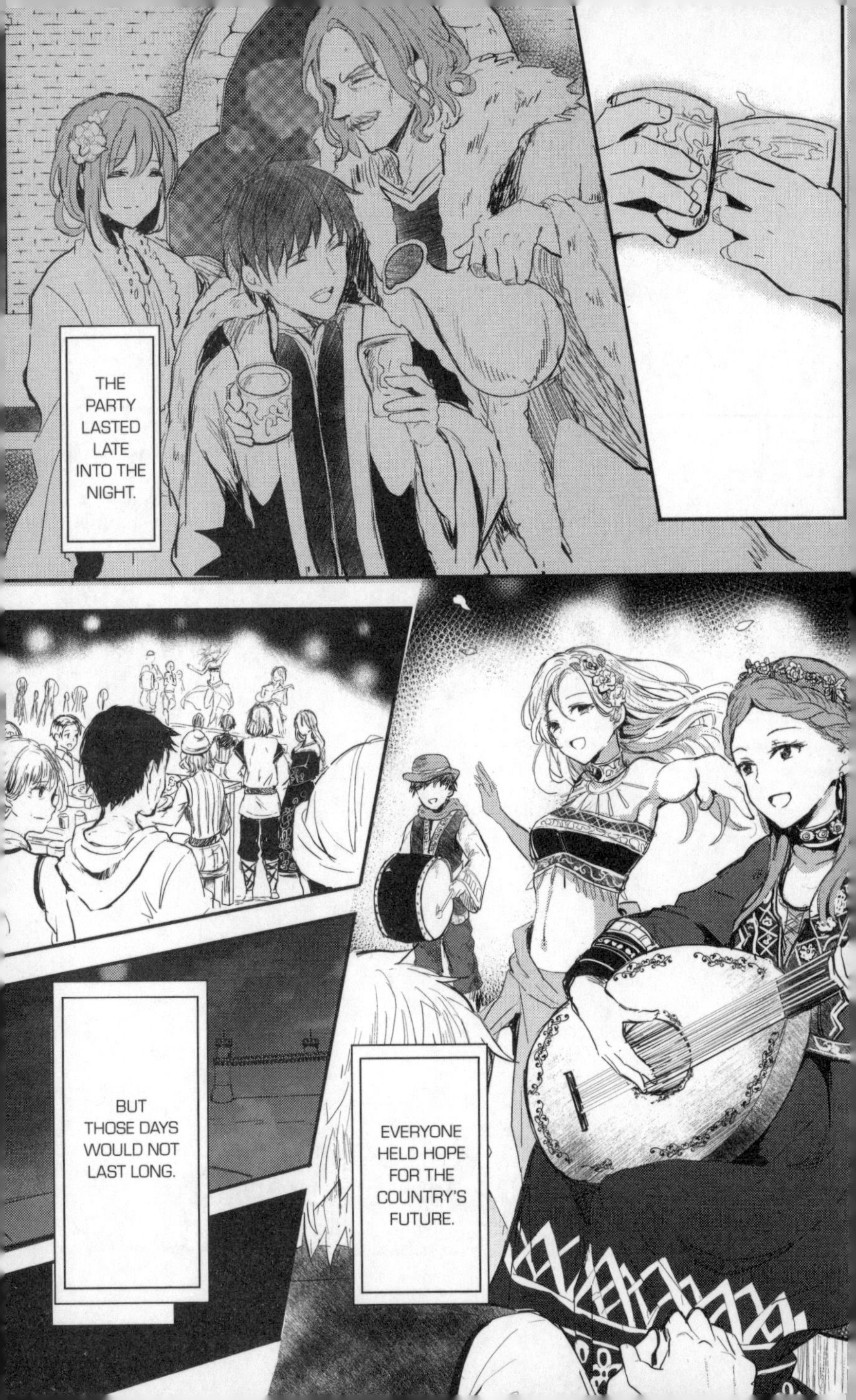
THE PARTY LASTED LATE INTO THE NIGHT.
EVERYONE HELD HOPE FOR THE COUNTRY'S FUTURE.
BUT THOSE DAYS WOULD NOT LAST LONG.

HER Royal Highness seems to be angry

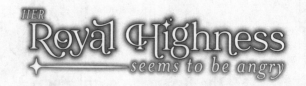

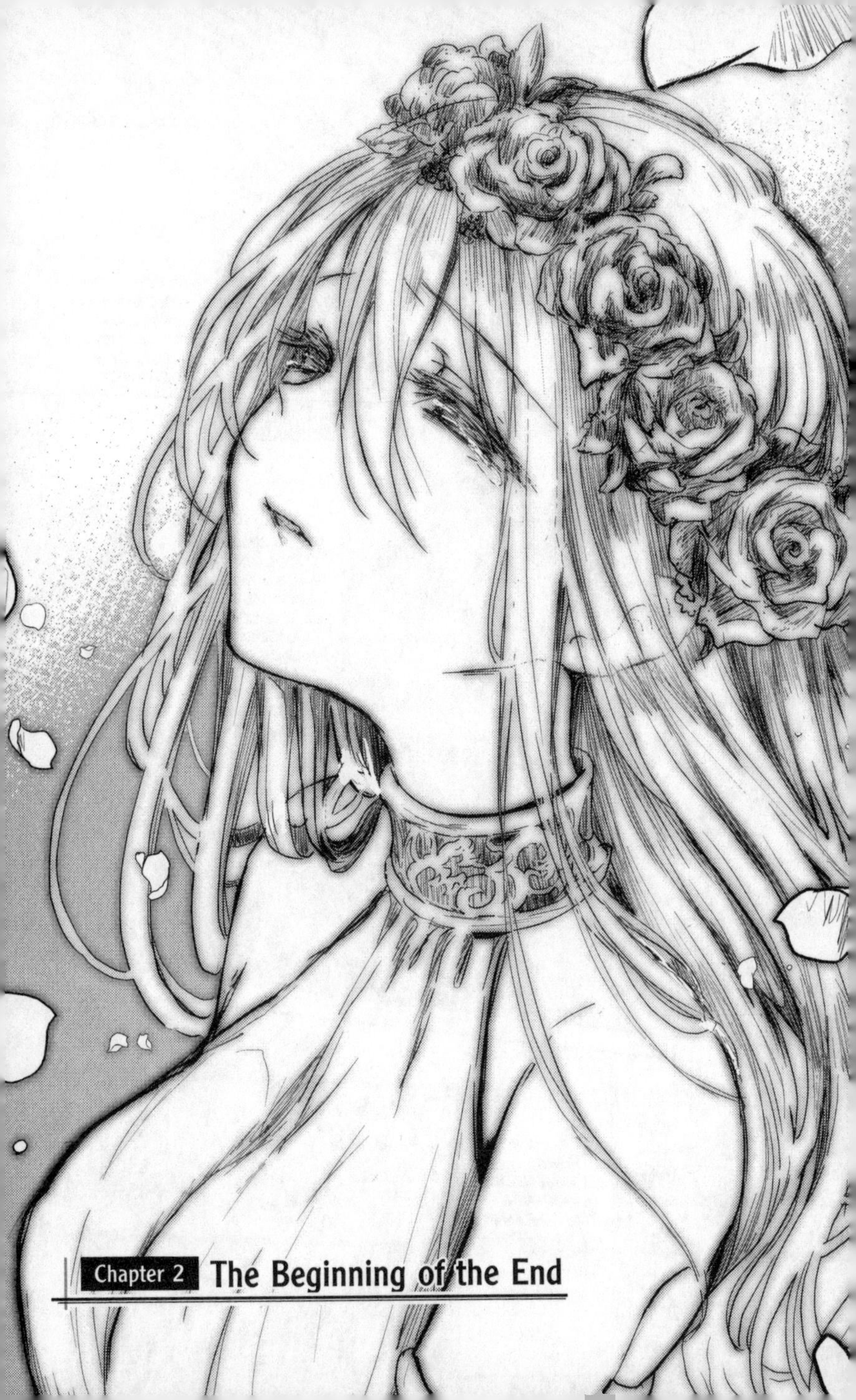

Chapter 2 The Beginning of the End

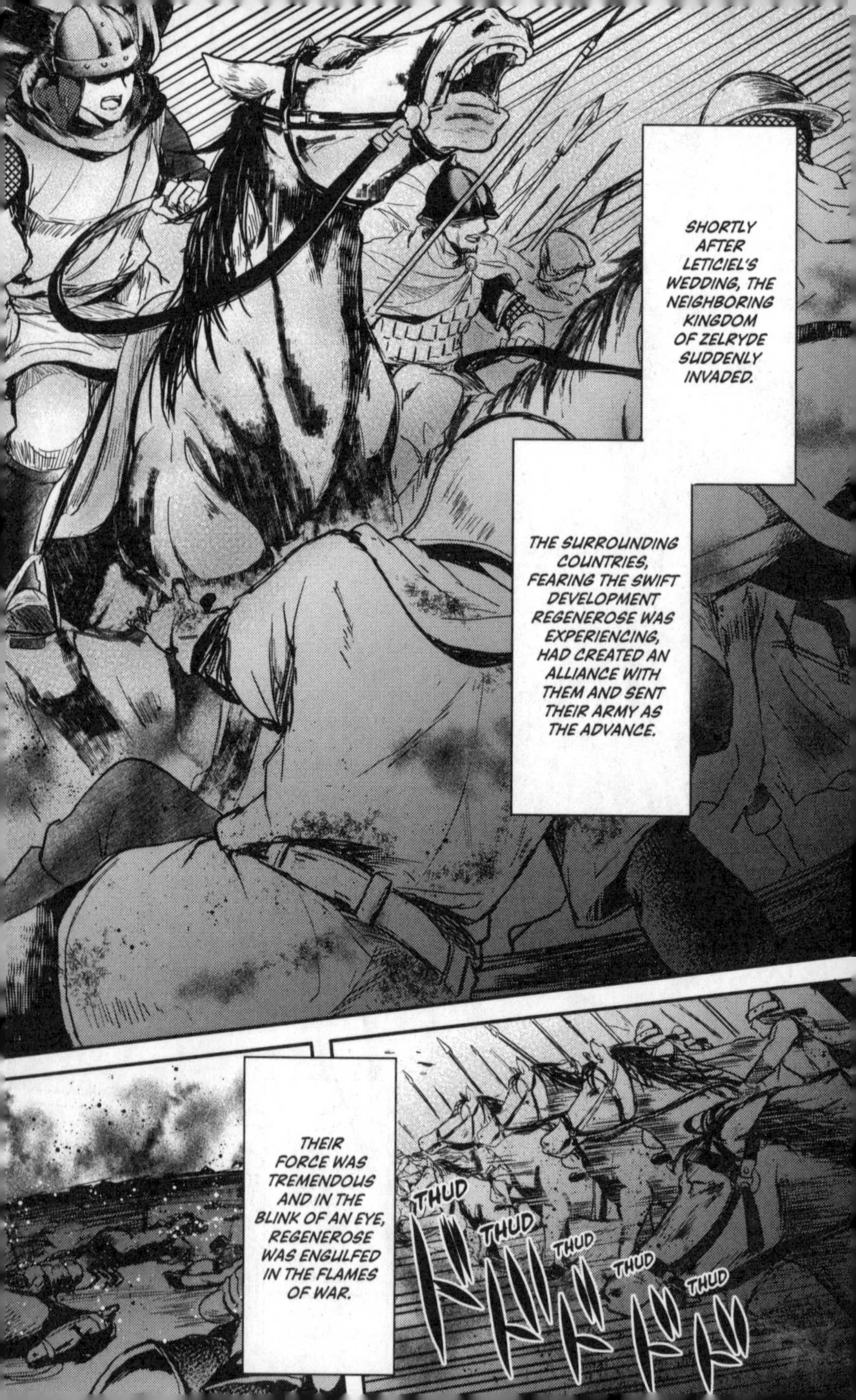
SHORTLY AFTER LETICIEL'S WEDDING, THE NEIGHBORING KINGDOM OF ZELRYDE SUDDENLY INVADED.
THE SURROUNDING COUNTRIES, FEARING THE SWIFT DEVELOPMENT REGENEROSE WAS EXPERIENCING, HAD CREATED AN ALLIANCE WITH THEM AND SENT THEIR ARMY AS THE ADVANCE.
THEIR FORCE WAS TREMENDOUS AND IN THE BLINK OF AN EYE, REGENEROSE WAS ENGULFED IN THE FLAMES OF WAR.
THUD
THUD
THUD
THUD
THUD

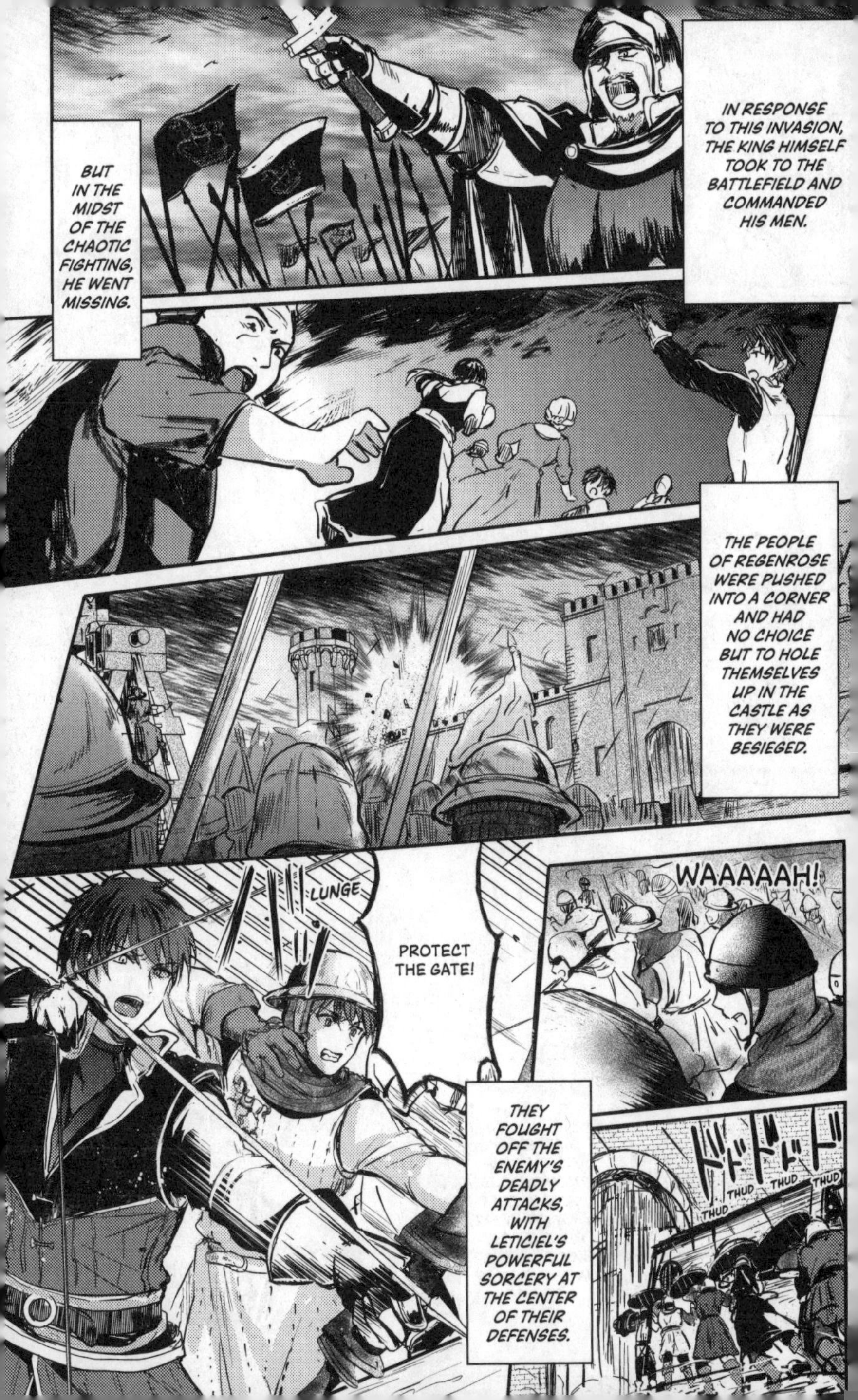
IN RESPONSE TO THIS INVASION, THE KING HIMSELF TOOK TO THE BATTLEFIELD AND COMMANDED HIS MEN.
BUT IN THE MIDST OF THE CHAOTIC FIGHTING, HE WENT MISSING.
THE PEOPLE OF REGENROSE WERE PUSHED INTO A CORNER AND HAD NO CHOICE BUT TO HOLE THEMSELVES UP IN THE CASTLE AS THEY WERE BESIEGED.
WAAAAAH!
ドドドドド
THUD THUD THUD THUD
THEY FOUGHT OFF THE ENEMY'S DEADLY ATTACKS, WITH LETICIEL'S POWERFUL SORCERY AT THE CENTER OF THEIR DEFENSES.
PROTECT THE GATE!
LUNGE

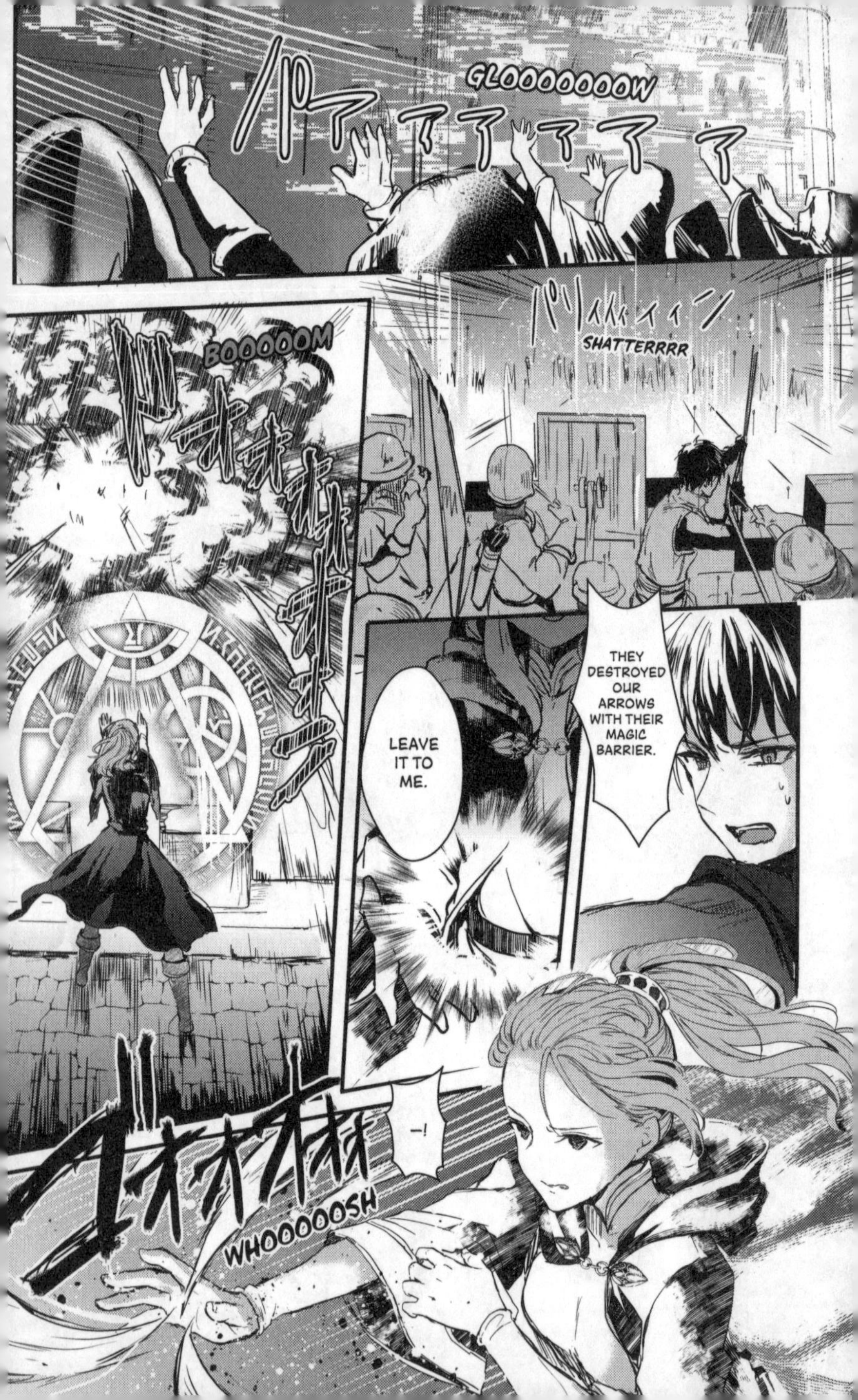
GLOOOOOOOW
SHATTERRRR
THEY DESTROYED OUR ARROWS WITH THEIR MAGIC BARRIER.
LEAVE IT TO ME.
BOOOOOM
—!
WHOOOOOSH

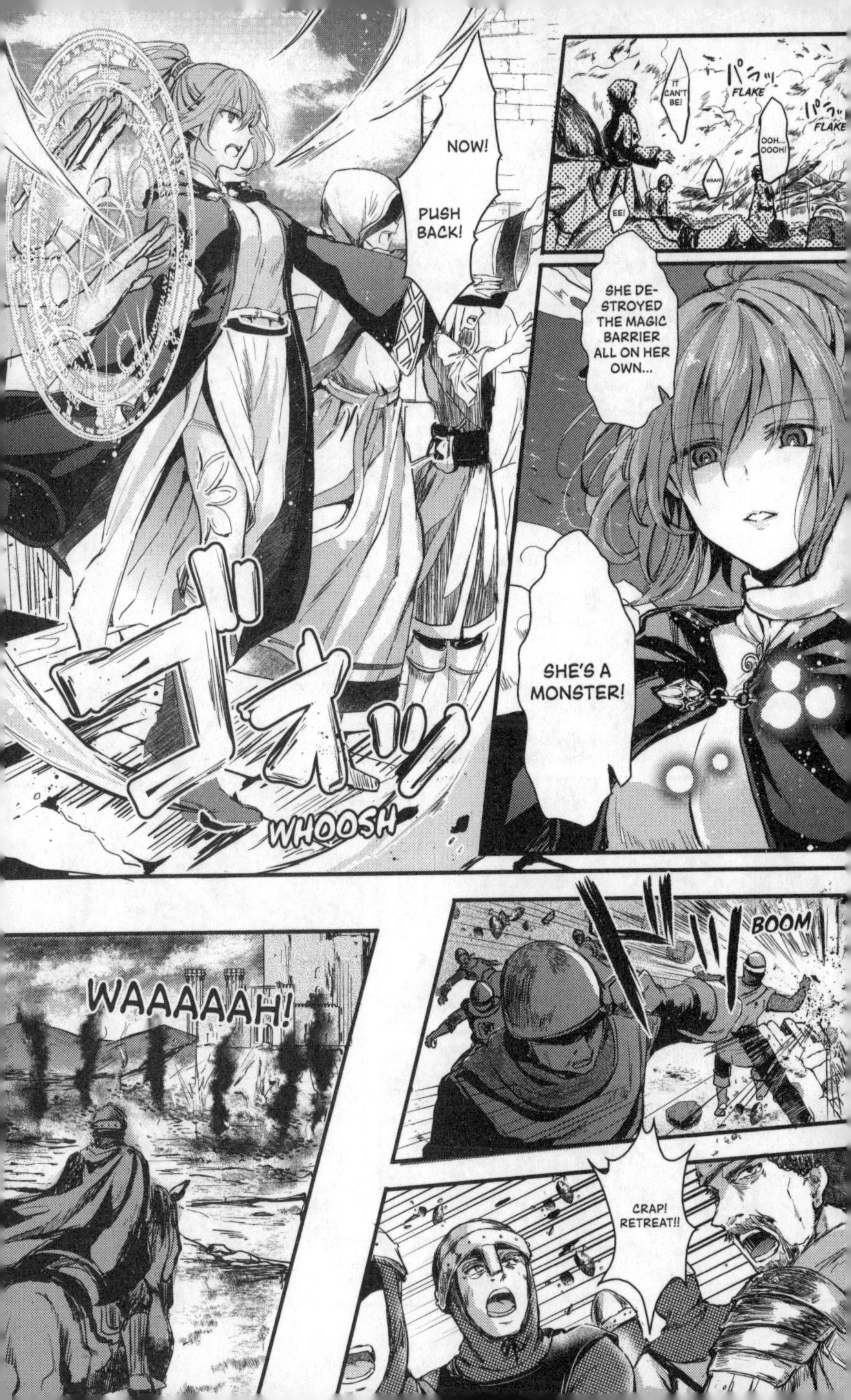
IT CAN'T BE!
パラッ
FLAKE
パラッ
FLAKE
OOH... OOOH!
WAAH!
EE!
SHE DESTROYED THE MAGIC BARRIER ALL ON HER OWN...
SHE'S A MONSTER!
NOW!
PUSH BACK!
WHOOSH
BOOM
CRAP! RETREAT!!
WAAAAAH!

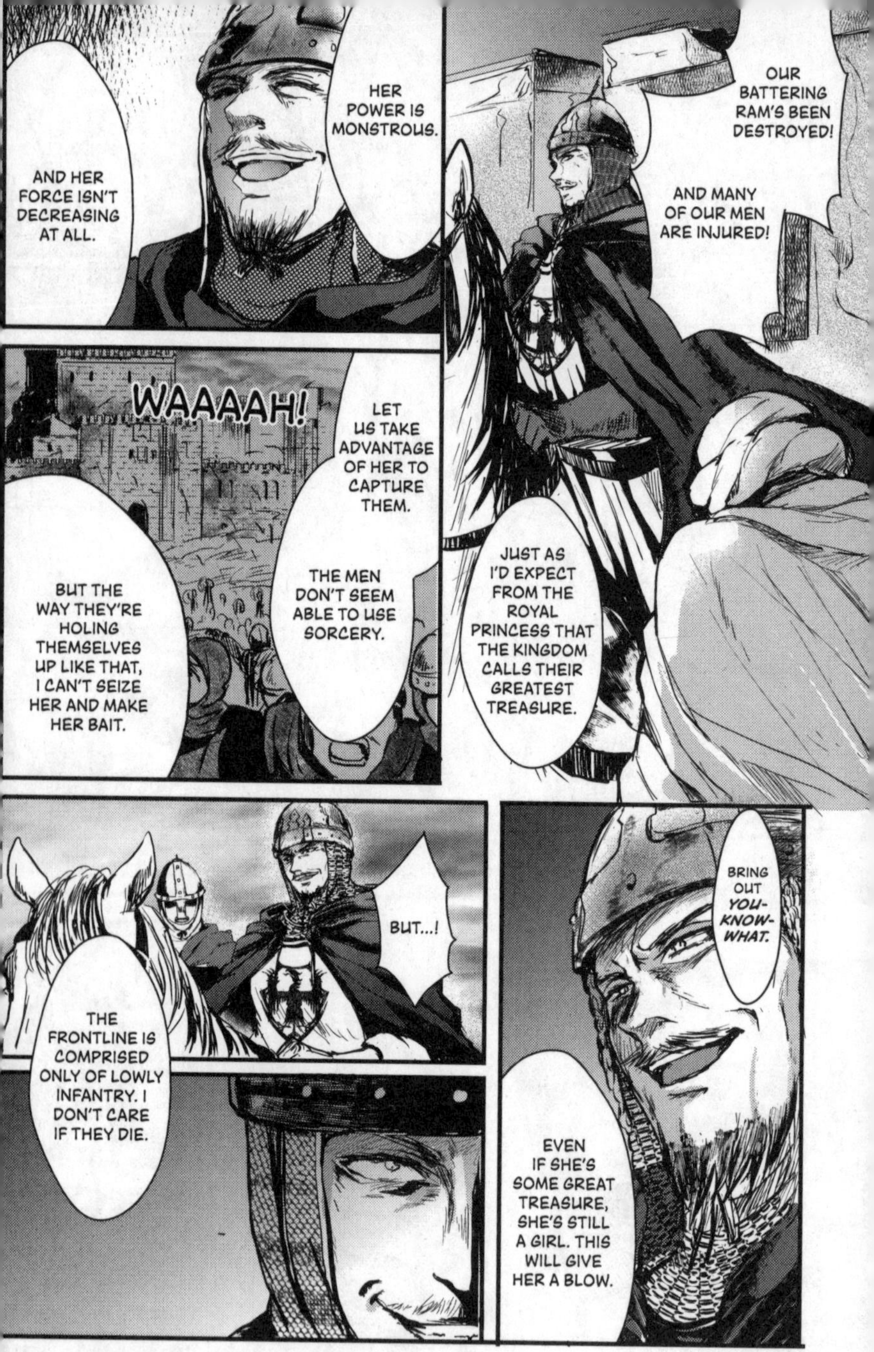
OUR BATTERING RAM'S BEEN DESTROYED!
AND MANY OF OUR MEN ARE INJURED!
JUST AS I'D EXPECT FROM THE ROYAL PRINCESS THAT THE KINGDOM CALLS THEIR GREATEST TREASURE.
HER POWER IS MONSTROUS.
AND HER FORCE ISN'T DECREASING AT ALL.
WAAAAH!
LET US TAKE ADVANTAGE OF HER TO CAPTURE THEM.
THE MEN DON'T SEEM ABLE TO USE SORCERY.
BUT THE WAY THEY'RE HOLING THEMSELVES UP LIKE THAT, I CAN'T SEIZE HER AND MAKE HER BAIT.
BRING OUT *YOU-KNOW-WHAT.*
EVEN IF SHE'S SOME GREAT TREASURE, SHE'S STILL A GIRL. THIS WILL GIVE HER A BLOW.
BUT...!
THE FRONTLINE IS COMPRISED ONLY OF LOWLY INFANTRY. I DON'T CARE IF THEY DIE.

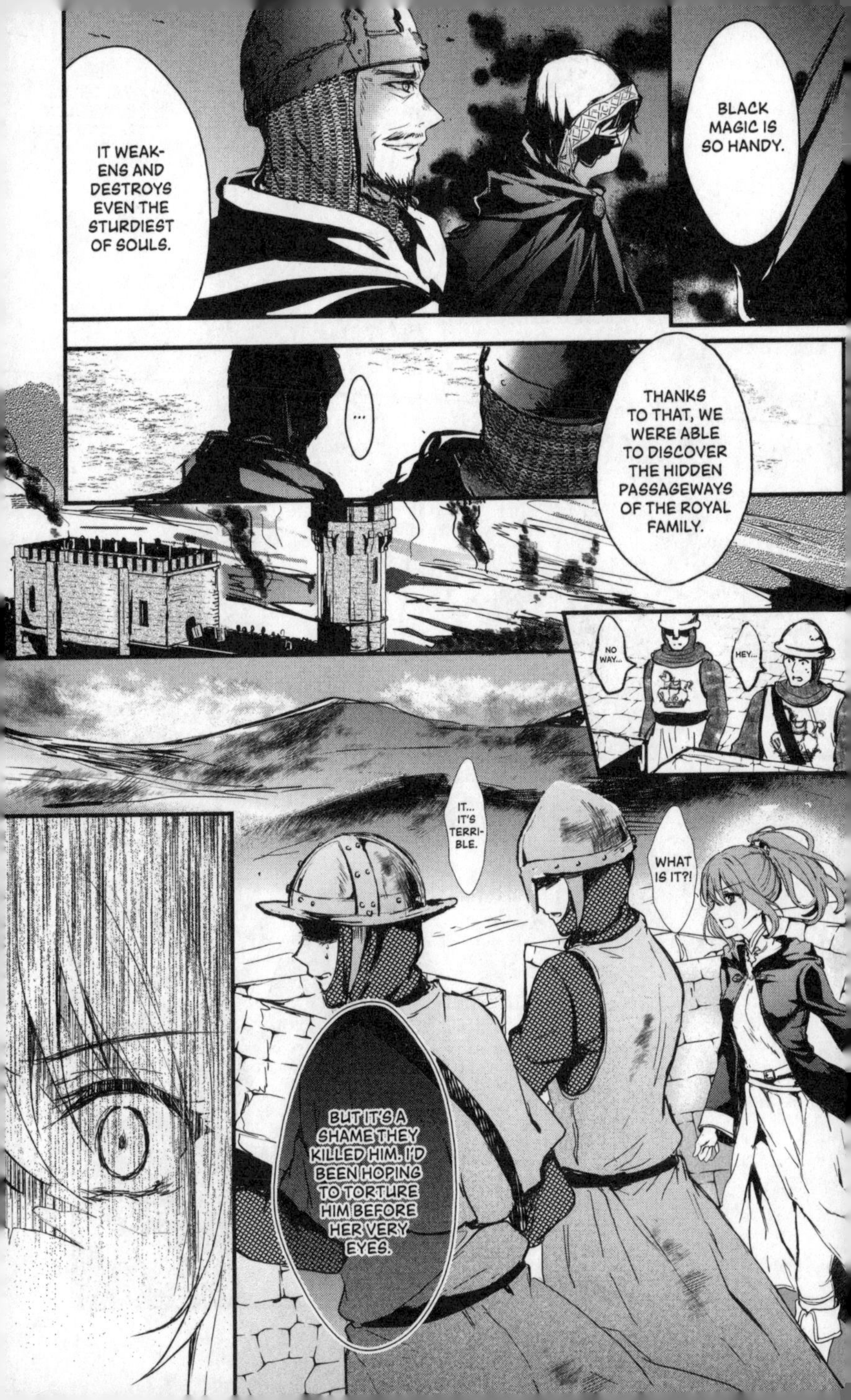
BLACK MAGIC IS SO HANDY.
IT WEAK-ENS AND DESTROYS EVEN THE STURDIEST OF SOULS.
THANKS TO THAT, WE WERE ABLE TO DISCOVER THE HIDDEN PASSAGEWAYS OF THE ROYAL FAMILY.
...
HEY...
NO WAY...
WHAT IS IT?!
IT... IT'S TERRI-BLE.
BUT IT'S A SHAME THEY KILLED HIM. I'D BEEN HOPING TO TORTURE HIM BEFORE HER VERY EYES.

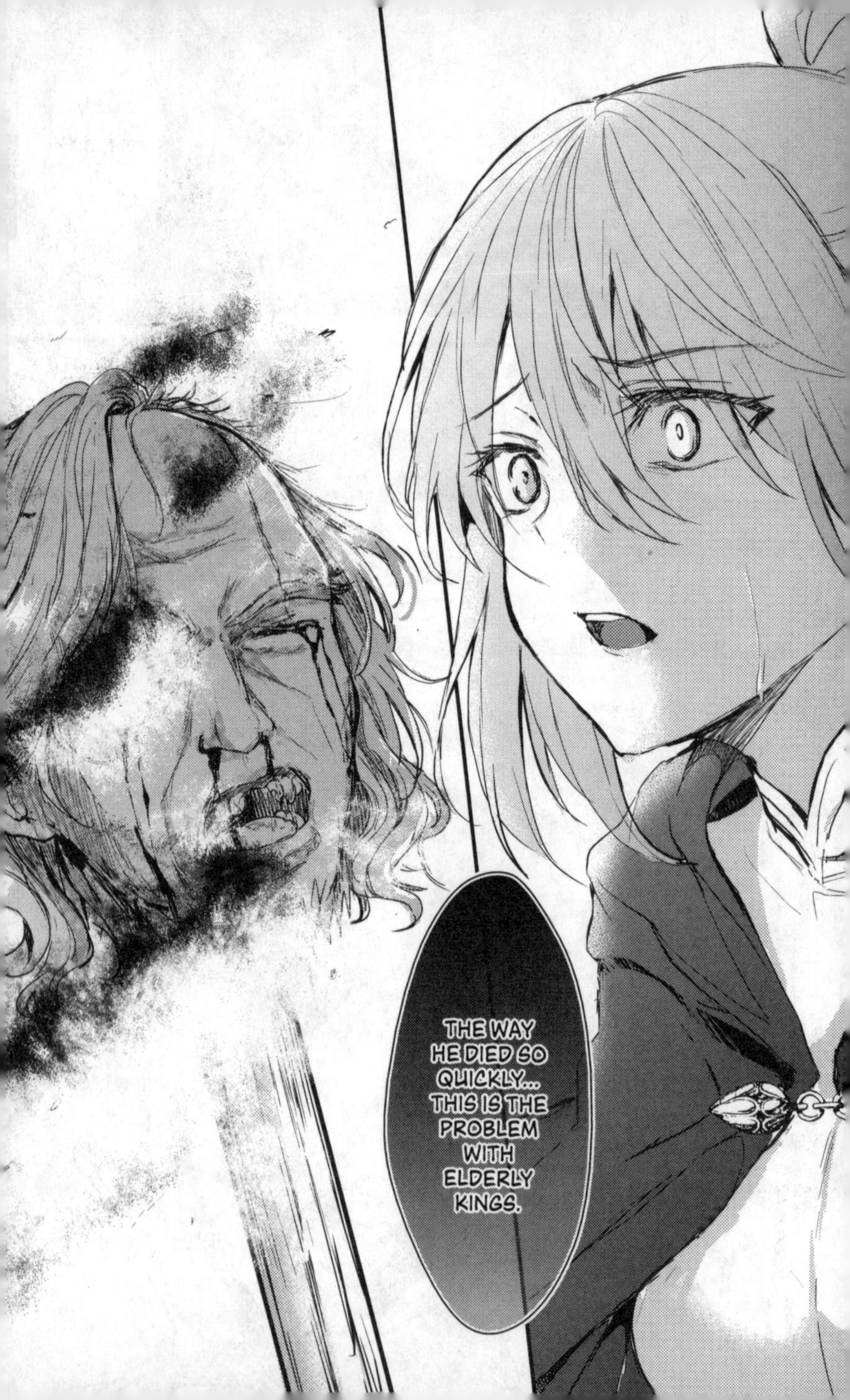
THE WAY HE DIED SO QUICKLY... THIS IS THE PROBLEM WITH ELDERLY KINGS.

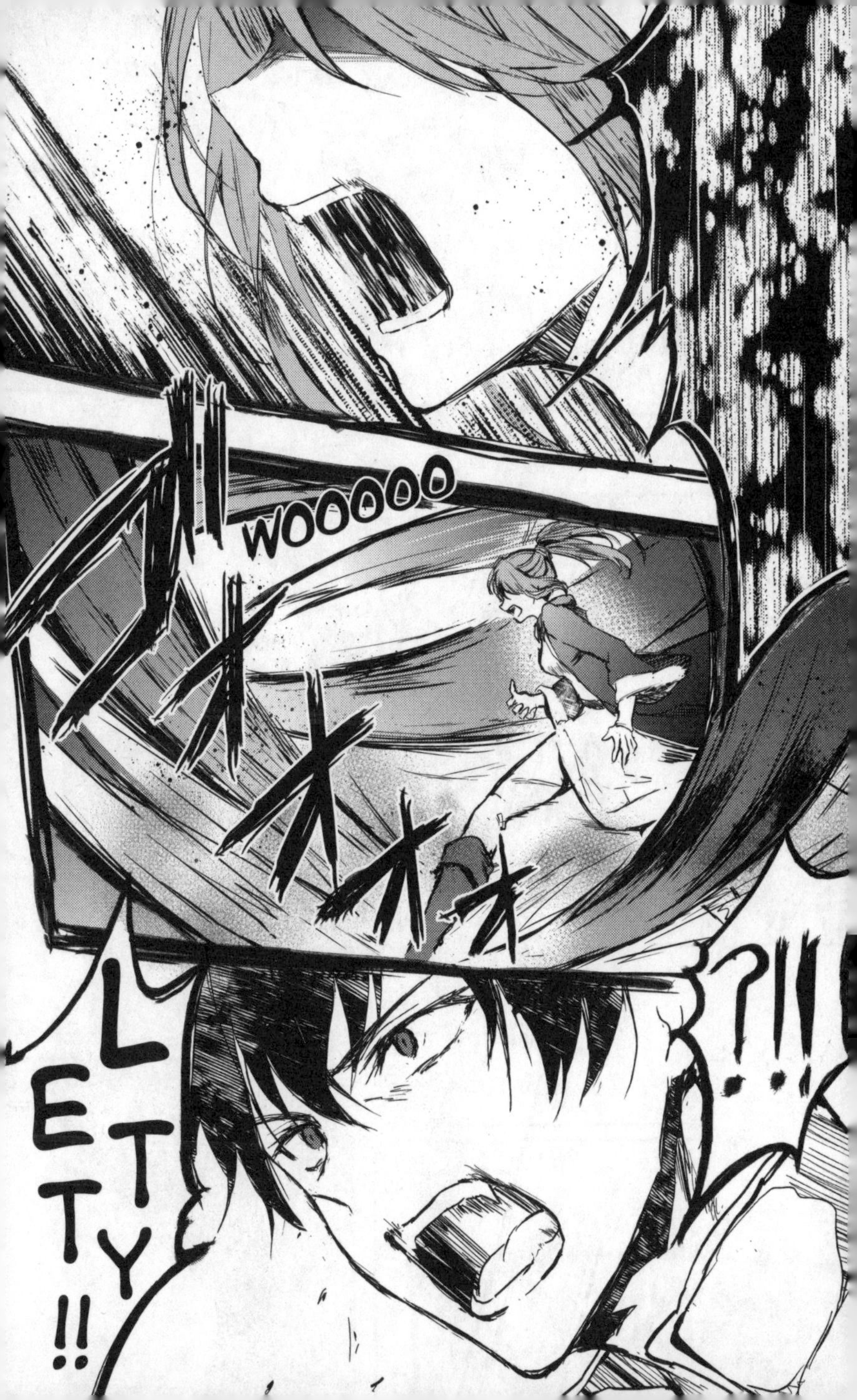
WOOOOO
?!!
LETTY!!

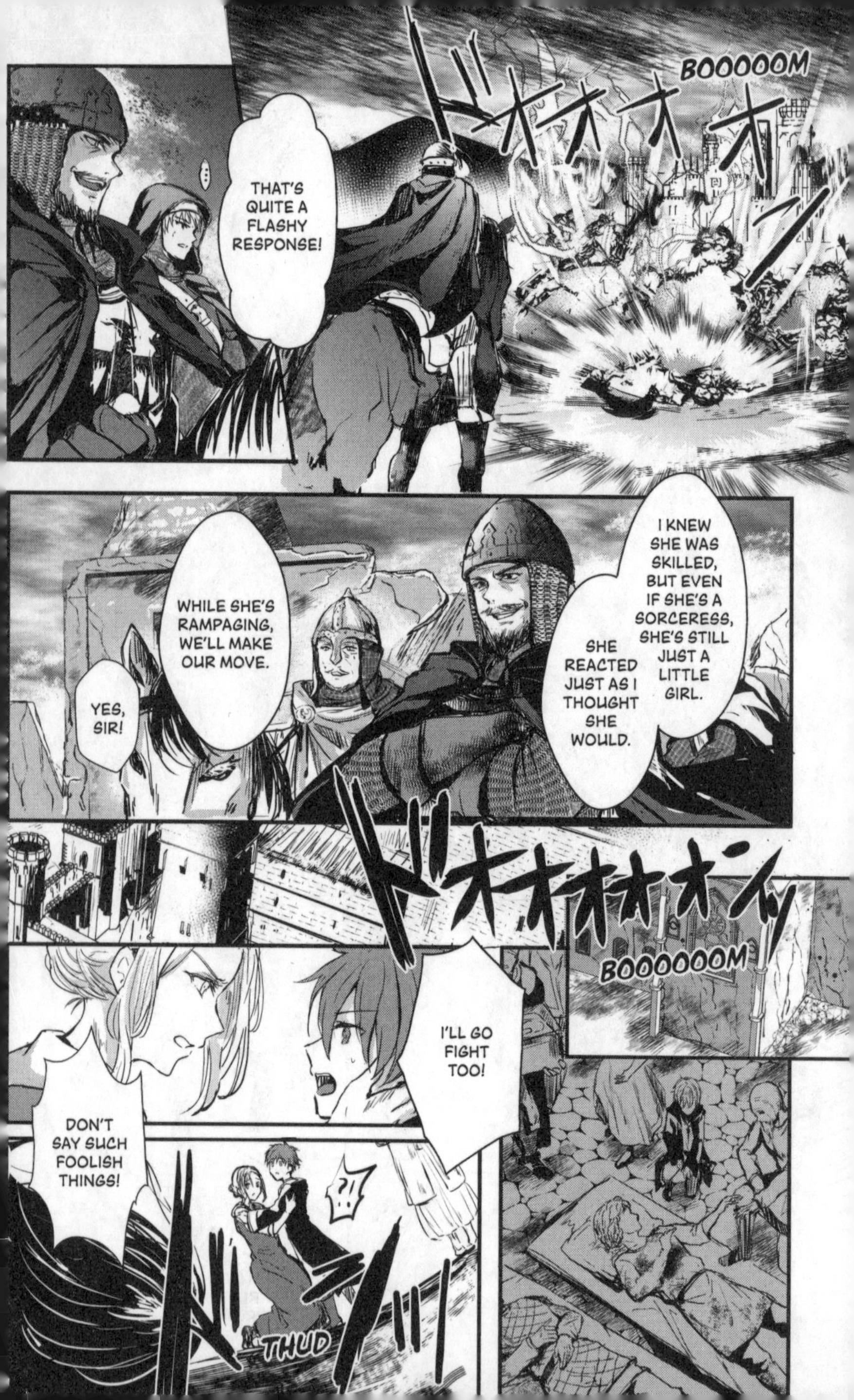
BOOOOOM
THAT'S QUITE A FLASHY RESPONSE!
…
I KNEW SHE WAS SKILLED, BUT EVEN IF SHE'S A SORCERESS, SHE'S STILL JUST A LITTLE GIRL.
SHE REACTED JUST AS I THOUGHT SHE WOULD.
WHILE SHE'S RAMPAGING, WE'LL MAKE OUR MOVE.
YES, SIR!
BOOOOOOM
I'LL GO FIGHT TOO!
DON'T SAY SUCH FOOLISH THINGS!
?!
THUD

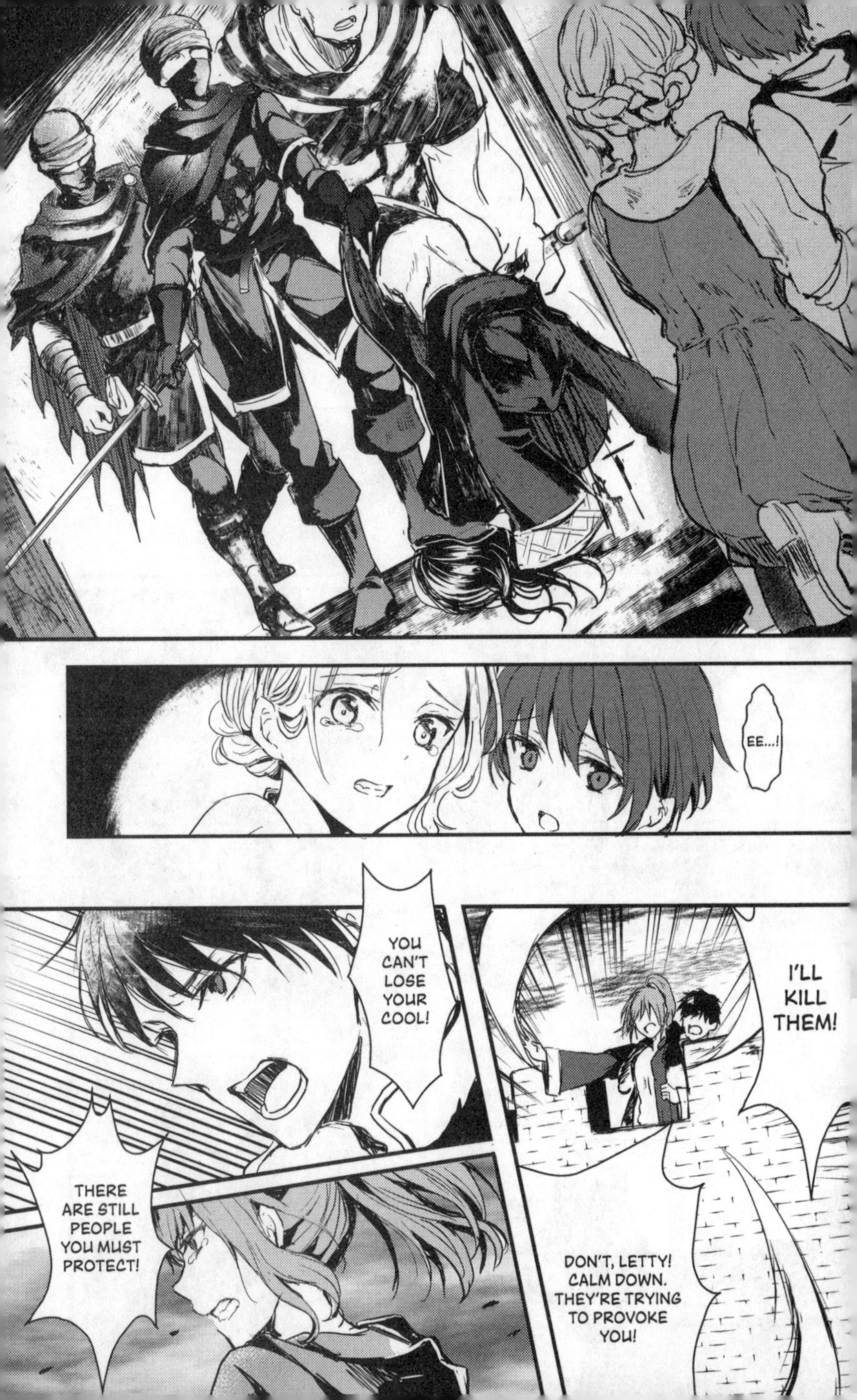
EE...!
I'LL KILL THEM!
DON'T, LETTY! CALM DOWN. THEY'RE TRYING TO PROVOKE YOU!
YOU CAN'T LOSE YOUR COOL!
THERE ARE STILL PEOPLE YOU MUST PROTECT!

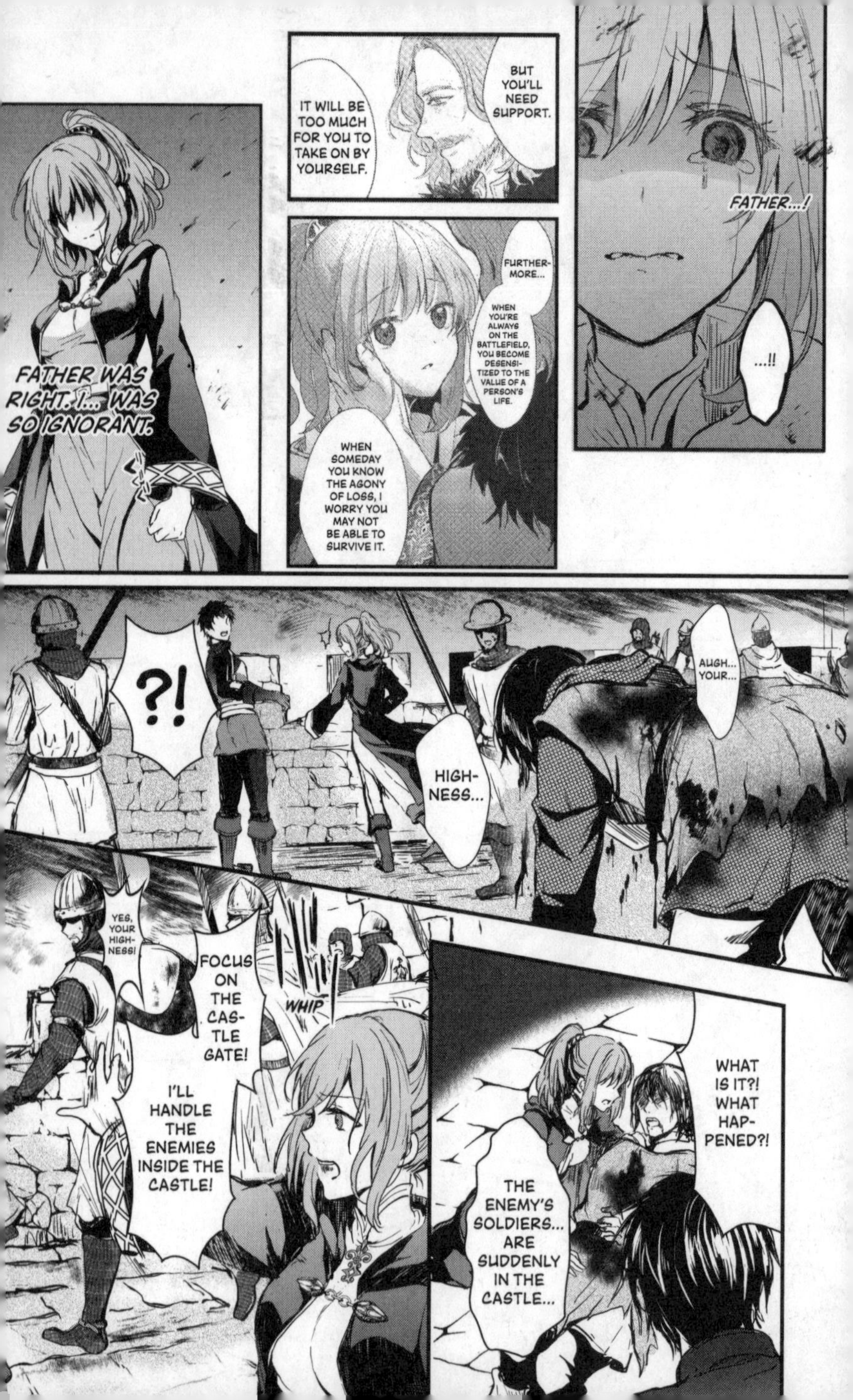
FATHER...!
...!!
BUT YOU'LL NEED SUPPORT.
IT WILL BE TOO MUCH FOR YOU TO TAKE ON BY YOURSELF.
FURTHER-MORE...
WHEN YOU'RE ALWAYS ON THE BATTLEFIELD, YOU BECOME DESENSI-TIZED TO THE VALUE OF A PERSON'S LIFE.
WHEN SOMEDAY YOU KNOW THE AGONY OF LOSS, I WORRY YOU MAY NOT BE ABLE TO SURVIVE IT.
FATHER WAS RIGHT. I... WAS SO IGNORANT.
AUGH... YOUR...
HIGH-NESS...
?!
WHAT IS IT?! WHAT HAP-PENED?!
THE ENEMY'S SOLDIERS... ARE SUDDENLY IN THE CASTLE...
FOCUS ON THE CAS-TLE GATE!
WHIP
I'LL HANDLE THE ENEMIES INSIDE THE CASTLE!
YES, YOUR HIGH-NESS!

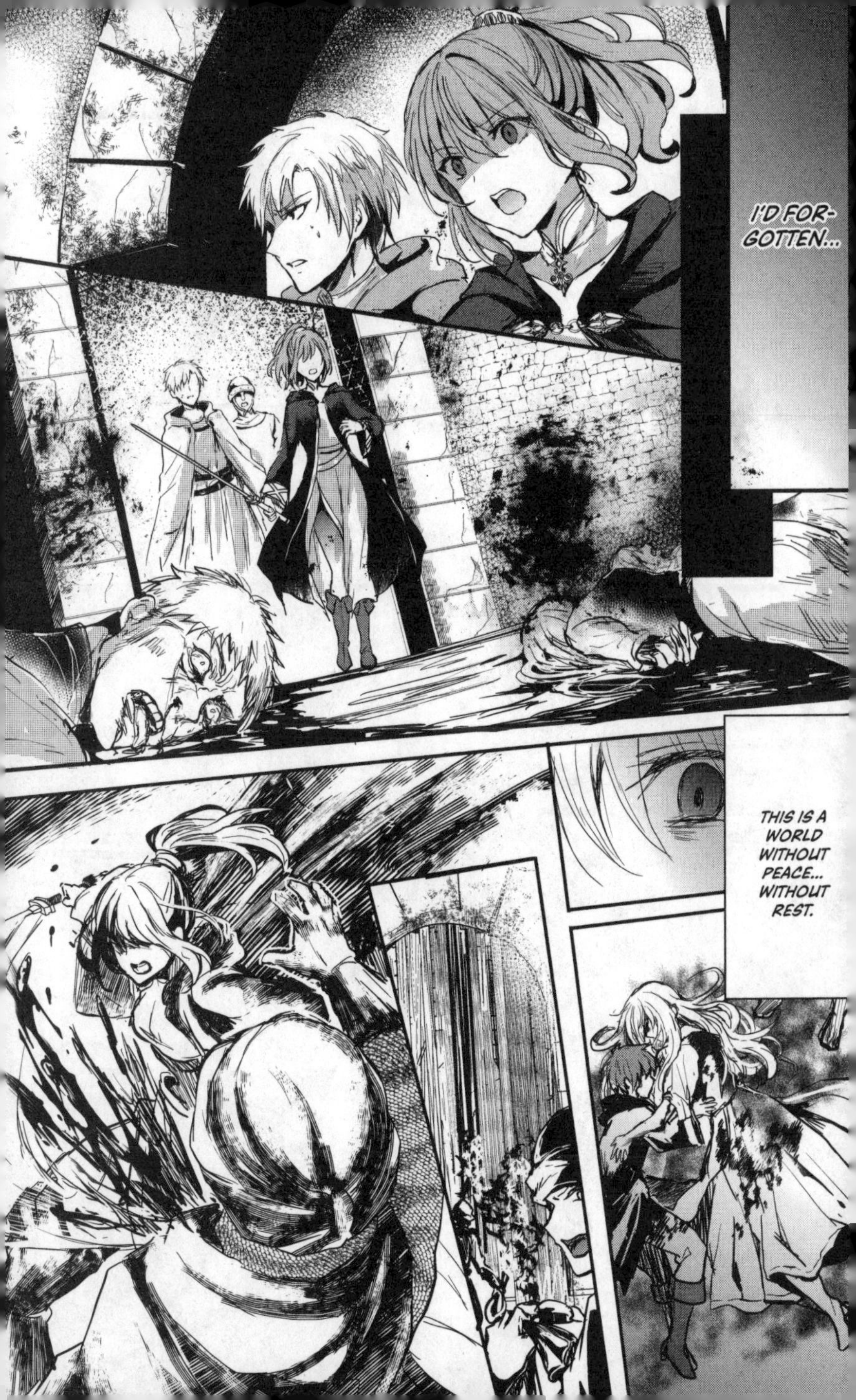
I'D FOR-
GOTTEN...
THIS IS A WORLD WITHOUT PEACE... WITHOUT REST.

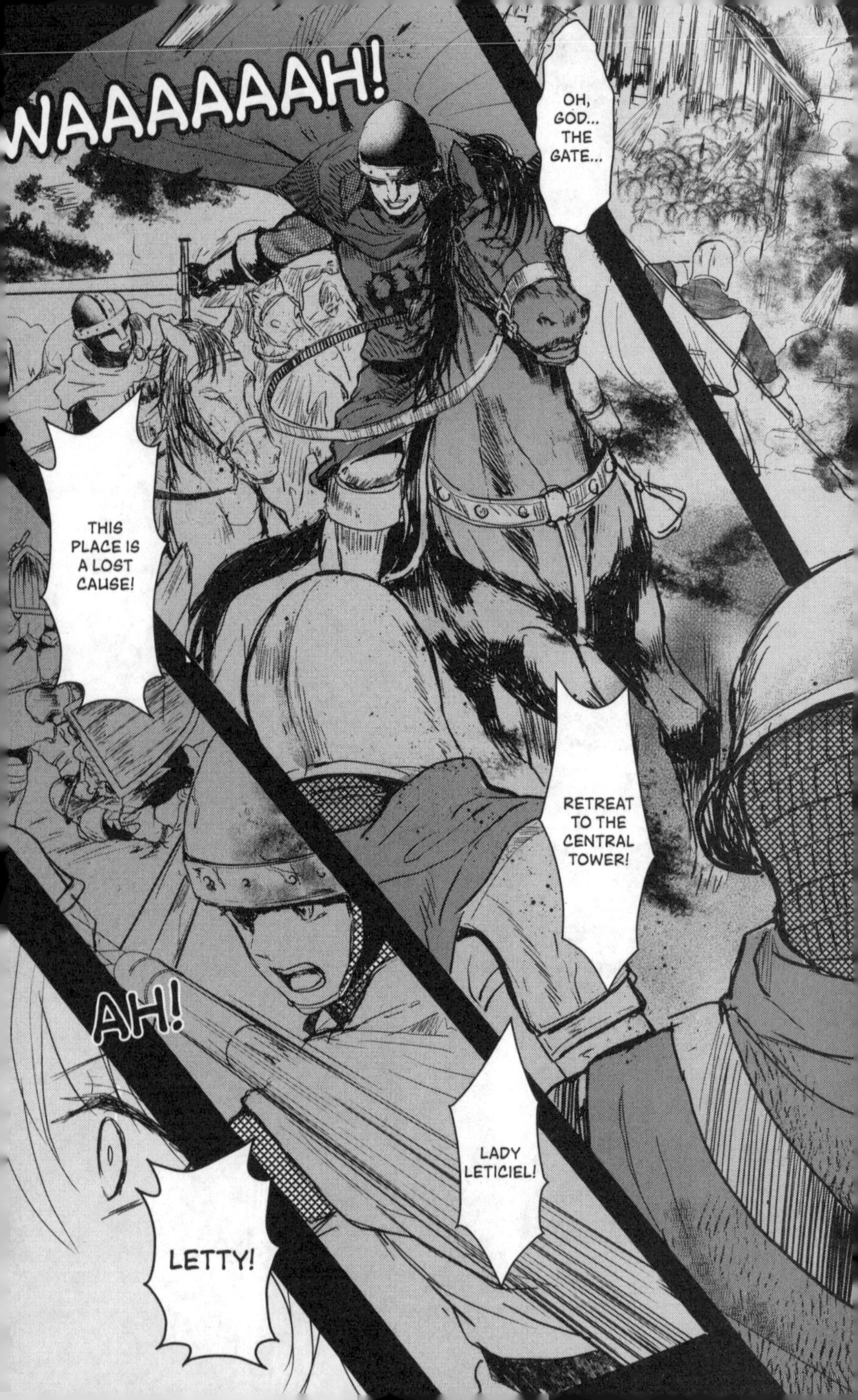
OH, GOD... THE GATE...
WAAAAAAH!
THIS PLACE IS A LOST CAUSE!
RETREAT TO THE CENTRAL TOWER!
AH!
LADY LETICIEL!
LETTY!

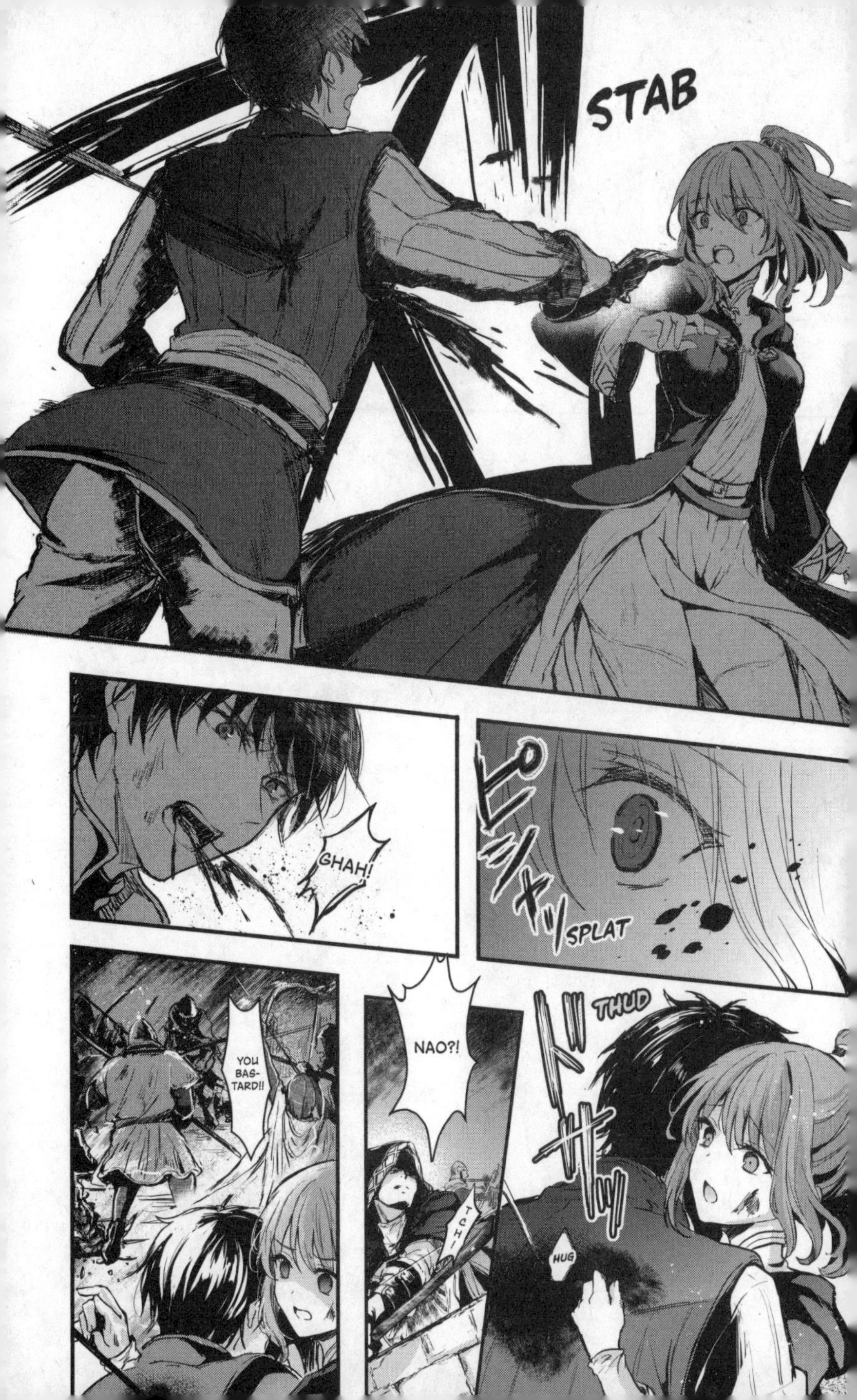
STAB
ピシャッ
SPLAT
GHAH!
THUD
HUG
NAO?!
TCH!
YOU BAS-TARD!!

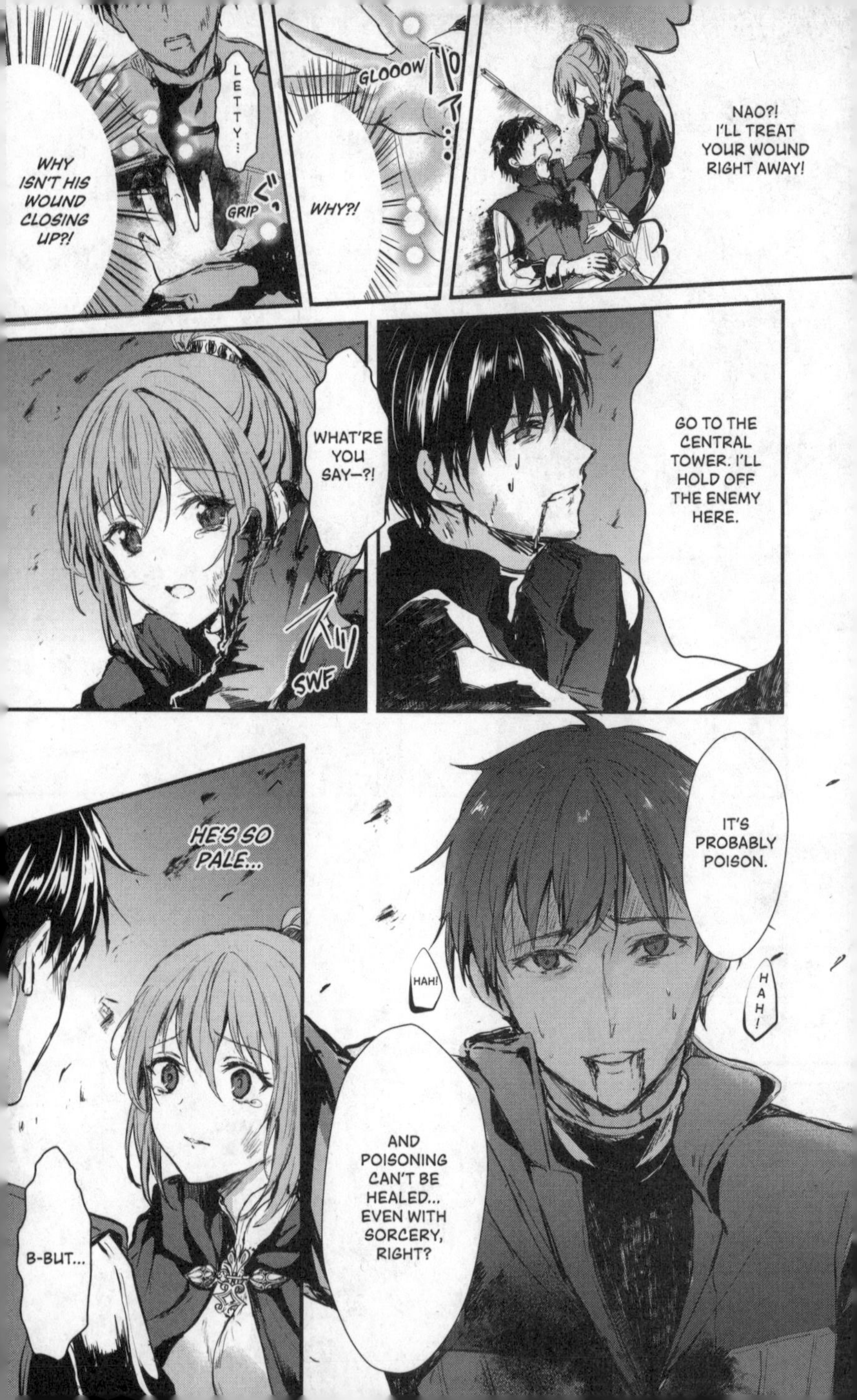
NAO?! I'LL TREAT YOUR WOUND RIGHT AWAY!
GLOOOW
WHY?!
LETTY...
GRIP
WHY ISN'T HIS WOUND CLOSING UP?!
GO TO THE CENTRAL TOWER. I'LL HOLD OFF THE ENEMY HERE.
WHAT'RE YOU SAY—?!
SWF
IT'S PROBABLY POISON.
HE'S SO PALE...
HAH!
HAH!
AND POISONING CAN'T BE HEALED... EVEN WITH SORCERY, RIGHT?
B-BUT...

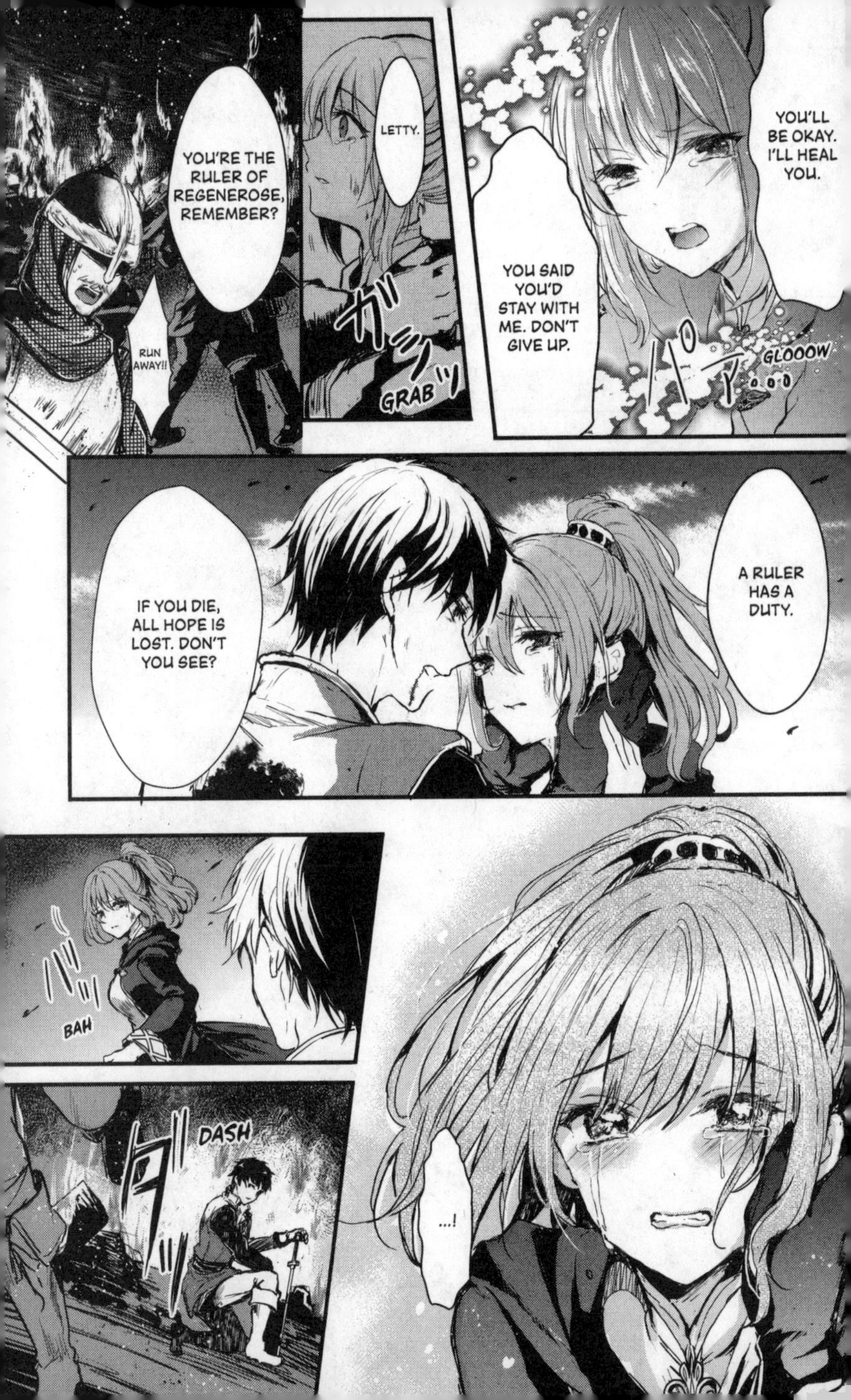
YOU'LL BE OKAY. I'LL HEAL YOU.
YOU SAID YOU'D STAY WITH ME. DON'T GIVE UP.
GLOOOW
LETTY.
GRAB
YOU'RE THE RULER OF REGENEROSE, REMEMBER?
RUN AWAY!!
A RULER HAS A DUTY.
IF YOU DIE, ALL HOPE IS LOST. DON'T YOU SEE?
...!
BAH
DASH

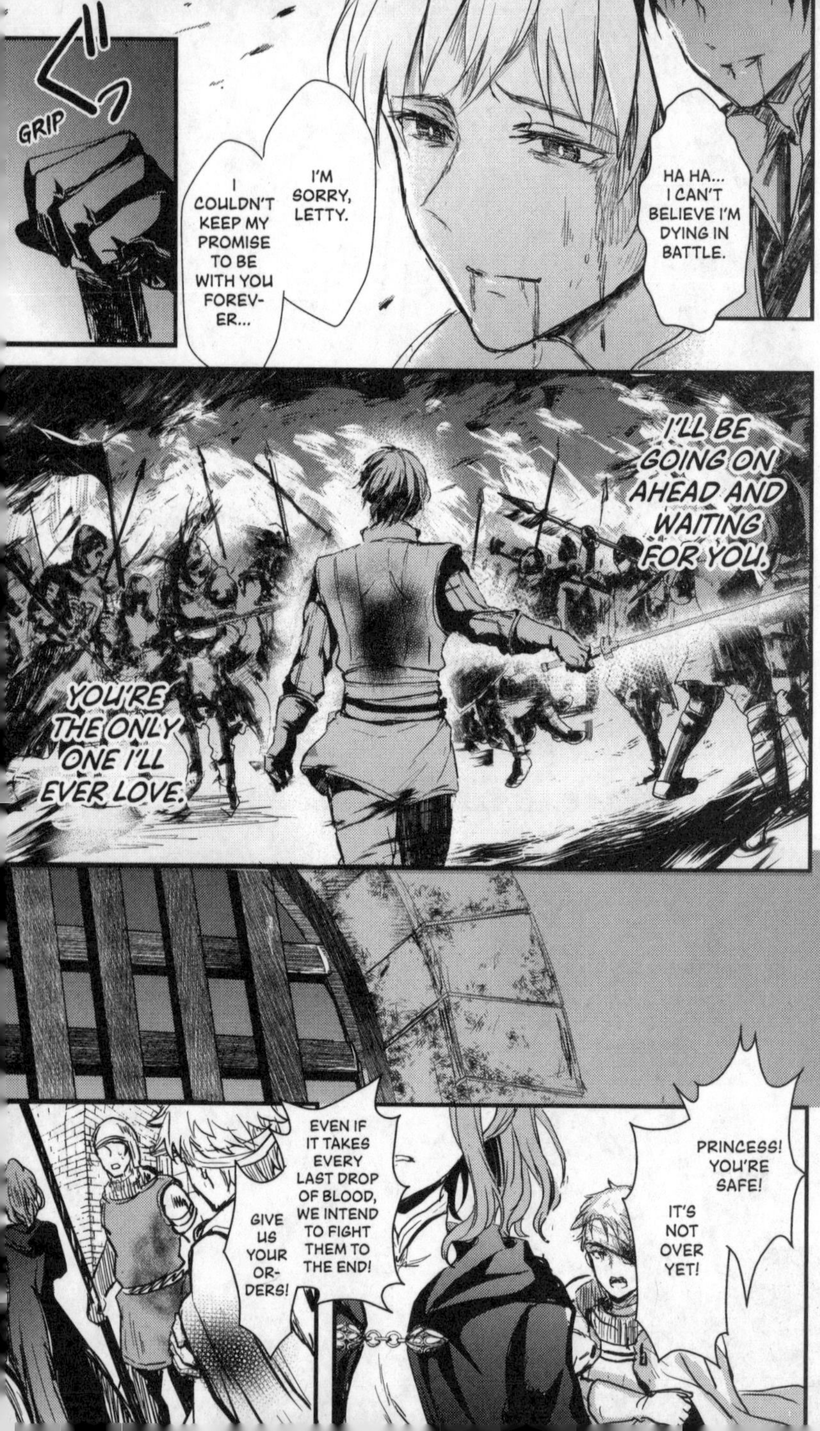
HA HA... I CAN'T BELIEVE I'M DYING IN BATTLE.
I'M SORRY, LETTY.
I COULDN'T KEEP MY PROMISE TO BE WITH YOU FOREVER-ER...
GRIP
I'LL BE GOING ON AHEAD AND WAITING FOR YOU.
YOU'RE THE ONLY ONE I'LL EVER LOVE.
PRINCESS! YOU'RE SAFE!
IT'S NOT OVER YET!
EVEN IF IT TAKES EVERY LAST DROP OF BLOOD, WE INTEND TO FIGHT THEM TO THE END!
GIVE US YOUR OR-DERS!

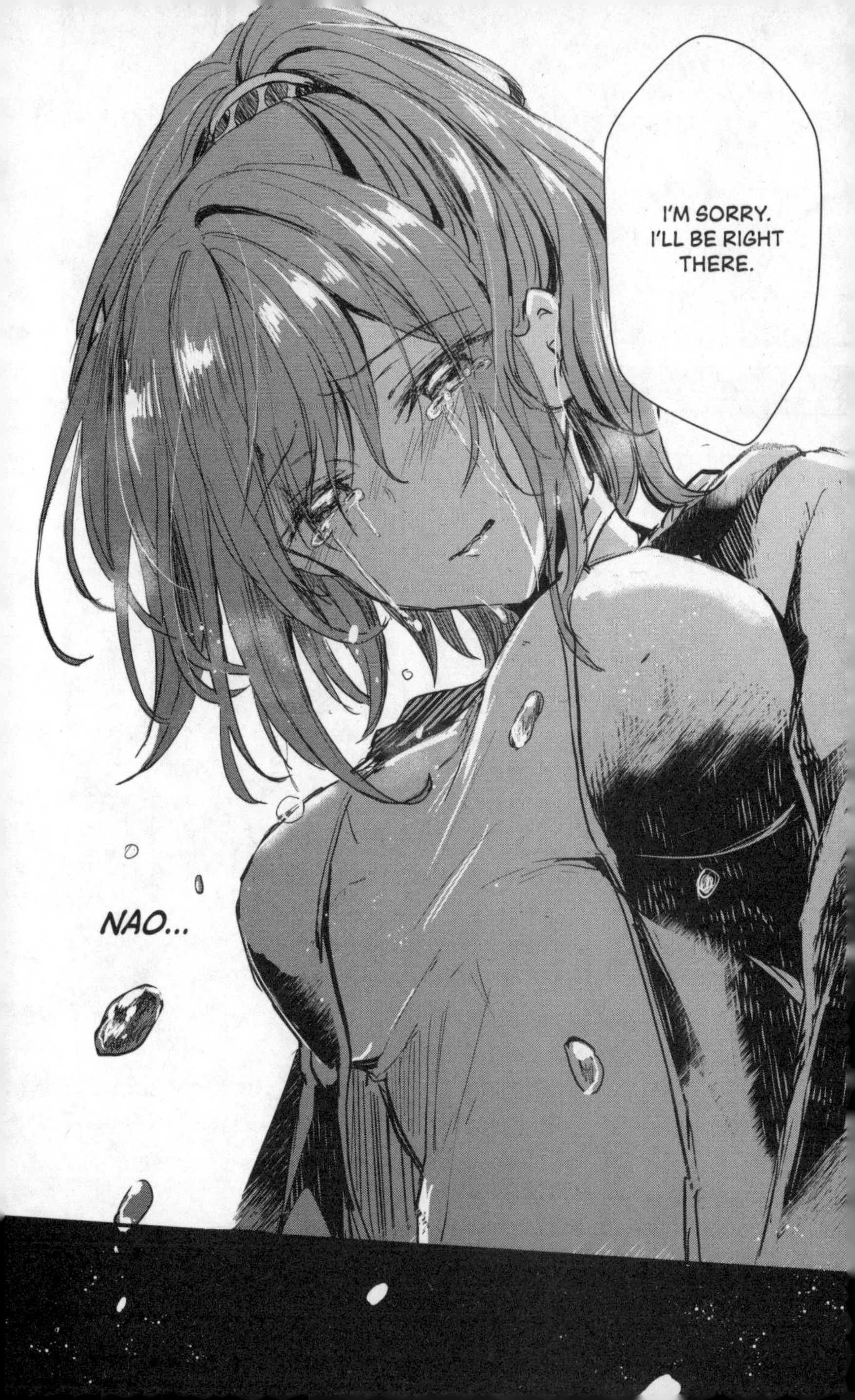
I'M SORRY. I'LL BE RIGHT THERE.
NAO...

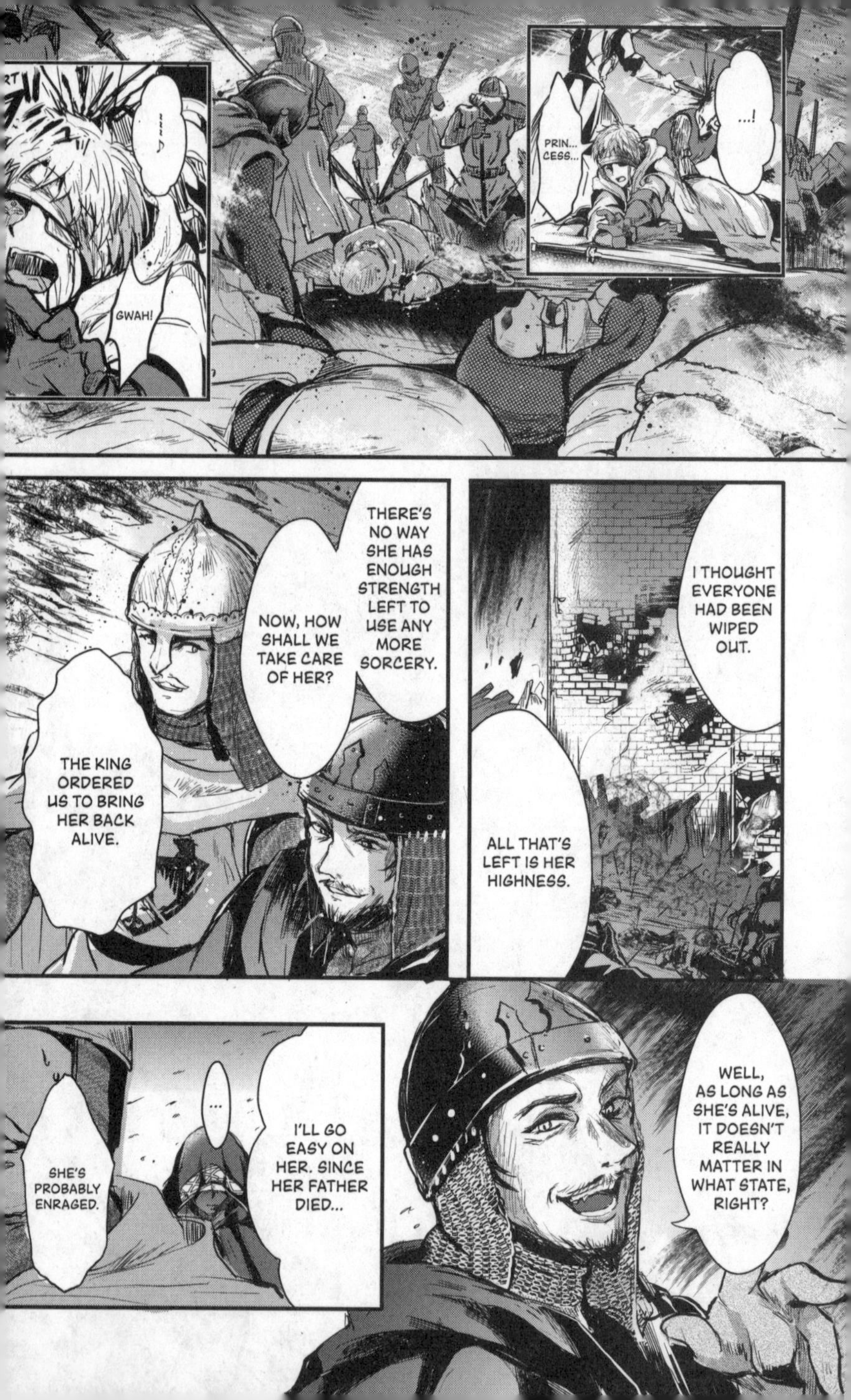
...!
PRIN... CESS...
GWAH!
I THOUGHT EVERYONE HAD BEEN WIPED OUT.
ALL THAT'S LEFT IS HER HIGHNESS.
THERE'S NO WAY SHE HAS ENOUGH STRENGTH LEFT TO USE ANY MORE SORCERY.
NOW, HOW SHALL WE TAKE CARE OF HER?
THE KING ORDERED US TO BRING HER BACK ALIVE.
WELL, AS LONG AS SHE'S ALIVE, IT DOESN'T REALLY MATTER IN WHAT STATE, RIGHT?
I'LL GO EASY ON HER. SINCE HER FATHER DIED...
...
SHE'S PROBABLY ENRAGED.

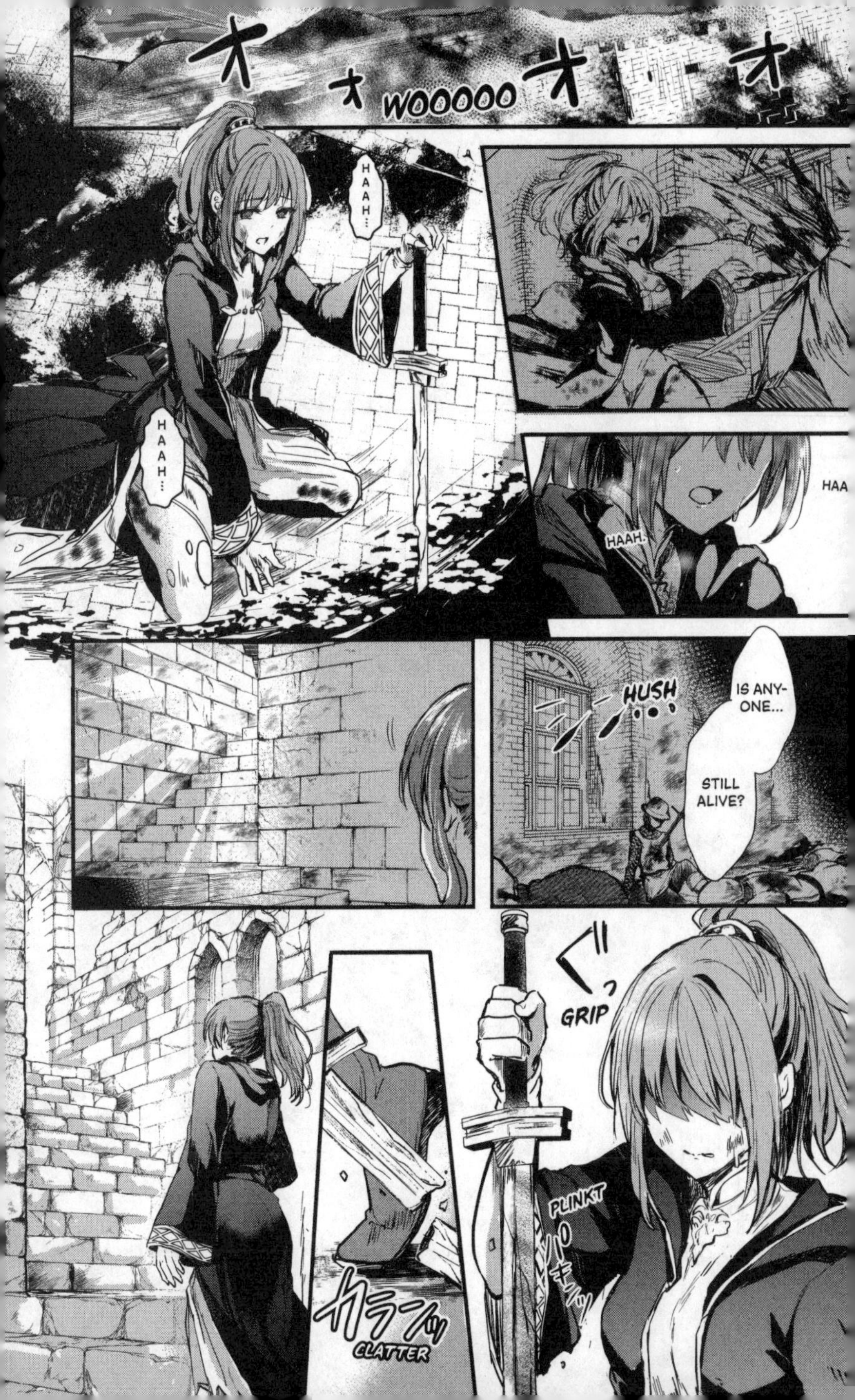
WOOOOO
HAA
HAAH.
HAAH...
HAAH...
HUSH
IS ANY-ONE...
STILL ALIVE?
GRIP
PLINKT
CLATTER

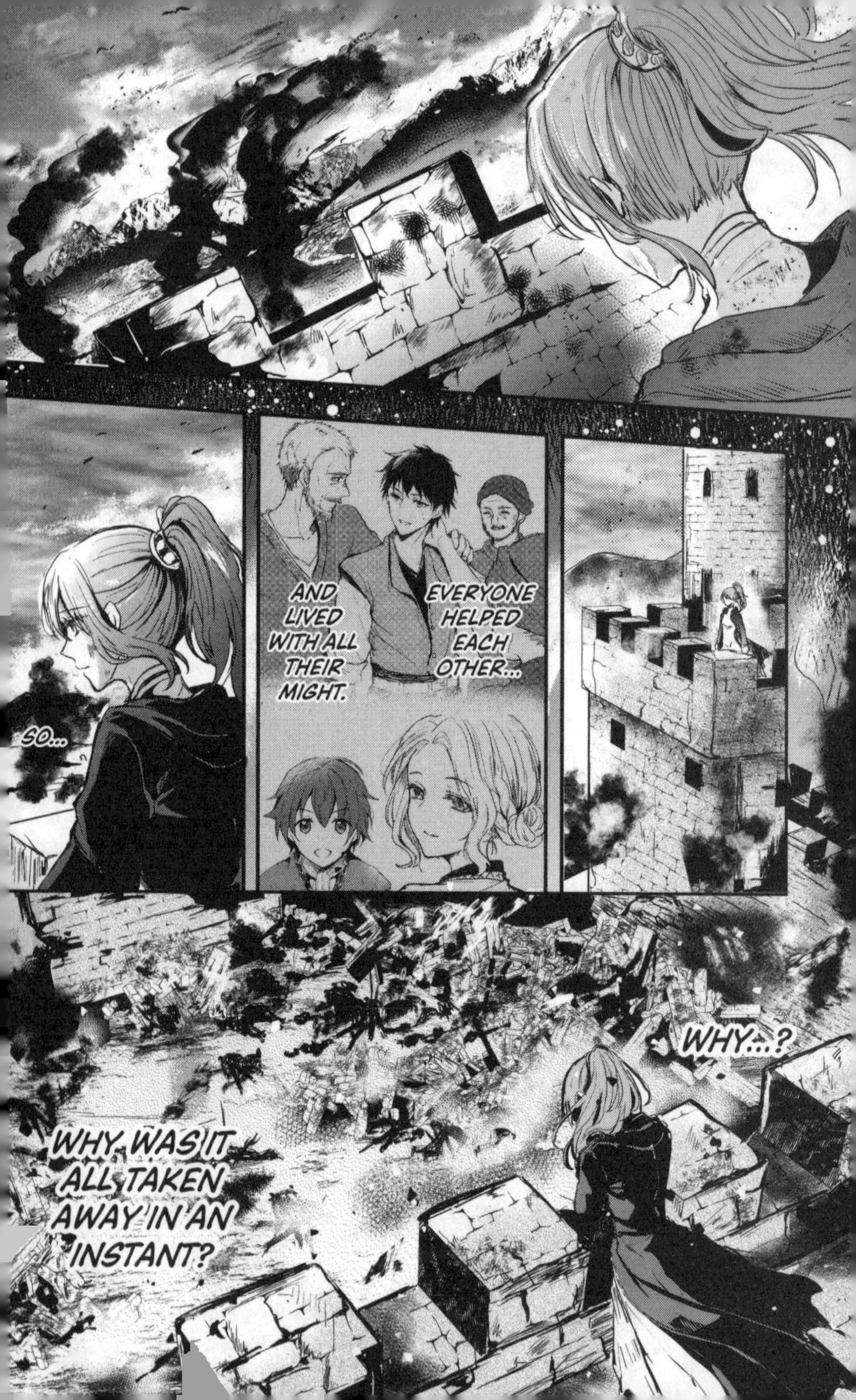
EVERYONE HELPED EACH OTHER...
AND LIVED WITH ALL THEIR MIGHT.
SO...
WHY...?
WHY WAS IT ALL TAKEN AWAY IN AN INSTANT?

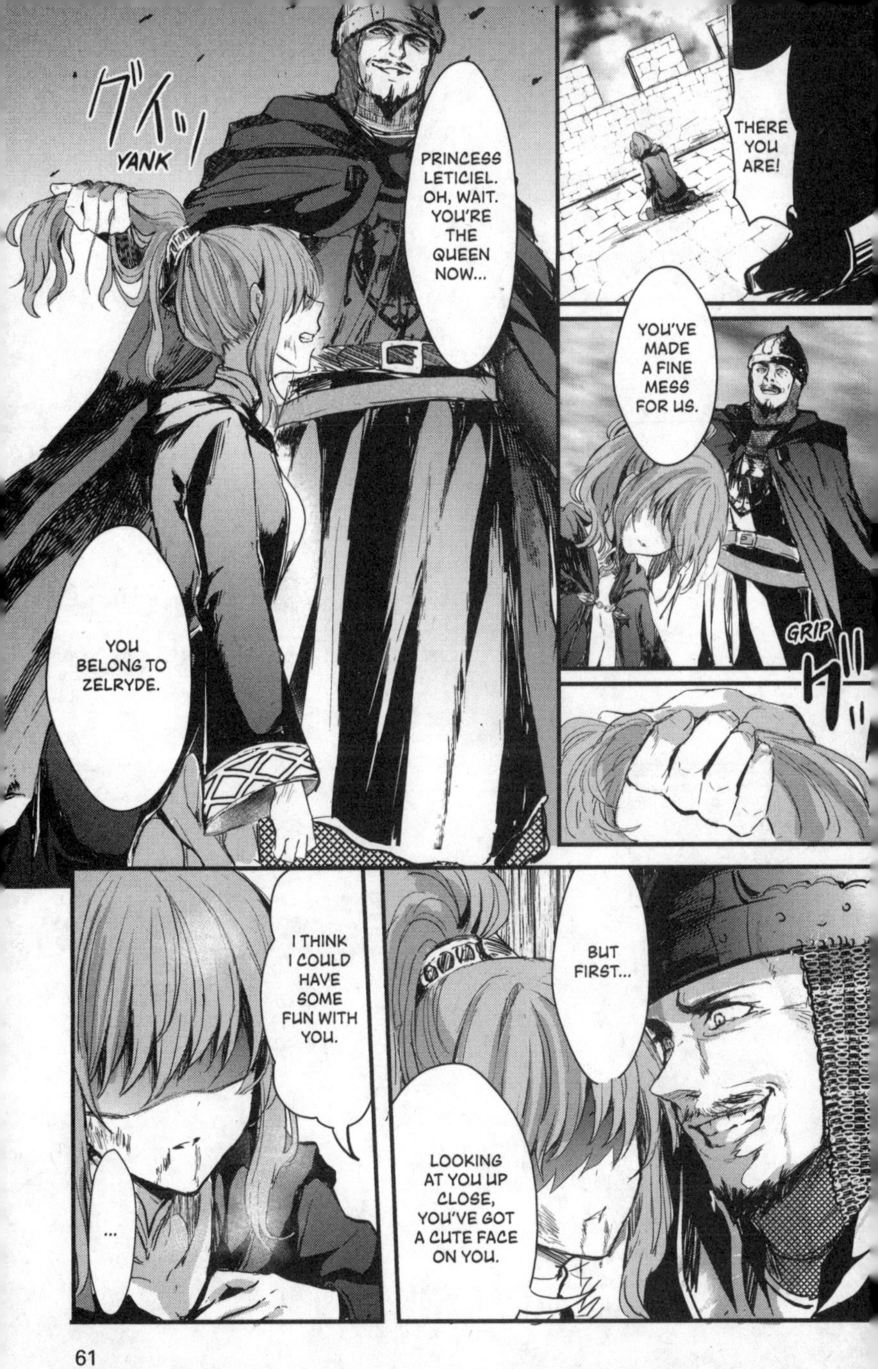
THERE YOU ARE!
YOU'VE MADE A FINE MESS FOR US.
GRIP
グイッ
YANK
PRINCESS LETICIEL. OH, WAIT. YOU'RE THE QUEEN NOW...
YOU BELONG TO ZELRYDE.
BUT FIRST...
LOOKING AT YOU UP CLOSE, YOU'VE GOT A CUTE FACE ON YOU.
I THINK I COULD HAVE SOME FUN WITH YOU.
...

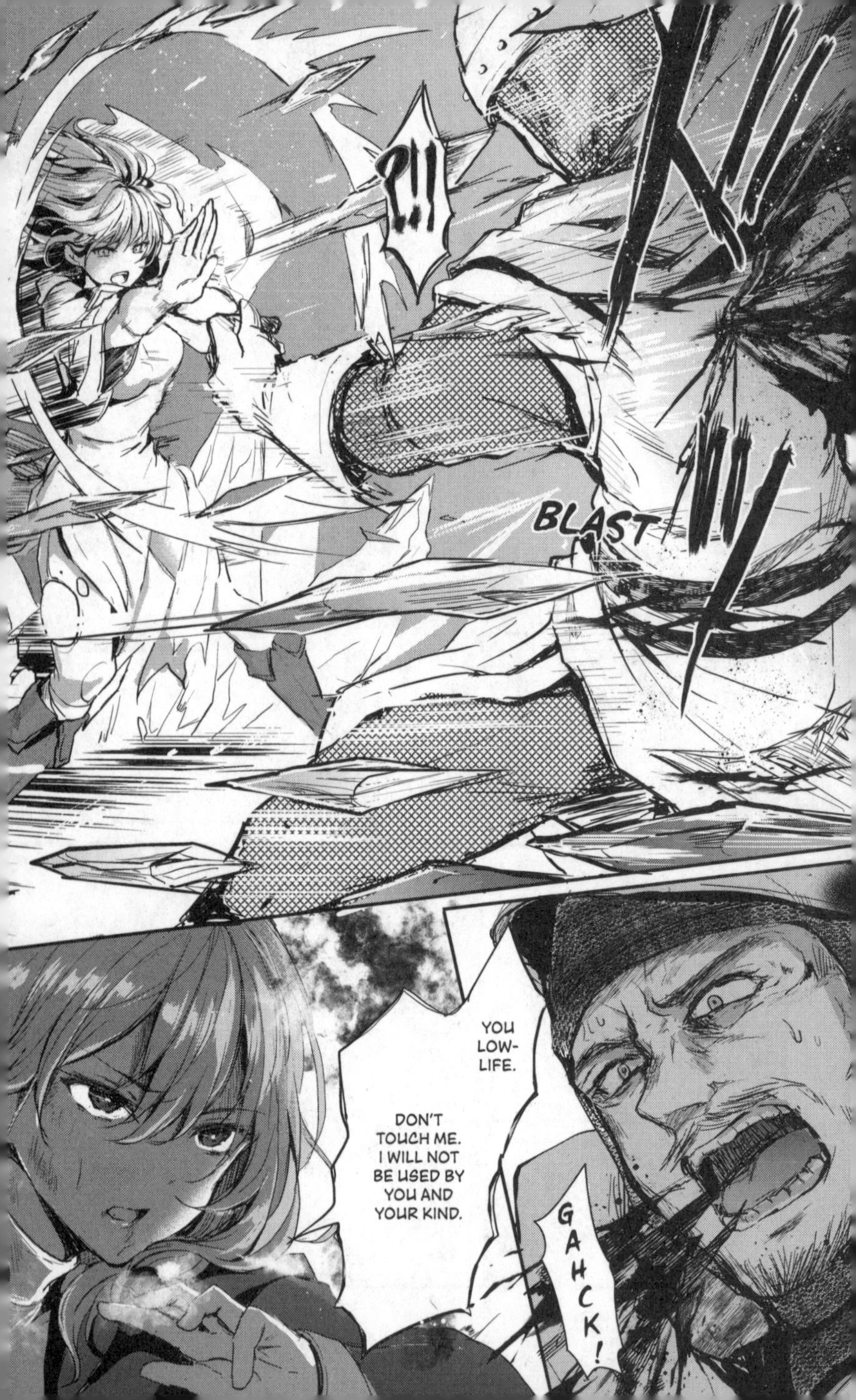
?!!
BLAST
YOU LOW-LIFE.
DON'T TOUCH ME. I WILL NOT BE USED BY YOU AND YOUR KIND.
GAHCK!

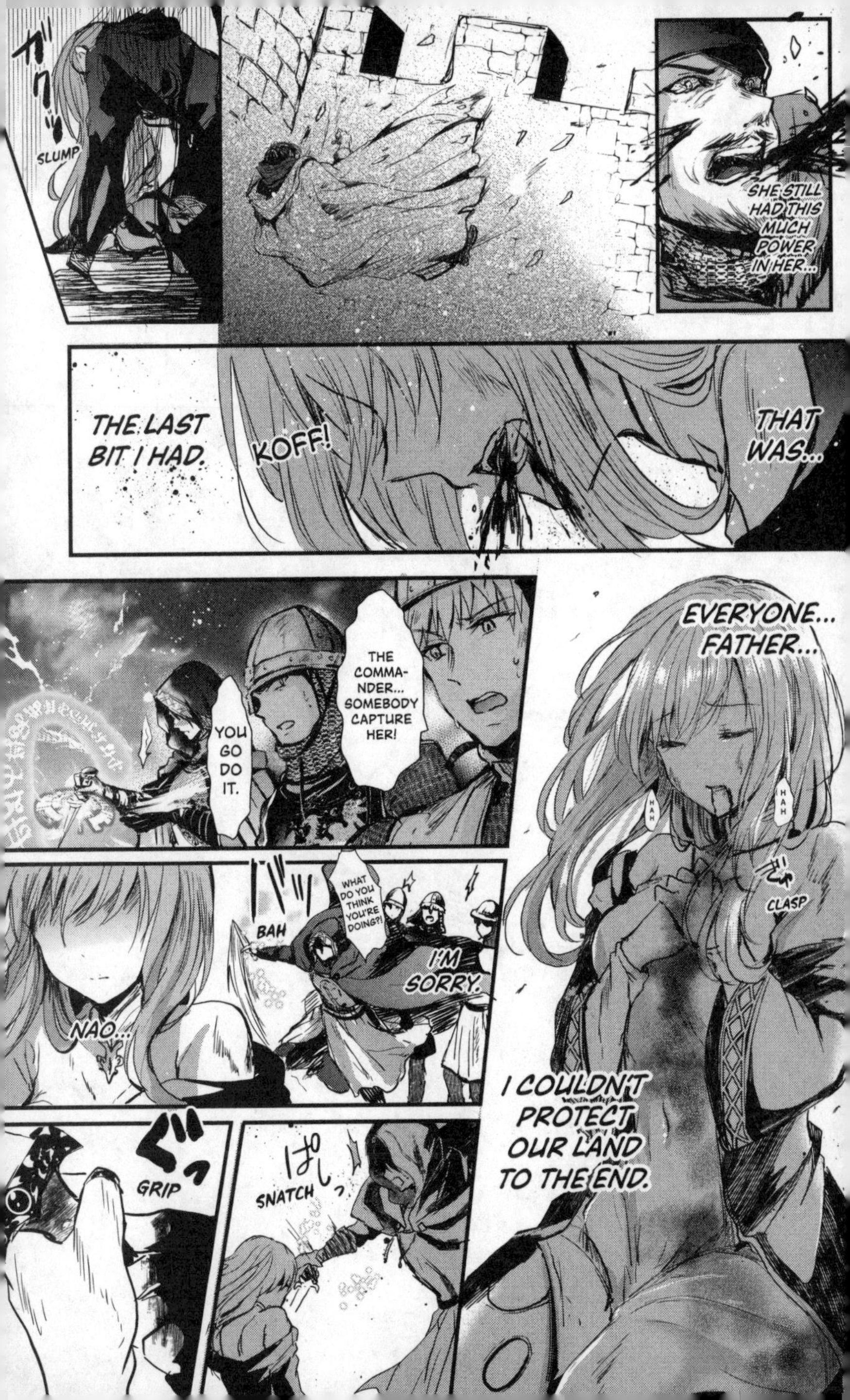

SHE STILL HAD THIS MUCH POWER IN HER...
SLUMP
THAT WAS...
KOFF!
THE LAST BIT I HAD.
EVERYONE... FATHER...
HAH
HAH
CLASP
I COULDN'T PROTECT OUR LAND TO THE END.
THE COMMANDER... SOMEBODY CAPTURE HER!
YOU GO DO IT.
WHAT DO YOU THINK YOU'RE DOING?!
I'M SORRY.
BAH
NAO...
SNATCH
GRIP

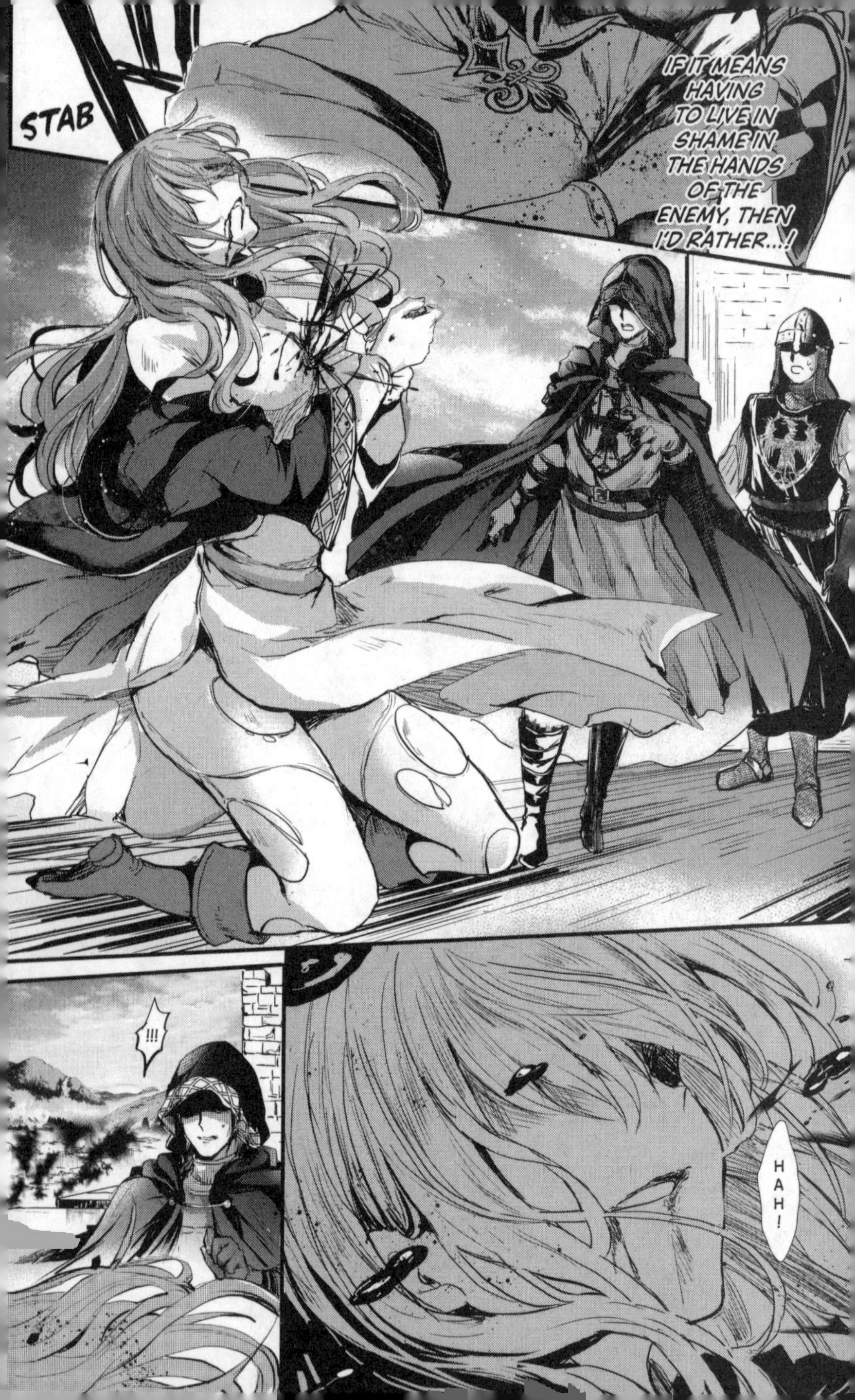
IF IT MEANS HAVING TO LIVE IN SHAME IN THE HANDS OF THE ENEMY, THEN I'D RATHER...!
STAB
HAH!
!!!

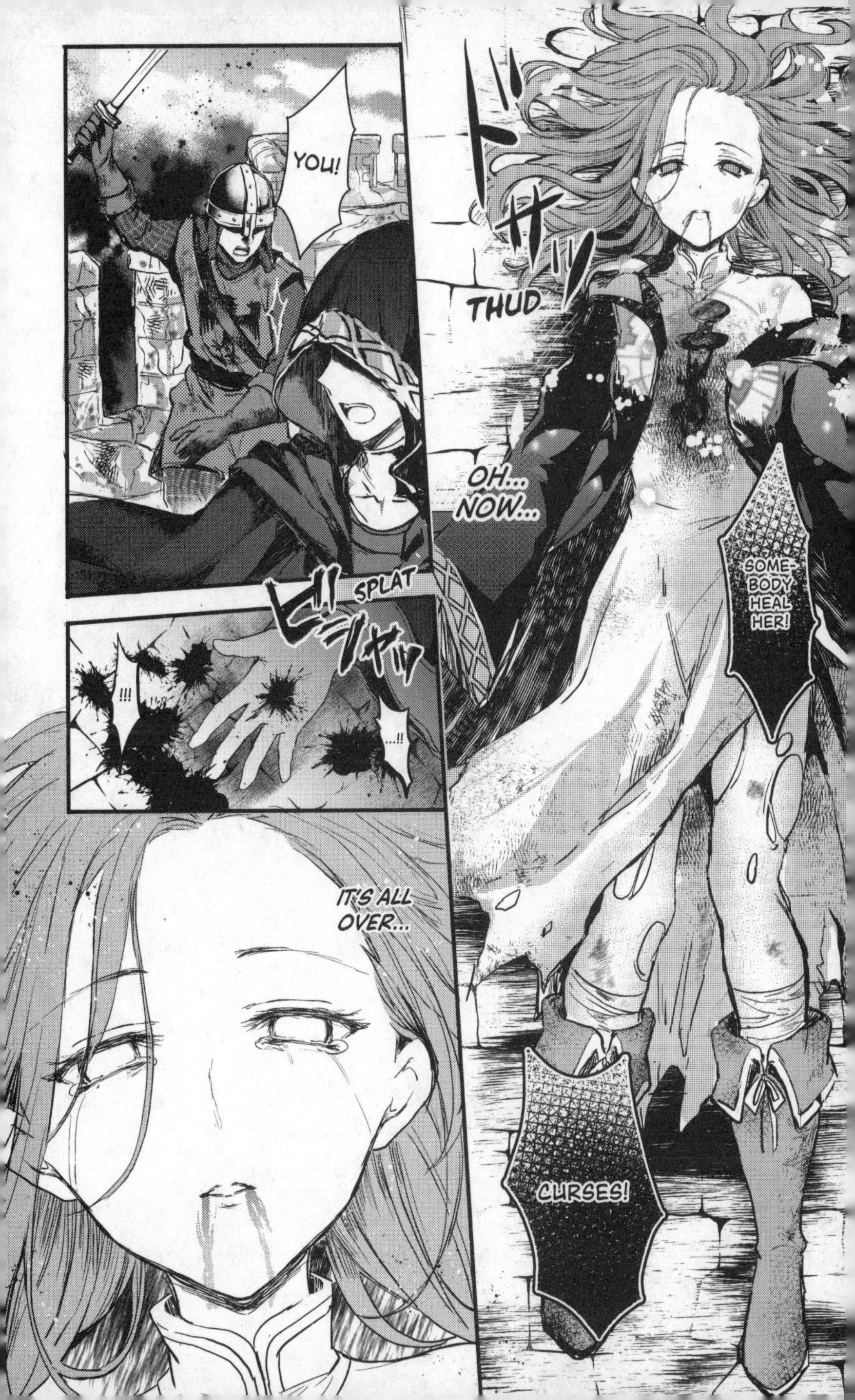
THUD
OH... NOW...
SOME-BODY HEAL HER!
CURSES!
YOU!
SPLAT
!!!
...!!
IT'S ALL OVER...

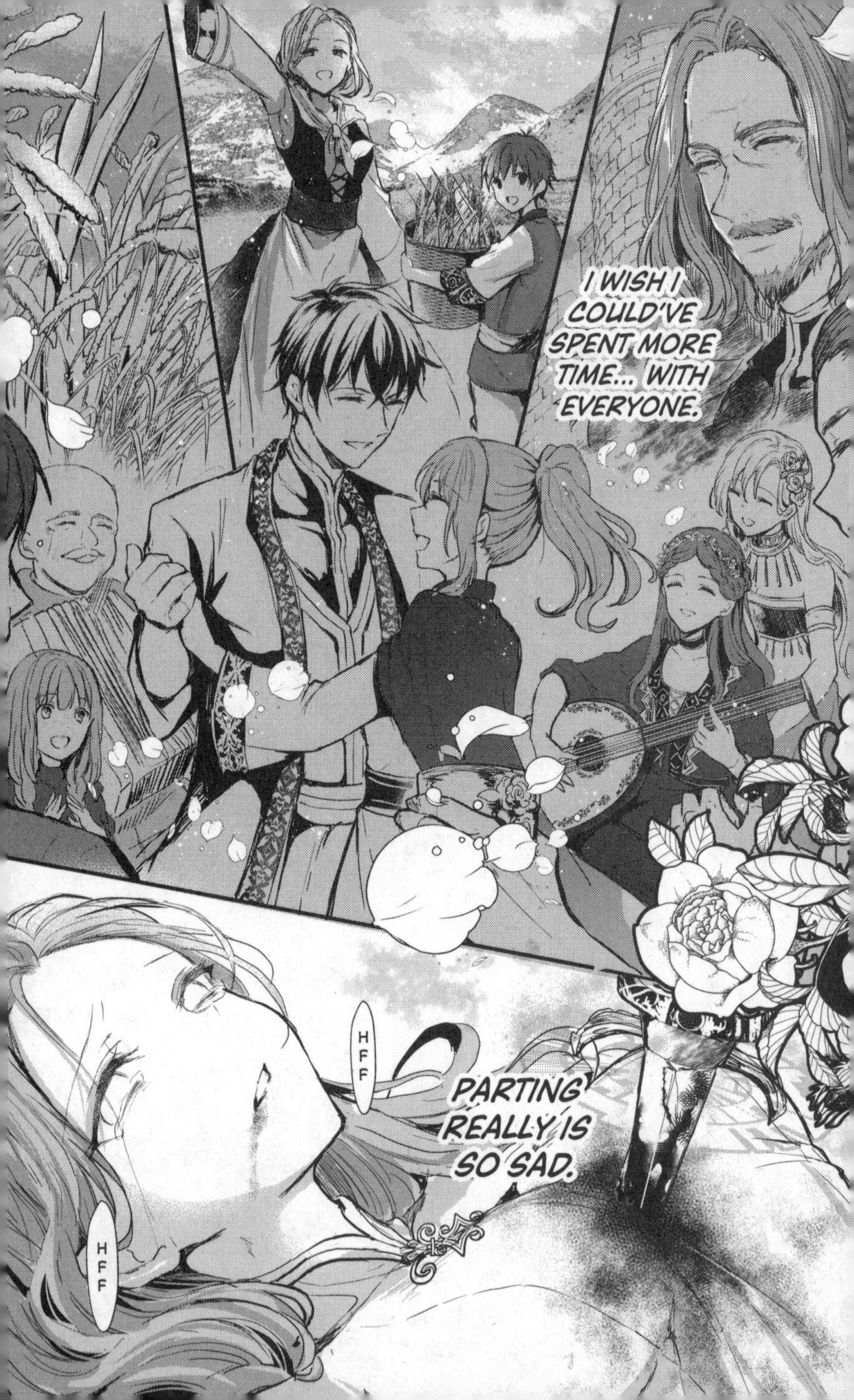
I WISH I COULD'VE SPENT MORE TIME... WITH EVERYONE.
PARTING REALLY IS SO SAD.
HFF
HFF

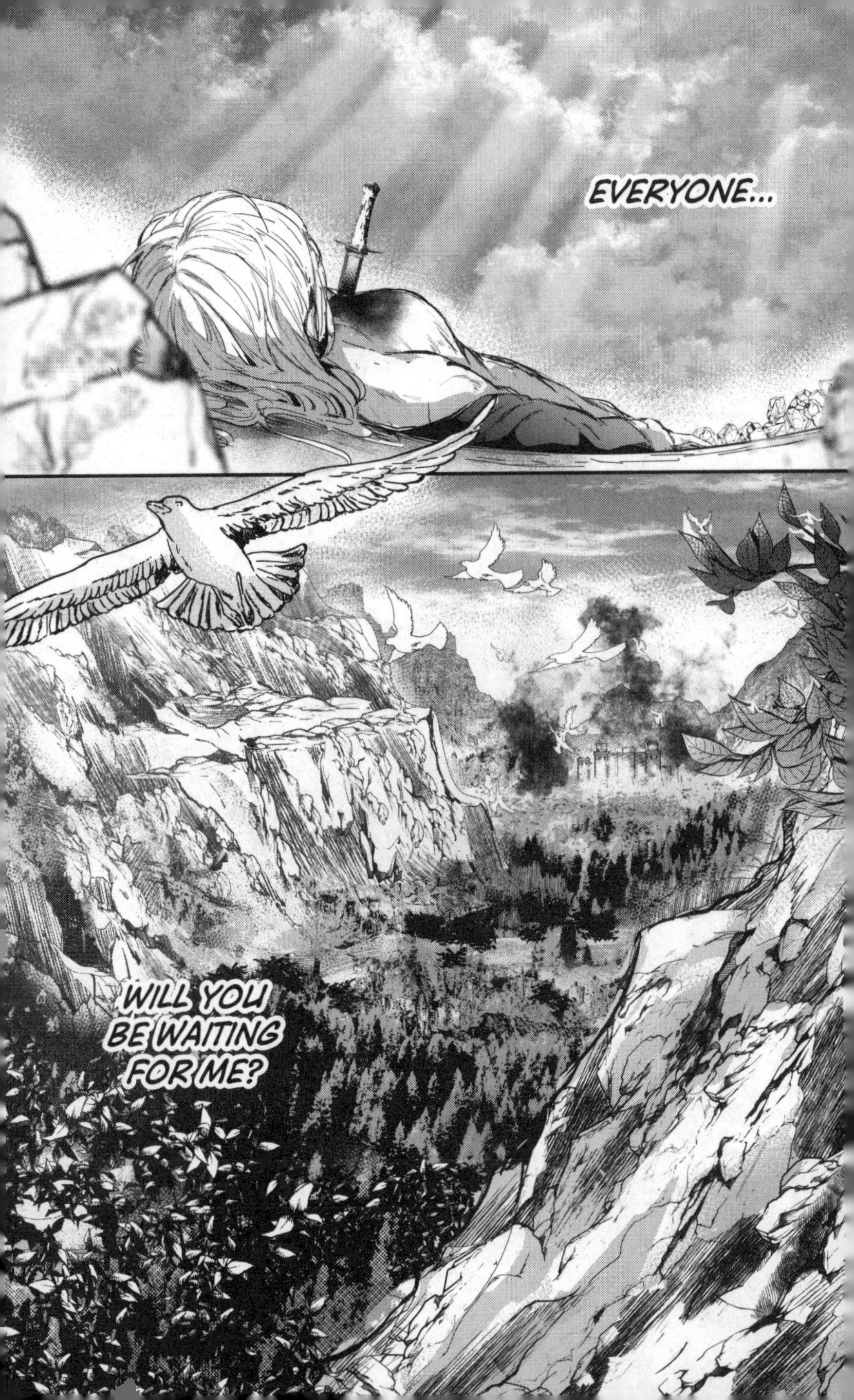
EVERYONE...
WILL YOU BE WAITING FOR ME?

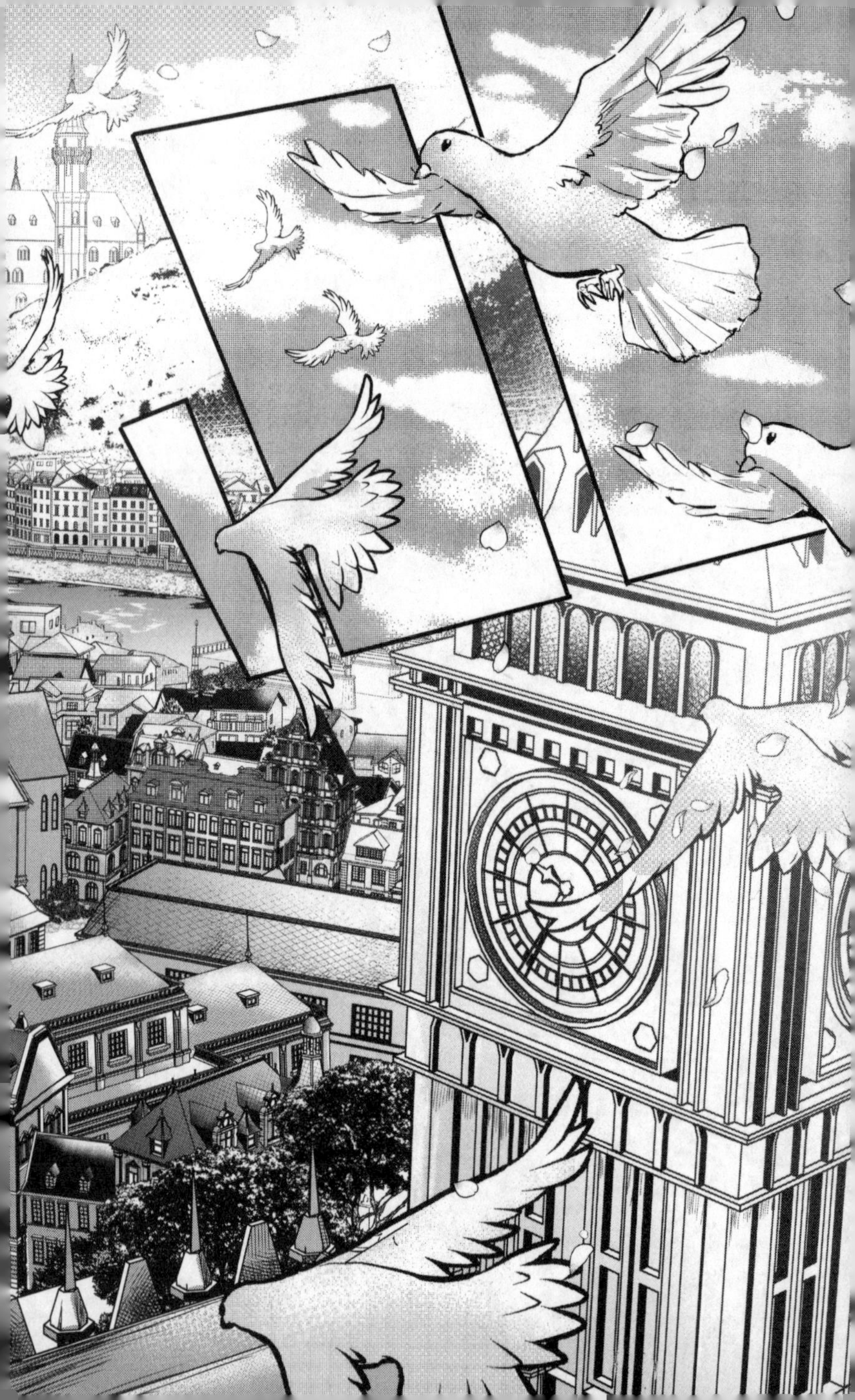

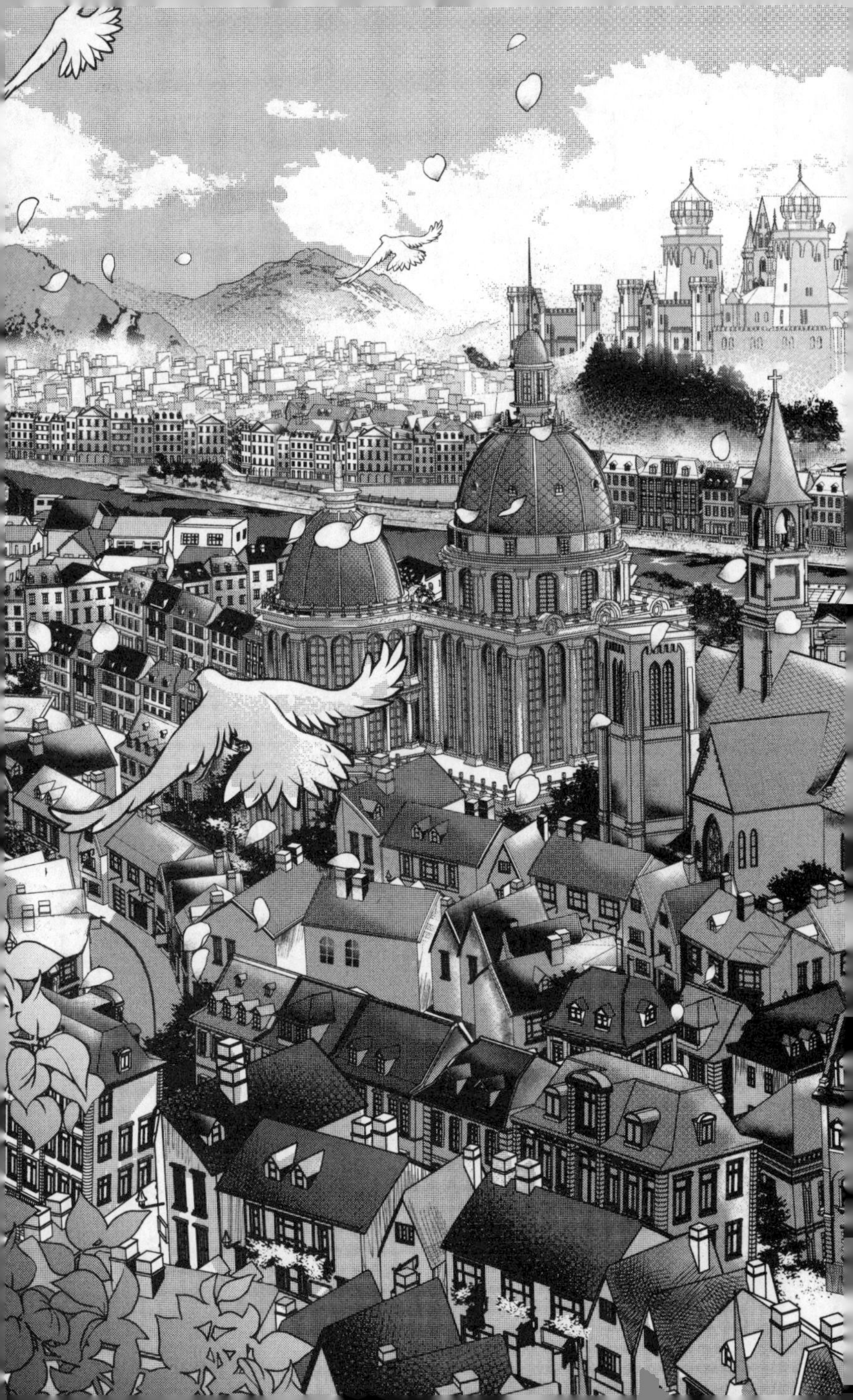

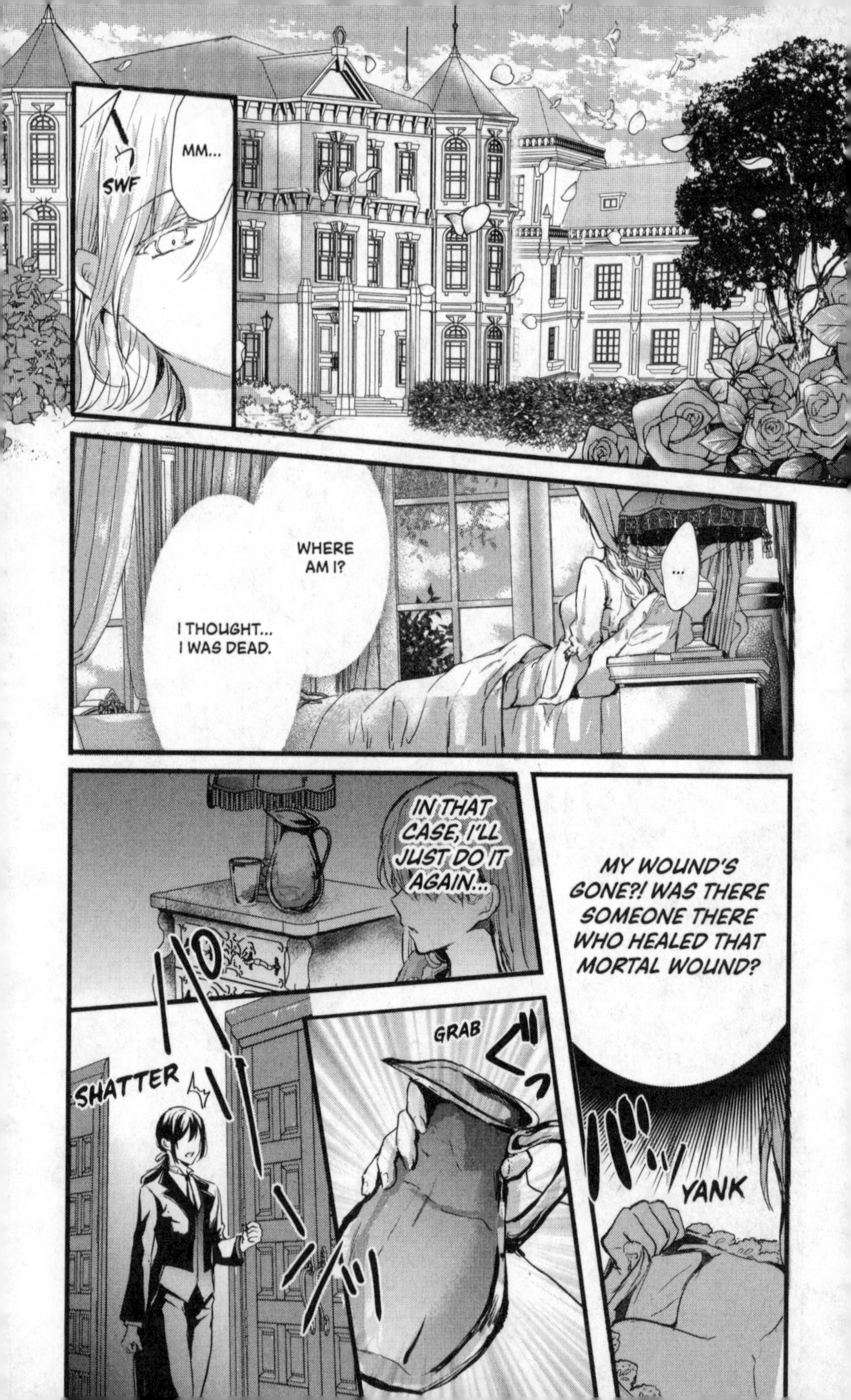
MM...
SWF
...
WHERE AM I?
I THOUGHT... I WAS DEAD.
MY WOUND'S GONE?! WAS THERE SOMEONE THERE WHO HEALED THAT MORTAL WOUND?
YANK
IN THAT CASE, I'LL JUST DO IT AGAIN...
GRAB
SHATTER

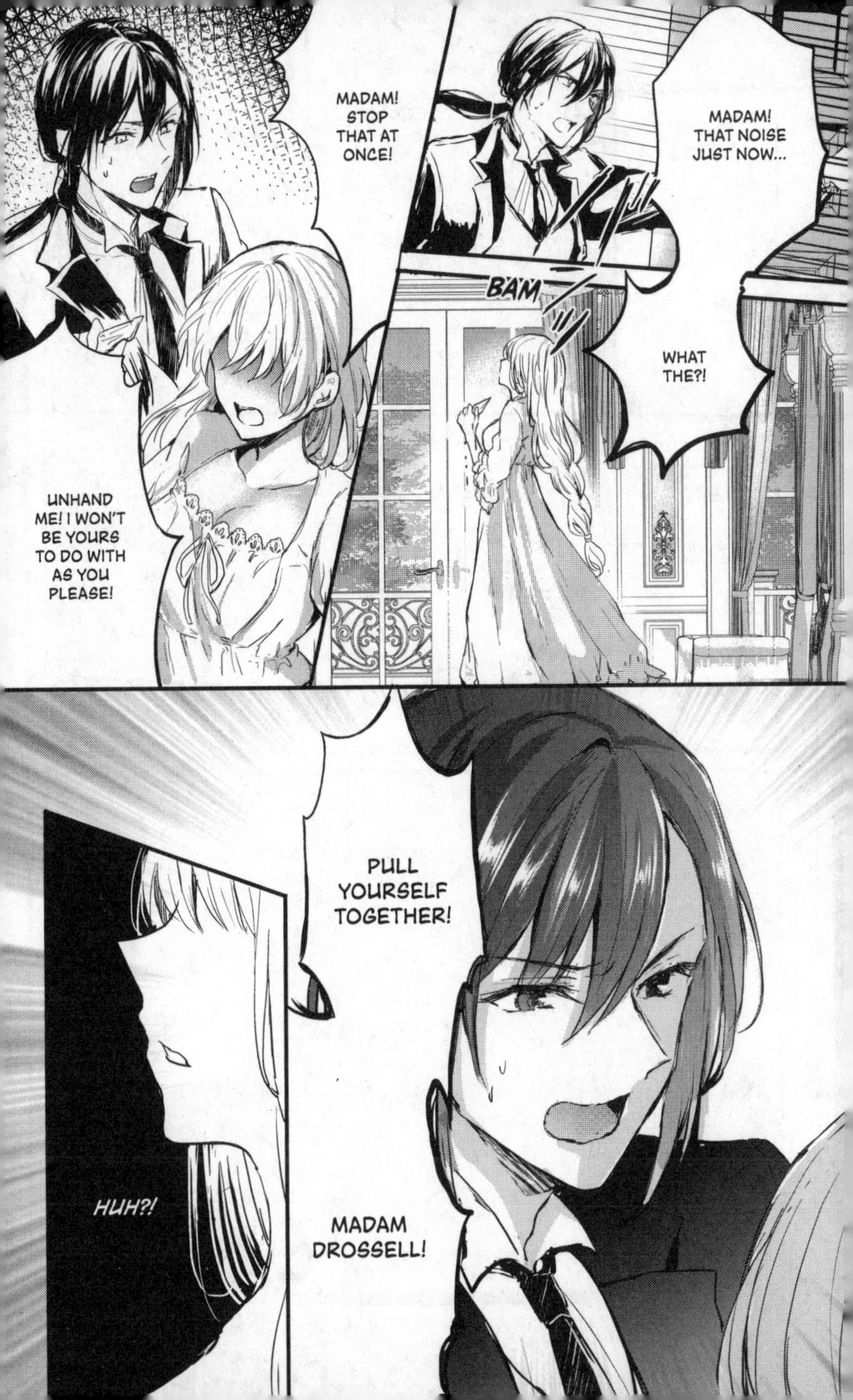
MADAM! THAT NOISE JUST NOW...
BAM
WHAT THE?!
MADAM! STOP THAT AT ONCE!
UNHAND ME! I WON'T BE YOURS TO DO WITH AS YOU PLEASE!
PULL YOURSELF TOGETHER!
MADAM DROSSELL!
HUH?!

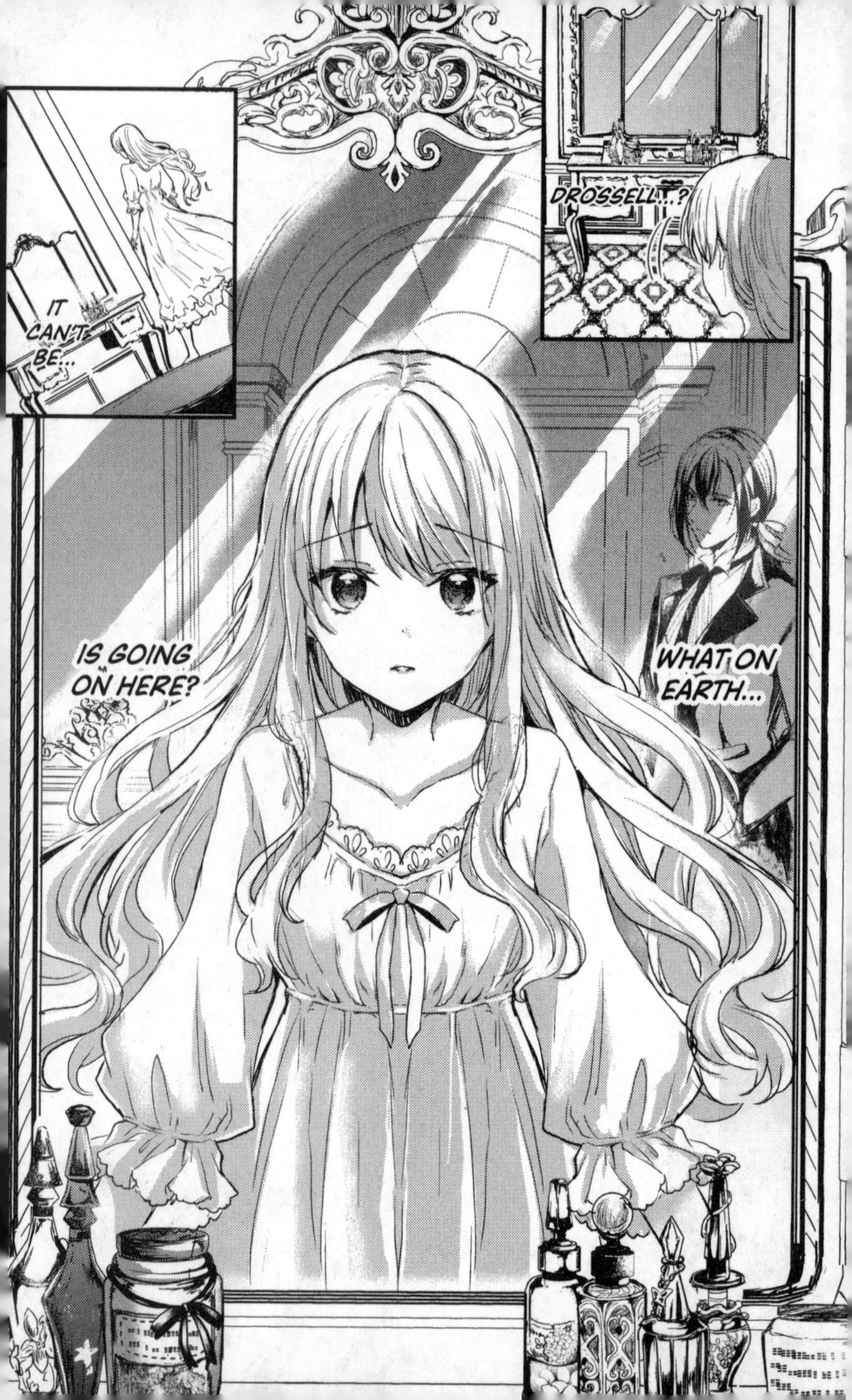
DROSSELL...?
IT CAN'T BE...
WHAT ON EARTH...
IS GOING ON HERE?

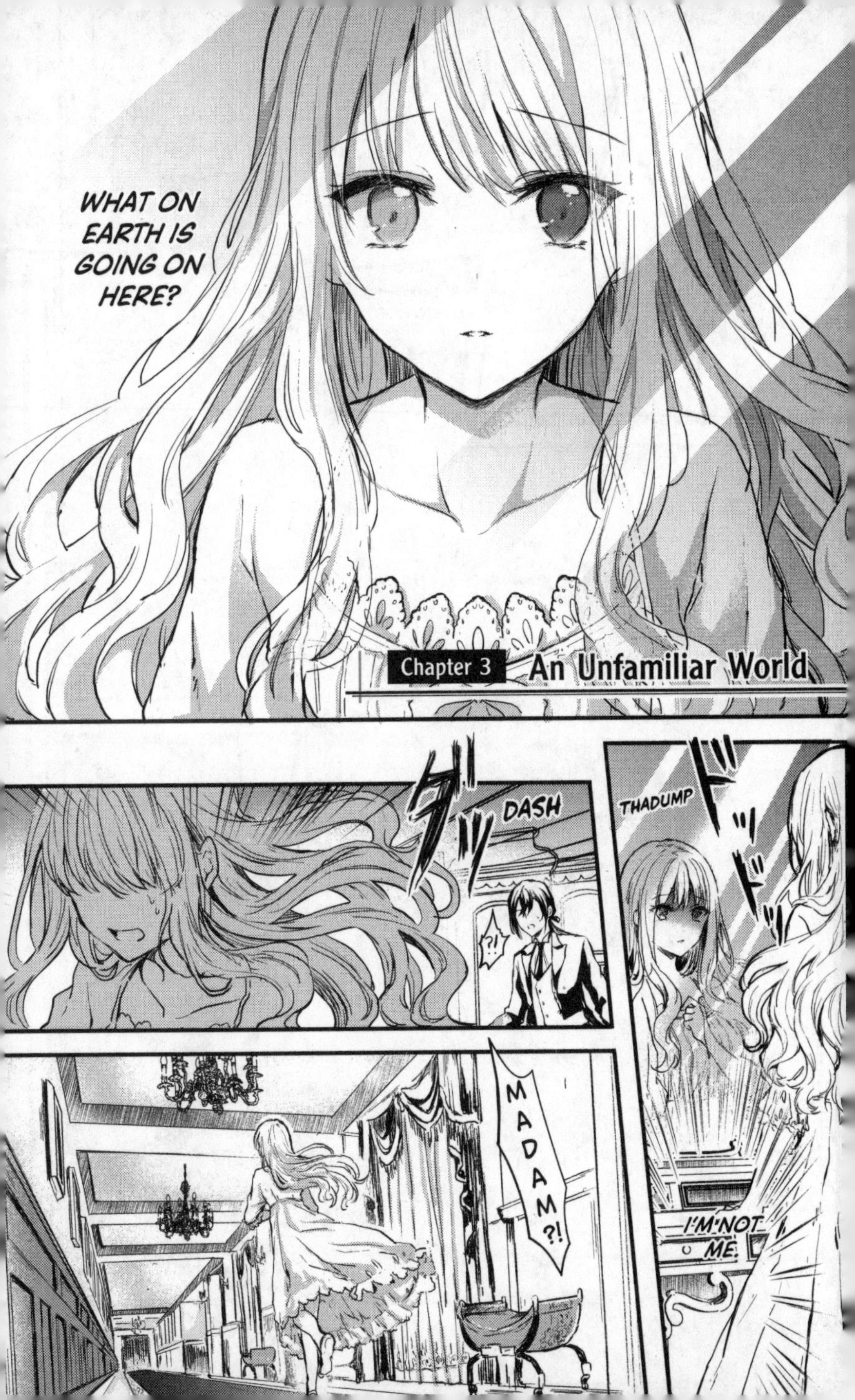
WHAT ON EARTH IS GOING ON HERE?
Chapter 3 An Unfamiliar World
THADUMP
I'M NOT ME.
DASH
?!
MADAM?!

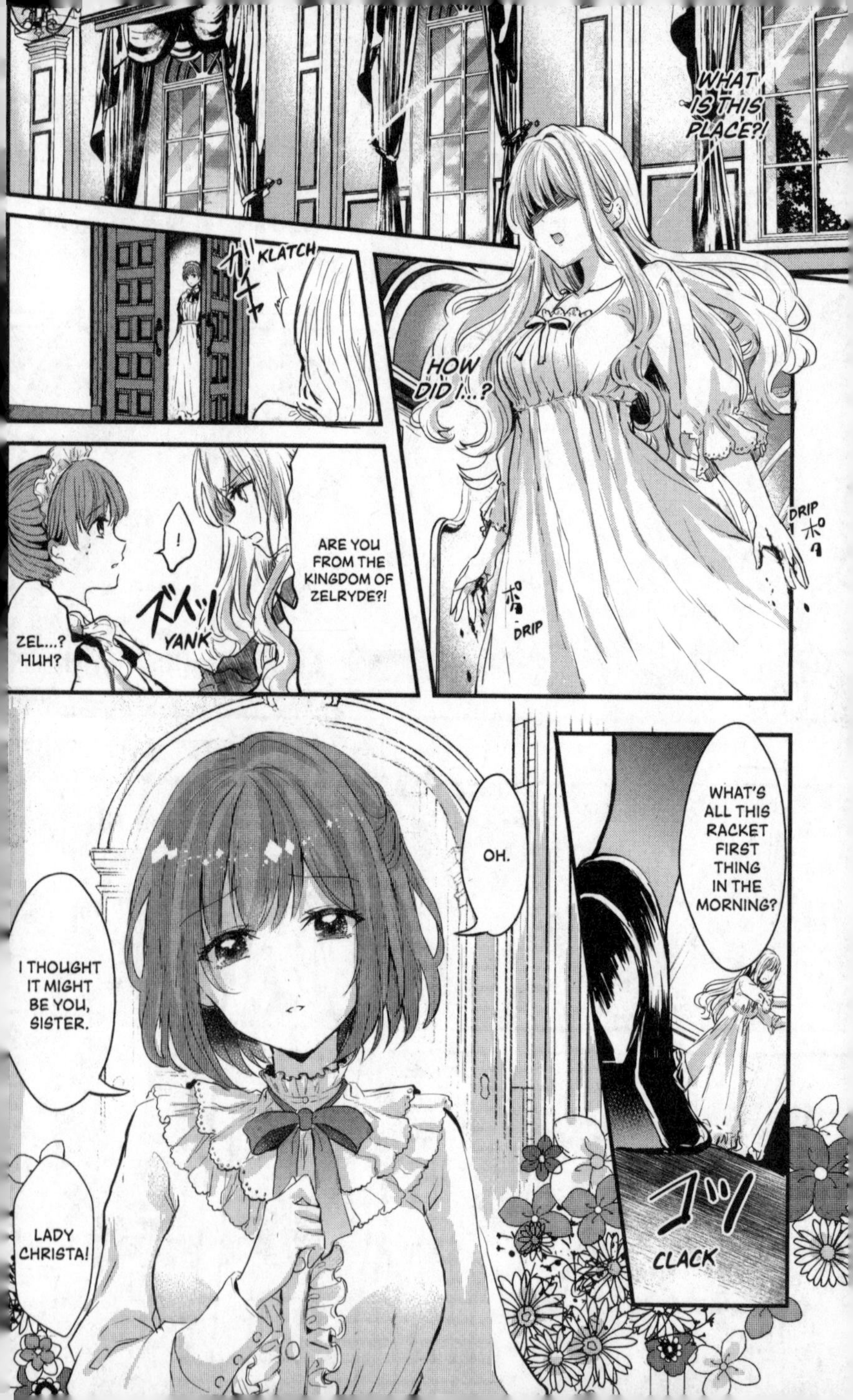
WHAT IS THIS PLACE?!
HOW DID I...?
DRIP
DRIP
KLATCH
ARE YOU FROM THE KINGDOM OF ZELRYDE?!
!
YANK
ZEL...? HUH?
WHAT'S ALL THIS RACKET FIRST THING IN THE MORNING?
CLACK
OH.
I THOUGHT IT MIGHT BE YOU, SISTER.
LADY CHRISTA!

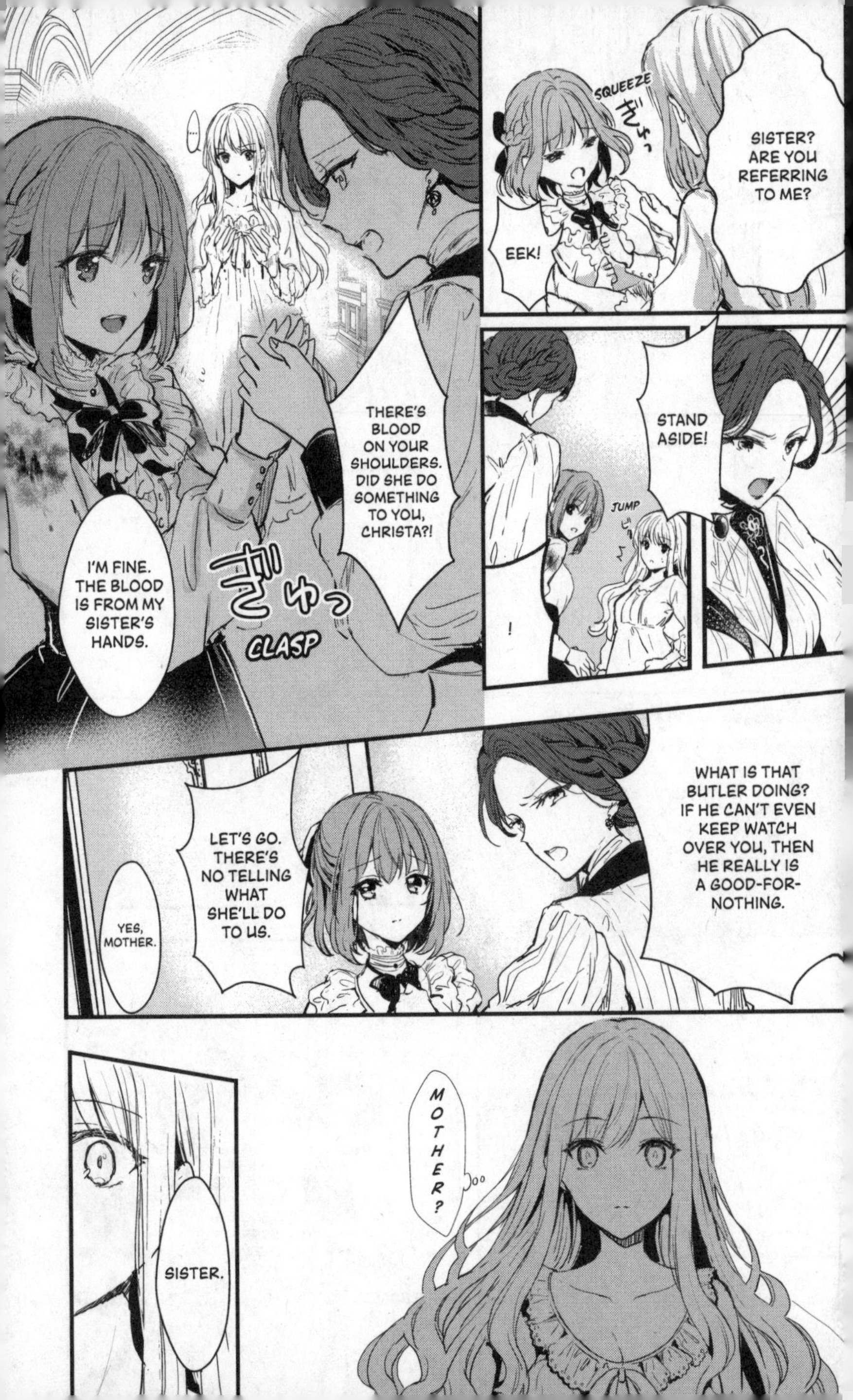
SISTER? ARE YOU REFERRING TO ME?
SQUEEZE
ぎゅっ
EEK!
STAND ASIDE!
JUMP
!
...
THERE'S BLOOD ON YOUR SHOULDERS. DID SHE DO SOMETHING TO YOU, CHRISTA?!
ぎゅっ
CLASP
I'M FINE. THE BLOOD IS FROM MY SISTER'S HANDS.
WHAT IS THAT BUTLER DOING? IF HE CAN'T EVEN KEEP WATCH OVER YOU, THEN HE REALLY IS A GOOD-FOR-NOTHING.
LET'S GO. THERE'S NO TELLING WHAT SHE'LL DO TO US.
YES, MOTHER.
MOTHER?
SISTER.

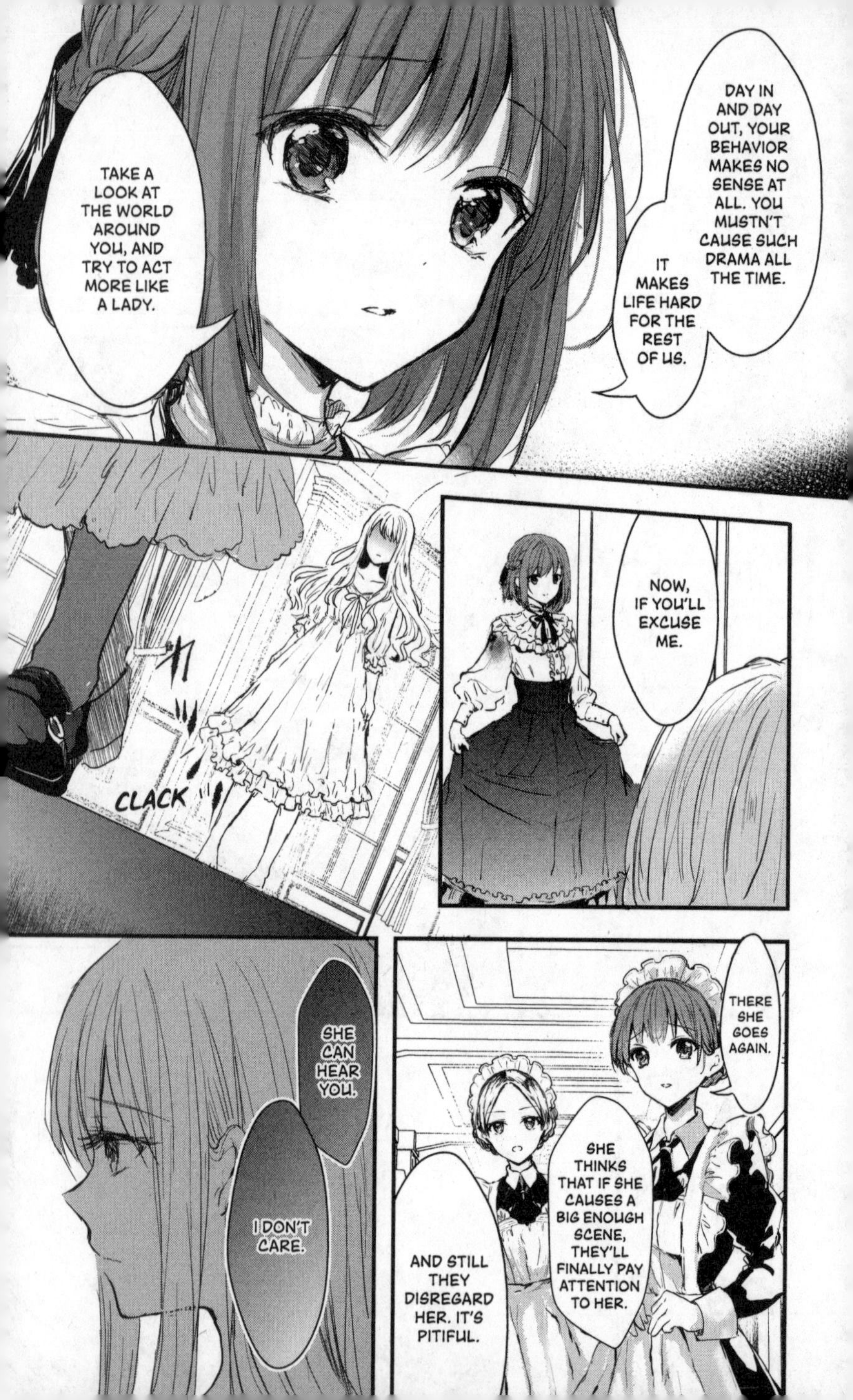
DAY IN AND DAY OUT, YOUR BEHAVIOR MAKES NO SENSE AT ALL. YOU MUSTN'T CAUSE SUCH DRAMA ALL THE TIME.
IT MAKES LIFE HARD FOR THE REST OF US.
TAKE A LOOK AT THE WORLD AROUND YOU, AND TRY TO ACT MORE LIKE A LADY.
NOW, IF YOU'LL EXCUSE ME.
CLACK
THERE SHE GOES AGAIN.
SHE THINKS THAT IF SHE CAUSES A BIG ENOUGH SCENE, THEY'LL FINALLY PAY ATTENTION TO HER.
AND STILL THEY DISREGARD HER. IT'S PITIFUL.
SHE CAN HEAR YOU.
I DON'T CARE.

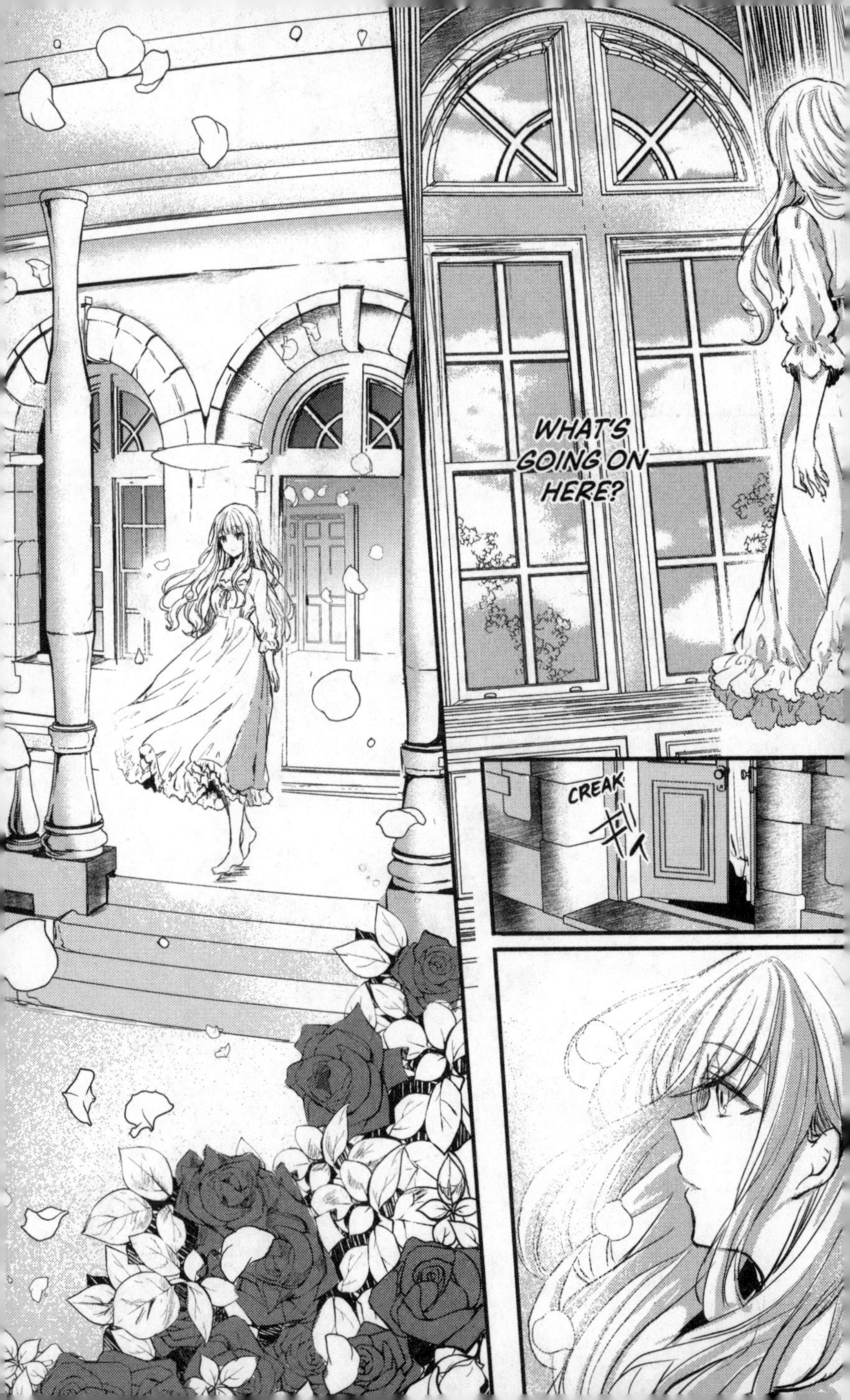
WHAT'S GOING ON HERE?
CREAK
ギィ

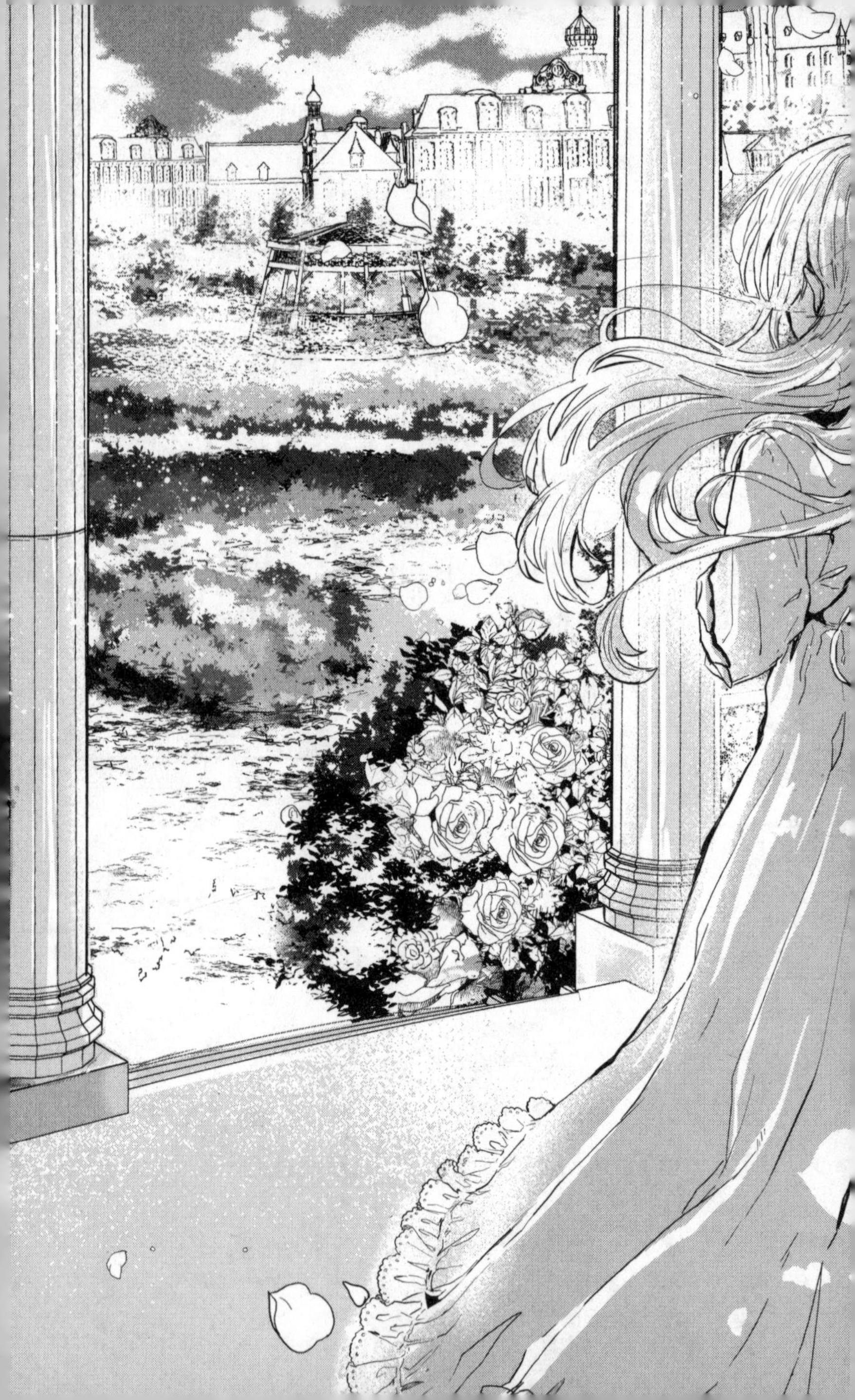

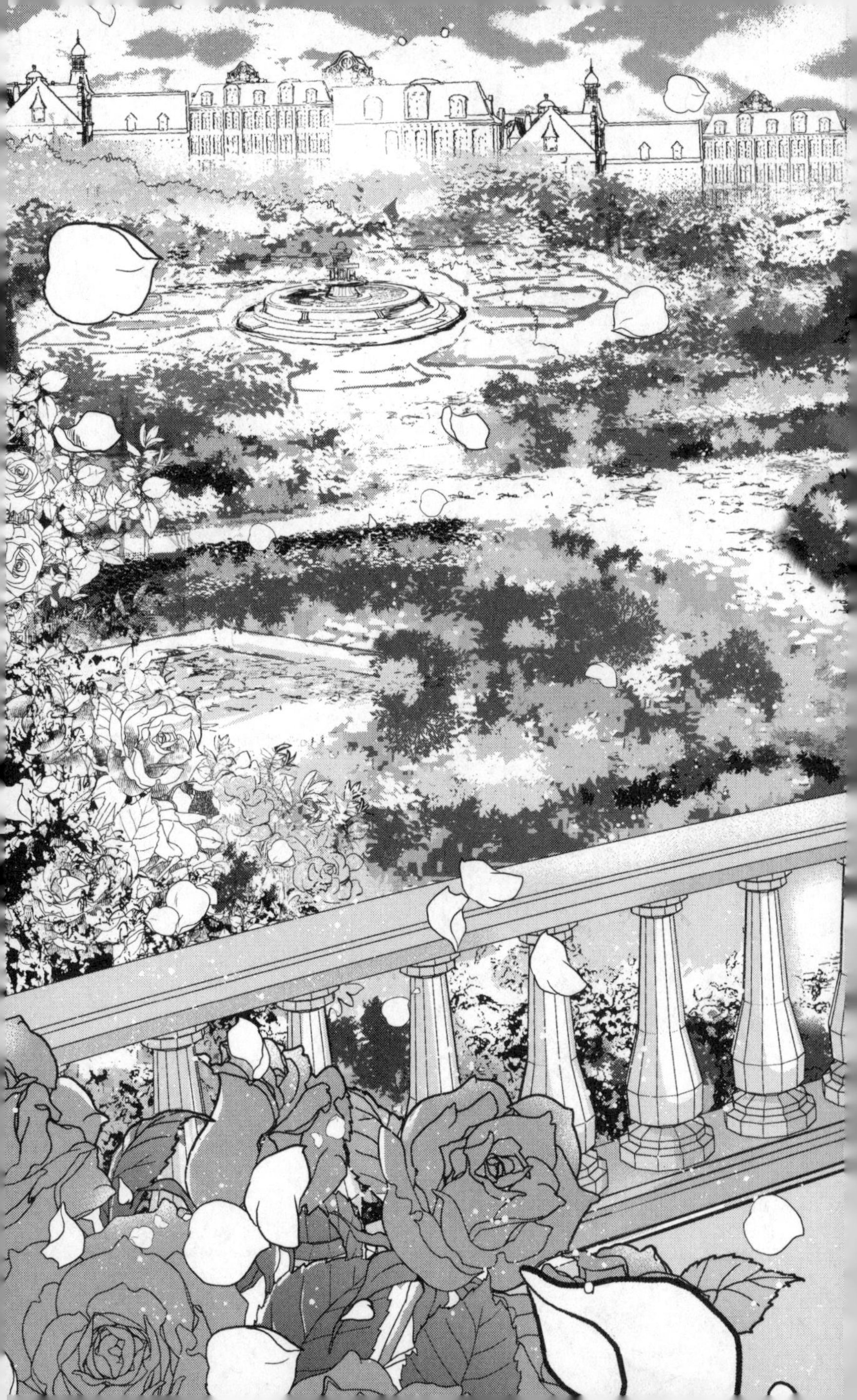

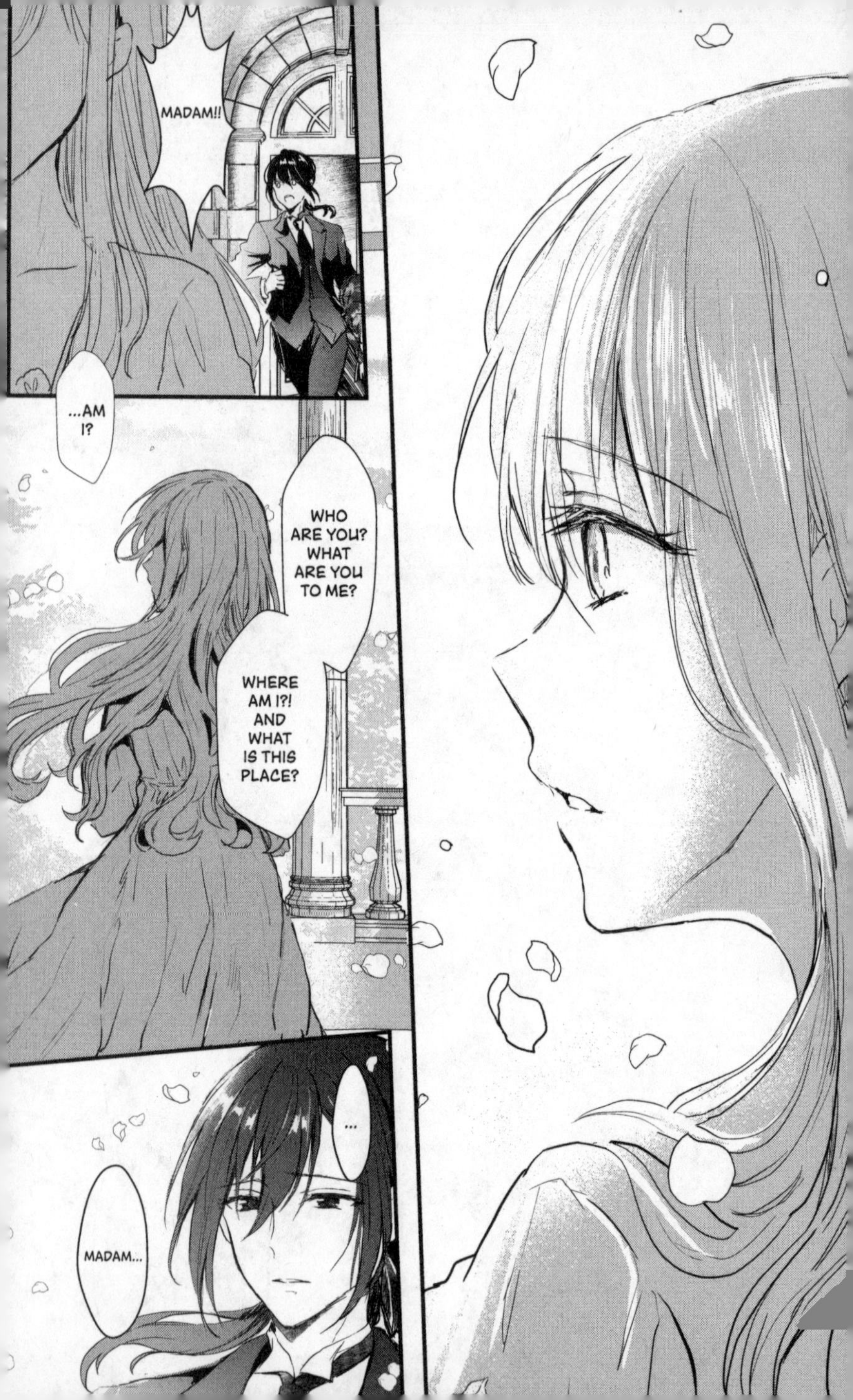
MADAM!!
WHO ARE YOU? WHAT ARE YOU TO ME?
WHERE AM I?! AND WHAT IS THIS PLACE?
...AM I?
...
MADAM...

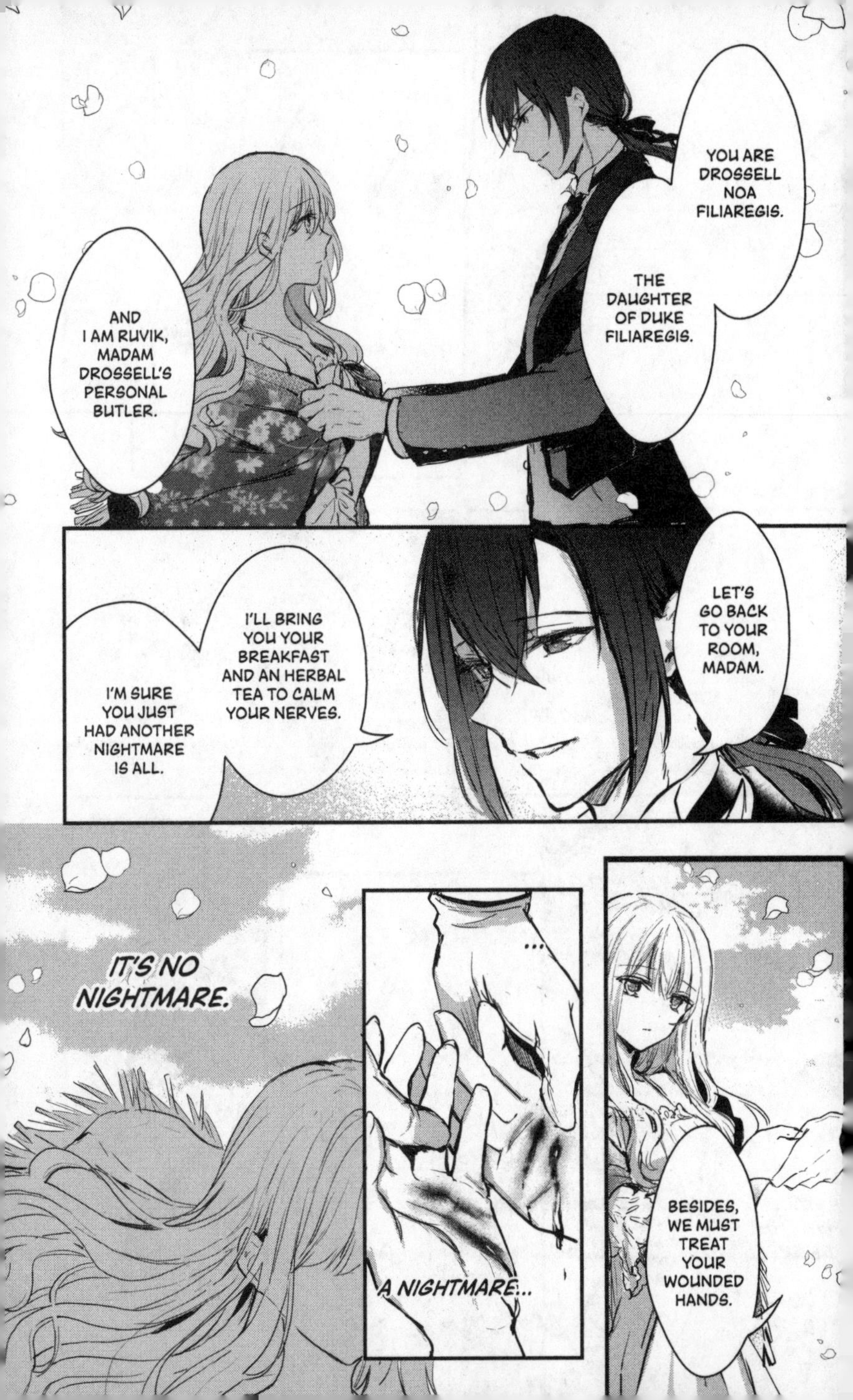
YOU ARE DROSSELL NOA FILIAREGIS.
THE DAUGHTER OF DUKE FILIAREGIS.
AND I AM RUVIK, MADAM DROSSELL'S PERSONAL BUTLER.
LET'S GO BACK TO YOUR ROOM, MADAM.
I'LL BRING YOU YOUR BREAKFAST AND AN HERBAL TEA TO CALM YOUR NERVES.
I'M SURE YOU JUST HAD ANOTHER NIGHTMARE IS ALL.
BESIDES, WE MUST TREAT YOUR WOUNDED HANDS.
...
A NIGHTMARE...
IT'S NO NIGHTMARE.

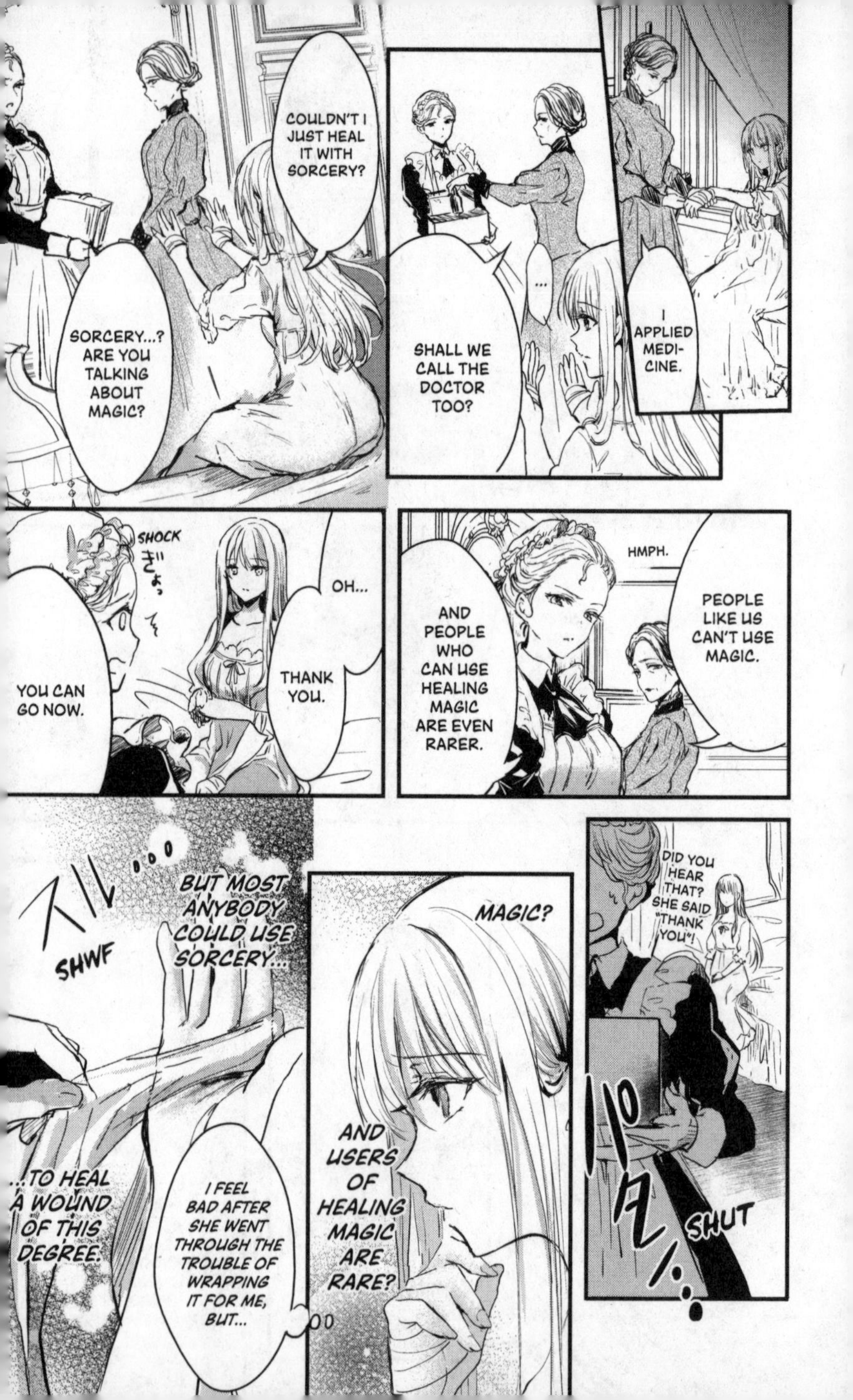
I APPLIED MEDICINE.
...
SHALL WE CALL THE DOCTOR TOO?
COULDN'T I JUST HEAL IT WITH SORCERY?
SORCERY...? ARE YOU TALKING ABOUT MAGIC?
HMPH.
PEOPLE LIKE US CAN'T USE MAGIC.
AND PEOPLE WHO CAN USE HEALING MAGIC ARE EVEN RARER.
OH...
THANK YOU.
SHOCK
ぎょっ
YOU CAN GO NOW.
DID YOU HEAR THAT? SHE SAID "THANK YOU"!
パタン...
SHUT
MAGIC?
AND USERS OF HEALING MAGIC ARE RARE?
BUT MOST ANYBODY COULD USE SORCERY...
スル...
SHWF
...TO HEAL A WOUND OF THIS DEGREE.
I FEEL BAD AFTER SHE WENT THROUGH THE TROUBLE OF WRAPPING IT FOR ME, BUT...

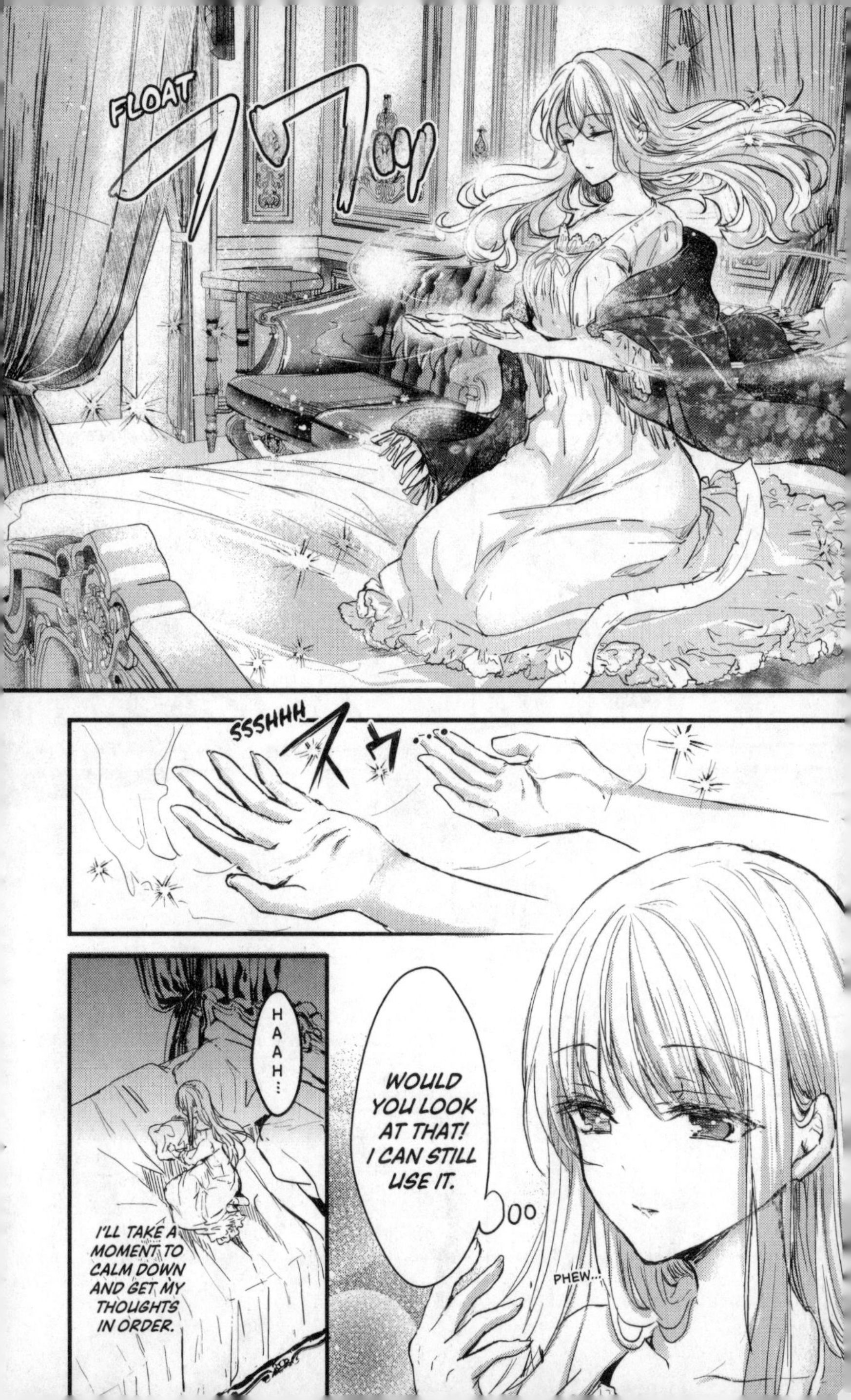
FLOAT
SSSHHH
HAAAH...
WOULD YOU LOOK AT THAT! I CAN STILL USE IT.
PHEW...
I'LL TAKE A MOMENT TO CALM DOWN AND GET MY THOUGHTS IN ORDER.

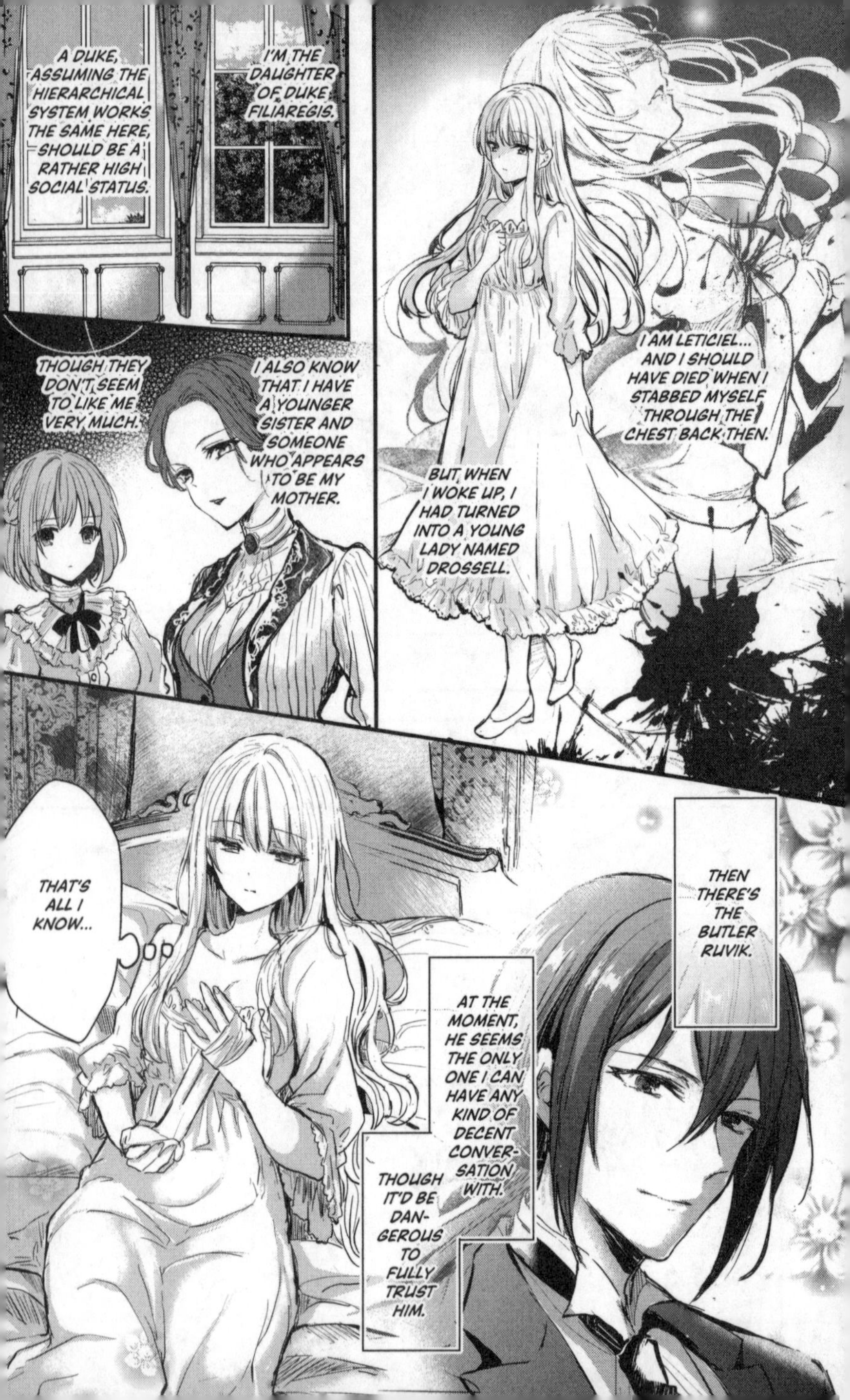
I AM LETICIEL... AND I SHOULD HAVE DIED WHEN I STABBED MYSELF THROUGH THE CHEST BACK THEN.
BUT, WHEN I WOKE UP, I HAD TURNED INTO A YOUNG LADY NAMED DROSSELL.
I'M THE DAUGHTER OF DUKE FILIAREGIS.
A DUKE, ASSUMING THE HIERARCHICAL SYSTEM WORKS THE SAME HERE, SHOULD BE A RATHER HIGH SOCIAL STATUS.
I ALSO KNOW THAT I HAVE A YOUNGER SISTER AND SOMEONE WHO APPEARS TO BE MY MOTHER.
THOUGH THEY DON'T SEEM TO LIKE ME VERY MUCH.
THEN THERE'S THE BUTLER RUVIK.
AT THE MOMENT, HE SEEMS THE ONLY ONE I CAN HAVE ANY KIND OF DECENT CONVER-SATION WITH.
THOUGH IT'D BE DAN-GEROUS TO FULLY TRUST HIM.
THAT'S ALL I KNOW...

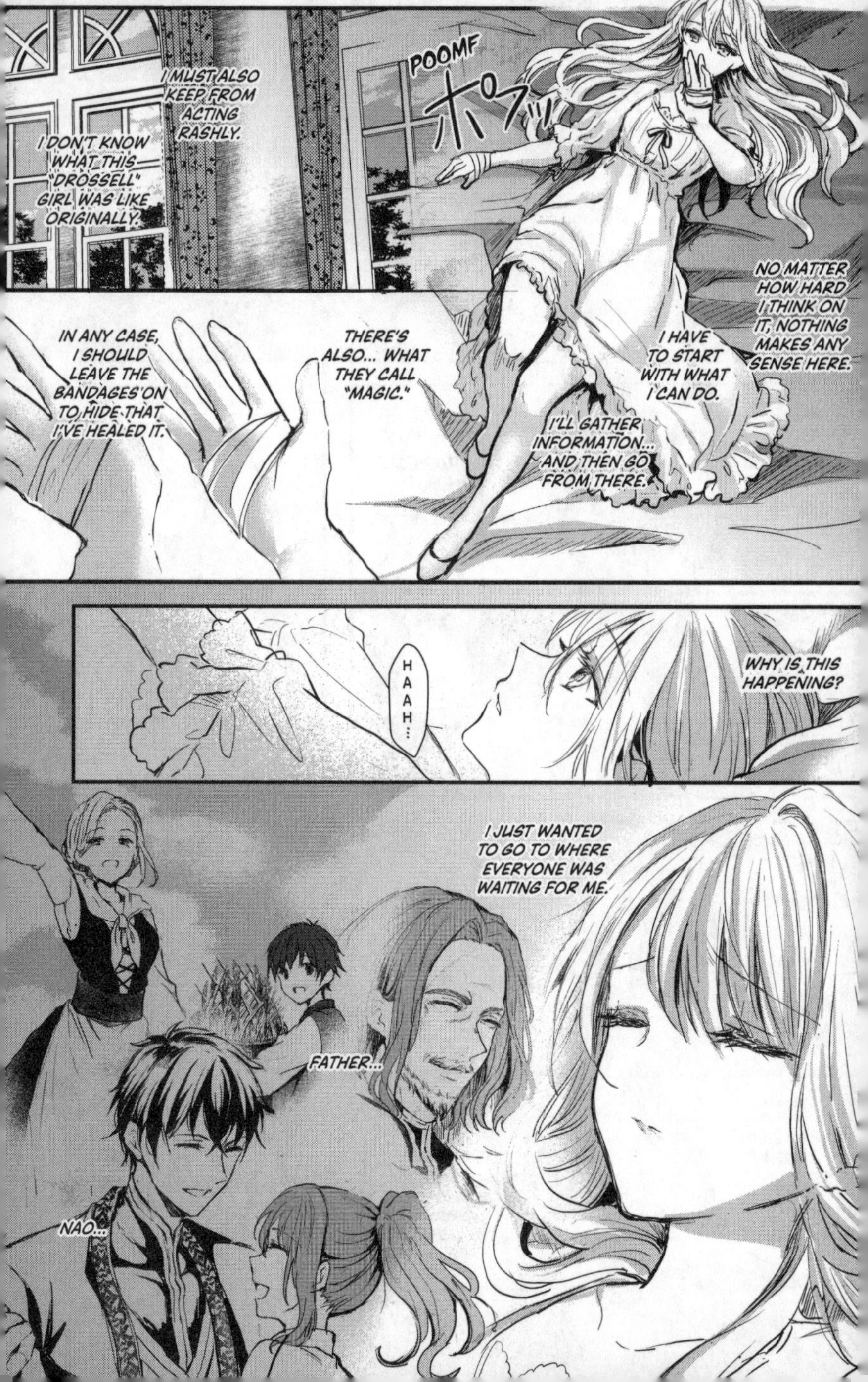

POOMF
ポフッ
I MUST ALSO KEEP FROM ACTING RASHLY.
I DON'T KNOW WHAT THIS "DROSSELL" GIRL WAS LIKE ORIGINALLY.
NO MATTER HOW HARD I THINK ON IT, NOTHING MAKES ANY SENSE HERE.
I HAVE TO START WITH WHAT I CAN DO.
I'LL GATHER INFORMATION... AND THEN GO FROM THERE.
THERE'S ALSO... WHAT THEY CALL "MAGIC."
IN ANY CASE, I SHOULD LEAVE THE BANDAGES ON TO HIDE THAT I'VE HEALED IT.
WHY IS THIS HAPPENING?
HAAH...
I JUST WANTED TO GO TO WHERE EVERYONE WAS WAITING FOR ME.
FATHER...
NAO...

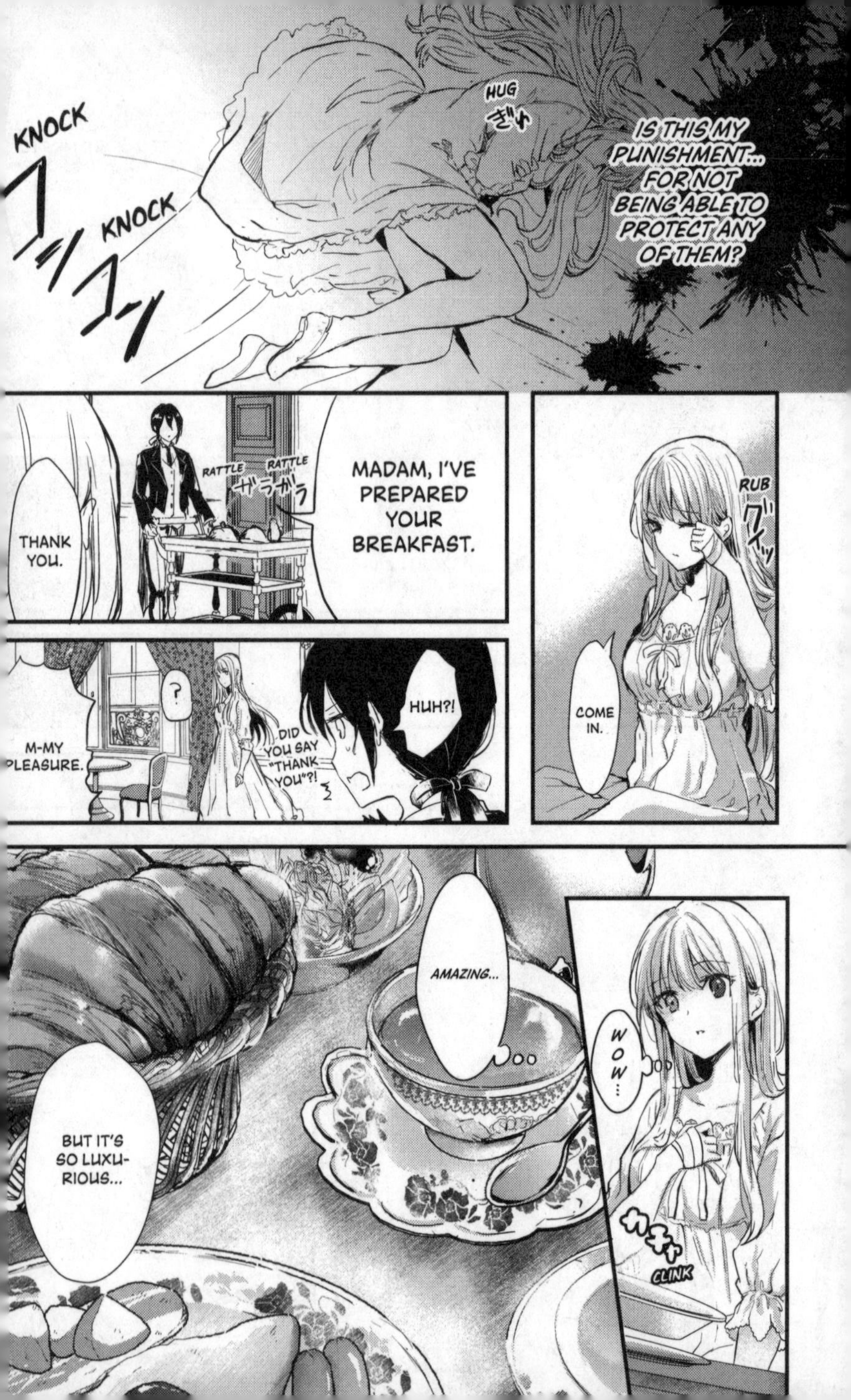
IS THIS MY PUNISHMENT... FOR NOT BEING ABLE TO PROTECT ANY OF THEM?
HUG
ぎゅ
KNOCK
コン
KNOCK
コン
RUB
グイッ
COME IN.
MADAM, I'VE PREPARED YOUR BREAKFAST.
RATTLE RATTLE
ガラガラ
THANK YOU.
HUH?!
DID YOU SAY "THANK YOU"?!
?
M-MY PLEASURE.
WOW...
カチャ
CLINK
AMAZING...
BUT IT'S SO LUXURIOUS...

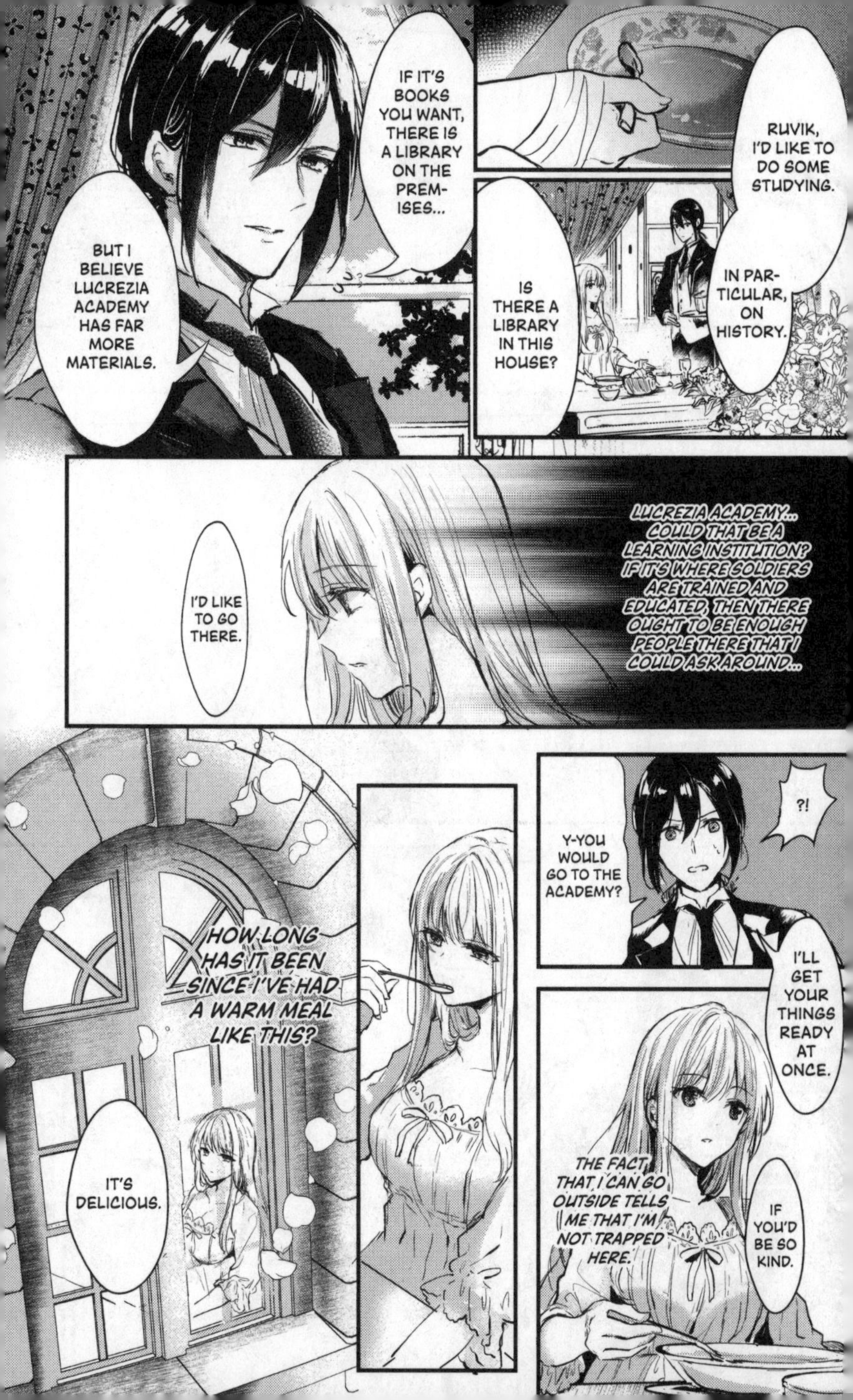
RUVIK, I'D LIKE TO DO SOME STUDYING.
IN PARTICULAR, ON HISTORY.
IS THERE A LIBRARY IN THIS HOUSE?
IF IT'S BOOKS YOU WANT, THERE IS A LIBRARY ON THE PREMISES...
BUT I BELIEVE LUCREZIA ACADEMY HAS FAR MORE MATERIALS.
LUCREZIA ACADEMY... COULD THAT BE A LEARNING INSTITUTION? IF IT'S WHERE SOLDIERS ARE TRAINED AND EDUCATED, THEN THERE OUGHT TO BE ENOUGH PEOPLE THERE THAT I COULD ASK AROUND...
I'D LIKE TO GO THERE.
?!
Y-YOU WOULD GO TO THE ACADEMY?
I'LL GET YOUR THINGS READY AT ONCE.
IF YOU'D BE SO KIND.
THE FACT THAT I CAN GO OUTSIDE TELLS ME THAT I'M NOT TRAPPED HERE.
HOW LONG HAS IT BEEN SINCE I'VE HAD A WARM MEAL LIKE THIS?
IT'S DELICIOUS.

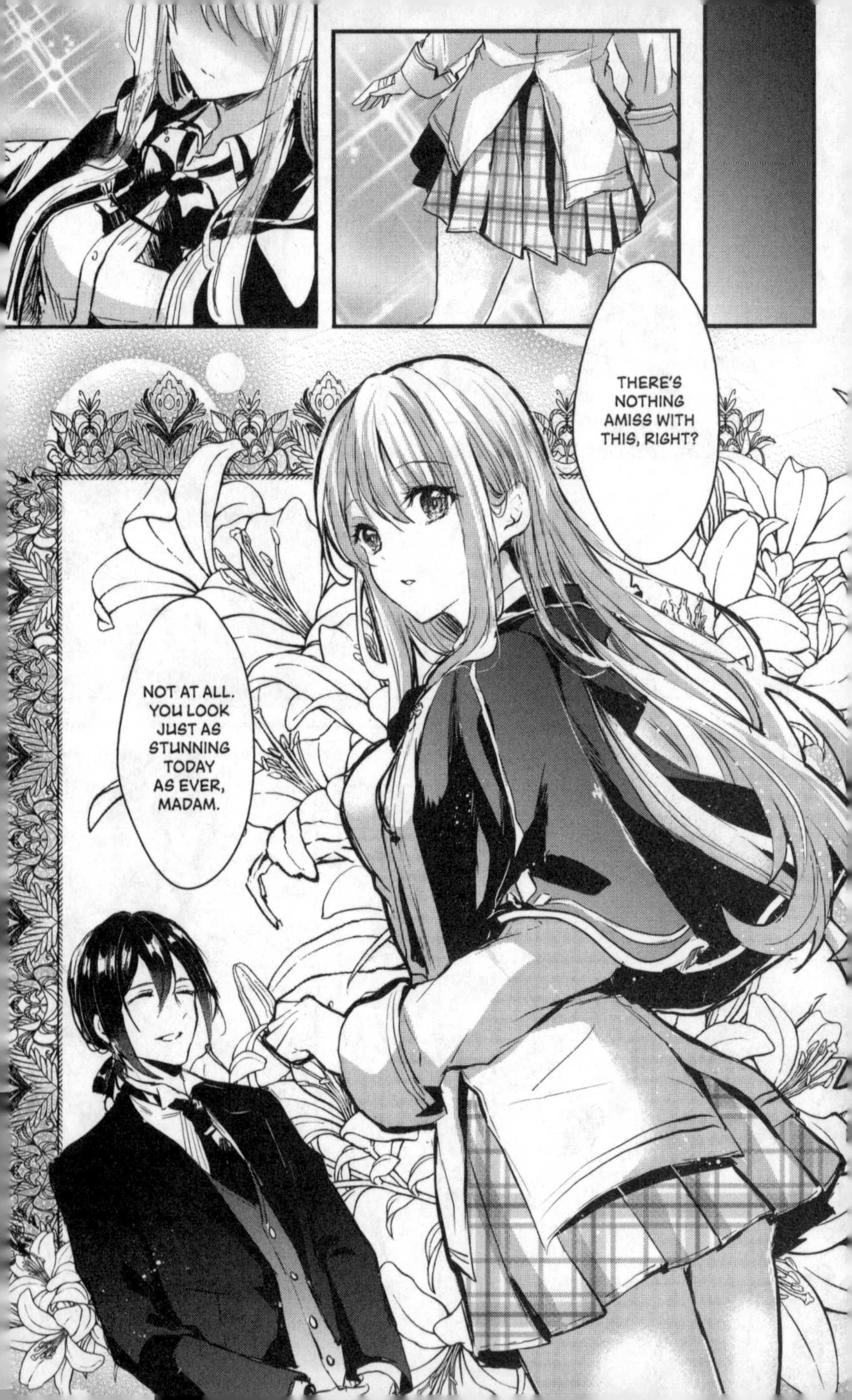
THERE'S NOTHING AMISS WITH THIS, RIGHT?
NOT AT ALL. YOU LOOK JUST AS STUNNING TODAY AS EVER, MADAM.

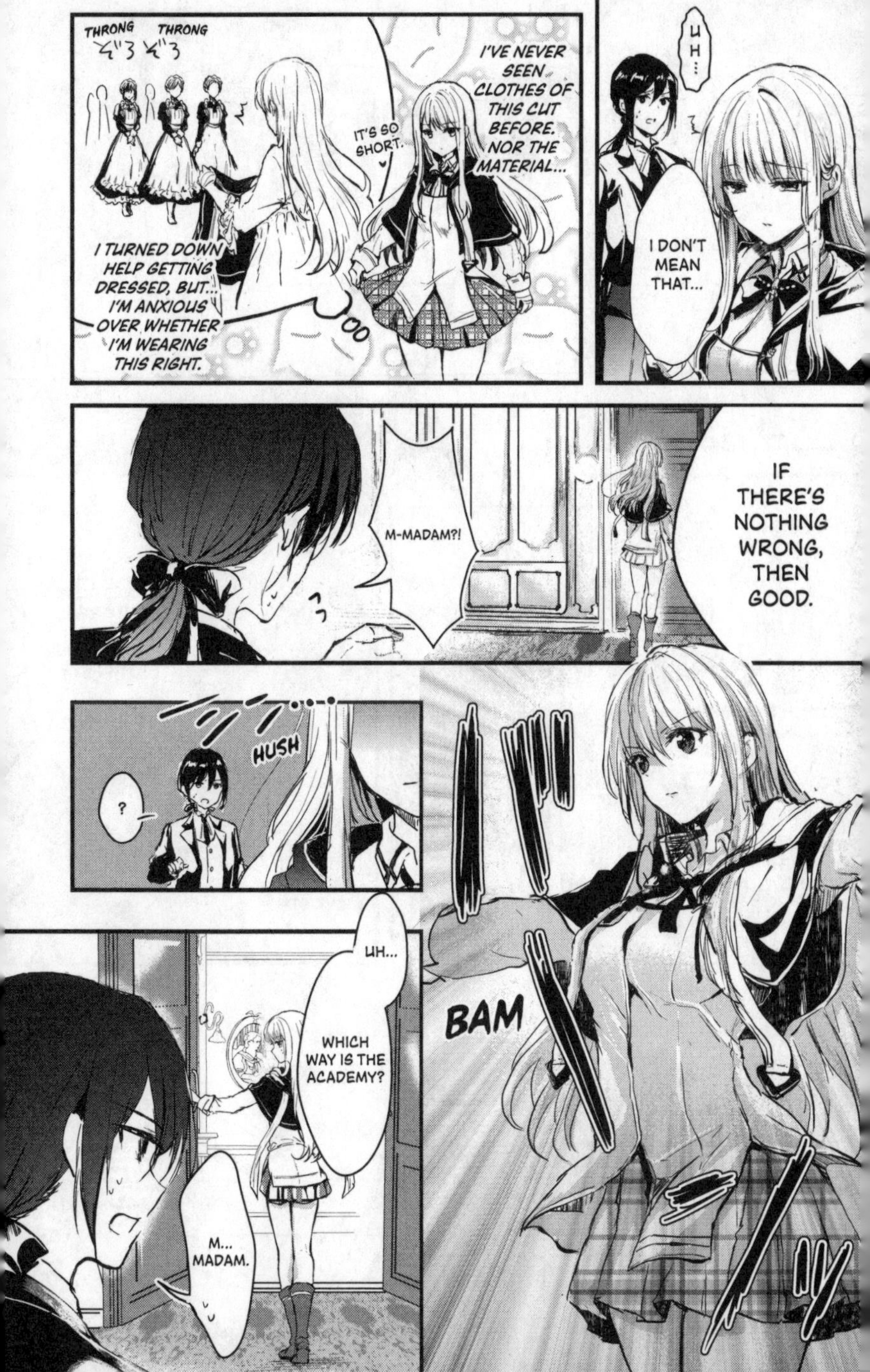
UH...
I DON'T MEAN THAT...
I'VE NEVER SEEN CLOTHES OF THIS CUT BEFORE. NOR THE MATERIAL...
IT'S SO SHORT.
THRONG THRONG
ぞろぞろ
I TURNED DOWN HELP GETTING DRESSED, BUT... I'M ANXIOUS OVER WHETHER I'M WEARING THIS RIGHT.
IF THERE'S NOTHING WRONG, THEN GOOD.
M-MADAM?!
BAM
HUSH
?
UH...
WHICH WAY IS THE ACADEMY?
M... MADAM.

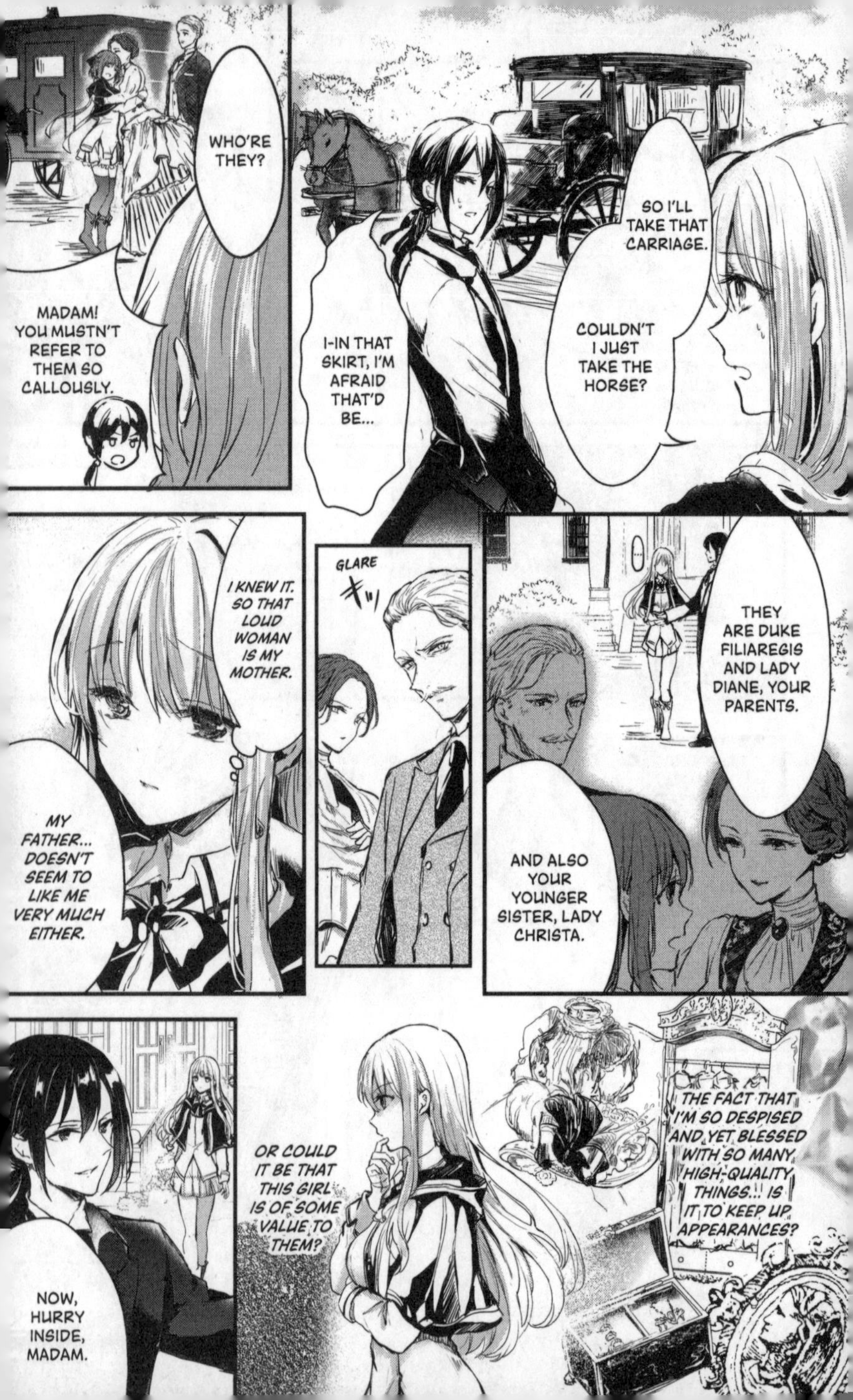
SO I'LL TAKE THAT CARRIAGE.
COULDN'T I JUST TAKE THE HORSE?
I-IN THAT SKIRT, I'M AFRAID THAT'D BE...
WHO'RE THEY?
MADAM! YOU MUSTN'T REFER TO THEM SO CALLOUSLY.
THEY ARE DUKE FILIAREGIS AND LADY DIANE, YOUR PARENTS.
AND ALSO YOUR YOUNGER SISTER, LADY CHRISTA.
GLARE
ギッ
I KNEW IT. SO THAT LOUD WOMAN IS MY MOTHER.
MY FATHER... DOESN'T SEEM TO LIKE ME VERY MUCH EITHER.
THE FACT THAT I'M SO DESPISED AND YET BLESSED WITH SO MANY HIGH-QUALITY THINGS... IS IT TO KEEP UP APPEARANCES?
OR COULD IT BE THAT THIS GIRL IS OF SOME VALUE TO THEM?
NOW, HURRY INSIDE, MADAM.

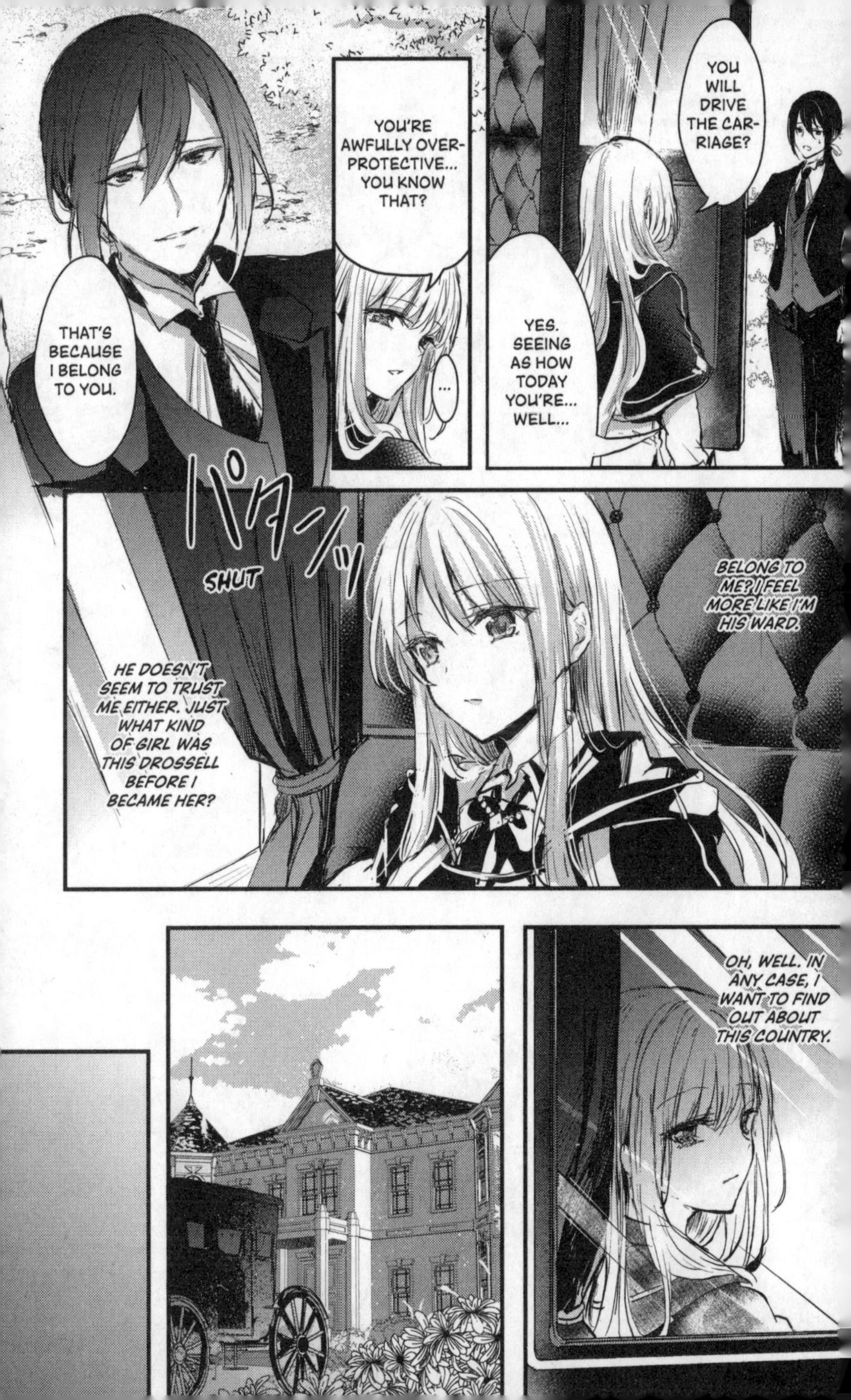
YOU WILL DRIVE THE CARRIAGE?
YES. SEEING AS HOW TODAY YOU'RE... WELL...
YOU'RE AWFULLY OVER-PROTECTIVE... YOU KNOW THAT?
...
THAT'S BECAUSE I BELONG TO YOU.
パタンッ
SHUT
BELONG TO ME? I FEEL MORE LIKE I'M HIS WARD.
HE DOESN'T SEEM TO TRUST ME EITHER. JUST WHAT KIND OF GIRL WAS THIS DROSSELL BEFORE I BECAME HER?
OH, WELL. IN ANY CASE, I WANT TO FIND OUT ABOUT THIS COUNTRY.

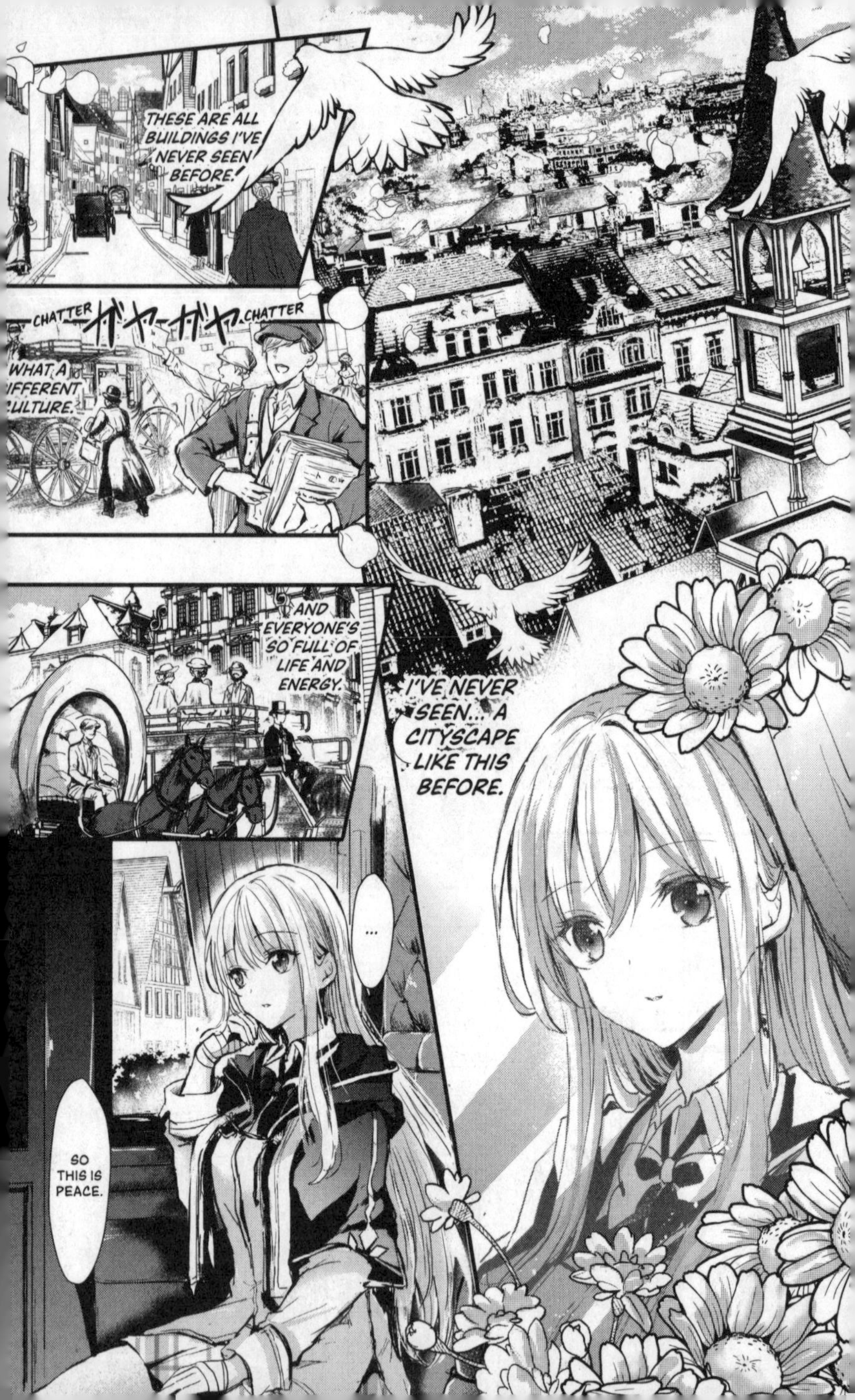
THESE ARE ALL BUILDINGS I'VE NEVER SEEN BEFORE!
CHATTER ガヤ CHATTER ガヤ
WHAT A DIFFERENT CULTURE.
AND EVERYONE'S SO FULL OF LIFE AND ENERGY.
I'VE NEVER SEEN... A CITYSCAPE LIKE THIS BEFORE.
...
SO THIS IS PEACE.

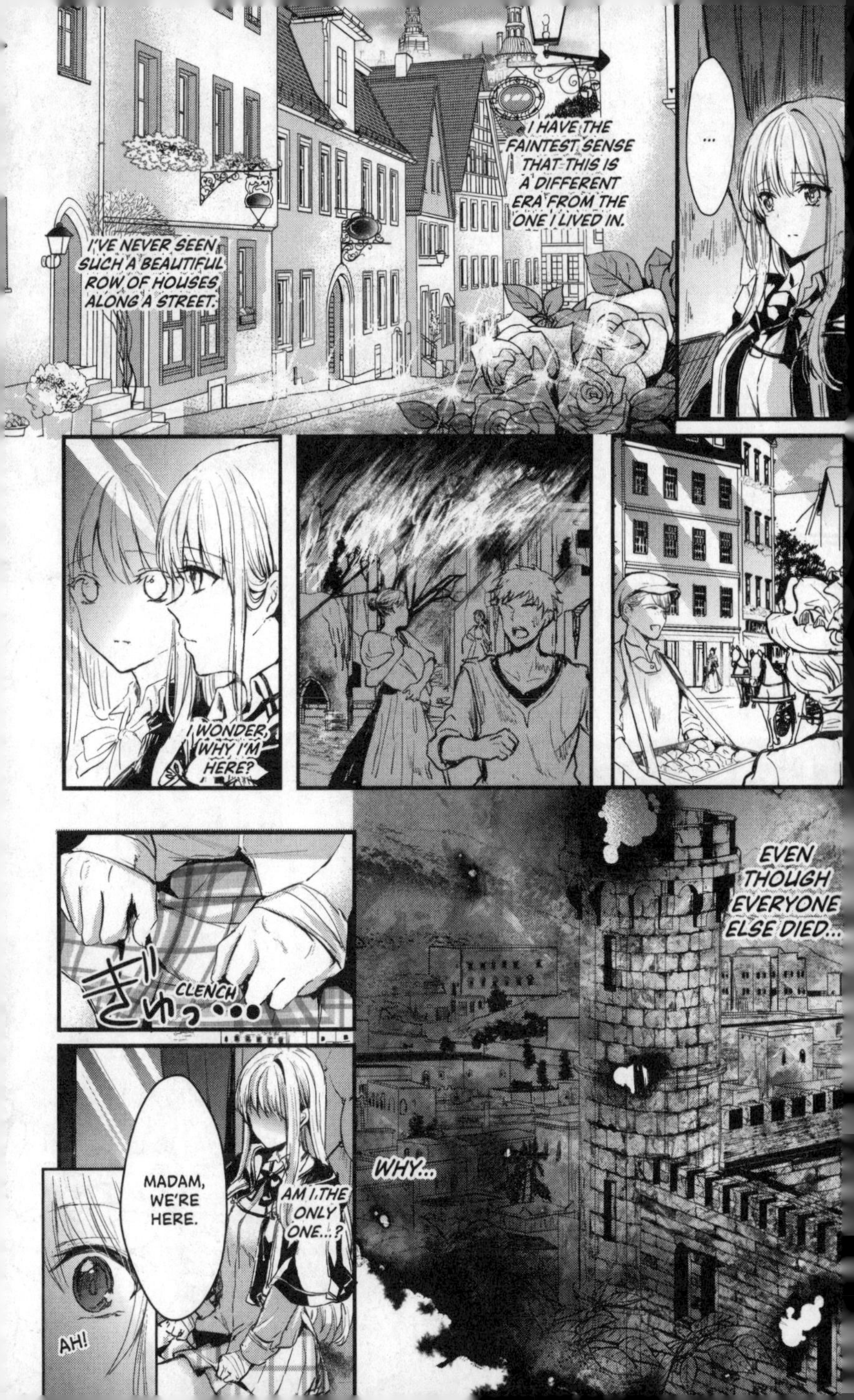
...
I HAVE THE FAINTEST SENSE THAT THIS IS A DIFFERENT ERA FROM THE ONE I LIVED IN.
I'VE NEVER SEEN SUCH A BEAUTIFUL ROW OF HOUSES ALONG A STREET.
I WONDER, WHY I'M HERE?
EVEN THOUGH EVERYONE ELSE DIED...
WHY...
ぎゅっ…
CLENCH
AM I THE ONLY ONE...?
MADAM, WE'RE HERE.
AH!

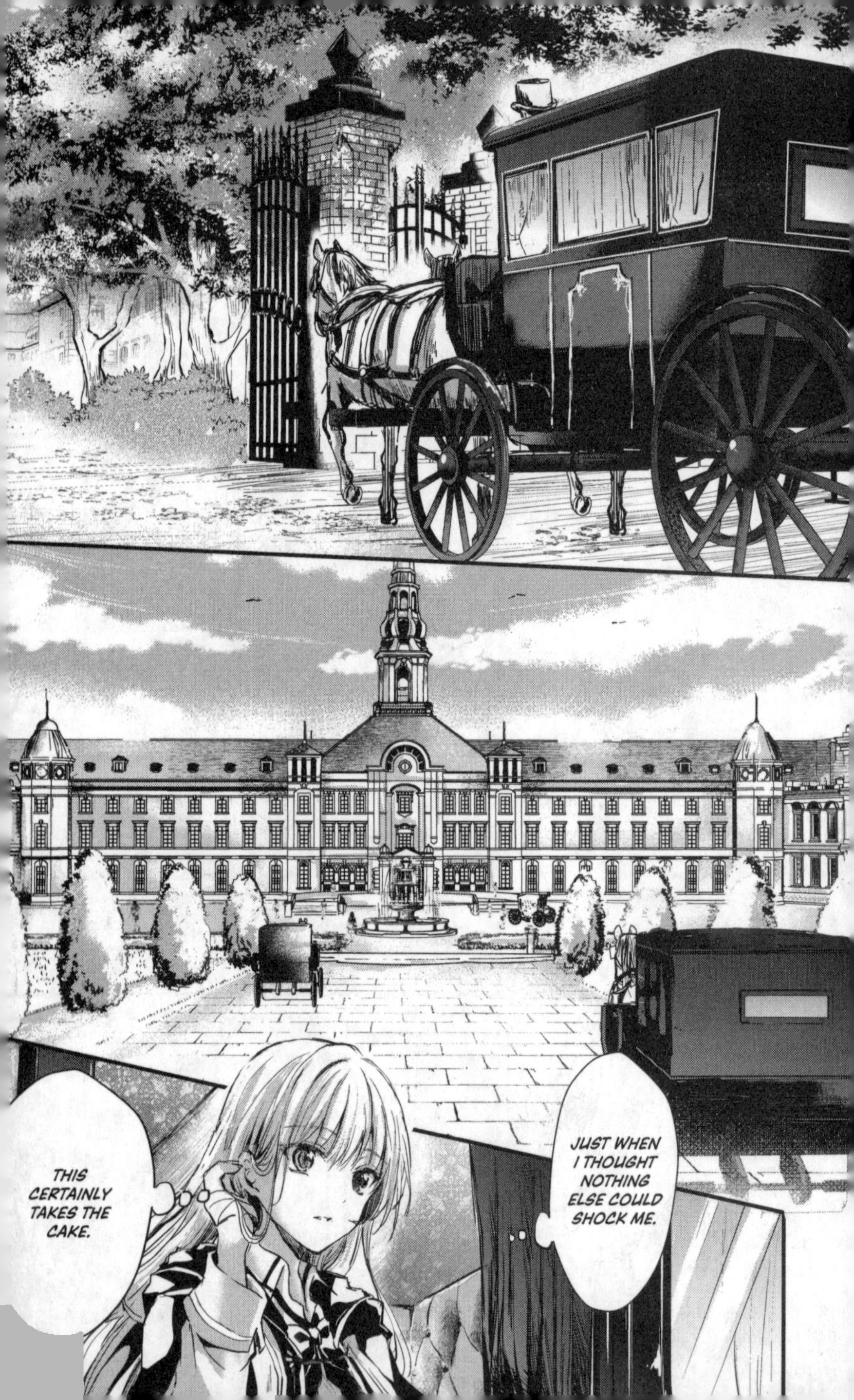
JUST WHEN I THOUGHT NOTHING ELSE COULD SHOCK ME.
THIS CERTAINLY TAKES THE CAKE.

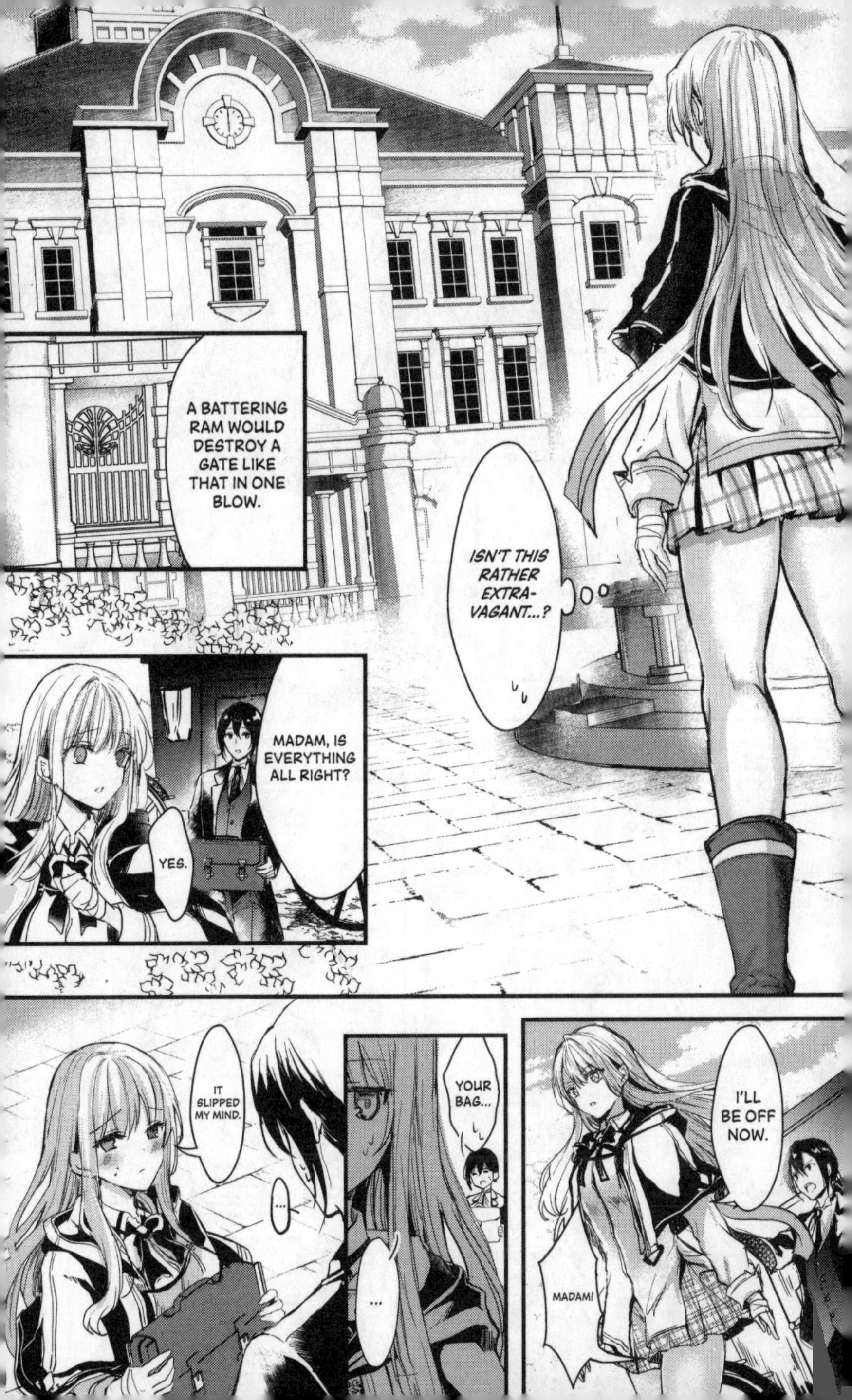
ISN'T THIS RATHER EXTRA-VAGANT...?
A BATTERING RAM WOULD DESTROY A GATE LIKE THAT IN ONE BLOW.
MADAM, IS EVERYTHING ALL RIGHT?
YES.
I'LL BE OFF NOW.
MADAM!
YOUR BAG...
...
IT SLIPPED MY MIND.
...

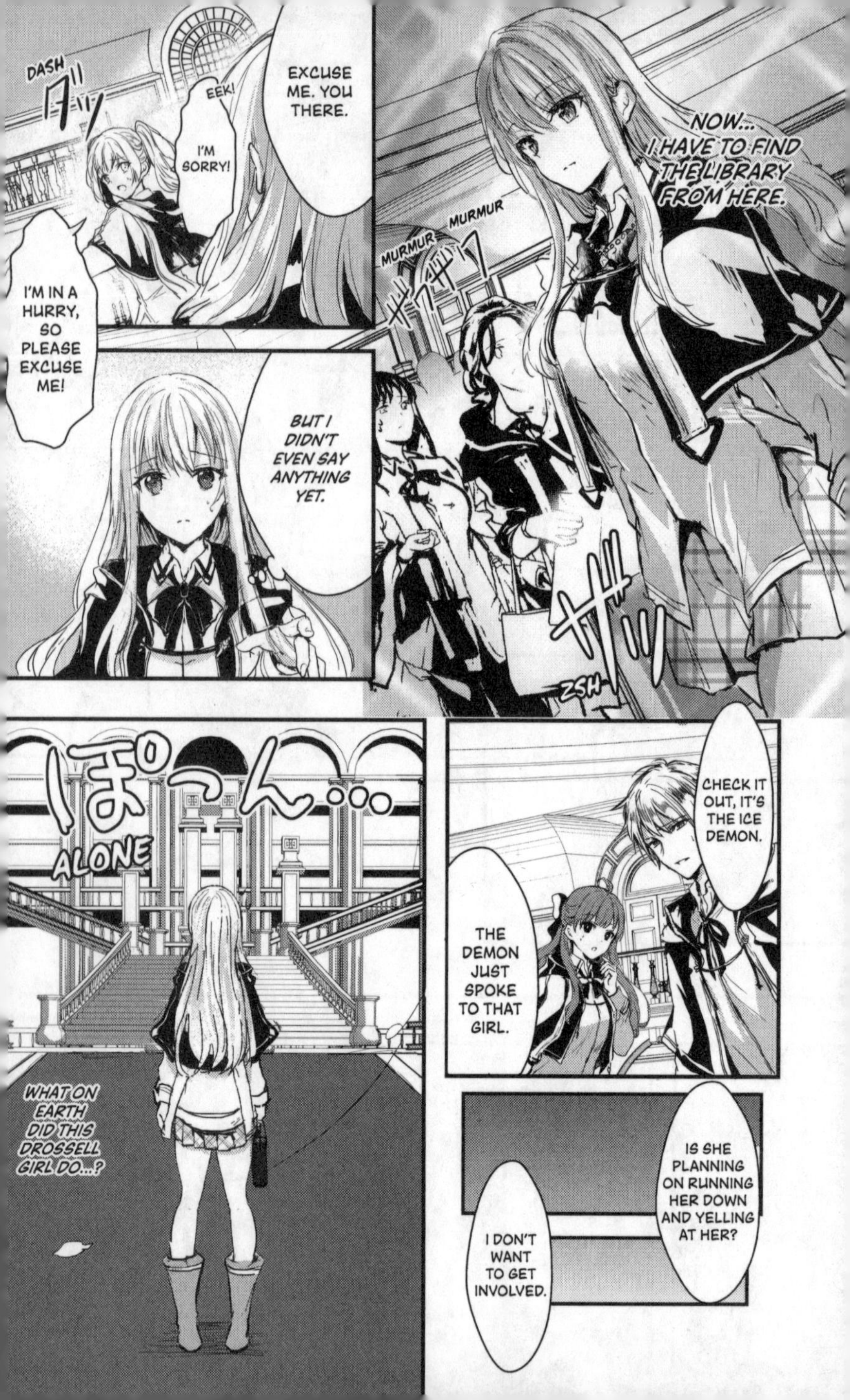
NOW... I HAVE TO FIND THE LIBRARY FROM HERE.
MURMUR
MURMUR
ZSH
EXCUSE ME. YOU THERE.
EEK!
I'M SORRY!
DASH
I'M IN A HURRY, SO PLEASE EXCUSE ME!
BUT I DIDN'T EVEN SAY ANYTHING YET.
CHECK IT OUT, IT'S THE ICE DEMON.
THE DEMON JUST SPOKE TO THAT GIRL.
IS SHE PLANNING ON RUNNING HER DOWN AND YELLING AT HER?
I DON'T WANT TO GET INVOLVED.
ぽつん...
ALONE
WHAT ON EARTH DID THIS DROSSELL GIRL DO...?

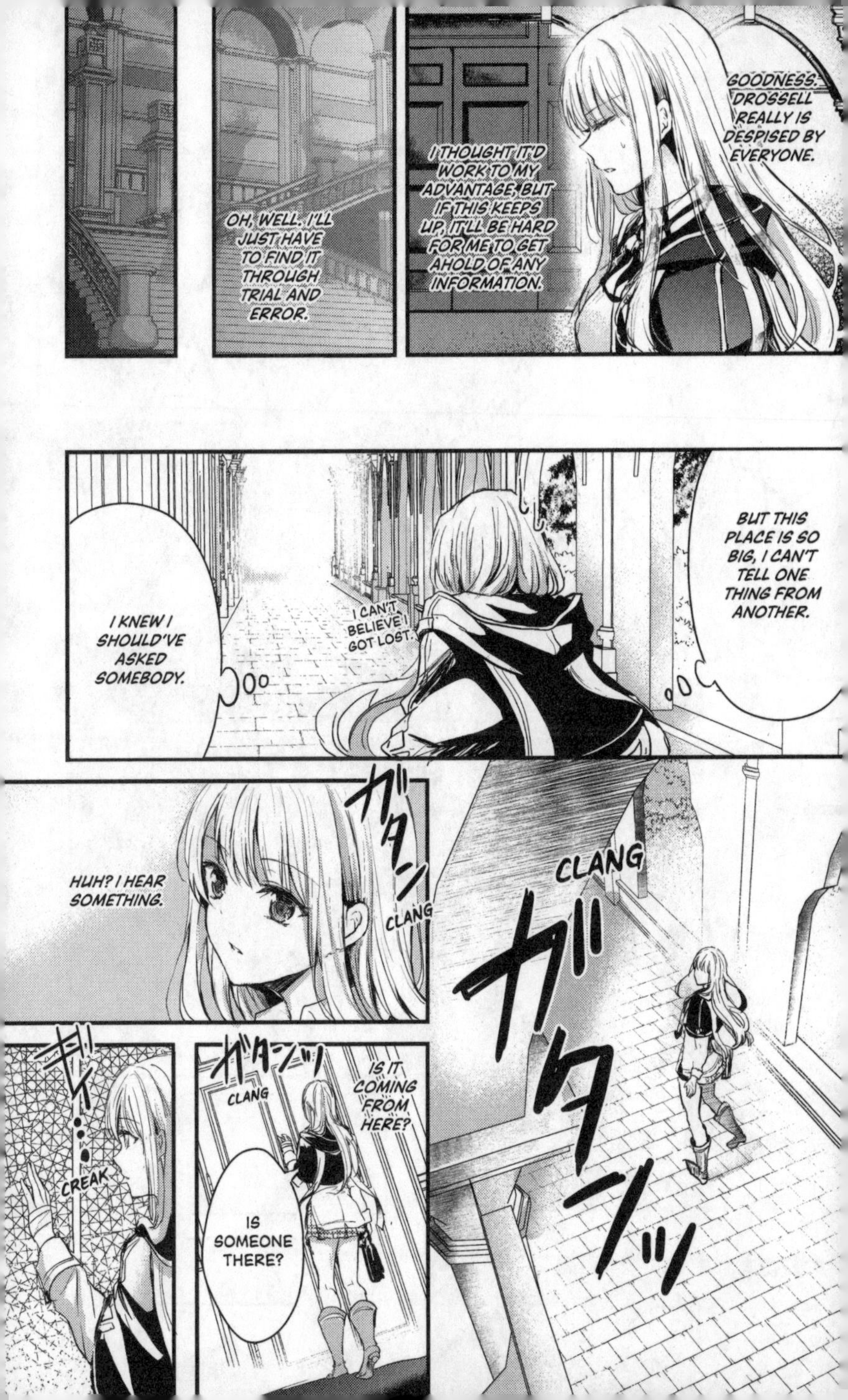
GOODNESS. DROSSELL REALLY IS DESPISED BY EVERYONE.
I THOUGHT IT'D WORK TO MY ADVANTAGE, BUT IF THIS KEEPS UP, IT'LL BE HARD FOR ME TO GET AHOLD OF ANY INFORMATION.
OH, WELL. I'LL JUST HAVE TO FIND IT THROUGH TRIAL AND ERROR.
BUT THIS PLACE IS SO BIG, I CAN'T TELL ONE THING FROM ANOTHER.
I CAN'T BELIEVE I GOT LOST.
I KNEW I SHOULD'VE ASKED SOMEBODY.
ガタンッ
CLANG
ガタン
CLANG
HUH? I HEAR SOMETHING.
ガタンッ
CLANG
IS IT COMING FROM HERE?
IS SOMEONE THERE?
ギィ…
CREAK

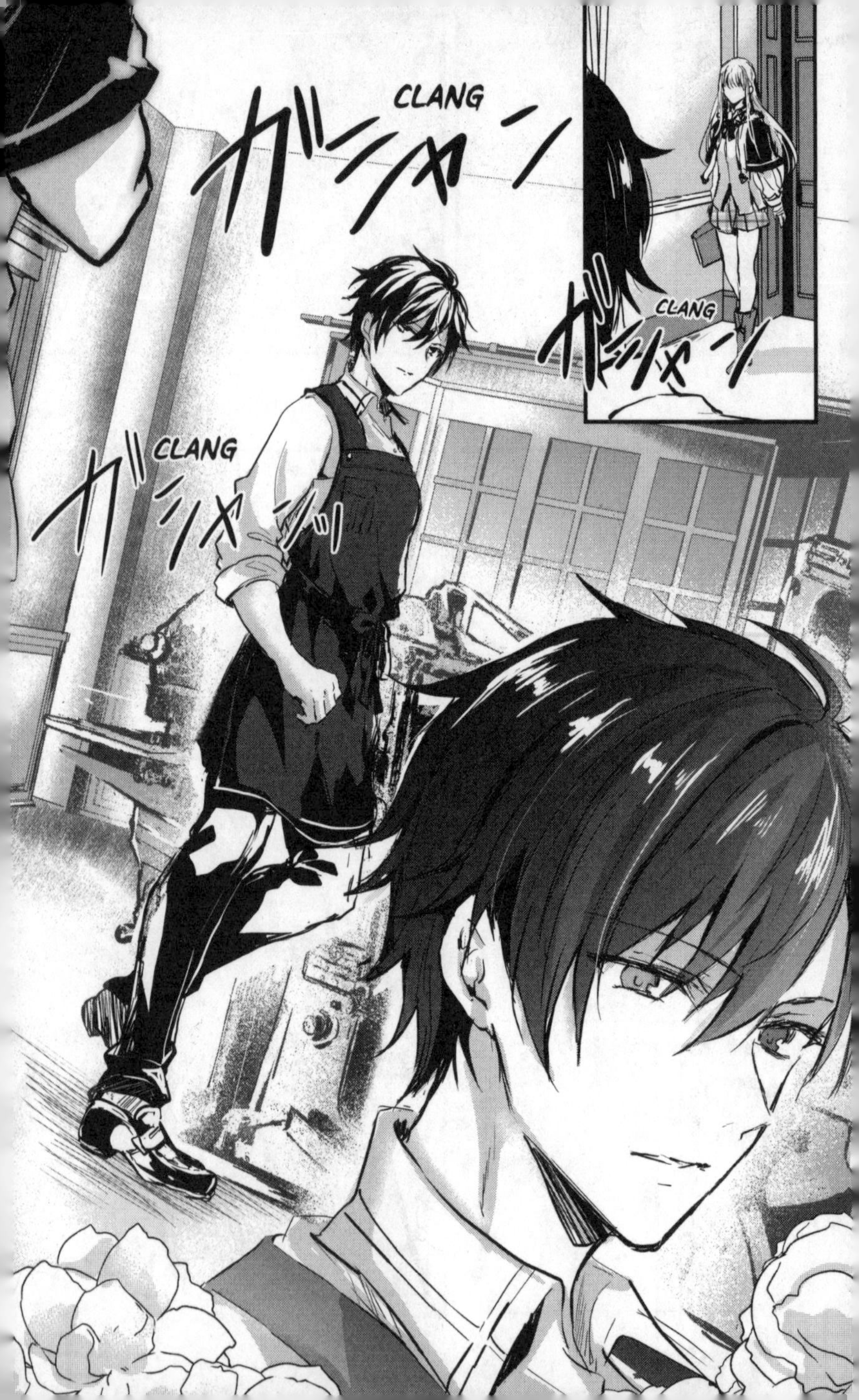
ガシャーン
CLANG
ガシャーン
CLANG
CLANG

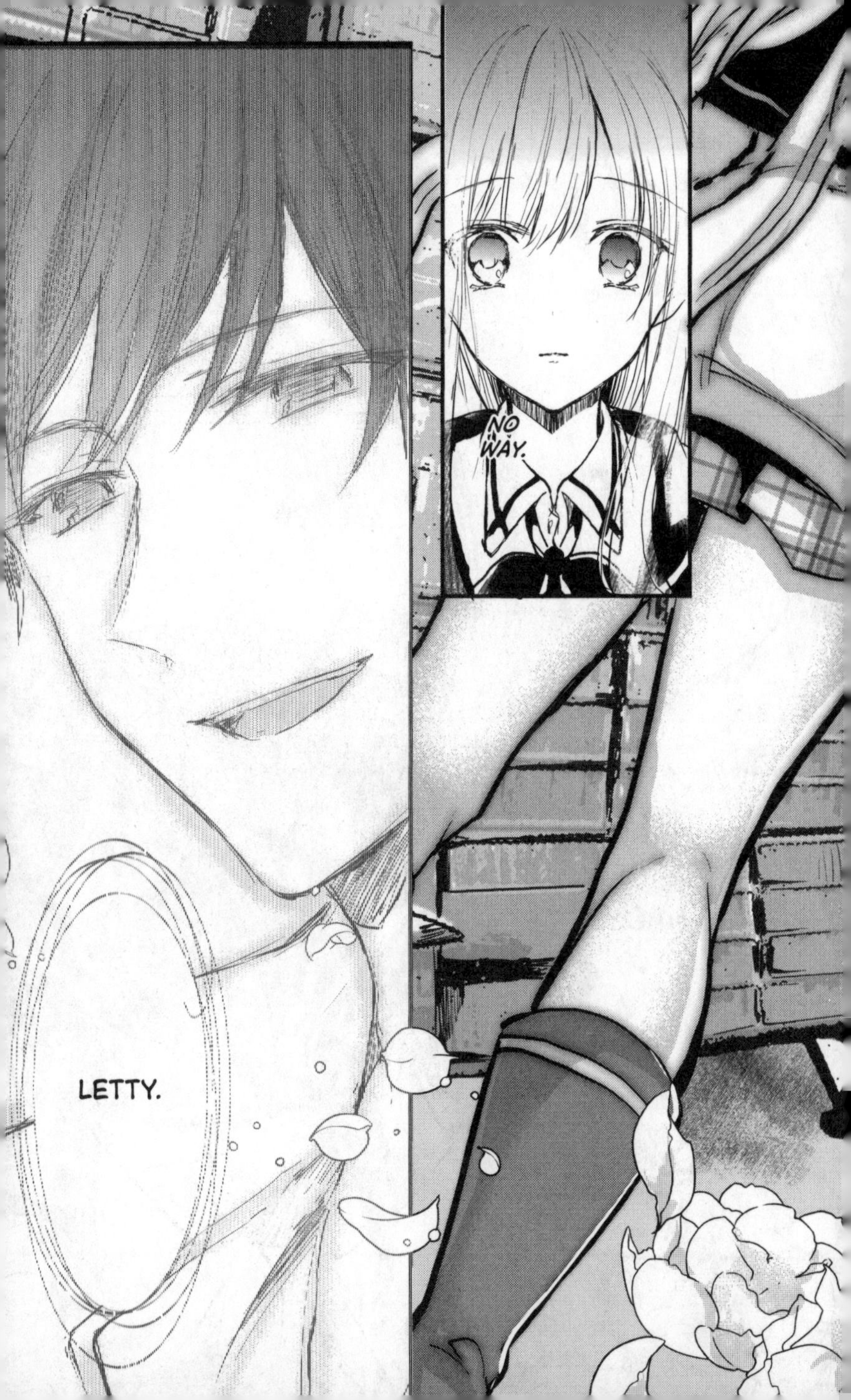
NO WAY.
LETTY.

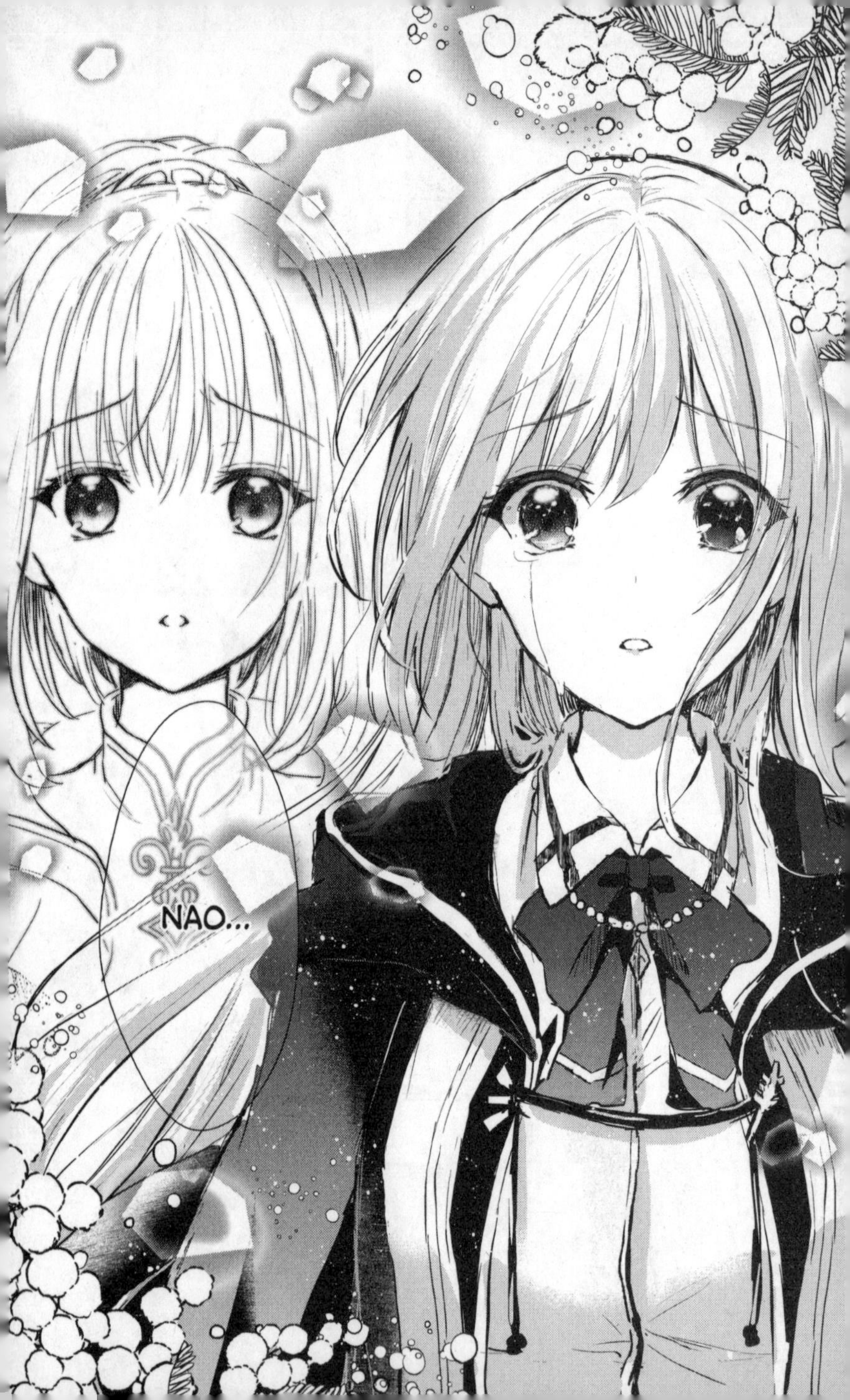
NAO...

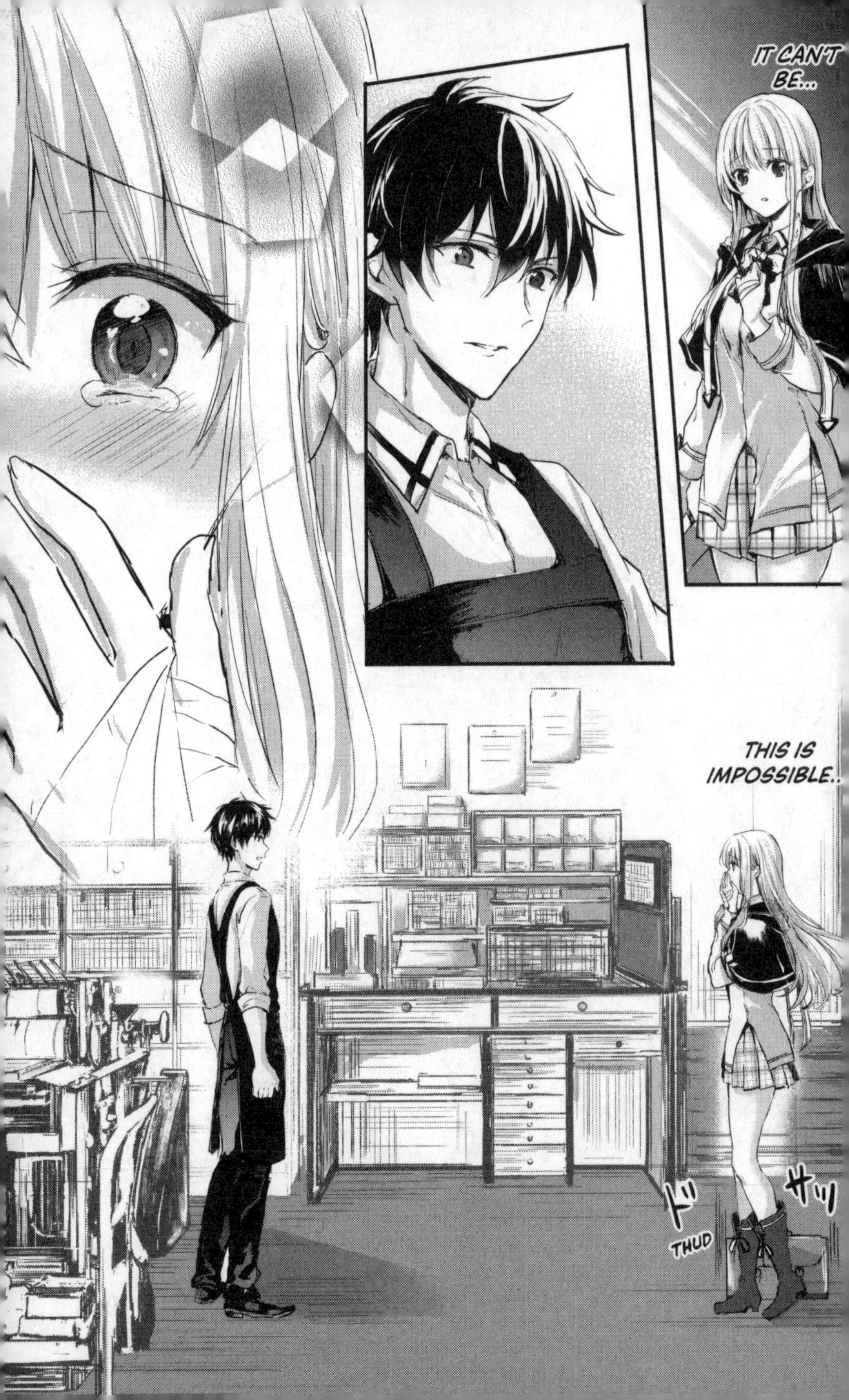
IT CAN'T BE...
THIS IS IMPOSSIBLE..
ドド
THUD
サッ

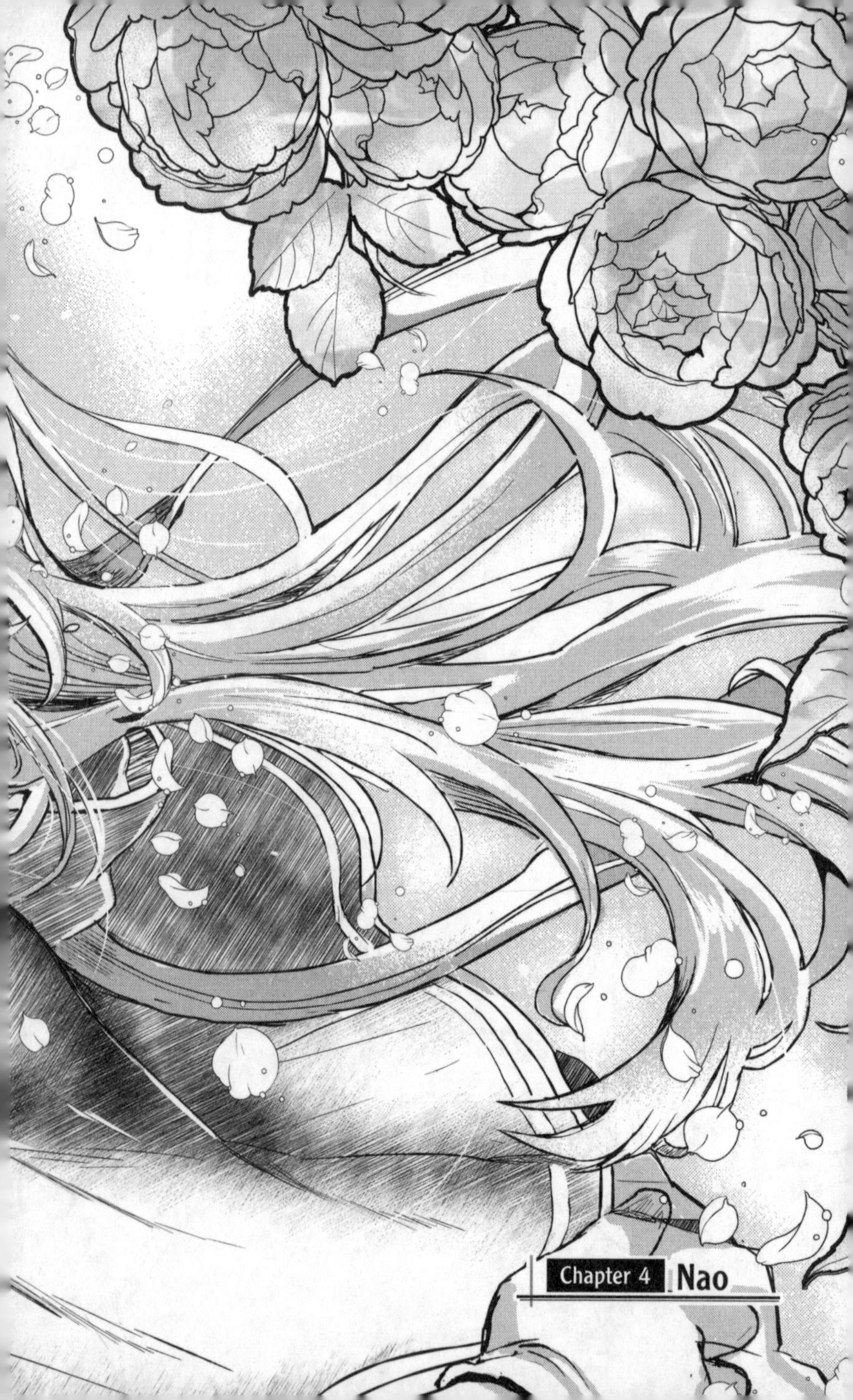
Chapter 4 Nao

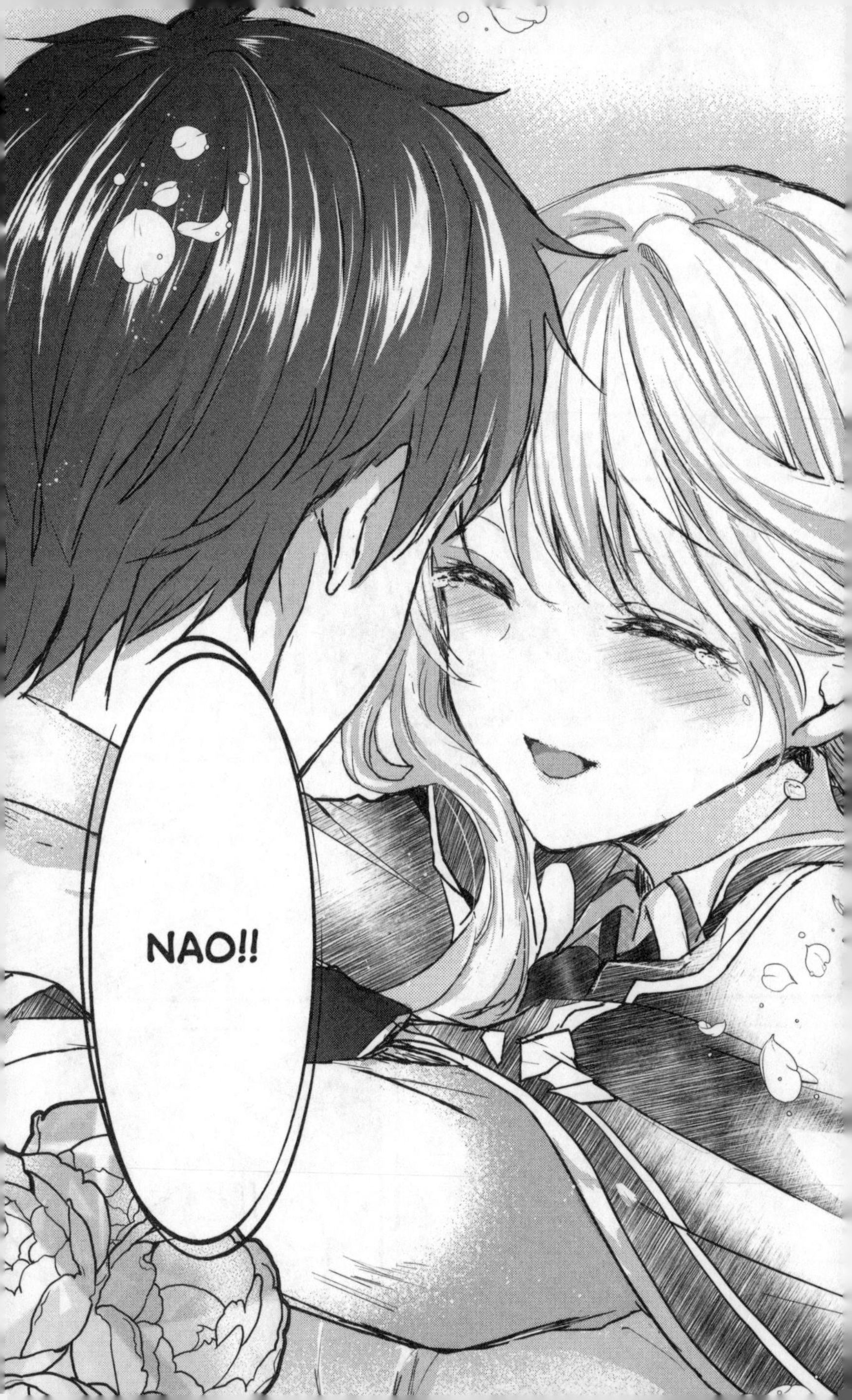
NAO!!

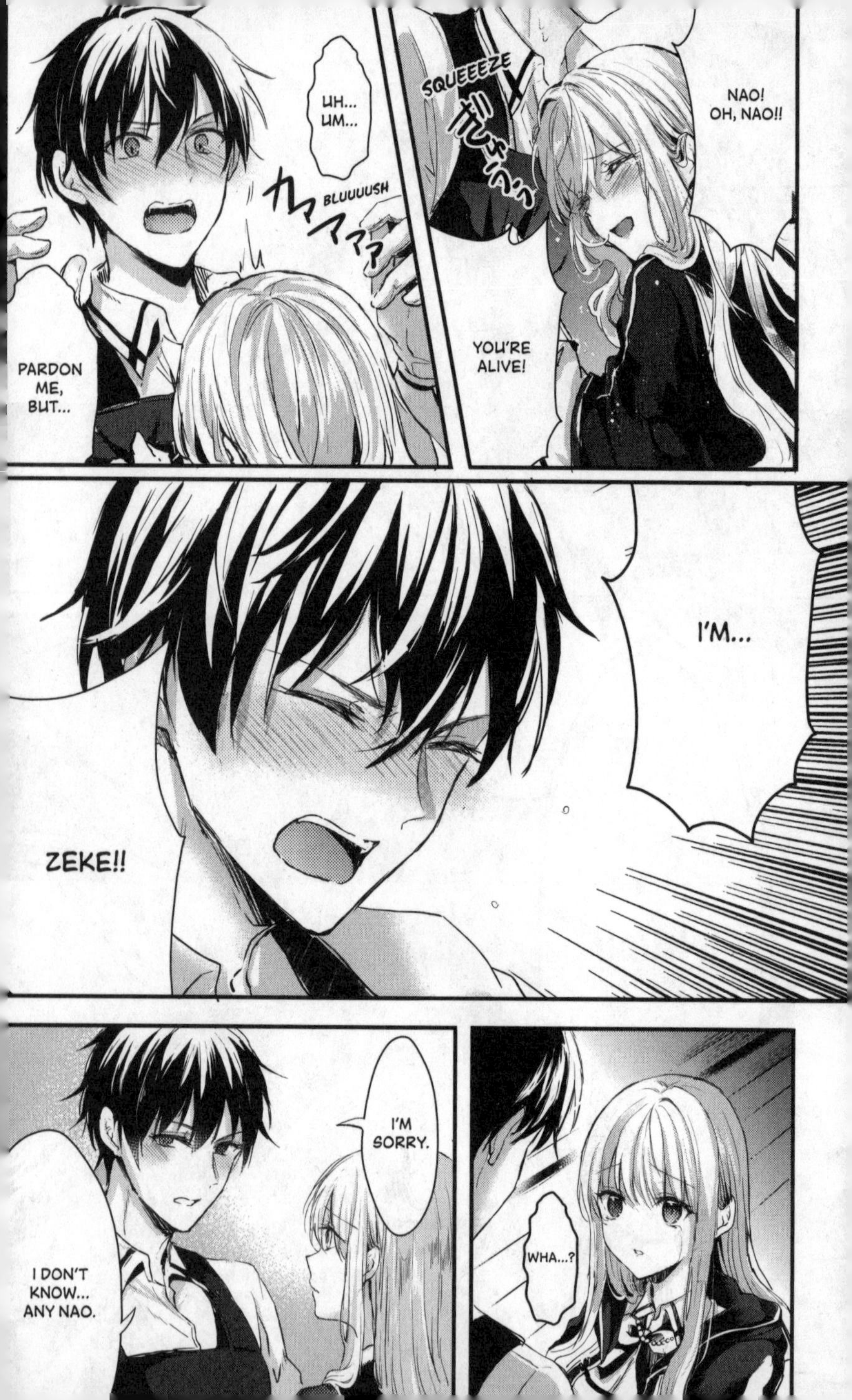
NAO!
OH, NAO!!
SQUEEEZE
YOU'RE ALIVE!
UH... UM...
BLUUUUSH
PARDON ME, BUT...
I'M...
ZEKE!!
WHA...?
I'M SORRY.
I DON'T KNOW... ANY NAO.

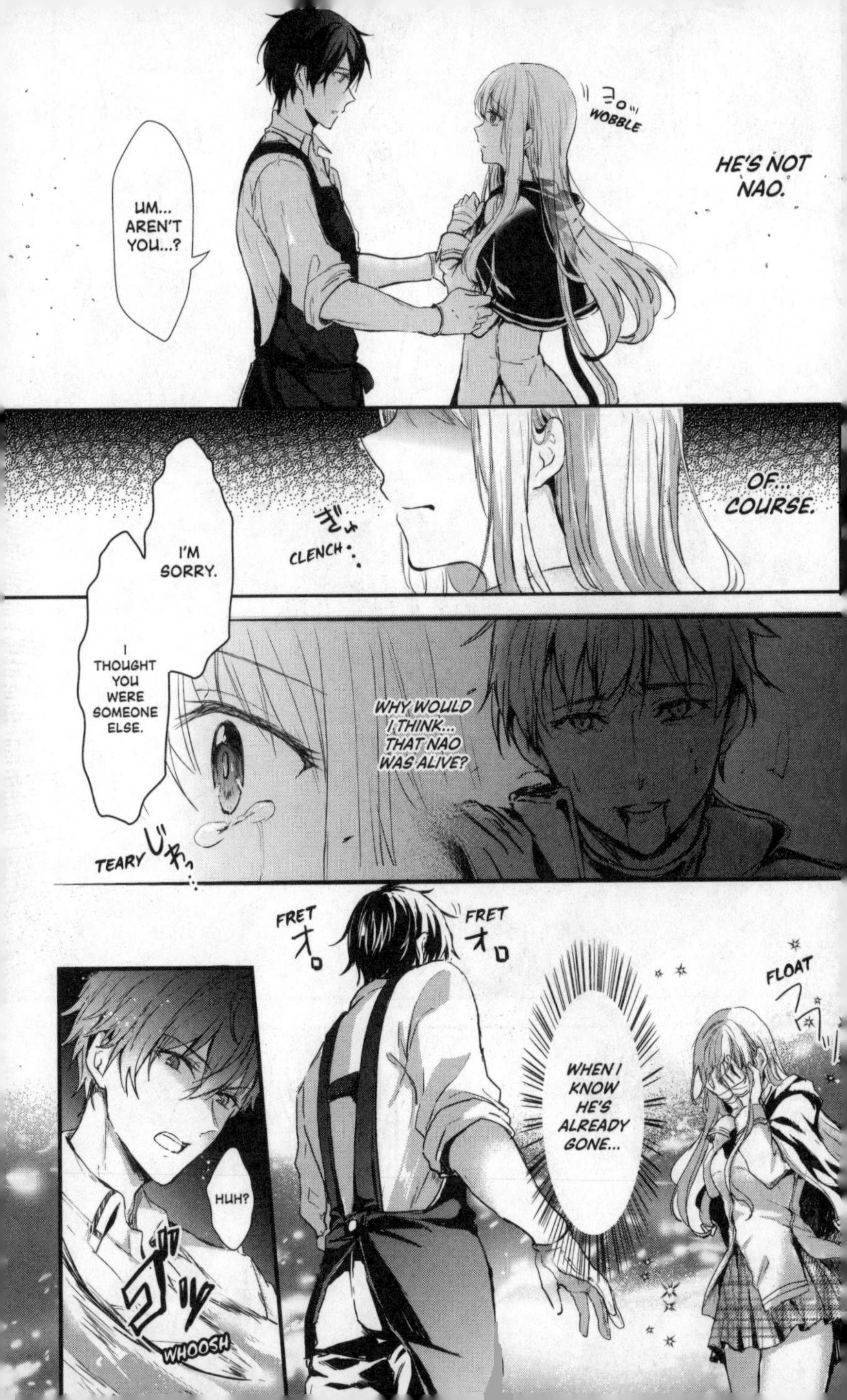
HE'S NOT NAO.
ヨロ
WOBBLE
UM... AREN'T YOU...?
OF... COURSE.
ぎゅ
CLENCH...
I'M SORRY.
WHY WOULD I THINK... THAT NAO WAS ALIVE?
I THOUGHT YOU WERE SOMEONE ELSE.
じわっ
TEARY
FLOAT
WHEN I KNOW HE'S ALREADY GONE...
FRET
オロ
FRET
オロ
HUH?
WHOOSH

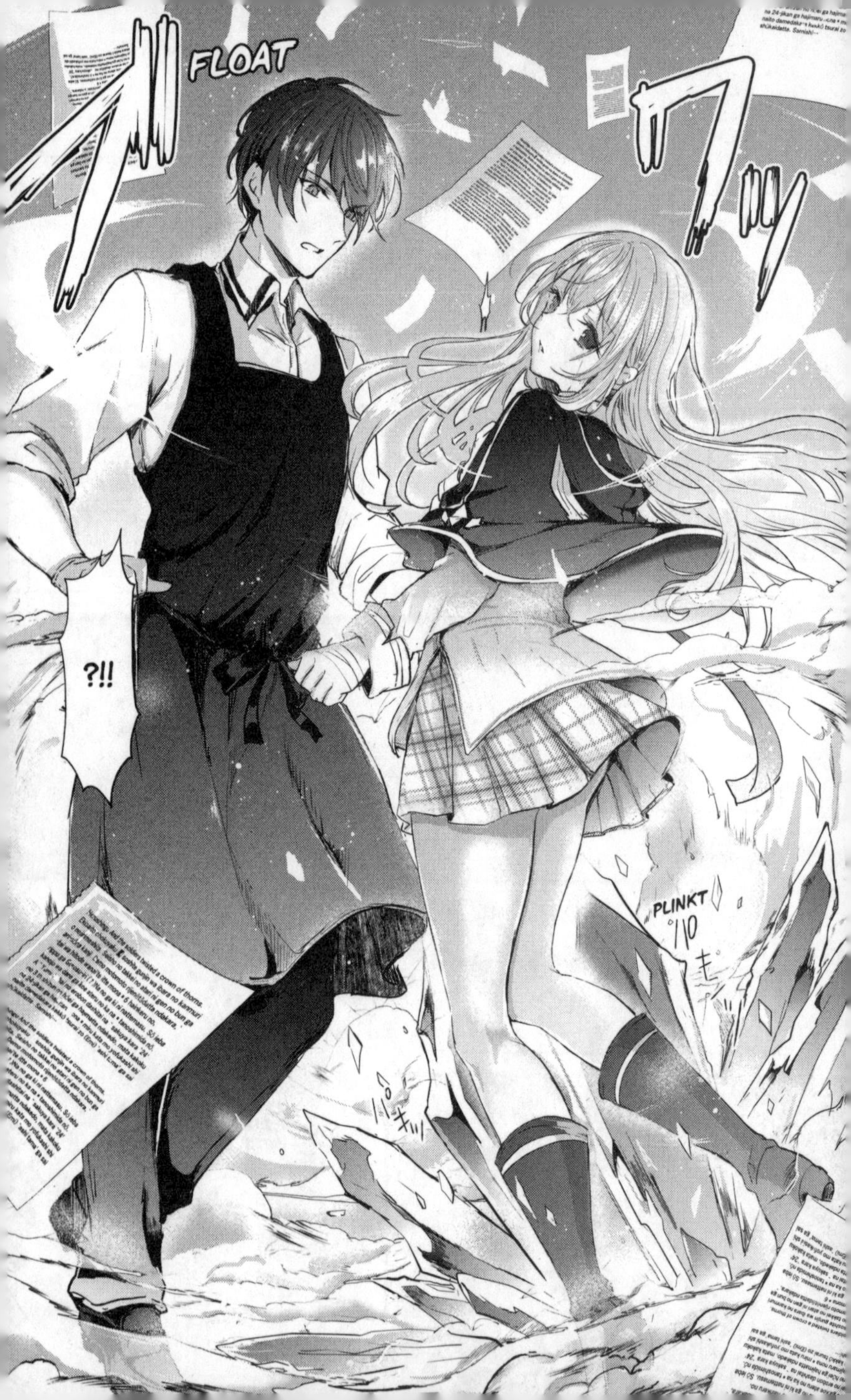
FLOAT
?!!
PLINKT

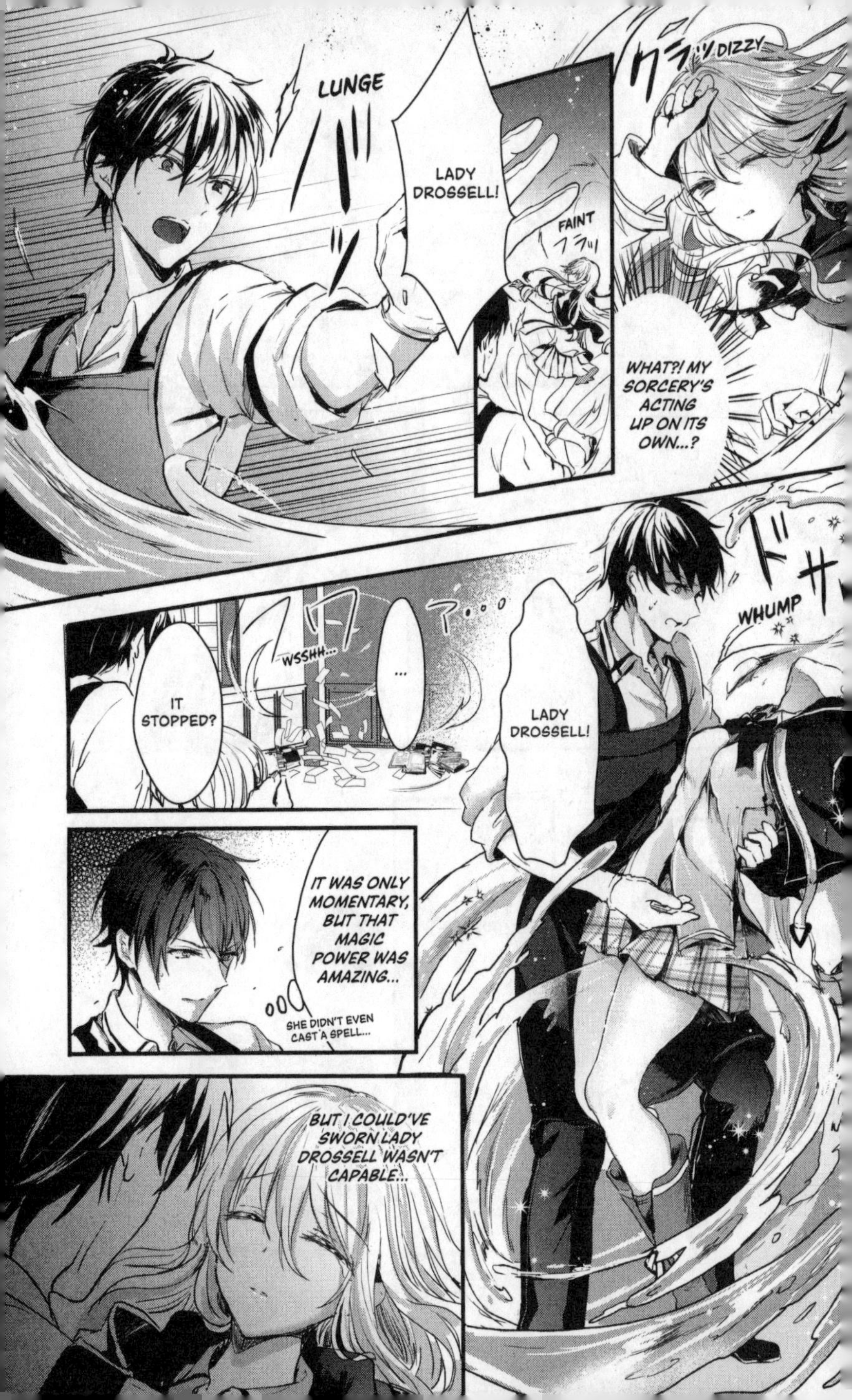
DIZZY
FAINT
WHAT?! MY SORCERY'S ACTING UP ON ITS OWN...?
LUNGE
LADY DROSSELL!
WHUMP
LADY DROSSELL!
...
WSSHH...
IT STOPPED?
IT WAS ONLY MOMENTARY, BUT THAT MAGIC POWER WAS AMAZING...
SHE DIDN'T EVEN CAST A SPELL...
BUT I COULD'VE SWORN LADY DROSSELL WASN'T CAPABLE...

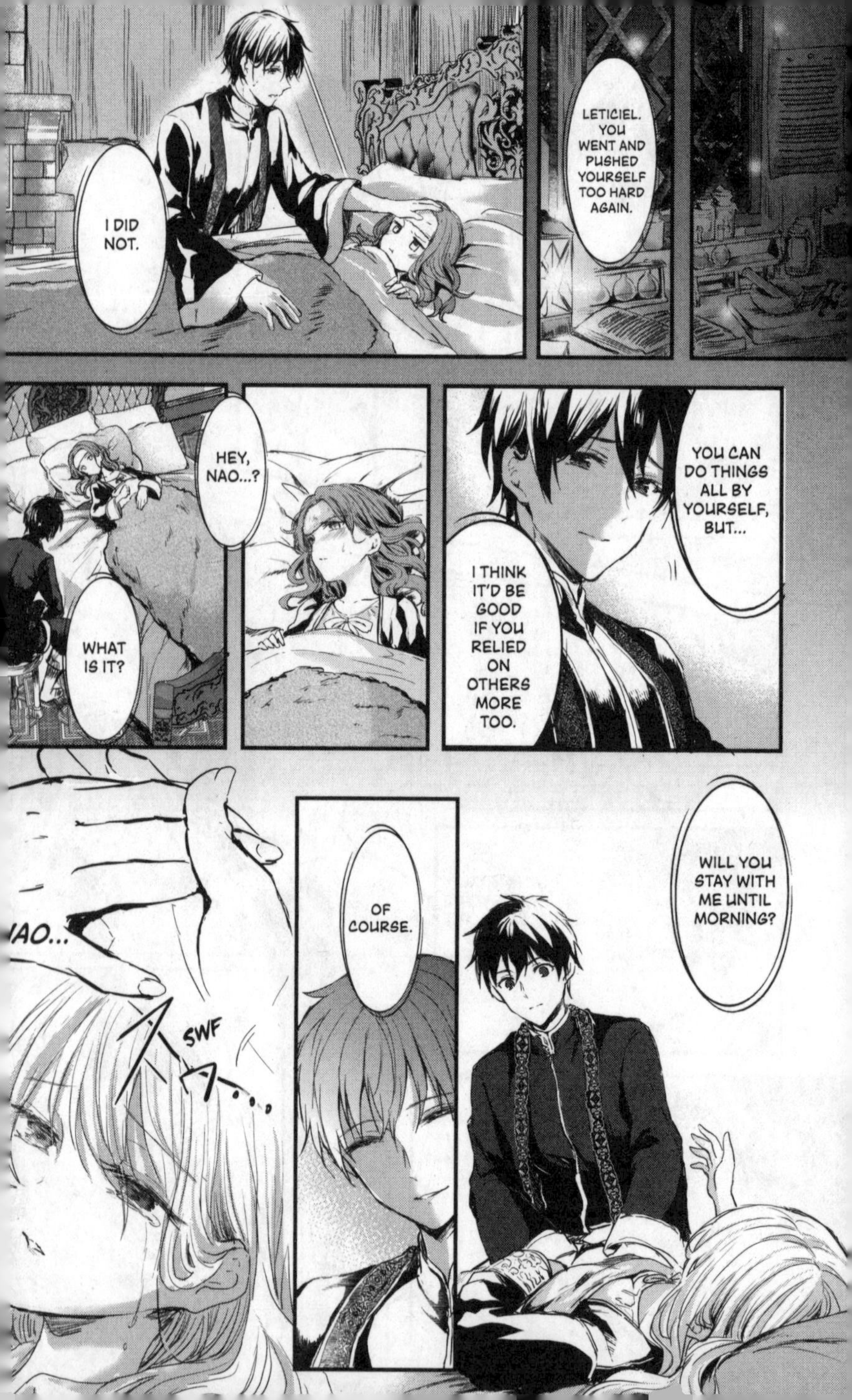
LETICIEL. YOU WENT AND PUSHED YOURSELF TOO HARD AGAIN.
I DID NOT.
YOU CAN DO THINGS ALL BY YOURSELF, BUT...
I THINK IT'D BE GOOD IF YOU RELIED ON OTHERS MORE TOO.
HEY, NAO...?
WHAT IS IT?
WILL YOU STAY WITH ME UNTIL MORNING?
OF COURSE.
NAO...
SWF

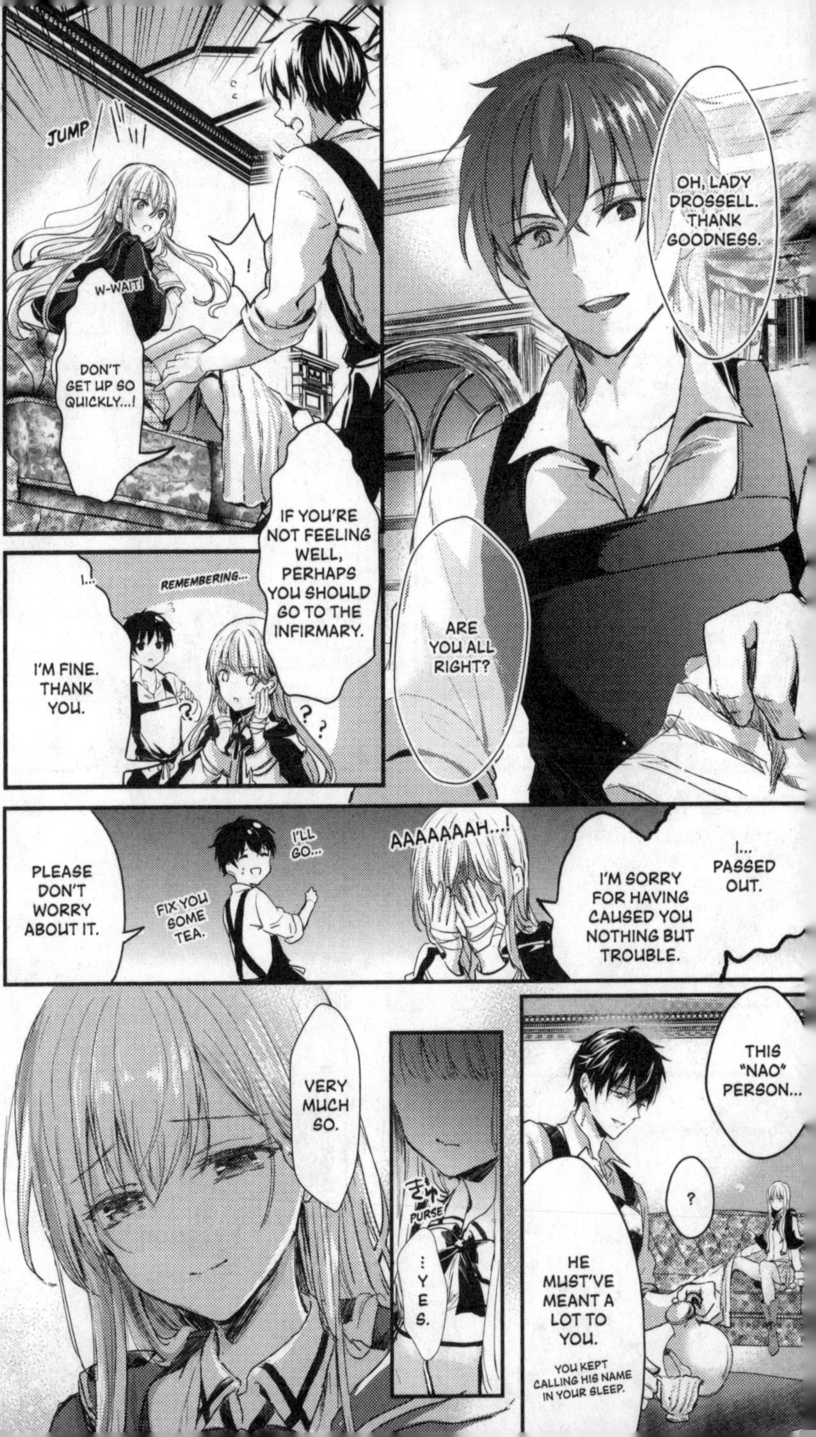
OH, LADY DROSSELL. THANK GOODNESS.
ARE YOU ALL RIGHT?
JUMP
!
W-WAIT!
DON'T GET UP SO QUICKLY...!
IF YOU'RE NOT FEELING WELL, PERHAPS YOU SHOULD GO TO THE INFIRMARY.
REMEMBERING...
I...!
I'M FINE. THANK YOU.
I... PASSED OUT.
I'M SORRY FOR HAVING CAUSED YOU NOTHING BUT TROUBLE.
AAAAAAAH...!
I'LL GO...
FIX YOU SOME TEA.
PLEASE DON'T WORRY ABOUT IT.
THIS "NAO" PERSON...
?
HE MUST'VE MEANT A LOT TO YOU.
YOU KEPT CALLING HIS NAME IN YOUR SLEEP.
PURSE
...YES.
VERY MUCH SO.

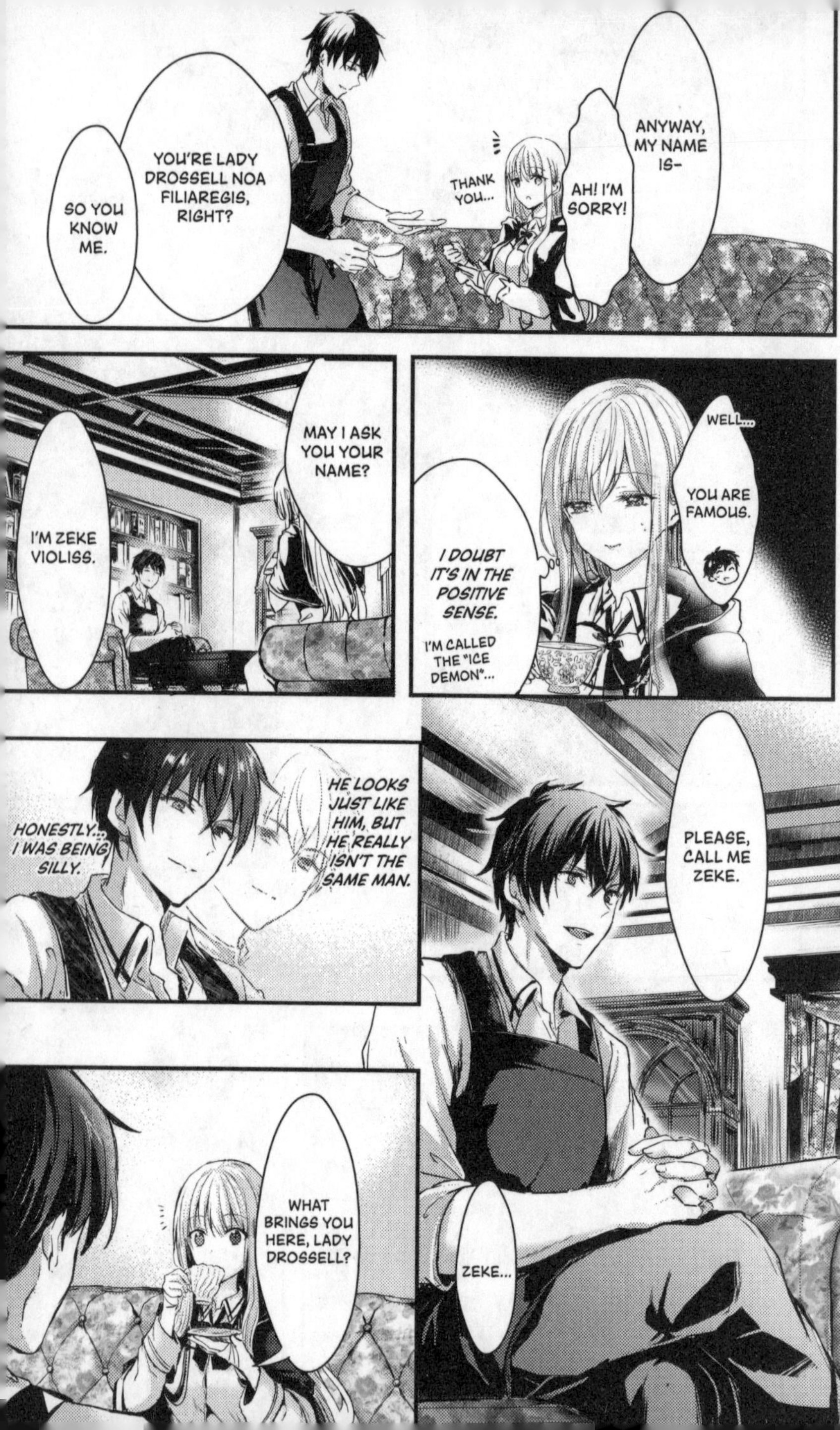
ANYWAY, MY NAME IS–
AH! I'M SORRY!
THANK YOU...
YOU'RE LADY DROSSELL NOA FILIAREGIS, RIGHT?
SO YOU KNOW ME.
WELL...
YOU ARE FAMOUS.
I DOUBT IT'S IN THE POSITIVE SENSE.
I'M CALLED THE "ICE DEMON"...
MAY I ASK YOU YOUR NAME?
I'M ZEKE VIOLISS.
PLEASE, CALL ME ZEKE.
ZEKE...
HE LOOKS JUST LIKE HIM, BUT HE REALLY ISN'T THE SAME MAN.
HONESTLY... I WAS BEING SILLY.
WHAT BRINGS YOU HERE, LADY DROSSELL?

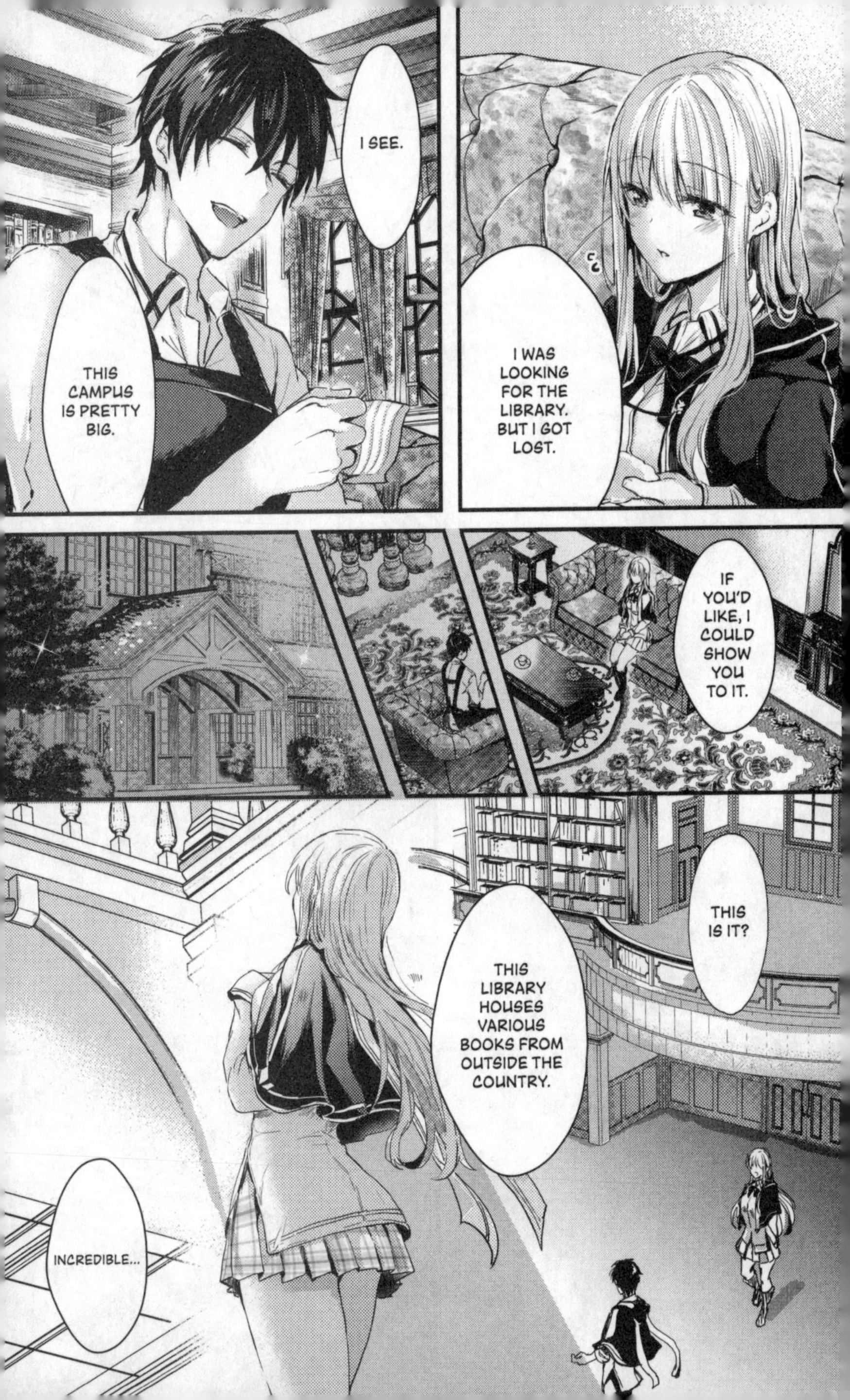
I WAS LOOKING FOR THE LIBRARY. BUT I GOT LOST.
I SEE.
THIS CAMPUS IS PRETTY BIG.
IF YOU'D LIKE, I COULD SHOW YOU TO IT.
THIS IS IT?
THIS LIBRARY HOUSES VARIOUS BOOKS FROM OUTSIDE THE COUNTRY.
INCREDIBLE...

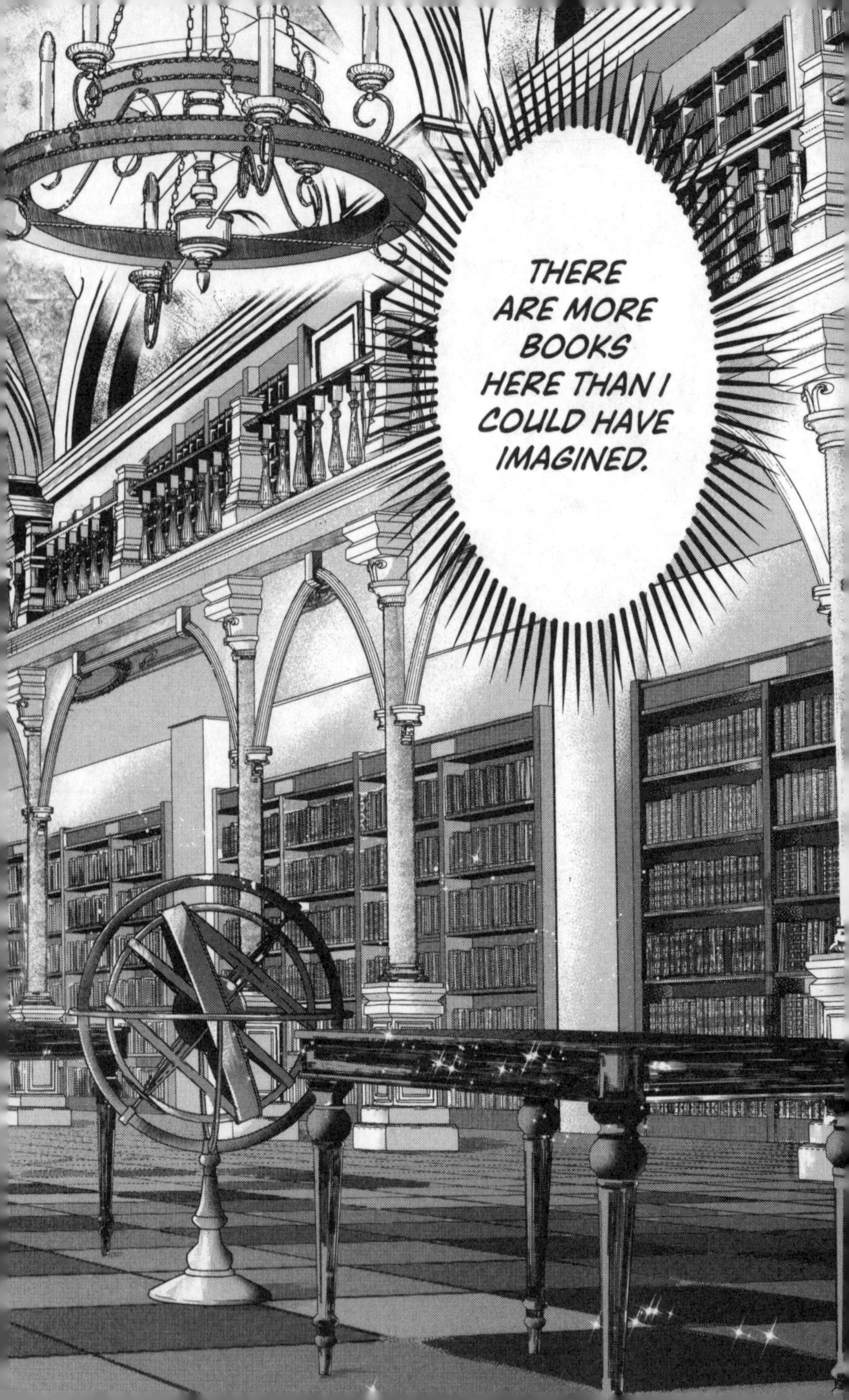
THERE ARE MORE BOOKS HERE THAN I COULD HAVE IMAGINED.

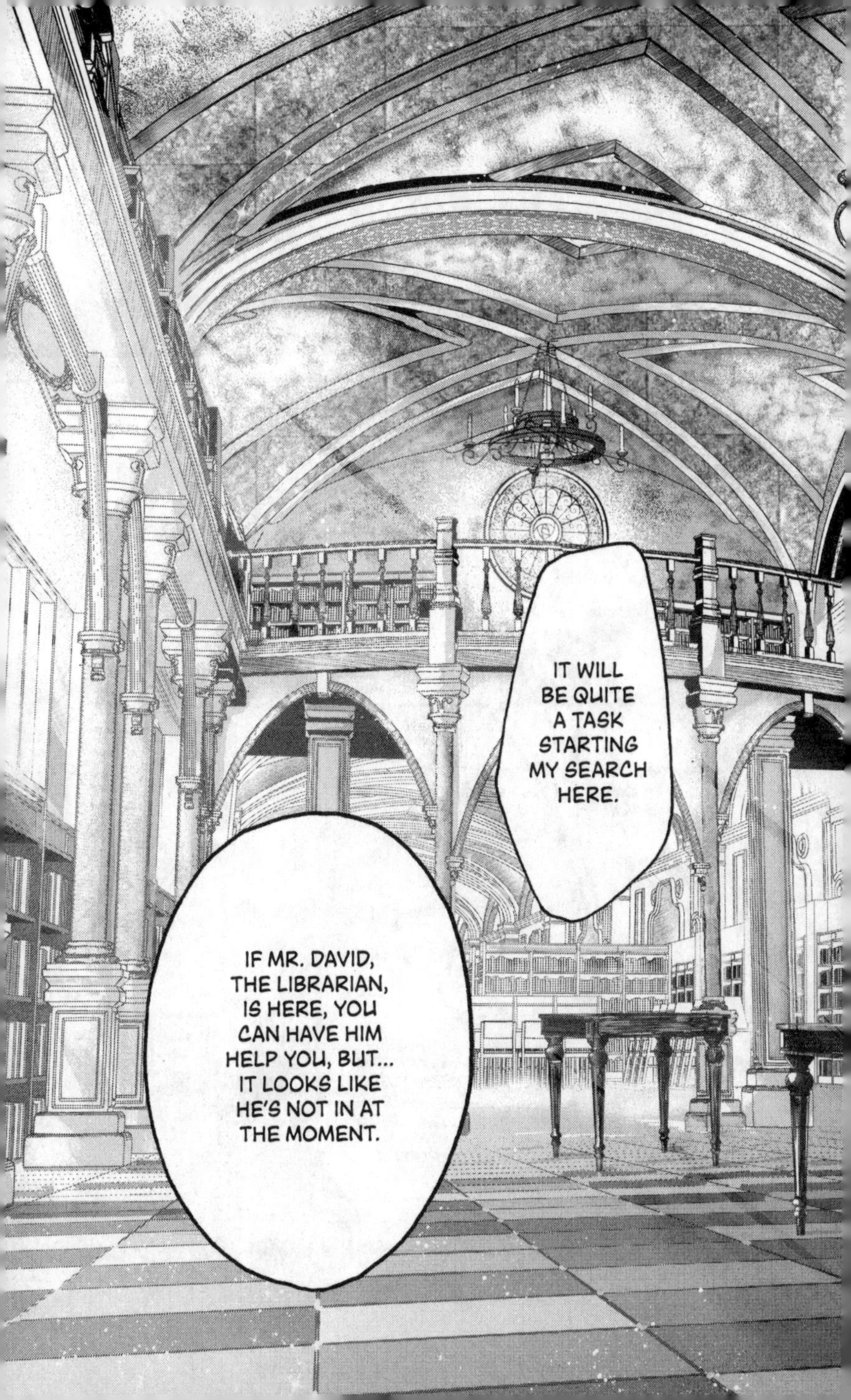
IT WILL BE QUITE A TASK STARTING MY SEARCH HERE.
IF MR. DAVID, THE LIBRARIAN, IS HERE, YOU CAN HAVE HIM HELP YOU, BUT... IT LOOKS LIKE HE'S NOT IN AT THE MOMENT.

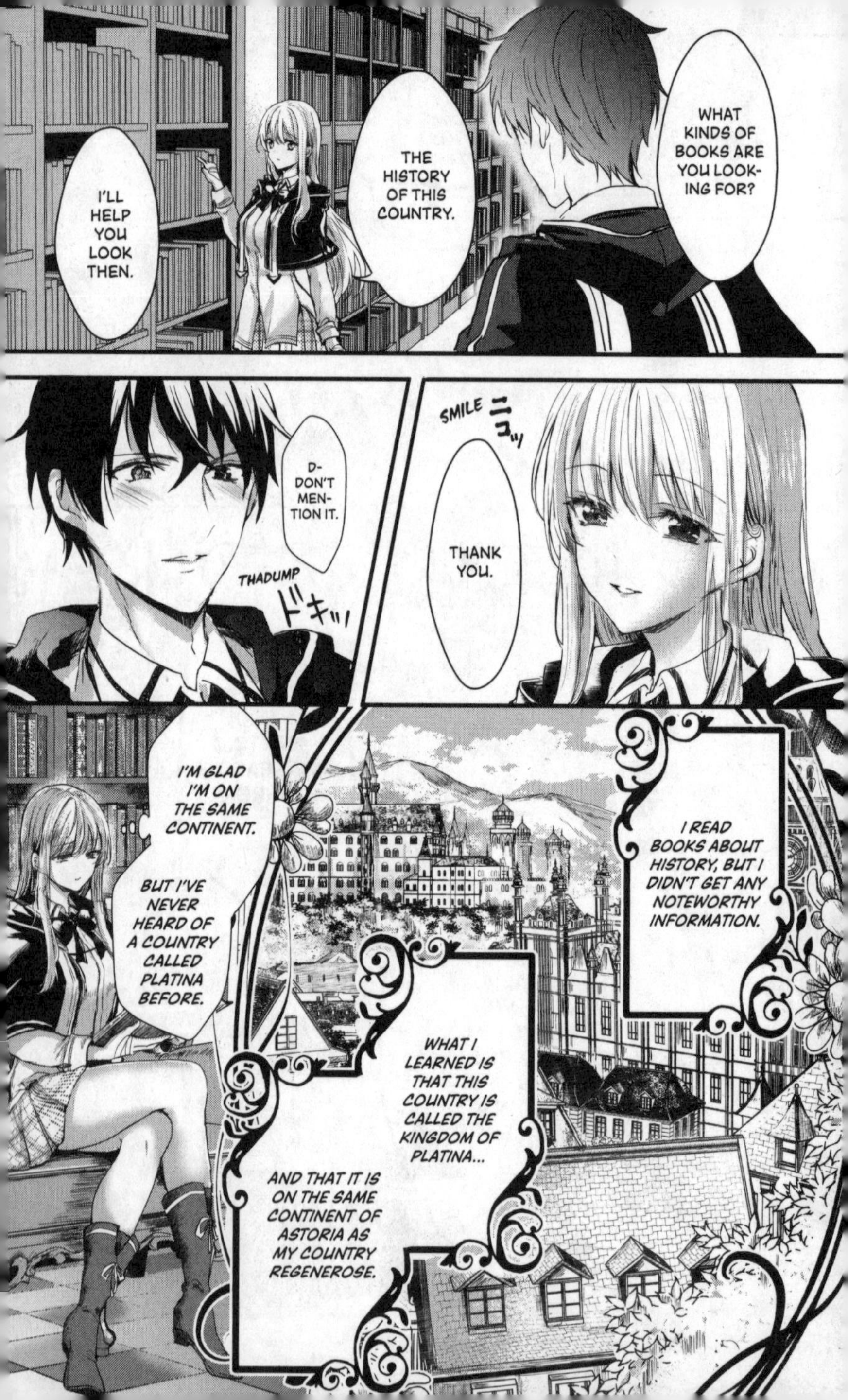
WHAT KINDS OF BOOKS ARE YOU LOOKING FOR?
THE HISTORY OF THIS COUNTRY.
I'LL HELP YOU LOOK THEN.
SMILE ニコッ
THANK YOU.
D-DON'T MENTION IT.
THADUMP ドキッ
I READ BOOKS ABOUT HISTORY, BUT I DIDN'T GET ANY NOTEWORTHY INFORMATION.
WHAT I LEARNED IS THAT THIS COUNTRY IS CALLED THE KINGDOM OF PLATINA...
AND THAT IT IS ON THE SAME CONTINENT OF ASTORIA AS MY COUNTRY REGENEROSE.
I'M GLAD I'M ON THE SAME CONTINENT.
BUT I'VE NEVER HEARD OF A COUNTRY CALLED PLATINA BEFORE.

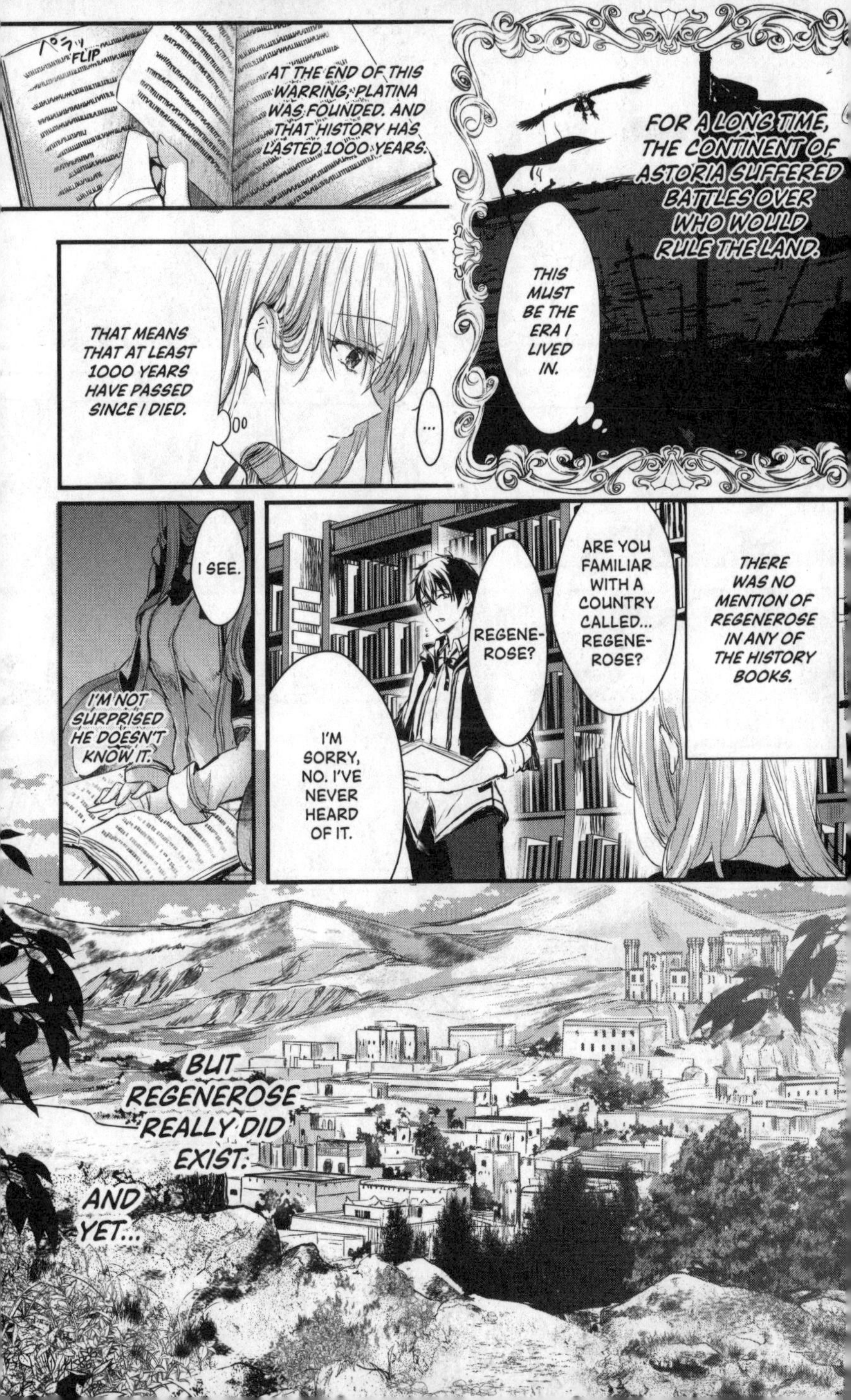
FOR A LONG TIME, THE CONTINENT OF ASTORIA SUFFERED BATTLES OVER WHO WOULD RULE THE LAND.
THIS MUST BE THE ERA I LIVED IN.
ペラッ
FLIP
AT THE END OF THIS WARRING, PLATINA WAS FOUNDED. AND THAT HISTORY HAS LASTED 1000 YEARS.
...
THAT MEANS THAT AT LEAST 1000 YEARS HAVE PASSED SINCE I DIED.
THERE WAS NO MENTION OF REGENEROSE IN ANY OF THE HISTORY BOOKS.
ARE YOU FAMILIAR WITH A COUNTRY CALLED... REGENE-ROSE?
REGENE-ROSE?
I'M SORRY, NO. I'VE NEVER HEARD OF IT.
I SEE.
I'M NOT SURPRISED HE DOESN'T KNOW IT.
BUT REGENEROSE REALLY DID EXIST.
AND YET...

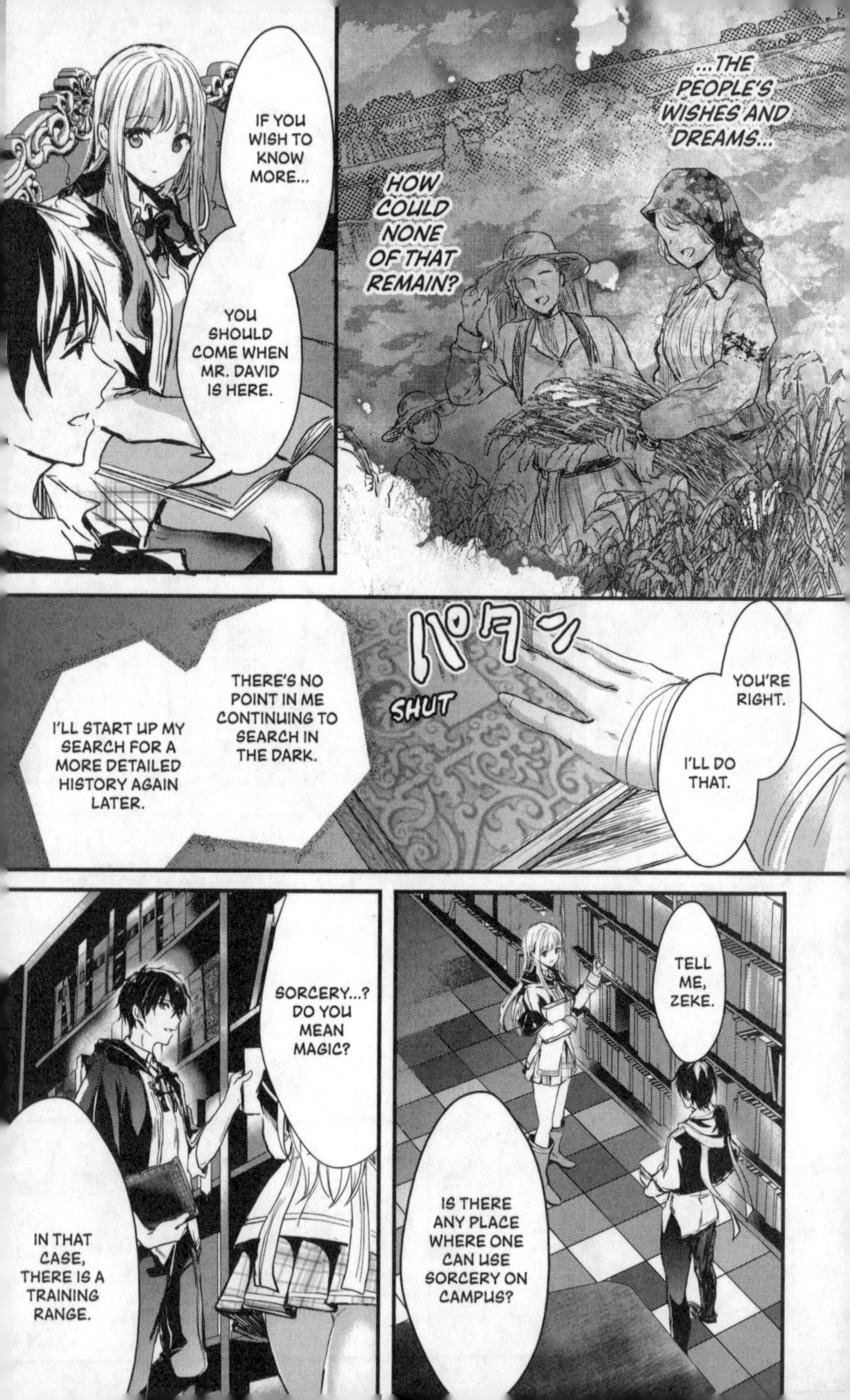
...THE PEOPLE'S WISHES AND DREAMS...
HOW COULD NONE OF THAT REMAIN?
IF YOU WISH TO KNOW MORE...
YOU SHOULD COME WHEN MR. DAVID IS HERE.
YOU'RE RIGHT.
I'LL DO THAT.
パタッ
SHUT
THERE'S NO POINT IN ME CONTINUING TO SEARCH IN THE DARK.
I'LL START UP MY SEARCH FOR A MORE DETAILED HISTORY AGAIN LATER.
TELL ME, ZEKE.
IS THERE ANY PLACE WHERE ONE CAN USE SORCERY ON CAMPUS?
SORCERY...? DO YOU MEAN MAGIC?
IN THAT CASE, THERE IS A TRAINING RANGE.

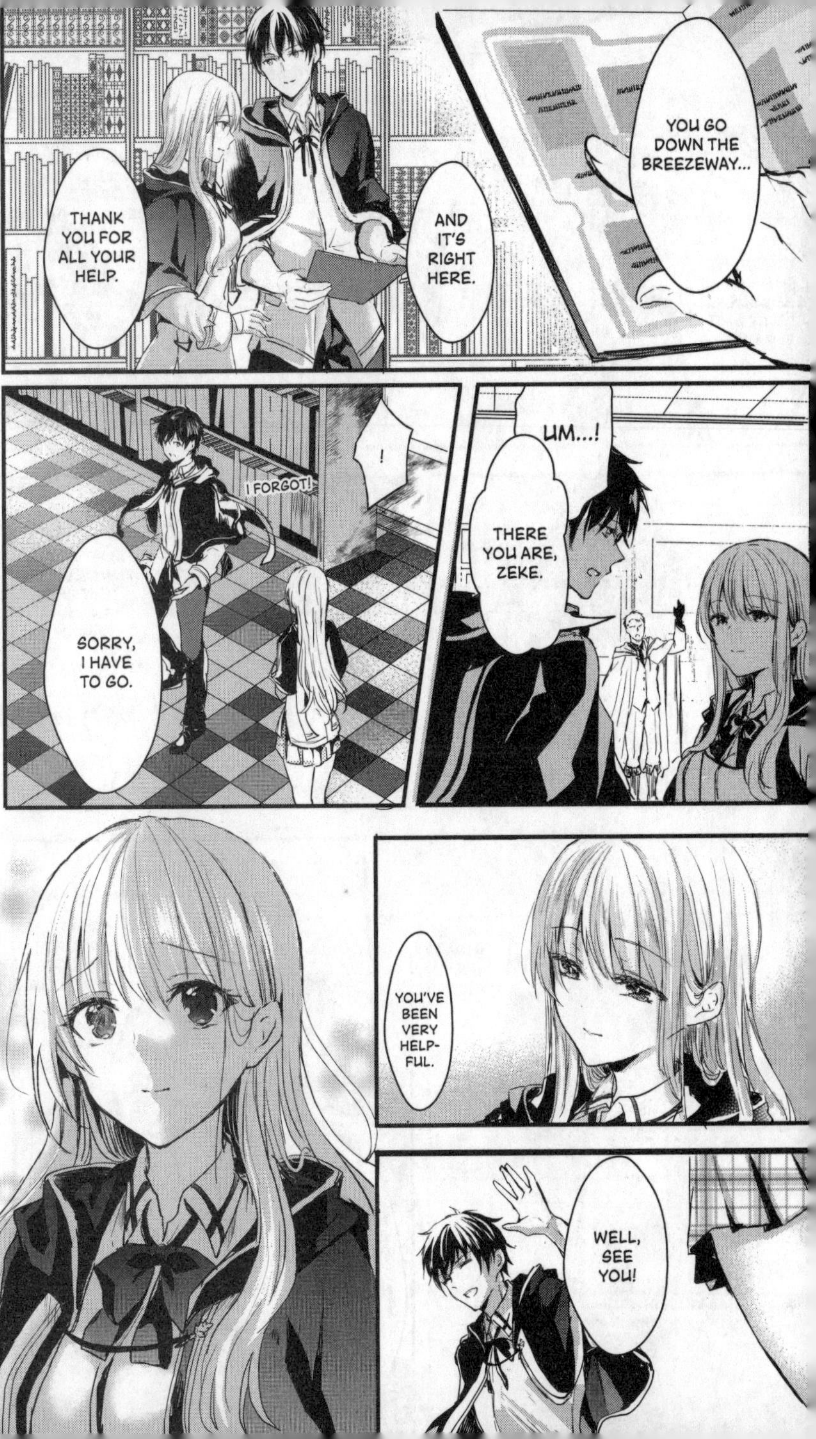
YOU GO DOWN THE BREEZEWAY...
AND IT'S RIGHT HERE.
THANK YOU FOR ALL YOUR HELP.
UM...!
THERE YOU ARE, ZEKE.
!
I FORGOT!
SORRY, I HAVE TO GO.
YOU'VE BEEN VERY HELP-FUL.
WELL, SEE YOU!

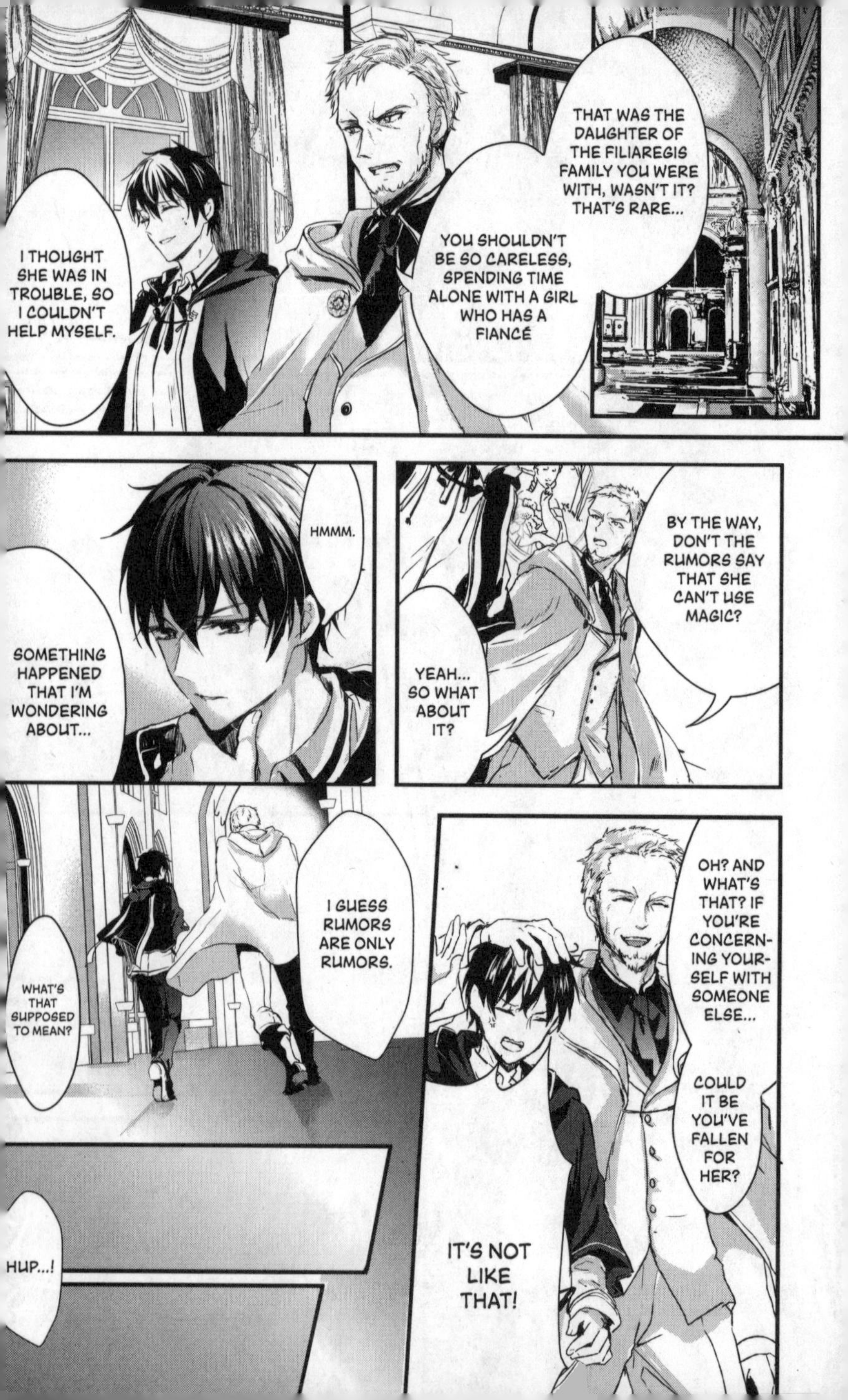
THAT WAS THE DAUGHTER OF THE FILIAREGIS FAMILY YOU WERE WITH, WASN'T IT? THAT'S RARE...
YOU SHOULDN'T BE SO CARELESS, SPENDING TIME ALONE WITH A GIRL WHO HAS A FIANCÉ
I THOUGHT SHE WAS IN TROUBLE, SO I COULDN'T HELP MYSELF.
BY THE WAY, DON'T THE RUMORS SAY THAT SHE CAN'T USE MAGIC?
YEAH... SO WHAT ABOUT IT?
HMMM.
SOMETHING HAPPENED THAT I'M WONDERING ABOUT...
OH? AND WHAT'S THAT? IF YOU'RE CONCERNING YOURSELF WITH SOMEONE ELSE...
COULD IT BE YOU'VE FALLEN FOR HER?
IT'S NOT LIKE THAT!
HUP...!
I GUESS RUMORS ARE ONLY RUMORS.
WHAT'S THAT SUPPOSED TO MEAN?

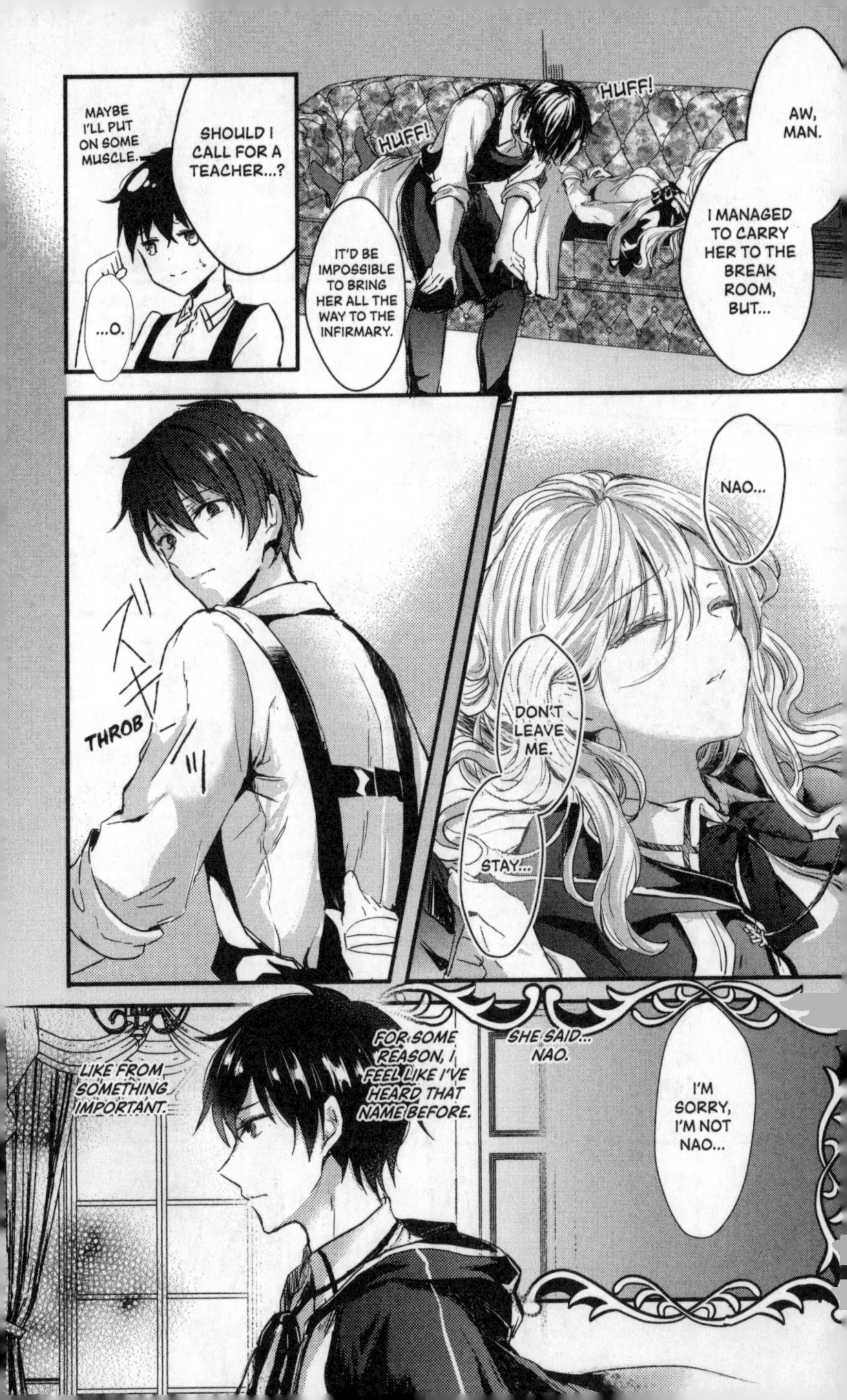
AW, MAN.
I MANAGED TO CARRY HER TO THE BREAK ROOM, BUT...
HUFF!
HUFF!
IT'D BE IMPOSSIBLE TO BRING HER ALL THE WAY TO THE INFIRMARY.
SHOULD I CALL FOR A TEACHER...?
MAYBE I'LL PUT ON SOME MUSCLE.
...O.
NAO...
DON'T LEAVE ME.
STAY...
THROB
I'M SORRY, I'M NOT NAO...
SHE SAID... NAO.
FOR SOME REASON, I FEEL LIKE I'VE HEARD THAT NAME BEFORE.
LIKE FROM SOMETHING IMPORTANT.

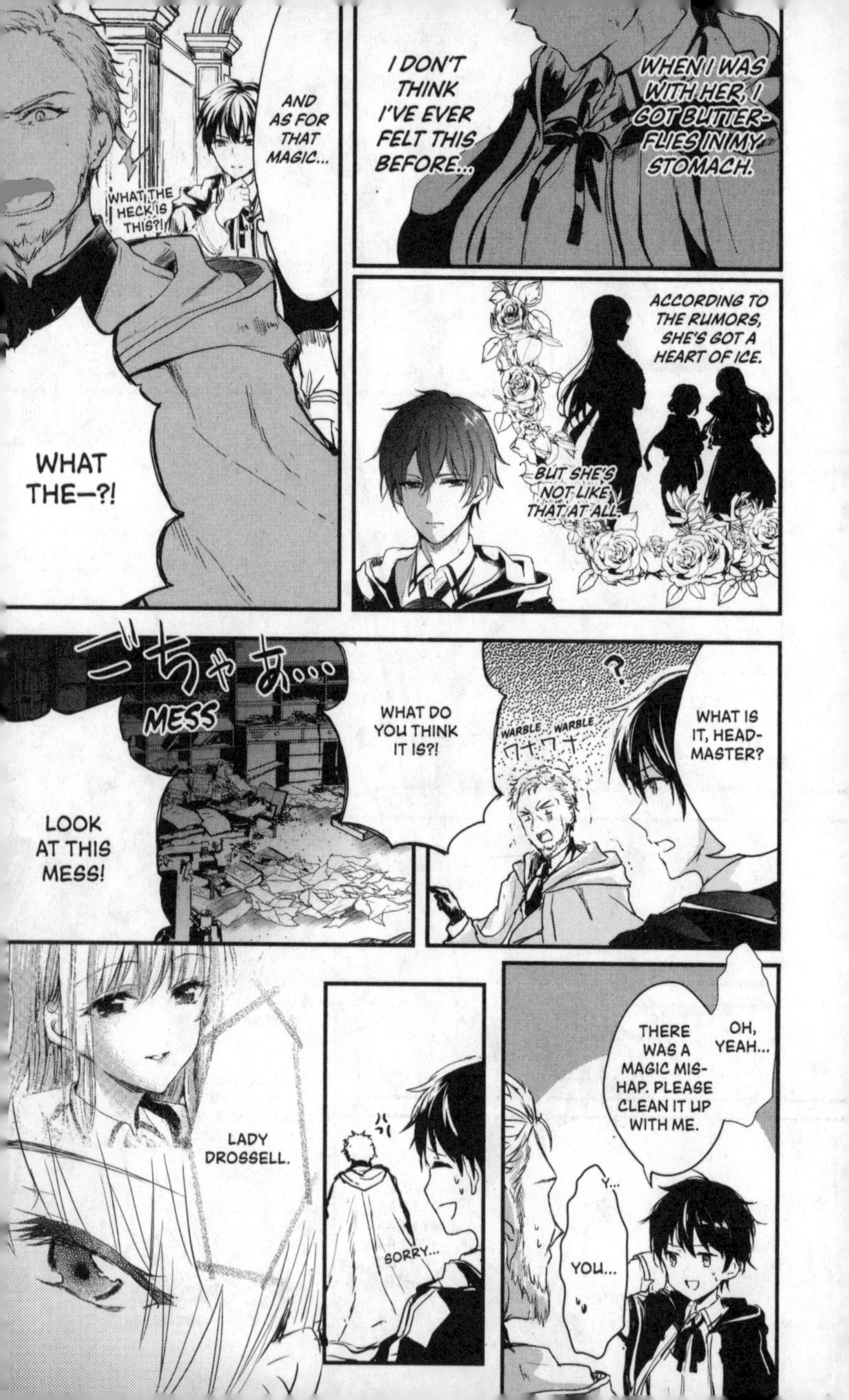
WHEN I WAS WITH HER, I GOT BUTTERFLIES IN MY STOMACH.
I DON'T THINK I'VE EVER FELT THIS BEFORE...
ACCORDING TO THE RUMORS, SHE'S GOT A HEART OF ICE.
BUT SHE'S NOT LIKE THAT AT ALL.
AND AS FOR THAT MAGIC...
WHAT THE HECK IS THIS?!
WHAT THE–?!
WHAT IS IT, HEAD-MASTER?
?
WARBLE WARBLE
WHAT DO YOU THINK IT IS?!
ごちゃあ…
MESS
LOOK AT THIS MESS!
OH, YEAH...
THERE WAS A MAGIC MIS-HAP. PLEASE CLEAN IT UP WITH ME.
Y...
YOU...
SORRY...
LADY DROSSELL.

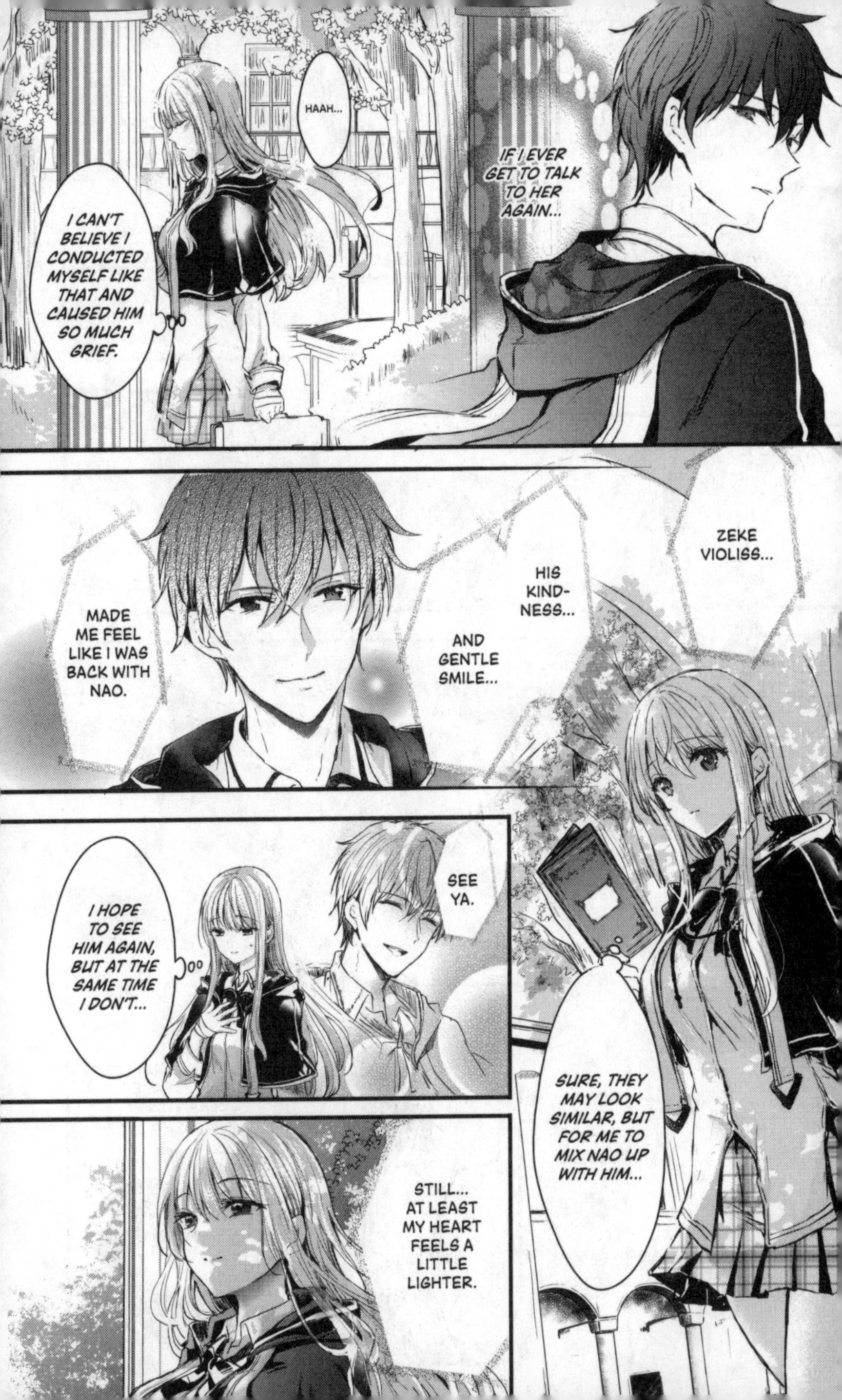
IF I EVER GET TO TALK TO HER AGAIN...
HAAH...
I CAN'T BELIEVE I CONDUCTED MYSELF LIKE THAT AND CAUSED HIM SO MUCH GRIEF.
ZEKE VIOLISS...
HIS KIND-NESS...
AND GENTLE SMILE...
MADE ME FEEL LIKE I WAS BACK WITH NAO.
SURE, THEY MAY LOOK SIMILAR, BUT FOR ME TO MIX NAO UP WITH HIM...
SEE YA.
I HOPE TO SEE HIM AGAIN, BUT AT THE SAME TIME I DON'T...
STILL... AT LEAST MY HEART FEELS A LITTLE LIGHTER.

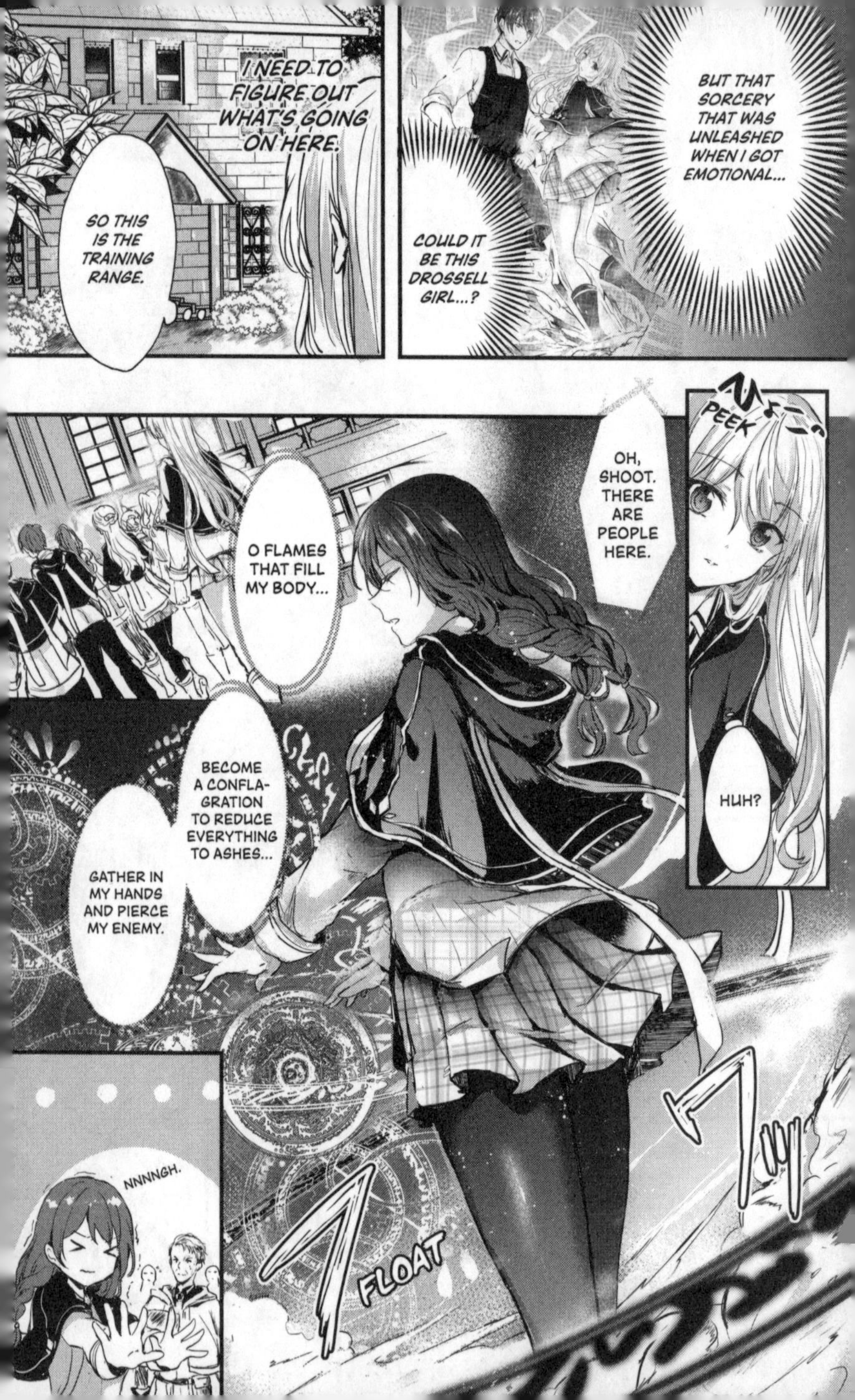
BUT THAT SORCERY THAT WAS UNLEASHED WHEN I GOT EMOTIONAL...
COULD IT BE THIS DROSSELL GIRL...?
I NEED TO FIGURE OUT WHAT'S GOING ON HERE.
SO THIS IS THE TRAINING RANGE.
PEEK
OH, SHOOT. THERE ARE PEOPLE HERE.
HUH?
O FLAMES THAT FILL MY BODY...
BECOME A CONFLAGRATION TO REDUCE EVERYTHING TO ASHES...
GATHER IN MY HANDS AND PIERCE MY ENEMY.
FLOAT
NNNNGH.

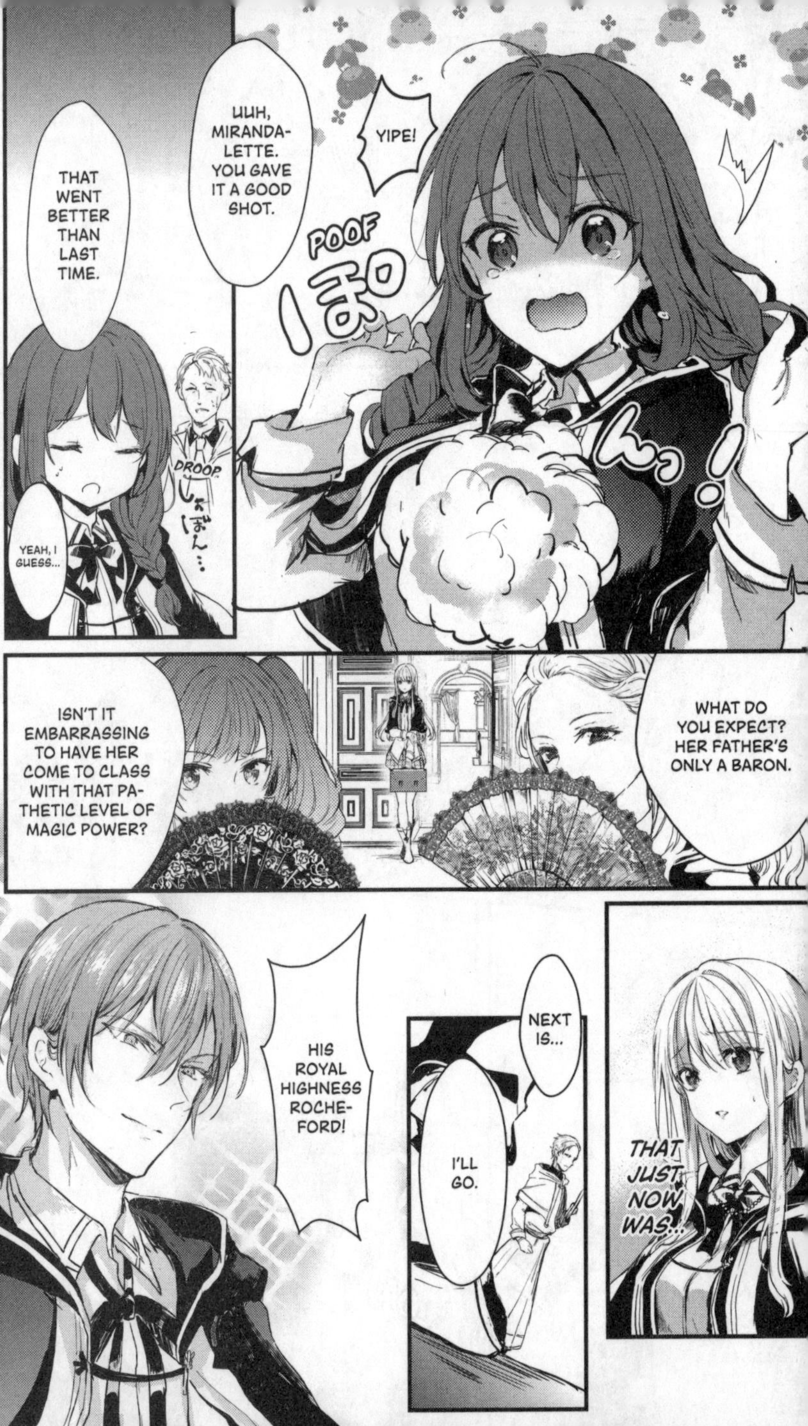
YIPE!
POOF
んっ!
UUH, MIRANDA-LETTE. YOU GAVE IT A GOOD SHOT.
THAT WENT BETTER THAN LAST TIME.
DROOP
しょぼん…
YEAH, I GUESS...
WHAT DO YOU EXPECT? HER FATHER'S ONLY A BARON.
ISN'T IT EMBARRASSING TO HAVE HER COME TO CLASS WITH THAT PA-THETIC LEVEL OF MAGIC POWER?
THAT JUST NOW WAS...
NEXT IS...
I'LL GO.
HIS ROYAL HIGHNESS ROCHE-FORD!

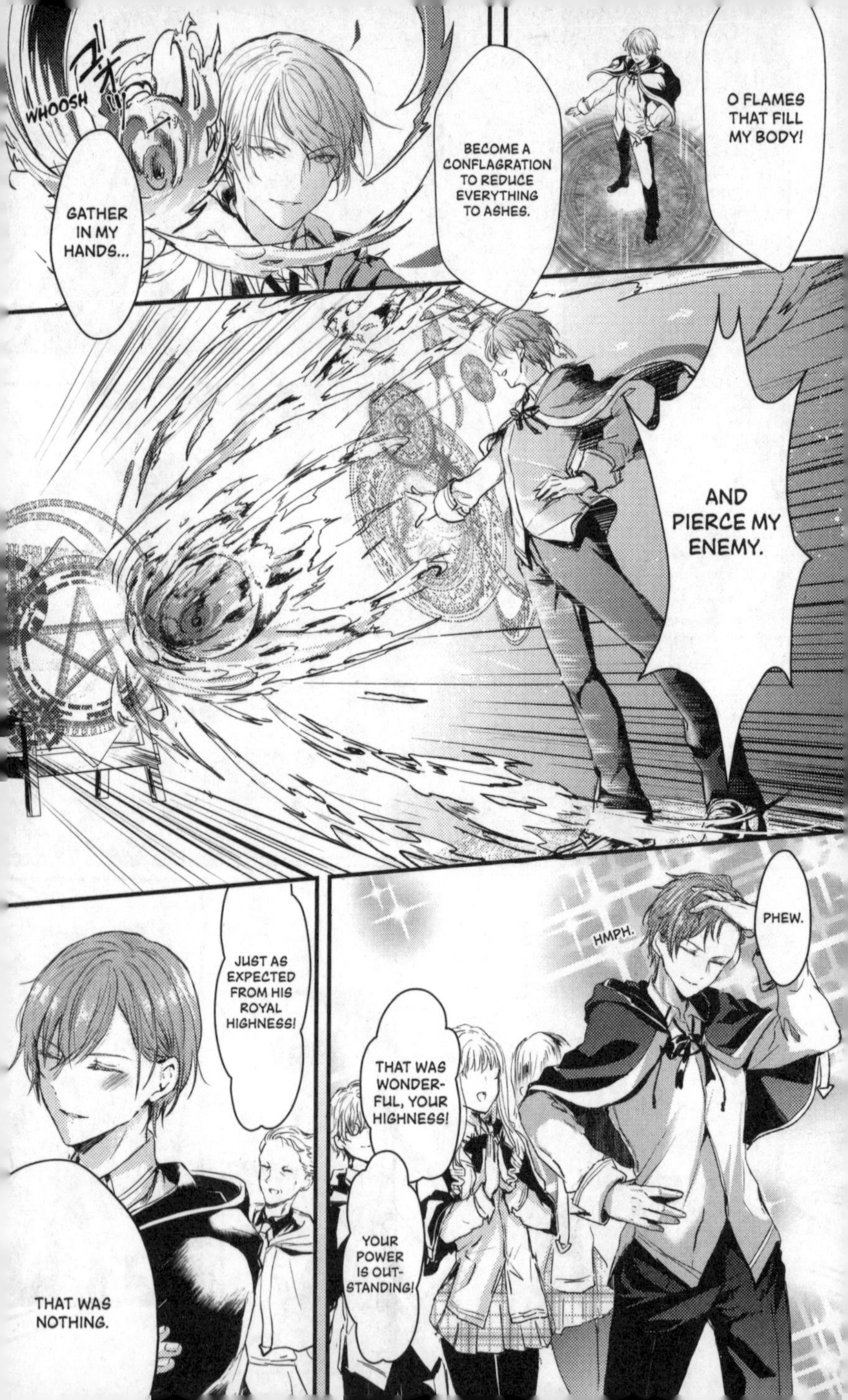

O FLAMES THAT FILL MY BODY!
BECOME A CONFLAGRATION TO REDUCE EVERYTHING TO ASHES.
ゴォッ
WHOOSH
GATHER IN MY HANDS...
AND PIERCE MY ENEMY.
PHEW.
HMPH.
THAT WAS WONDERFUL, YOUR HIGHNESS!
YOUR POWER IS OUTSTANDING!
JUST AS EXPECTED FROM HIS ROYAL HIGHNESS!
THAT WAS NOTHING.

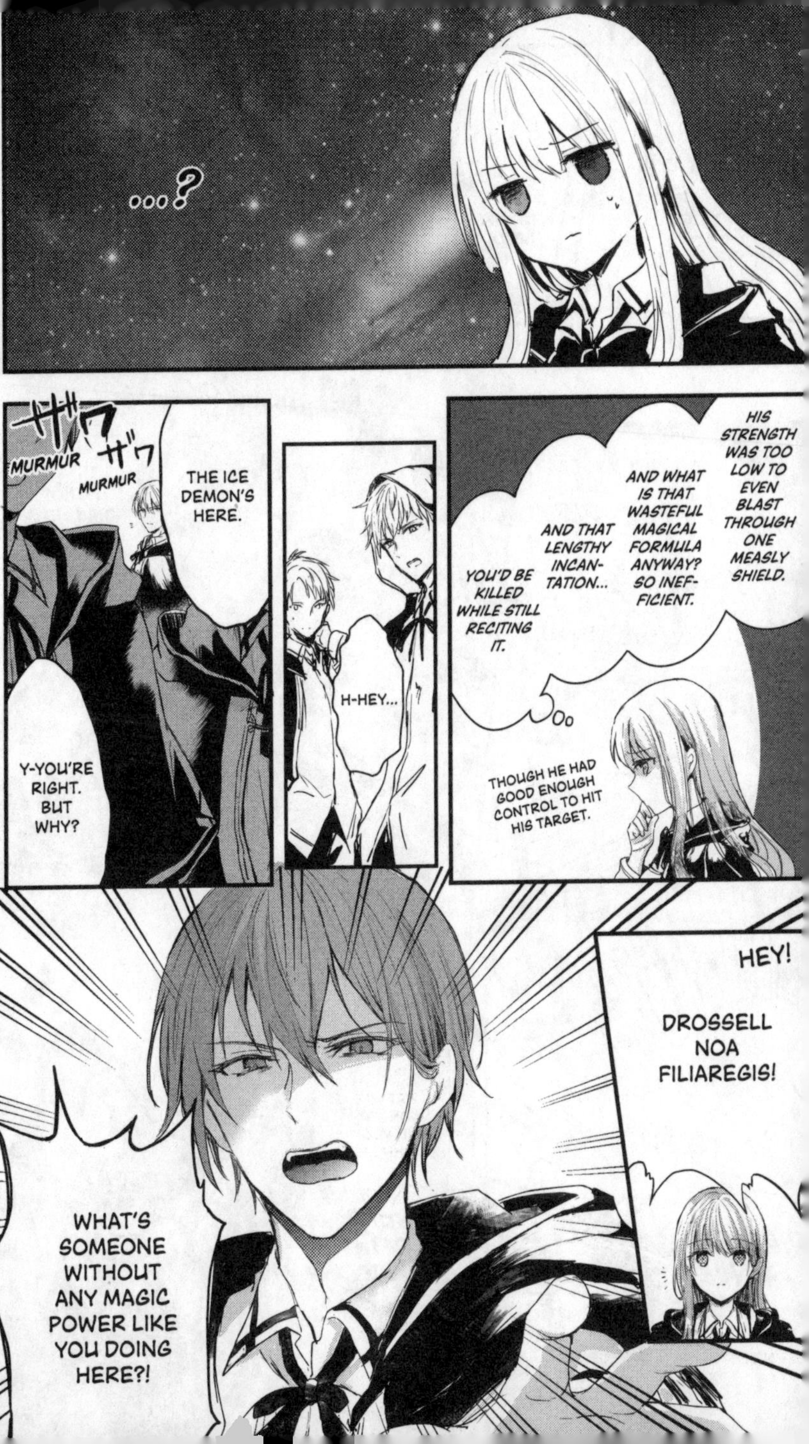
...?
HIS STRENGTH WAS TOO LOW TO EVEN BLAST THROUGH ONE MEASLY SHIELD.
AND WHAT IS THAT WASTEFUL MAGICAL FORMULA ANYWAY? SO INEFFICIENT.
AND THAT LENGTHY INCANTATION...
YOU'D BE KILLED WHILE STILL RECITING IT.
THOUGH HE HAD GOOD ENOUGH CONTROL TO HIT HIS TARGET.
H-HEY...
ザワ
MURMUR
ザワ
MURMUR
THE ICE DEMON'S HERE.
Y-YOU'RE RIGHT. BUT WHY?
HEY!
DROSSELL NOA FILIAREGIS!
WHAT'S SOMEONE WITHOUT ANY MAGIC POWER LIKE YOU DOING HERE?!

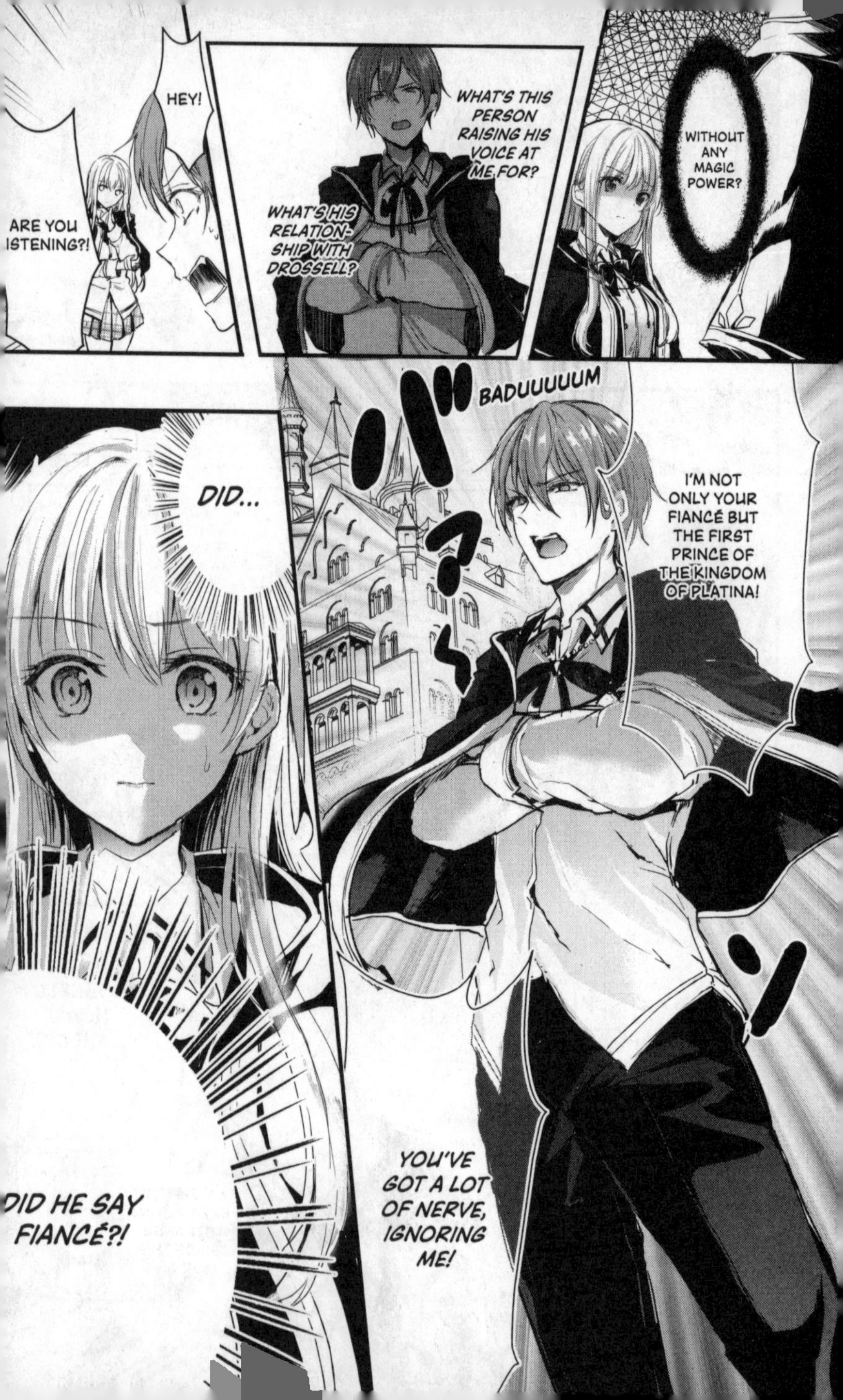
WITHOUT ANY MAGIC POWER?
WHAT'S THIS PERSON RAISING HIS VOICE AT ME FOR?
WHAT'S HIS RELATIONSHIP WITH DROSSELL?
HEY!
ARE YOU ISTENING?!
BADUUUUUM
I'M NOT ONLY YOUR FIANCÉ BUT THE FIRST PRINCE OF THE KINGDOM OF PLATINA!
YOU'VE GOT A LOT OF NERVE, IGNORING ME!
DID...
DID HE SAY FIANCÉ?!

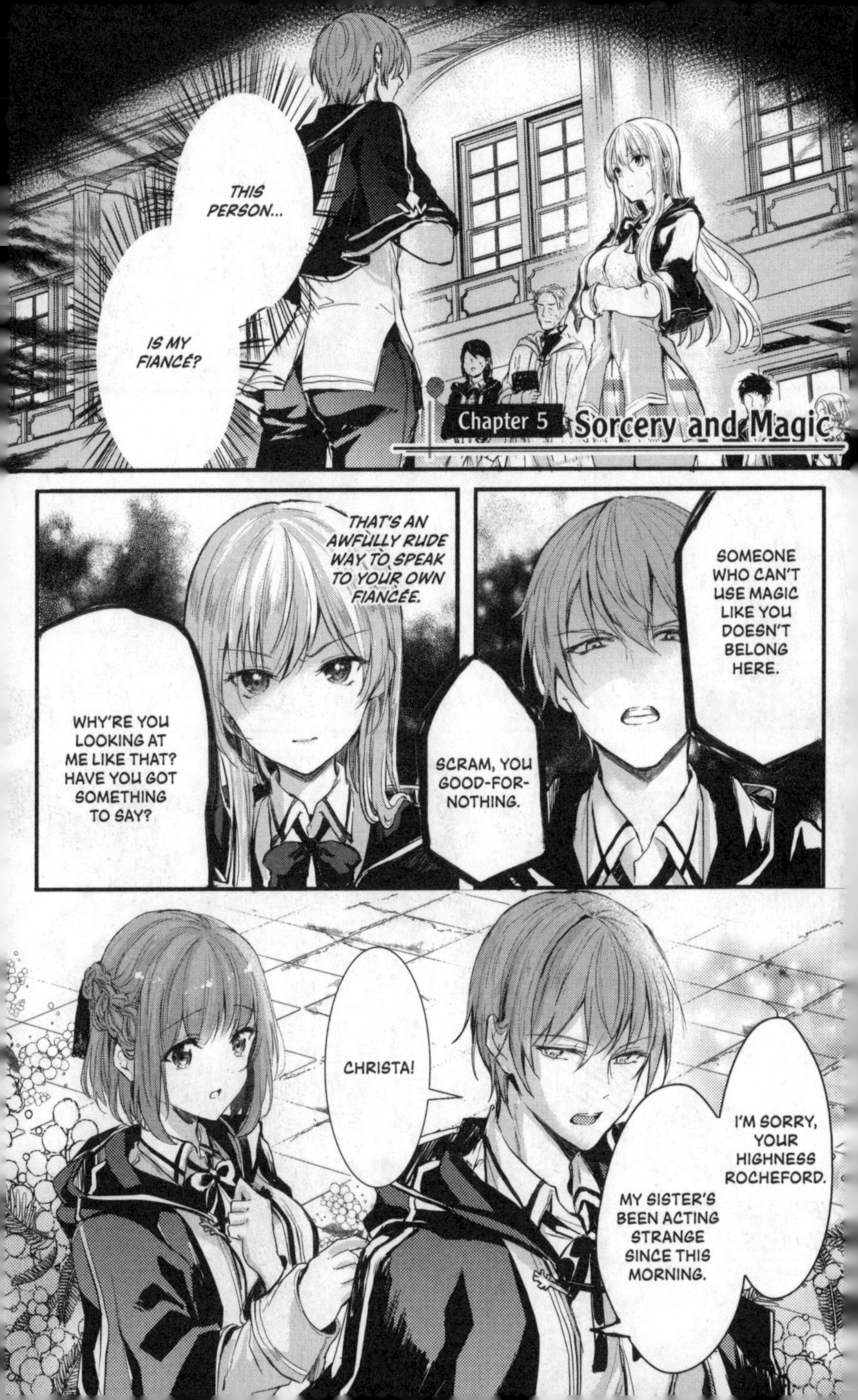
THIS PERSON...
IS MY FIANCÉ?
Chapter 5 Sorcery and Magic
SOMEONE WHO CAN'T USE MAGIC LIKE YOU DOESN'T BELONG HERE.
SCRAM, YOU GOOD-FOR-NOTHING.
THAT'S AN AWFULLY RUDE WAY TO SPEAK TO YOUR OWN FIANCÉE.
WHY'RE YOU LOOKING AT ME LIKE THAT? HAVE YOU GOT SOMETHING TO SAY?
I'M SORRY, YOUR HIGHNESS ROCHEFORD.
MY SISTER'S BEEN ACTING STRANGE SINCE THIS MORNING.
CHRISTA!

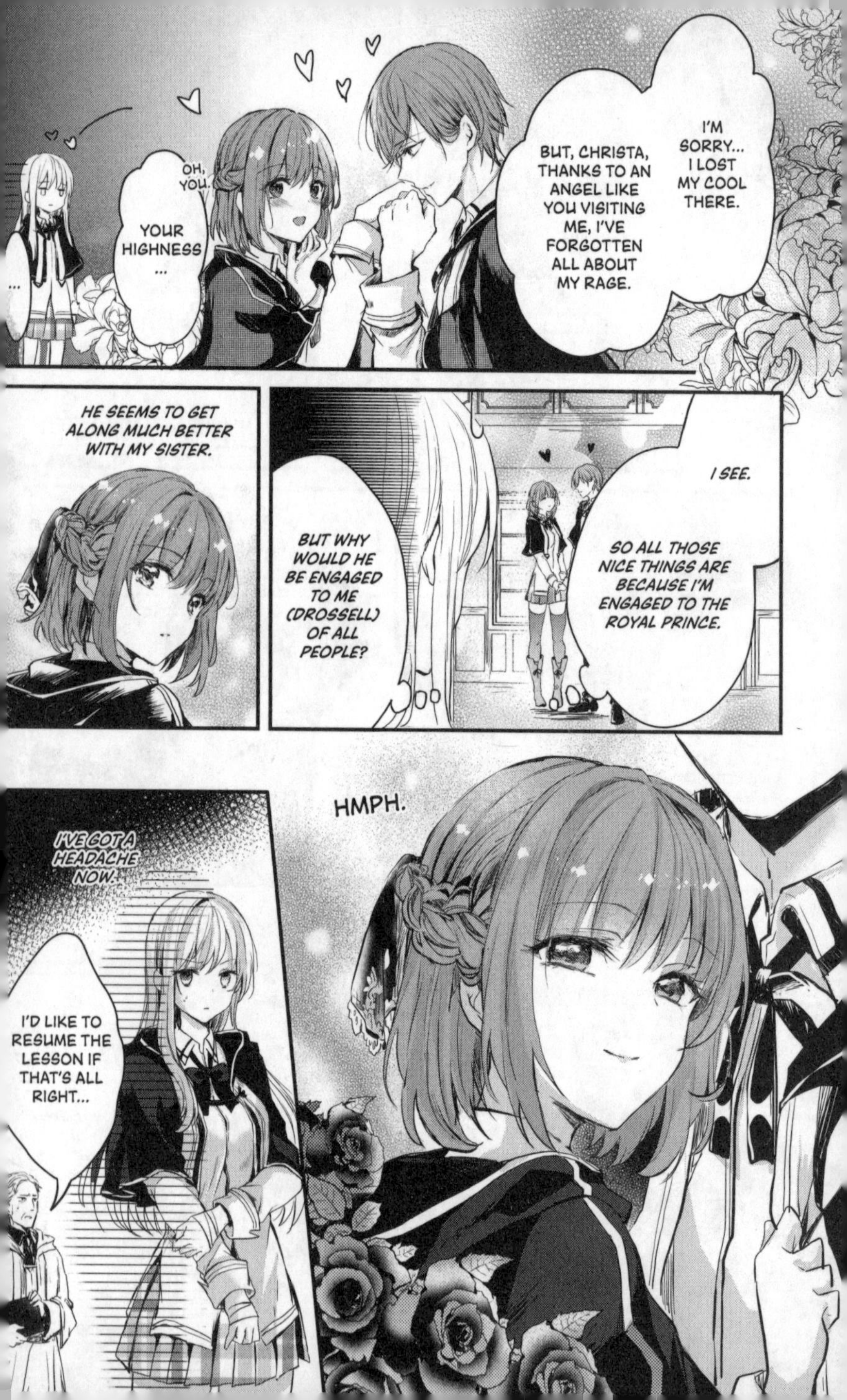
I'M SORRY... I LOST MY COOL THERE.
BUT, CHRISTA, THANKS TO AN ANGEL LIKE YOU VISITING ME, I'VE FORGOTTEN ALL ABOUT MY RAGE.
OH, YOU.
YOUR HIGHNESS ...
...
I SEE.
SO ALL THOSE NICE THINGS ARE BECAUSE I'M ENGAGED TO THE ROYAL PRINCE.
BUT WHY WOULD HE BE ENGAGED TO ME (DROSSELL) OF ALL PEOPLE?
HE SEEMS TO GET ALONG MUCH BETTER WITH MY SISTER.
HMPH.
I'VE GOT A HEADACHE NOW.
I'D LIKE TO RESUME THE LESSON IF THAT'S ALL RIGHT...

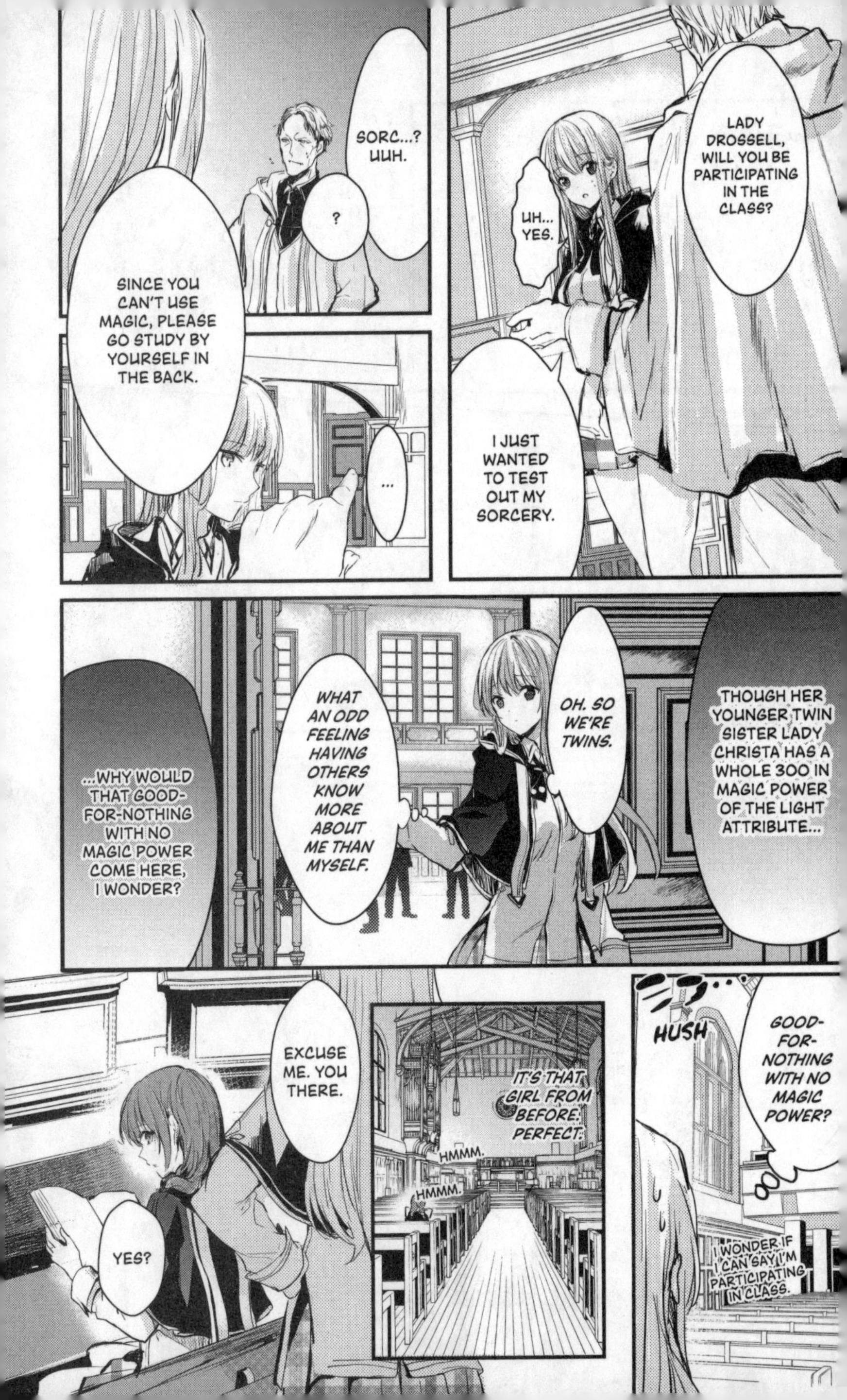
LADY DROSSELL, WILL YOU BE PARTICIPATING IN THE CLASS?
UH... YES.
I JUST WANTED TO TEST OUT MY SORCERY.
SORC...? UUH.
?
SINCE YOU CAN'T USE MAGIC, PLEASE GO STUDY BY YOURSELF IN THE BACK.
...
THOUGH HER YOUNGER TWIN SISTER LADY CHRISTA HAS A WHOLE 300 IN MAGIC POWER OF THE LIGHT ATTRIBUTE...
OH. SO WE'RE TWINS.
WHAT AN ODD FEELING HAVING OTHERS KNOW MORE ABOUT ME THAN MYSELF.
...WHY WOULD THAT GOOD-FOR-NOTHING WITH NO MAGIC POWER COME HERE, I WONDER?
GOOD-FOR-NOTHING WITH NO MAGIC POWER?
HUSH
I WONDER IF I CAN SAY I'M PARTICIPATING IN CLASS.
IT'S THAT GIRL FROM BEFORE. PERFECT.
HMMM.
HMMM.
EXCUSE ME. YOU THERE.
YES?

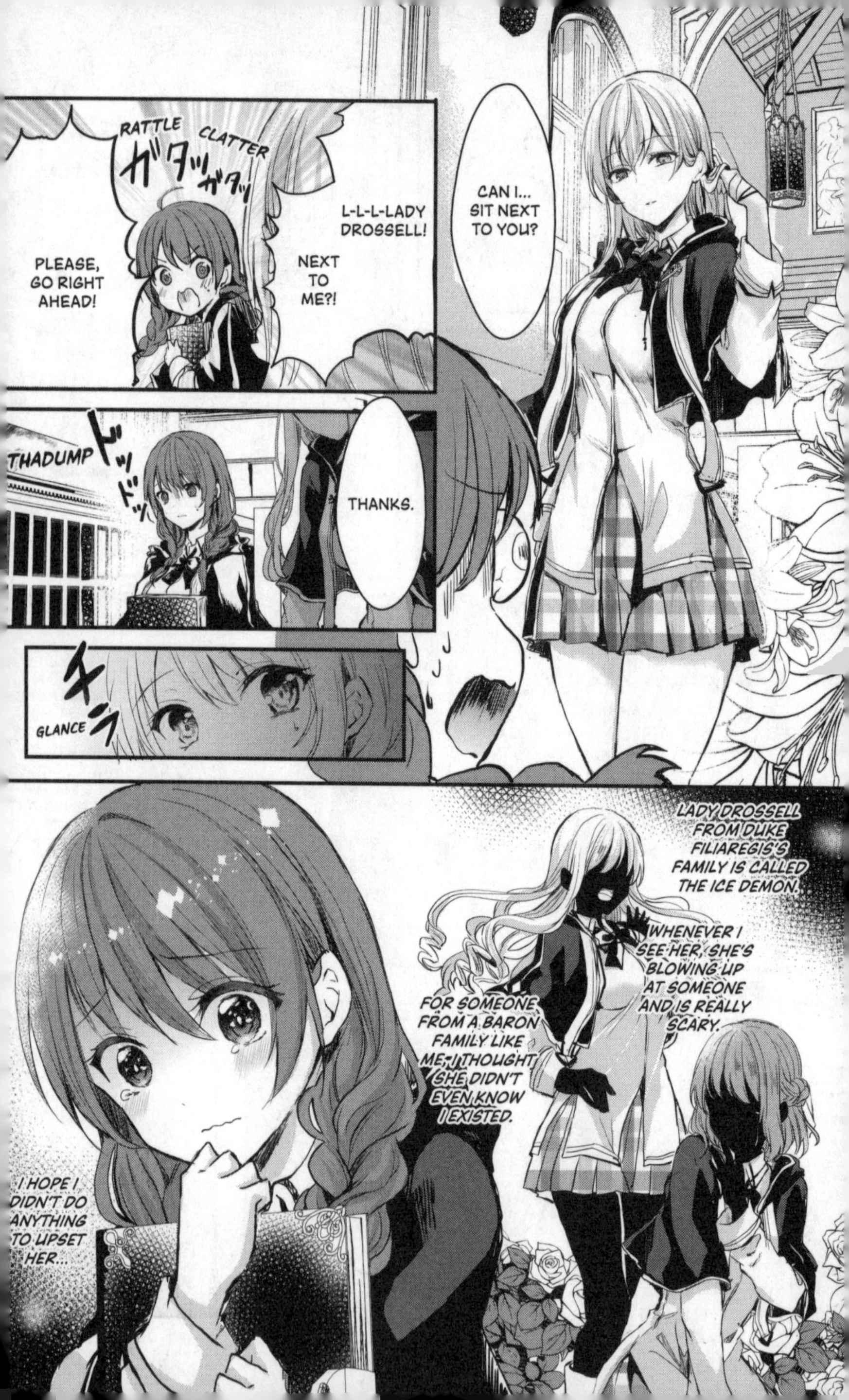
CAN I... SIT NEXT TO YOU?
RATTLE
ガタッ
CLATTER
ガタッ
L-L-L-LADY DROSSELL!
NEXT TO ME?!
PLEASE, GO RIGHT AHEAD!
THANKS.
THADUMP
ドッドッ
GLANCE
チラ
LADY DROSSELL FROM DUKE FILIAREGIS'S FAMILY IS CALLED THE ICE DEMON.
WHENEVER I SEE HER, SHE'S BLOWING UP AT SOMEONE AND IS REALLY SCARY.
FOR SOMEONE FROM A BARON FAMILY LIKE ME, I THOUGHT SHE DIDN'T EVEN KNOW I EXISTED.
I HOPE I DIDN'T DO ANYTHING TO UPSET HER...

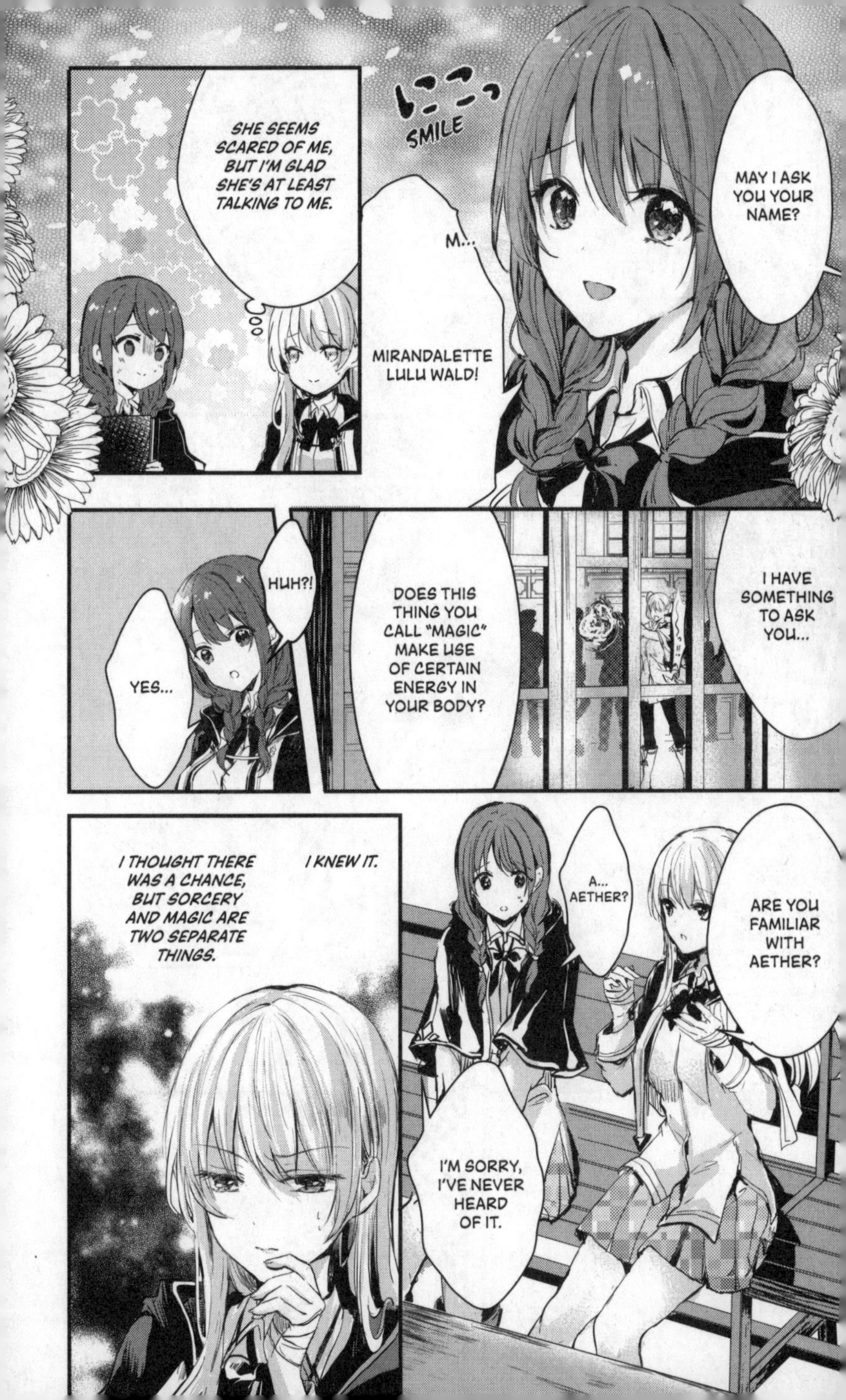

にこっ
SMILE
MAY I ASK YOU YOUR NAME?
M...
MIRANDALETTE LULU WALD!
SHE SEEMS SCARED OF ME, BUT I'M GLAD SHE'S AT LEAST TALKING TO ME.
I HAVE SOMETHING TO ASK YOU...
DOES THIS THING YOU CALL "MAGIC" MAKE USE OF CERTAIN ENERGY IN YOUR BODY?
HUH?!
YES...
ARE YOU FAMILIAR WITH AETHER?
A... AETHER?
I'M SORRY, I'VE NEVER HEARD OF IT.
I KNEW IT.
I THOUGHT THERE WAS A CHANCE, BUT SORCERY AND MAGIC ARE TWO SEPARATE THINGS.

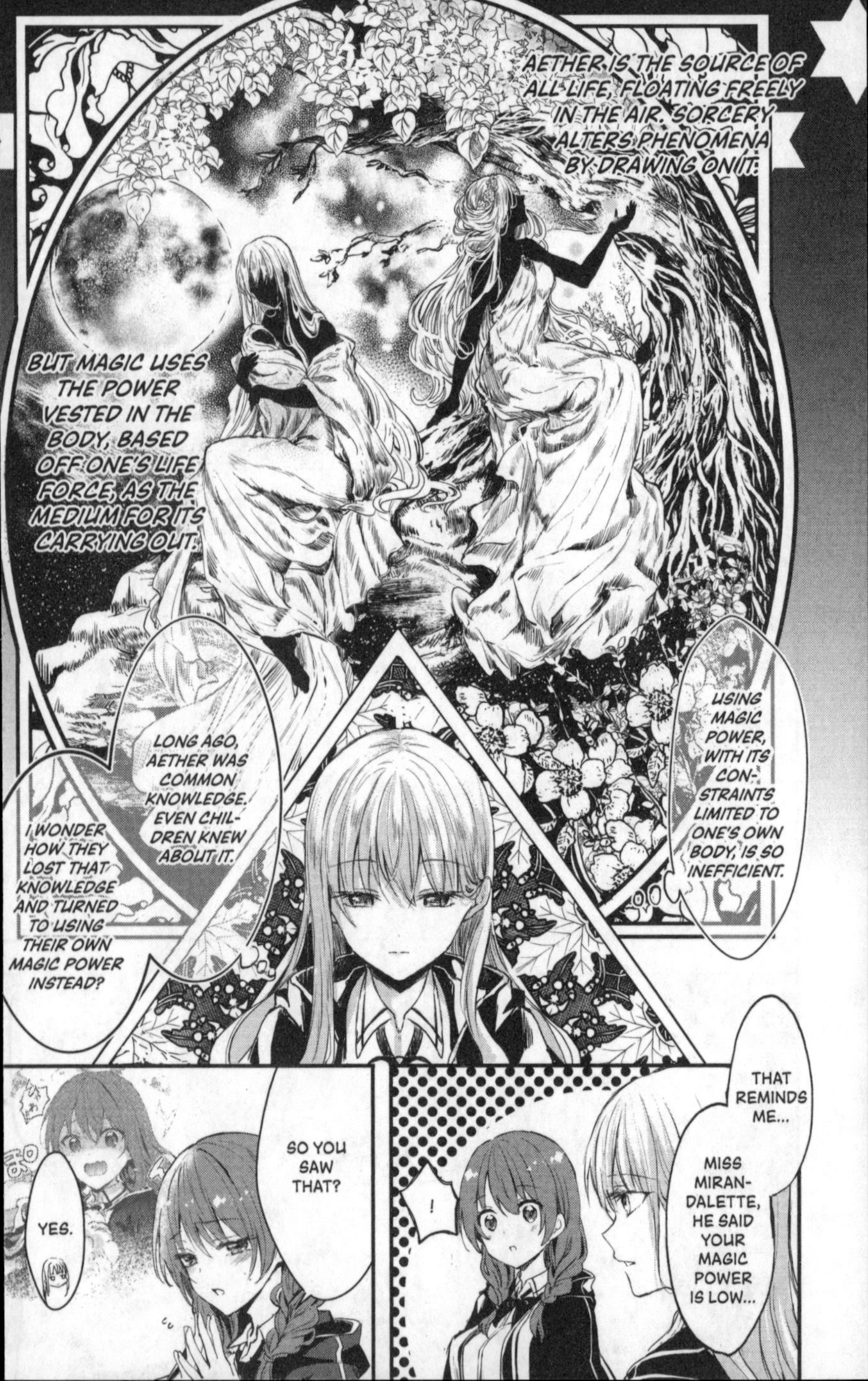
AETHER IS THE SOURCE OF ALL LIFE, FLOATING FREELY IN THE AIR. SORCERY ALTERS PHENOMENA BY DRAWING ON IT.
BUT MAGIC USES THE POWER VESTED IN THE BODY, BASED OFF ONE'S LIFE FORCE, AS THE MEDIUM FOR ITS CARRYING OUT.
USING MAGIC POWER, WITH ITS CON-STRAINTS LIMITED TO ONE'S OWN BODY, IS SO INEFFICIENT.
LONG AGO, AETHER WAS COMMON KNOWLEDGE. EVEN CHIL-DREN KNEW ABOUT IT.
I WONDER HOW THEY LOST THAT KNOWLEDGE AND TURNED TO USING THEIR OWN MAGIC POWER INSTEAD?
THAT REMINDS ME...
MISS MIRAN-DALETTE, HE SAID YOUR MAGIC POWER IS LOW...
!
SO YOU SAW THAT?
YES.

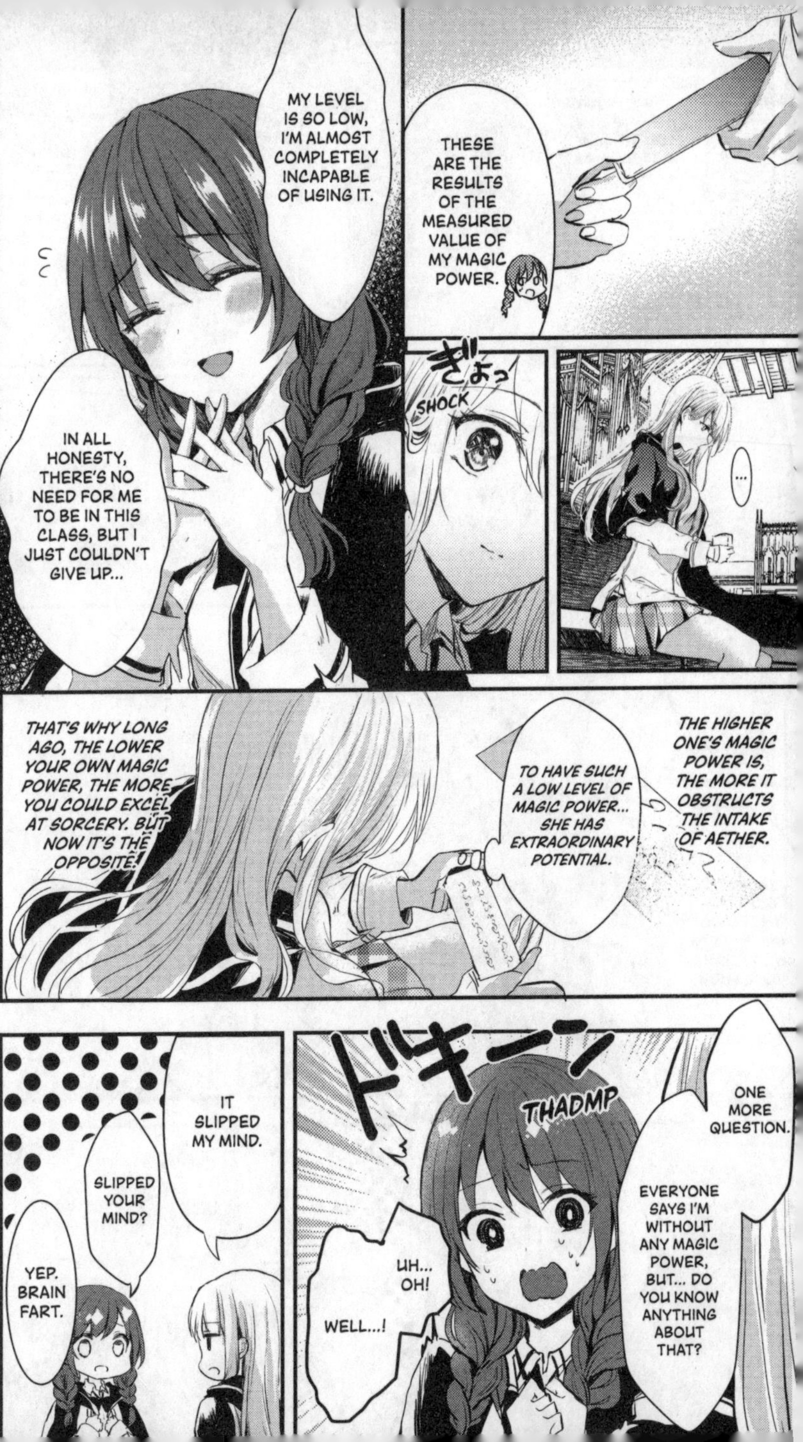
THESE ARE THE RESULTS OF THE MEASURED VALUE OF MY MAGIC POWER.
...
ぎょっ
SHOCK
MY LEVEL IS SO LOW, I'M ALMOST COMPLETELY INCAPABLE OF USING IT.
IN ALL HONESTY, THERE'S NO NEED FOR ME TO BE IN THIS CLASS, BUT I JUST COULDN'T GIVE UP...
THE HIGHER ONE'S MAGIC POWER IS, THE MORE IT OBSTRUCTS THE INTAKE OF AETHER.
TO HAVE SUCH A LOW LEVEL OF MAGIC POWER... SHE HAS EXTRAORDINARY POTENTIAL.
THAT'S WHY LONG AGO, THE LOWER YOUR OWN MAGIC POWER, THE MORE YOU COULD EXCEL AT SORCERY. BUT NOW IT'S THE OPPOSITE.
ONE MORE QUESTION.
EVERYONE SAYS I'M WITHOUT ANY MAGIC POWER, BUT... DO YOU KNOW ANYTHING ABOUT THAT?
ドキーー
THADMP
UH... OH!
WELL...!
IT SLIPPED MY MIND.
SLIPPED YOUR MIND?
YEP. BRAIN FART.

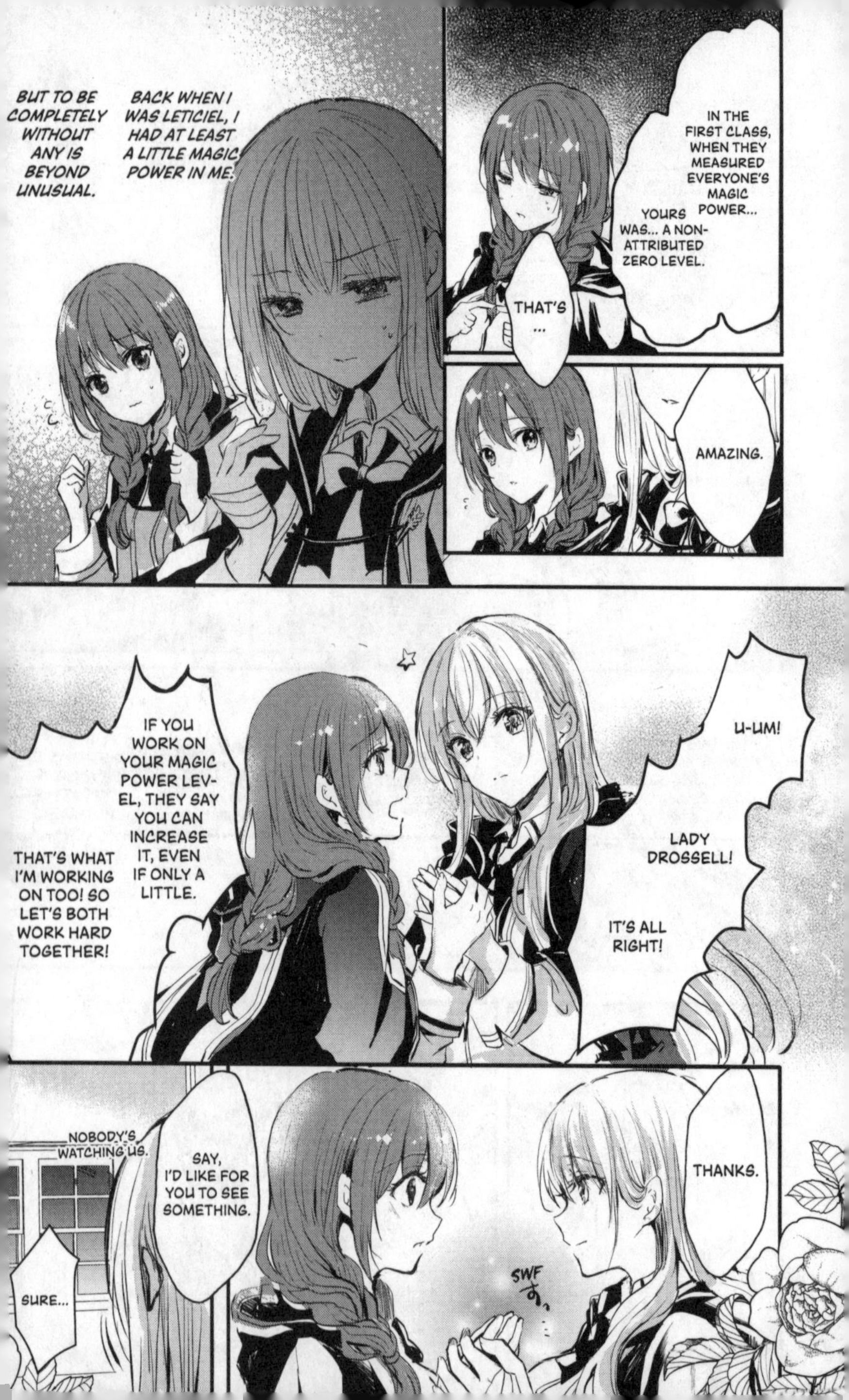
IN THE FIRST CLASS, WHEN THEY MEASURED EVERYONE'S MAGIC POWER...
YOURS WAS... A NON-ATTRIBUTED ZERO LEVEL.
THAT'S ...
AMAZING.
BACK WHEN I WAS LETICIEL, I HAD AT LEAST A LITTLE MAGIC POWER IN ME.
BUT TO BE COMPLETELY WITHOUT ANY IS BEYOND UNUSUAL.
U-UM!
LADY DROSSELL!
IT'S ALL RIGHT!
IF YOU WORK ON YOUR MAGIC POWER LEVEL, THEY SAY YOU CAN INCREASE IT, EVEN IF ONLY A LITTLE.
THAT'S WHAT I'M WORKING ON TOO! SO LET'S BOTH WORK HARD TOGETHER!
THANKS.
SAY, I'D LIKE FOR YOU TO SEE SOMETHING.
NOBODY'S WATCHING US.
SWF
SURE...

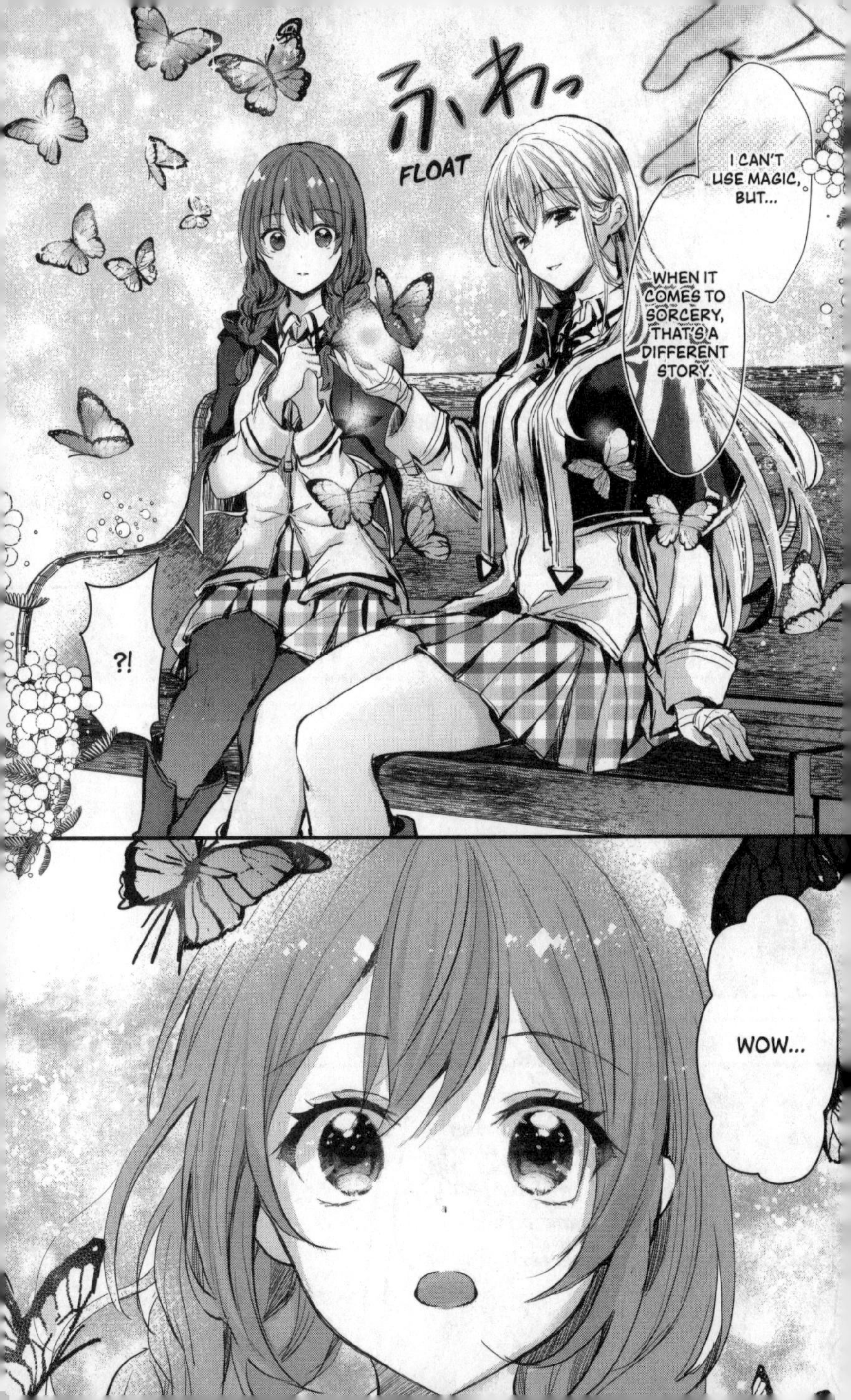
ふわっ
FLOAT
I CAN'T USE MAGIC, BUT...
WHEN IT COMES TO SORCERY, THAT'S A DIFFERENT STORY.
?!
WOW...

LOOKS LIKE I WAS RIGHT. THERE IS STILL AETHER HERE, AND I CAN USE IT.

WHEN I'M CALM, I CAN CONTROL IT TOO.

HOW PRETTY...

STILL...

THE FLIPSIDE OF "LACKING MAGIC POWER" IS THE LIMITLESS AETHER I CAN ABSORB. WHEN MY EMOTIONS BECOME UNSTABLE, THE AETHER FLOWS IN ON ITS OWN AND GOES BERSERK.

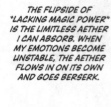

I HAVE TO BE CAREFUL.

NAO LOOKED THE SAME WAY...

THE FIRST TIME I SHOWED HIM SORCERY.

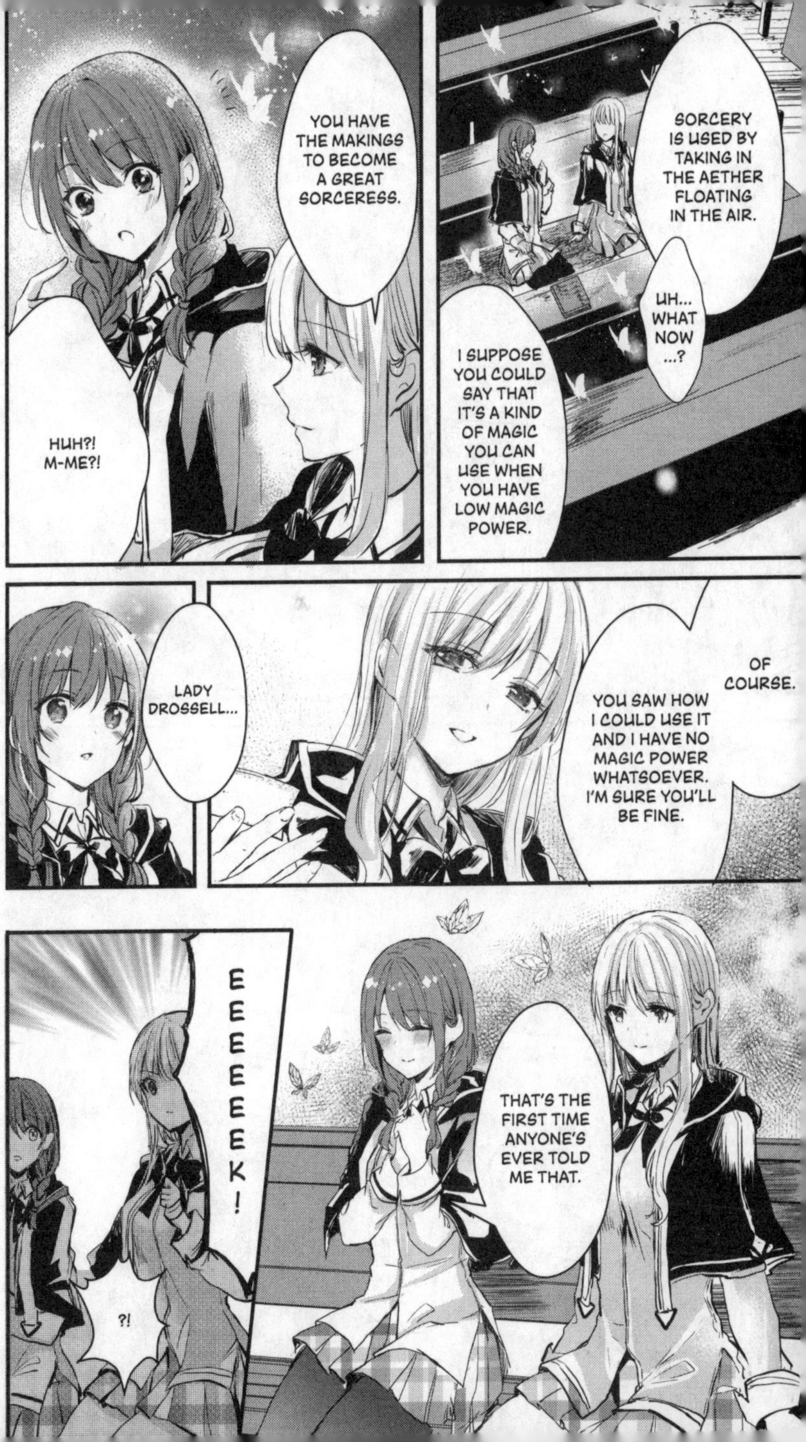
SORCERY IS USED BY TAKING IN THE AETHER FLOATING IN THE AIR.
UH... WHAT NOW ...?
I SUPPOSE YOU COULD SAY THAT IT'S A KIND OF MAGIC YOU CAN USE WHEN YOU HAVE LOW MAGIC POWER.
YOU HAVE THE MAKINGS TO BECOME A GREAT SORCERESS.
HUH?! M-ME?!
OF COURSE.
YOU SAW HOW I COULD USE IT AND I HAVE NO MAGIC POWER WHATSOEVER. I'M SURE YOU'LL BE FINE.
LADY DROSSELL...
THAT'S THE FIRST TIME ANYONE'S EVER TOLD ME THAT.
EEEEEEK!
?!

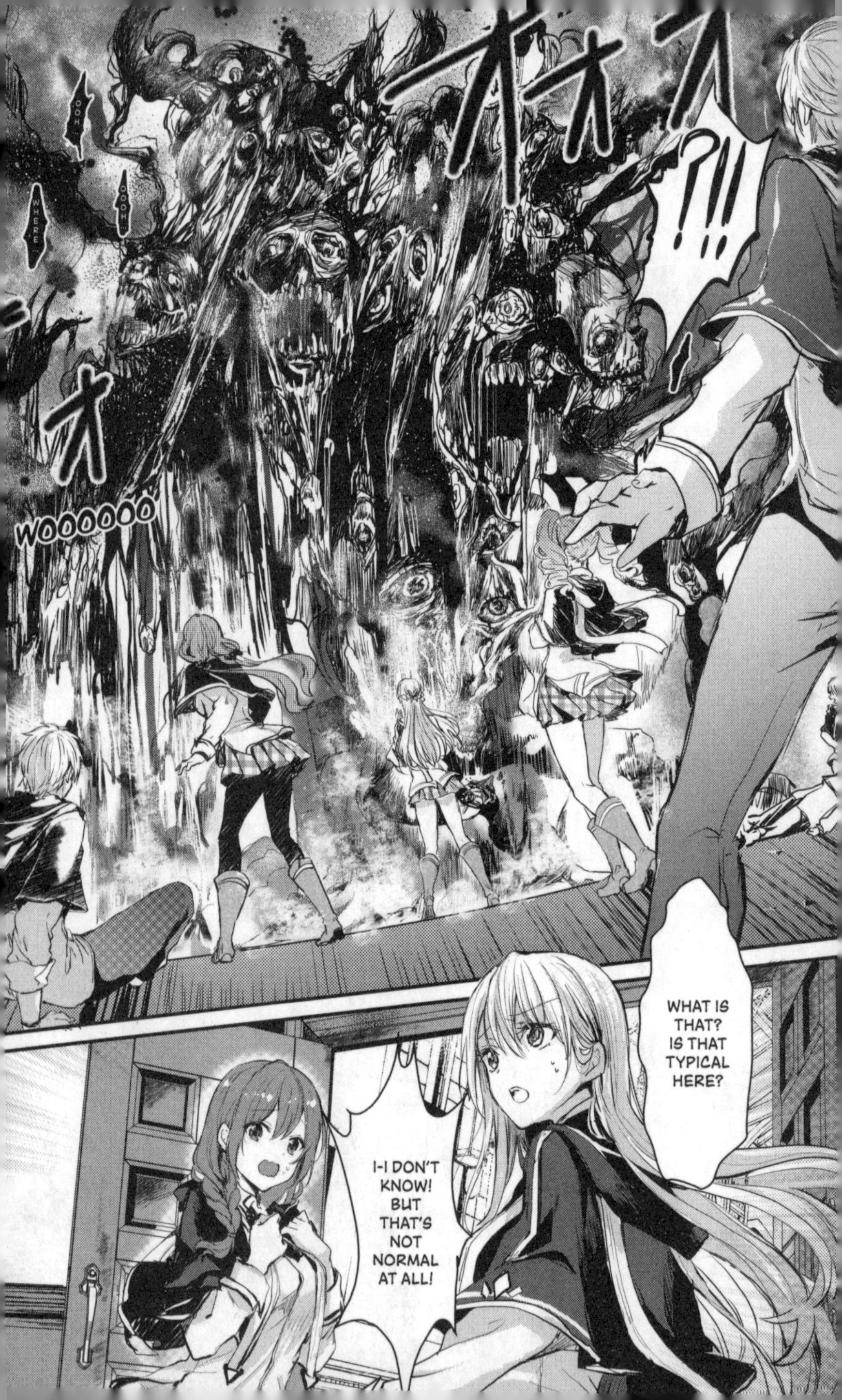
?!!
OOOH...
OOH...
WHERE...
WOOOOOO
WHAT IS THAT? IS THAT TYPICAL HERE?
I-I DON'T KNOW! BUT THAT'S NOT NORMAL AT ALL!

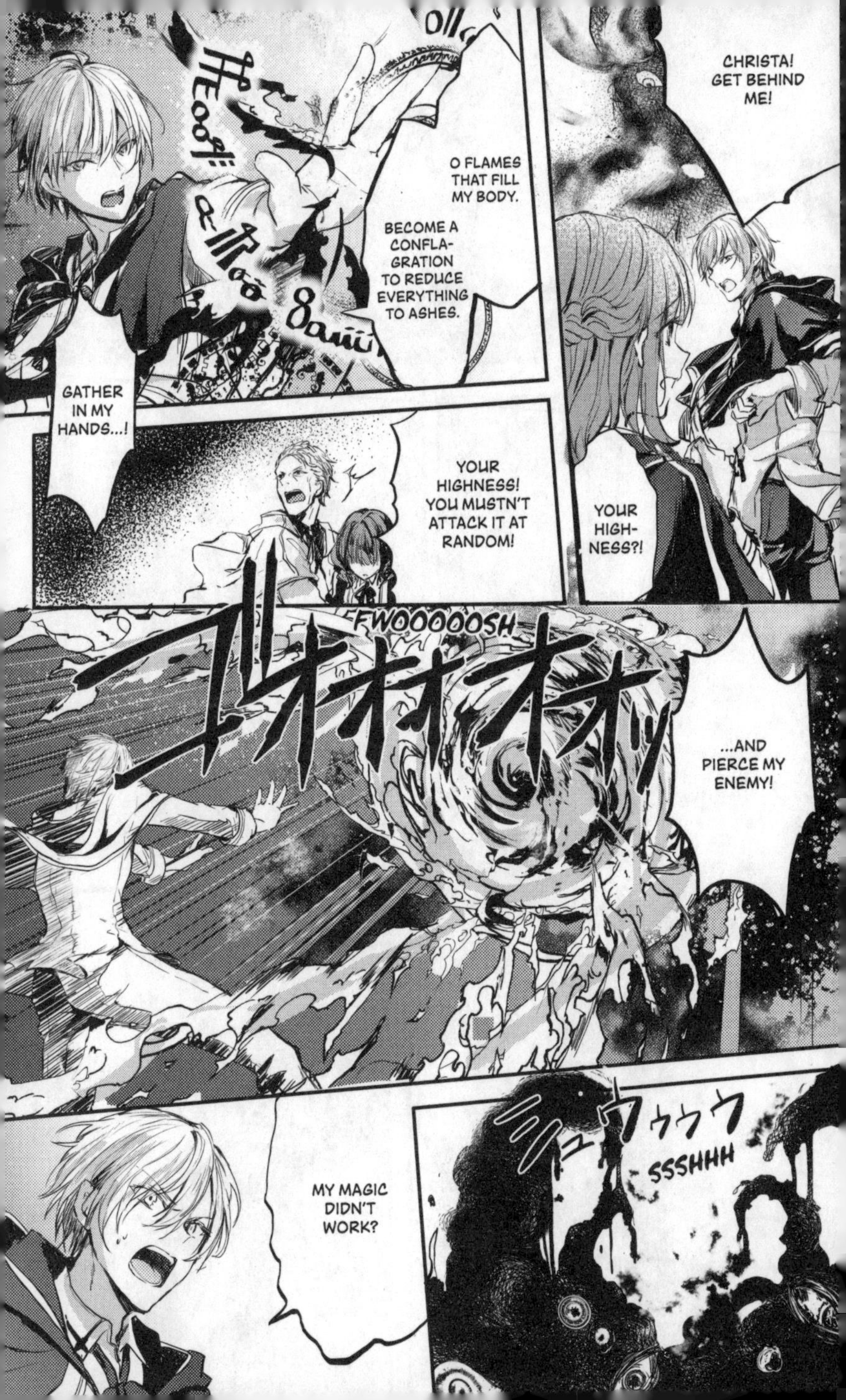
CHRISTA! GET BEHIND ME!
YOUR HIGHNESS?!
O FLAMES THAT FILL MY BODY.
BECOME A CONFLAGRATION TO REDUCE EVERYTHING TO ASHES.
GATHER IN MY HANDS...!
YOUR HIGHNESS! YOU MUSTN'T ATTACK IT AT RANDOM!
FWOOOOOSH
...AND PIERCE MY ENEMY!
SSSHHH
MY MAGIC DIDN'T WORK?

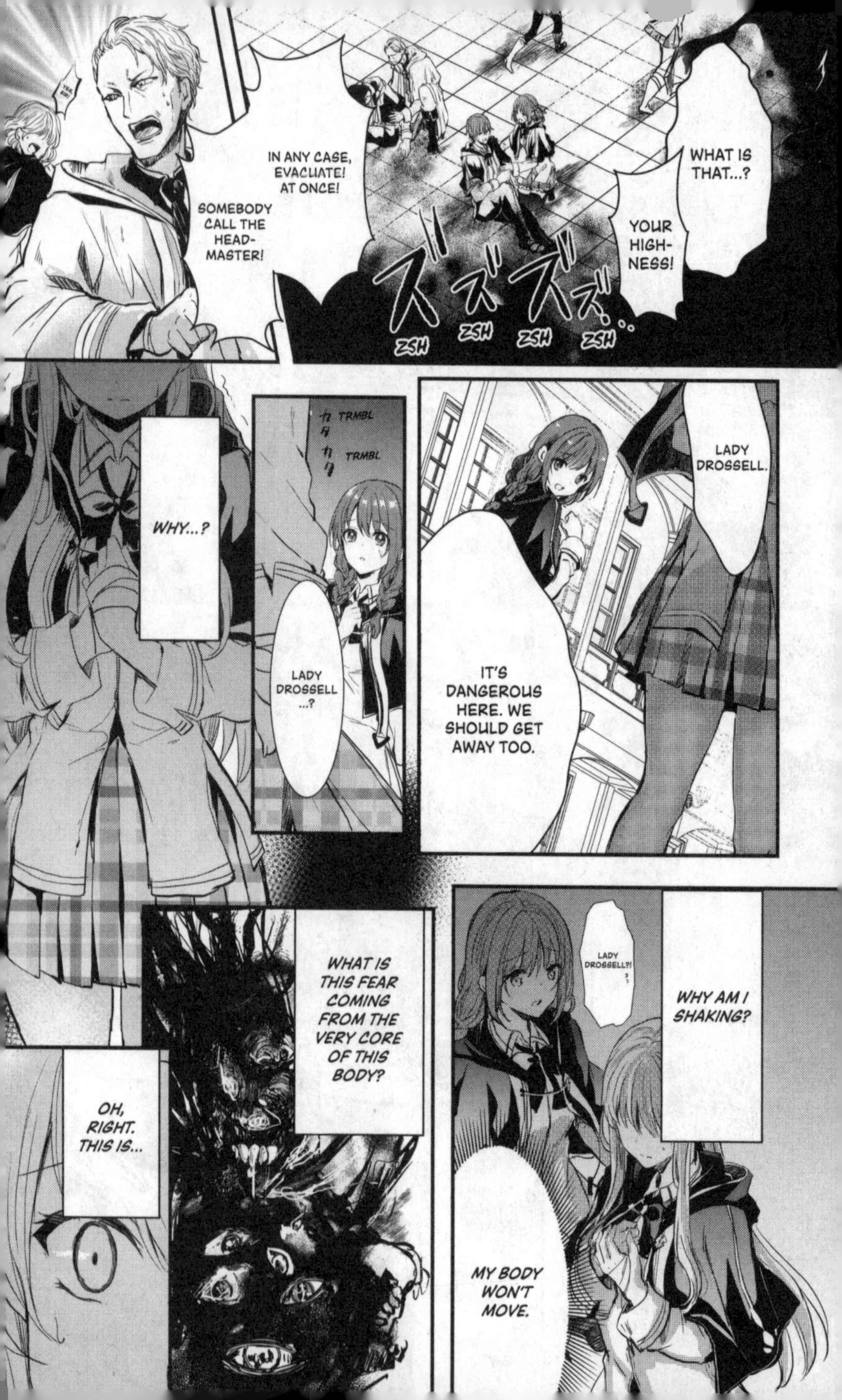
WHAT IS THAT...?
YOUR HIGH-NESS!
ズズズズ
ZSH ZSH ZSH ZSH
IN ANY CASE, EVACUATE! AT ONCE!
SOMEBODY CALL THE HEAD-MASTER!
LADY DROSSELL.
IT'S DANGEROUS HERE. WE SHOULD GET AWAY TOO.
カタカタ TRMBL TRMBL
LADY DROSSELL ...?
WHY...?
WHY AM I SHAKING?
LADY DROSSELL?!
MY BODY WON'T MOVE.
WHAT IS THIS FEAR COMING FROM THE VERY CORE OF THIS BODY?
OH, RIGHT. THIS IS...

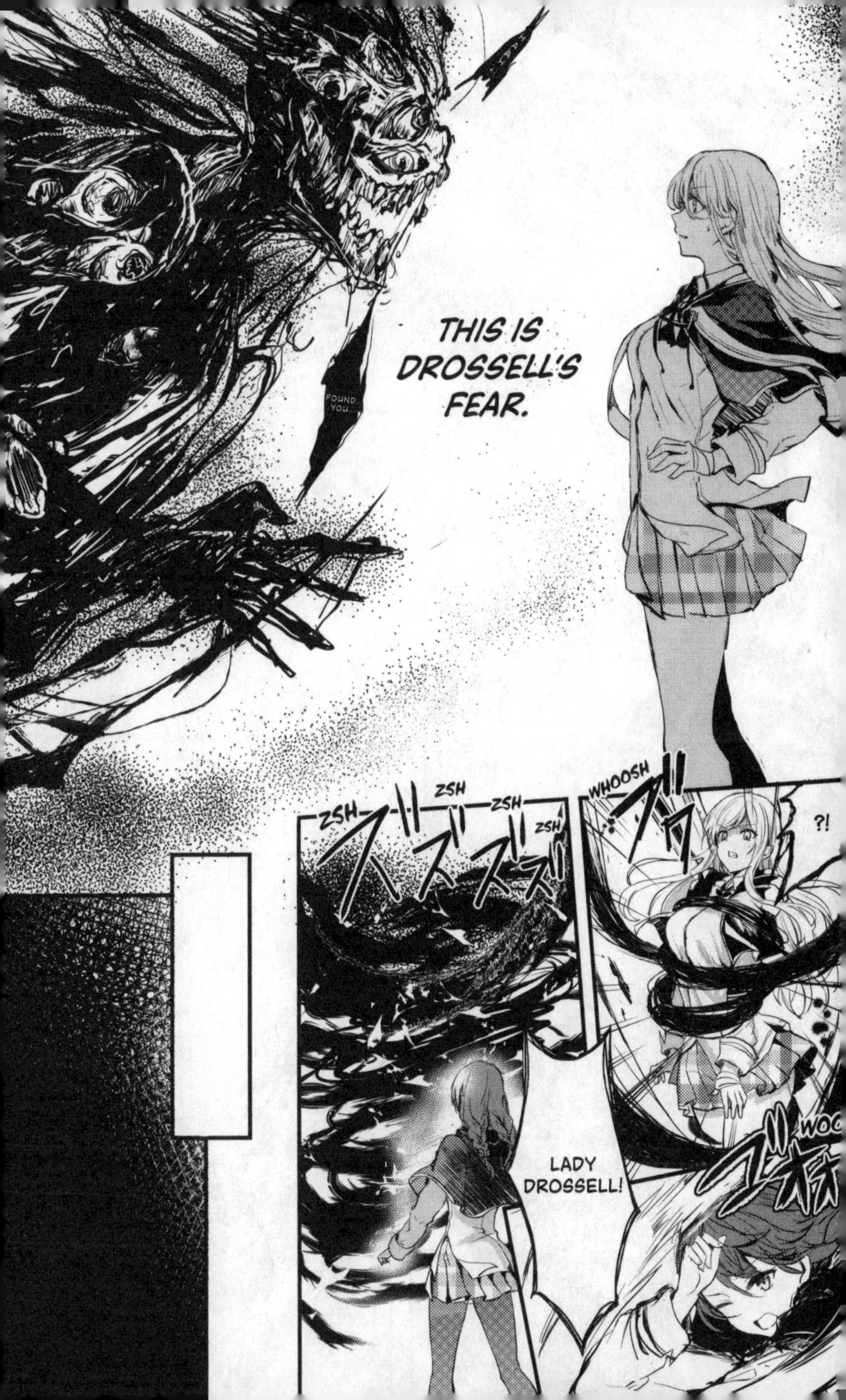
THIS IS DROSSELL'S FEAR.
FOUND YOU...
WHOOSH
?!
WOO
LADY DROSSELL!
ZSH
ZSH
ZSH
ZSH

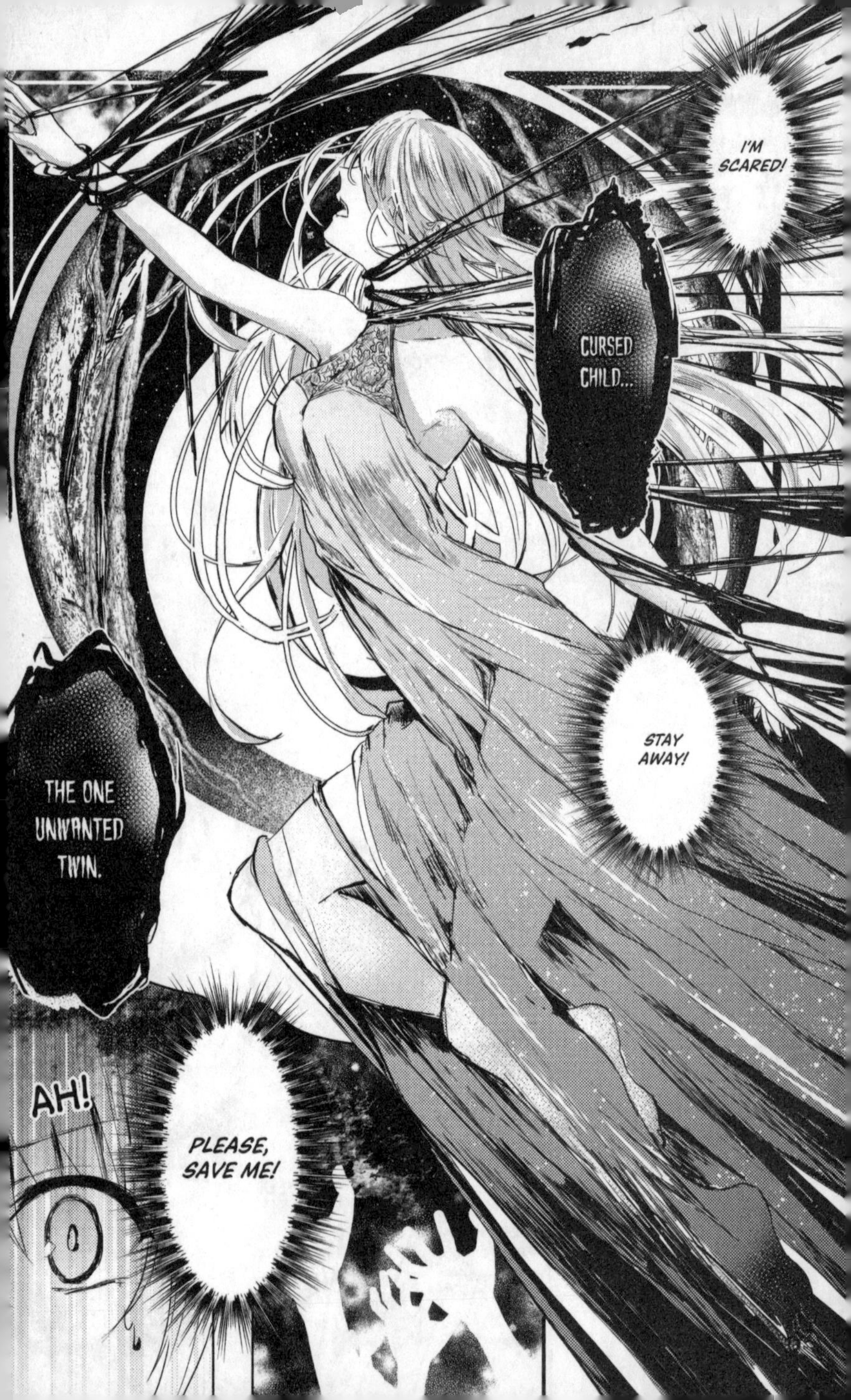
I'M SCARED!
CURSED CHILD...
STAY AWAY!
THE ONE UNWANTED TWIN.
PLEASE, SAVE ME!
AH!

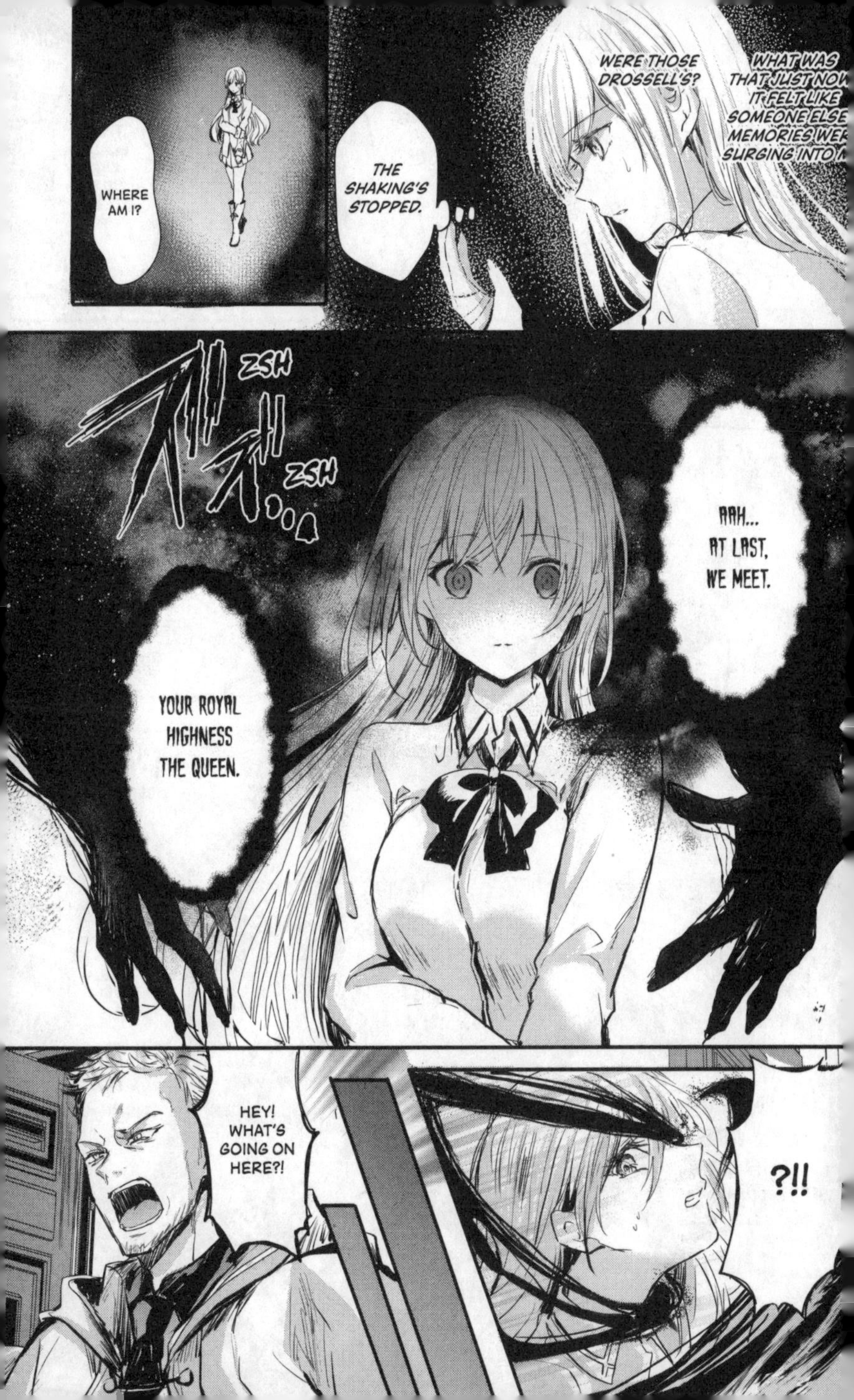
WHAT WAS THAT JUST NOW
IT FELT LIKE SOMEONE ELSE MEMORIES WER SURGING INTO M
WERE THOSE DROSSELL'S?
THE SHAKING'S STOPPED.
WHERE AM I?
ZSH
ZSH
AAH... AT LAST, WE MEET.
YOUR ROYAL HIGHNESS THE QUEEN.
?!!
HEY! WHAT'S GOING ON HERE?!

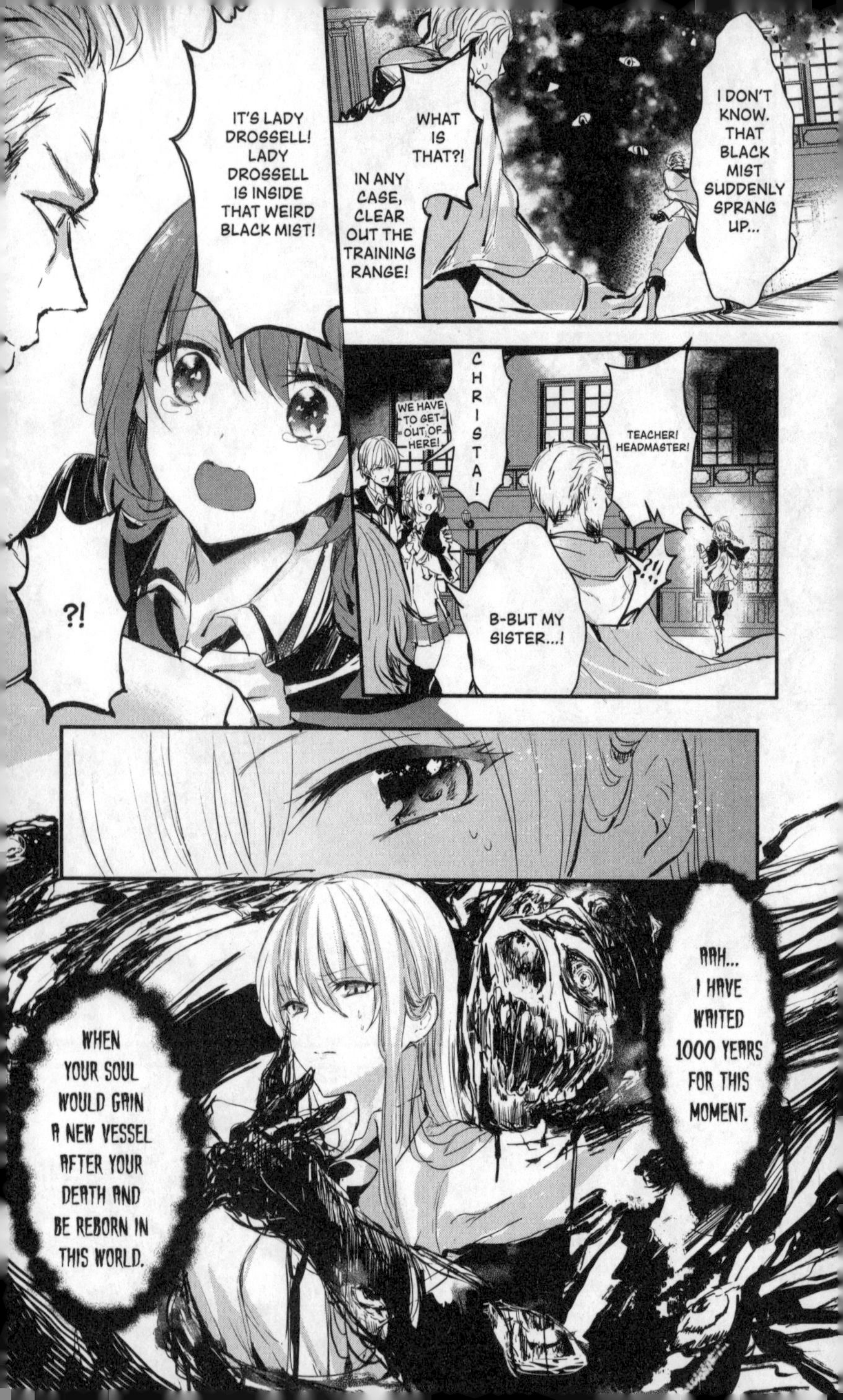
I DON'T KNOW. THAT BLACK MIST SUDDENLY SPRANG UP...
WHAT IS THAT?!
IN ANY CASE, CLEAR OUT THE TRAINING RANGE!
TEACHER! HEADMASTER!
!!
CHRISTA!
WE HAVE TO GET OUT OF HERE!
B-BUT MY SISTER...!
IT'S LADY DROSSELL! LADY DROSSELL IS INSIDE THAT WEIRD BLACK MIST!
?!
AAH... I HAVE WAITED 1000 YEARS FOR THIS MOMENT.
WHEN YOUR SOUL WOULD GAIN A NEW VESSEL AFTER YOUR DEATH AND BE REBORN IN THIS WORLD.

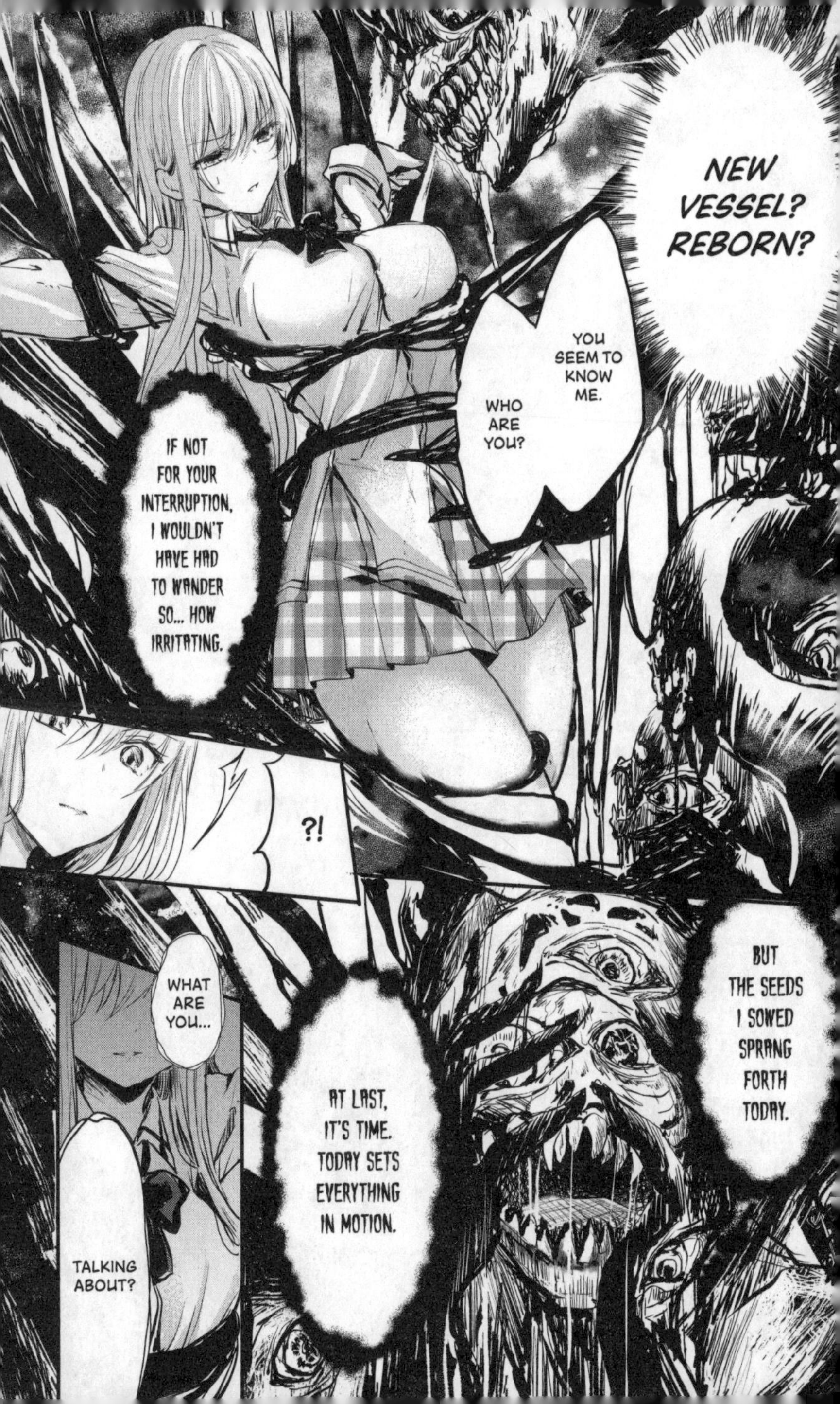
NEW VESSEL? REBORN?
YOU SEEM TO KNOW ME.
WHO ARE YOU?
IF NOT FOR YOUR INTERRUPTION, I WOULDN'T HAVE HAD TO WANDER SO... HOW IRRITATING.
?!
BUT THE SEEDS I SOWED SPRANG FORTH TODAY.
AT LAST, IT'S TIME. TODAY SETS EVERYTHING IN MOTION.
WHAT ARE YOU...
TALKING ABOUT?

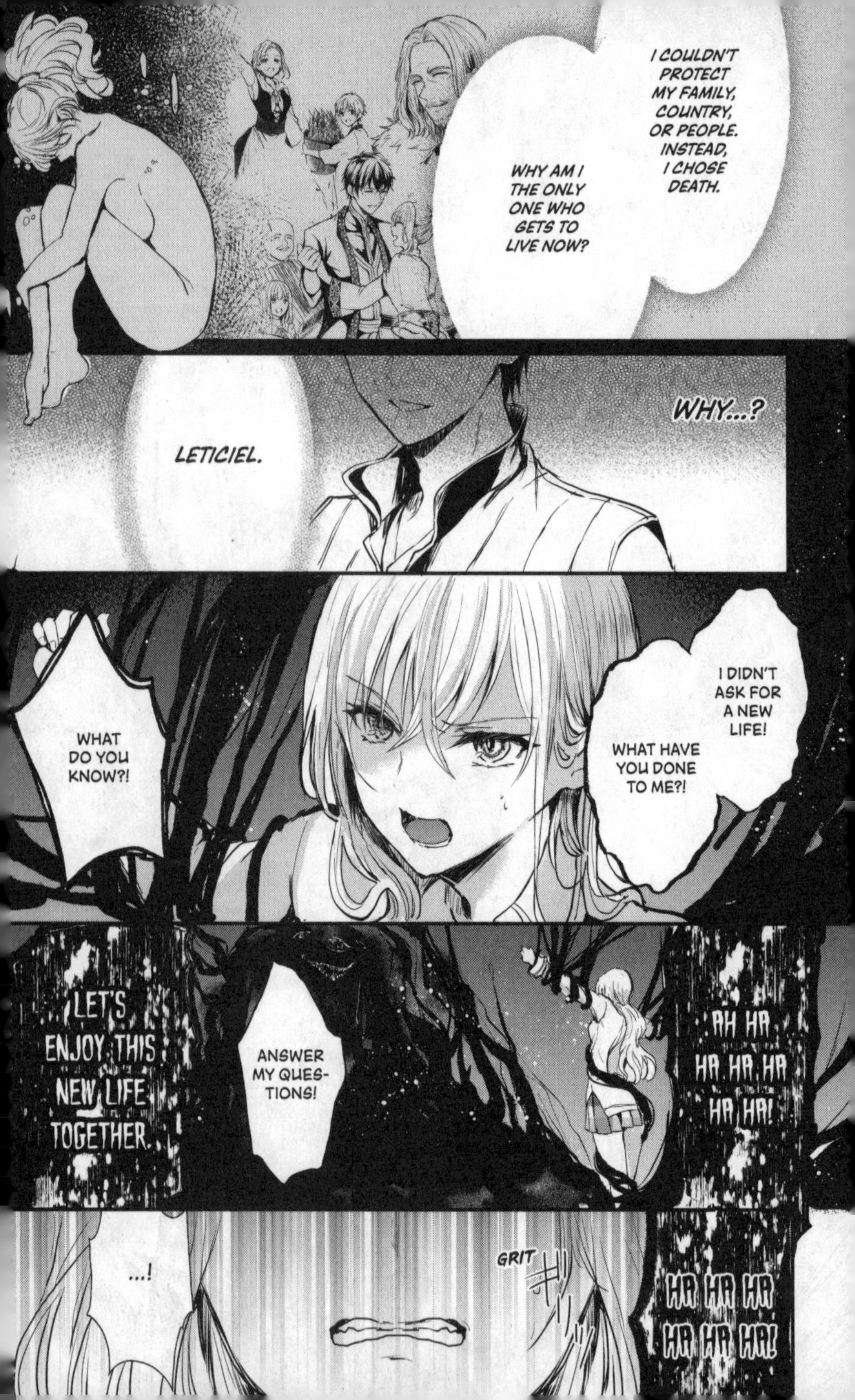
I COULDN'T PROTECT MY FAMILY, COUNTRY, OR PEOPLE. INSTEAD, I CHOSE DEATH.
WHY AM I THE ONLY ONE WHO GETS TO LIVE NOW?
WHY...?
LETICIEL.
I DIDN'T ASK FOR A NEW LIFE!
WHAT HAVE YOU DONE TO ME?!
WHAT DO YOU KNOW?!
AH HA HA HA HA HA HA!
ANSWER MY QUES-TIONS!
LET'S ENJOY THIS NEW LIFE TOGETHER.
HA HA HA HA HA HA!
GRIT
...!

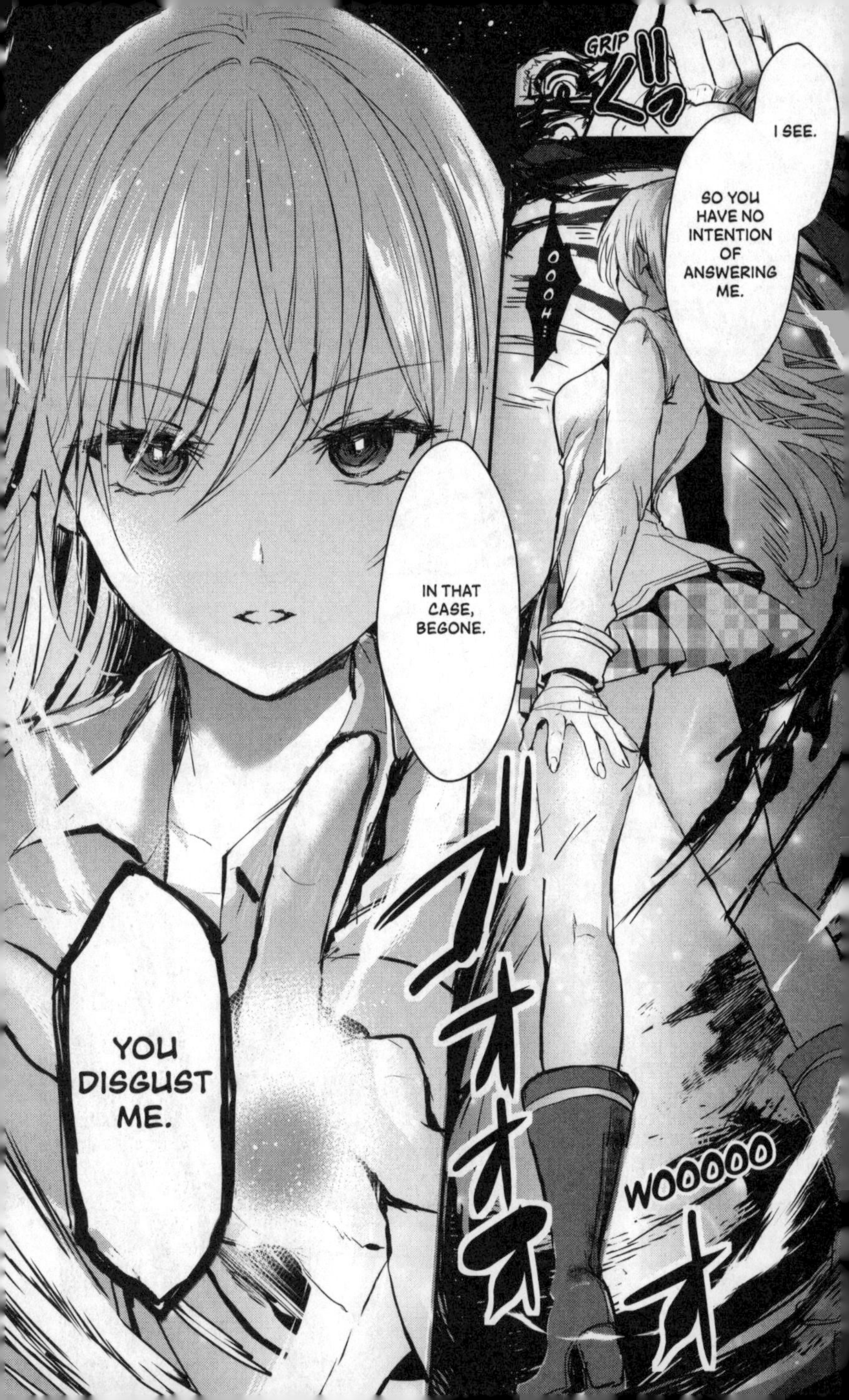
GRIP
I SEE.
SO YOU HAVE NO INTENTION OF ANSWERING ME.
OOOH...
IN THAT CASE, BEGONE.
YOU DISGUST ME.
WOOOOO

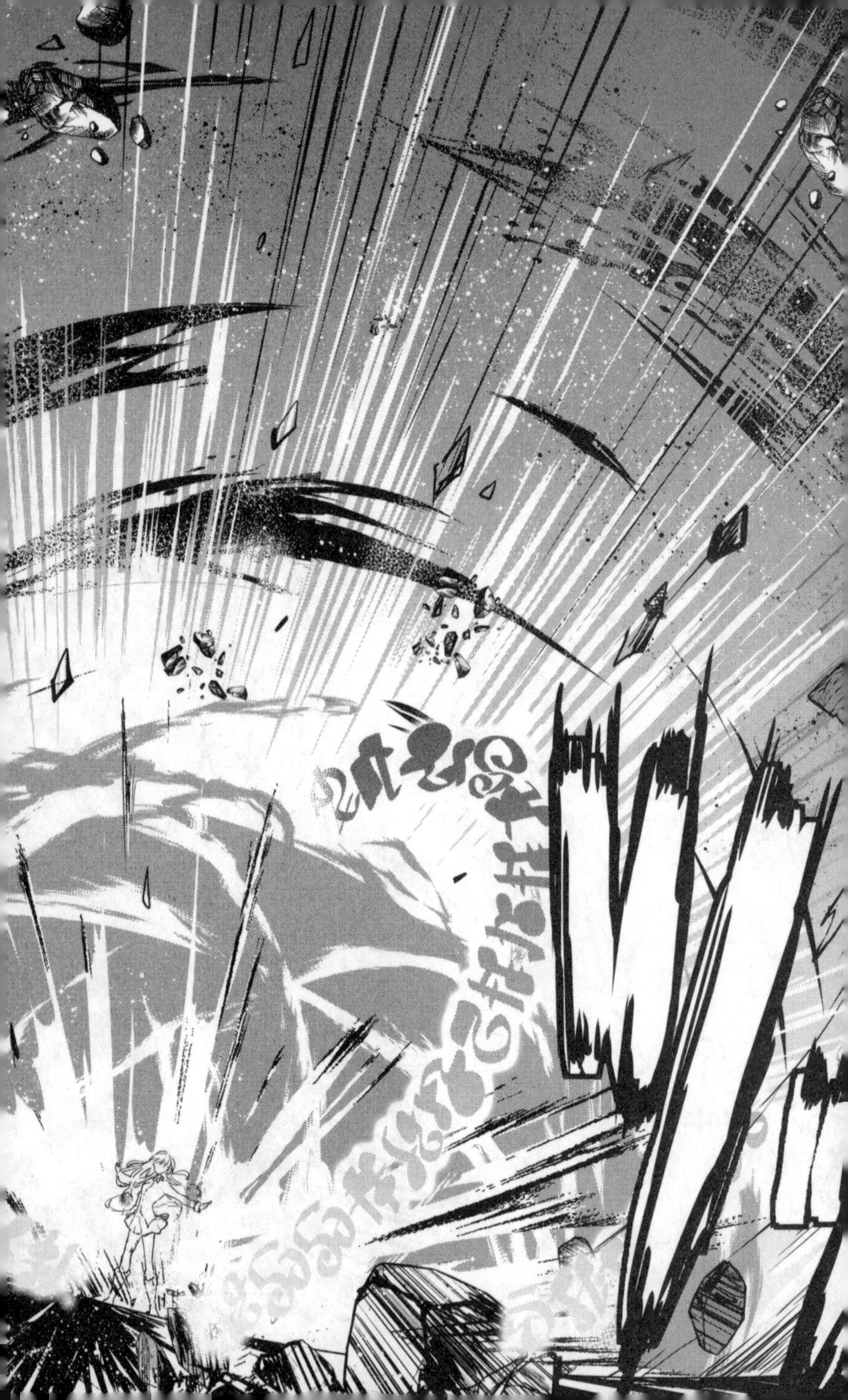

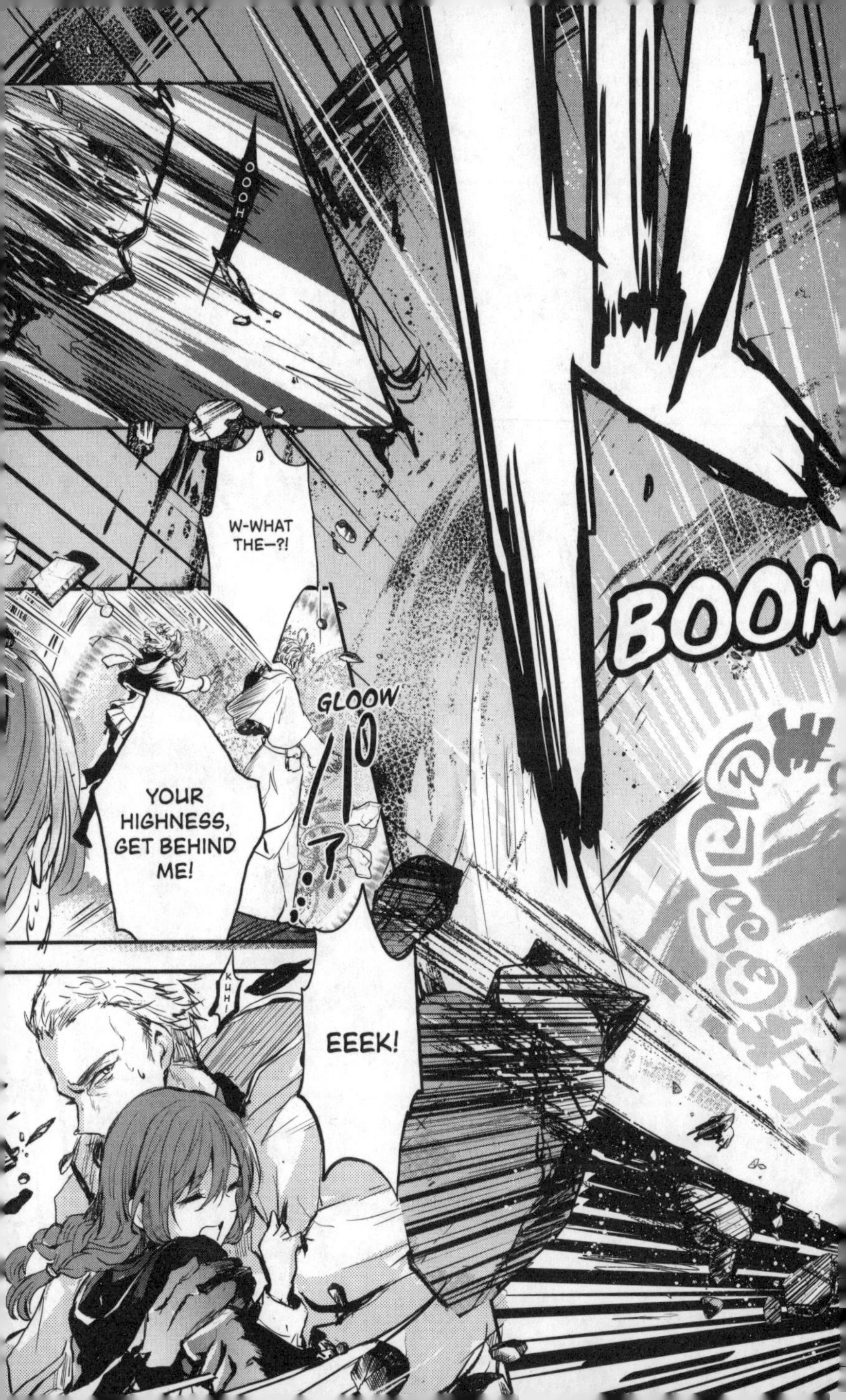
BOOM
OOOH...
W-WHAT THE—?!
GLOOW
YOUR HIGHNESS, GET BEHIND ME!
KUHI
EEEK!

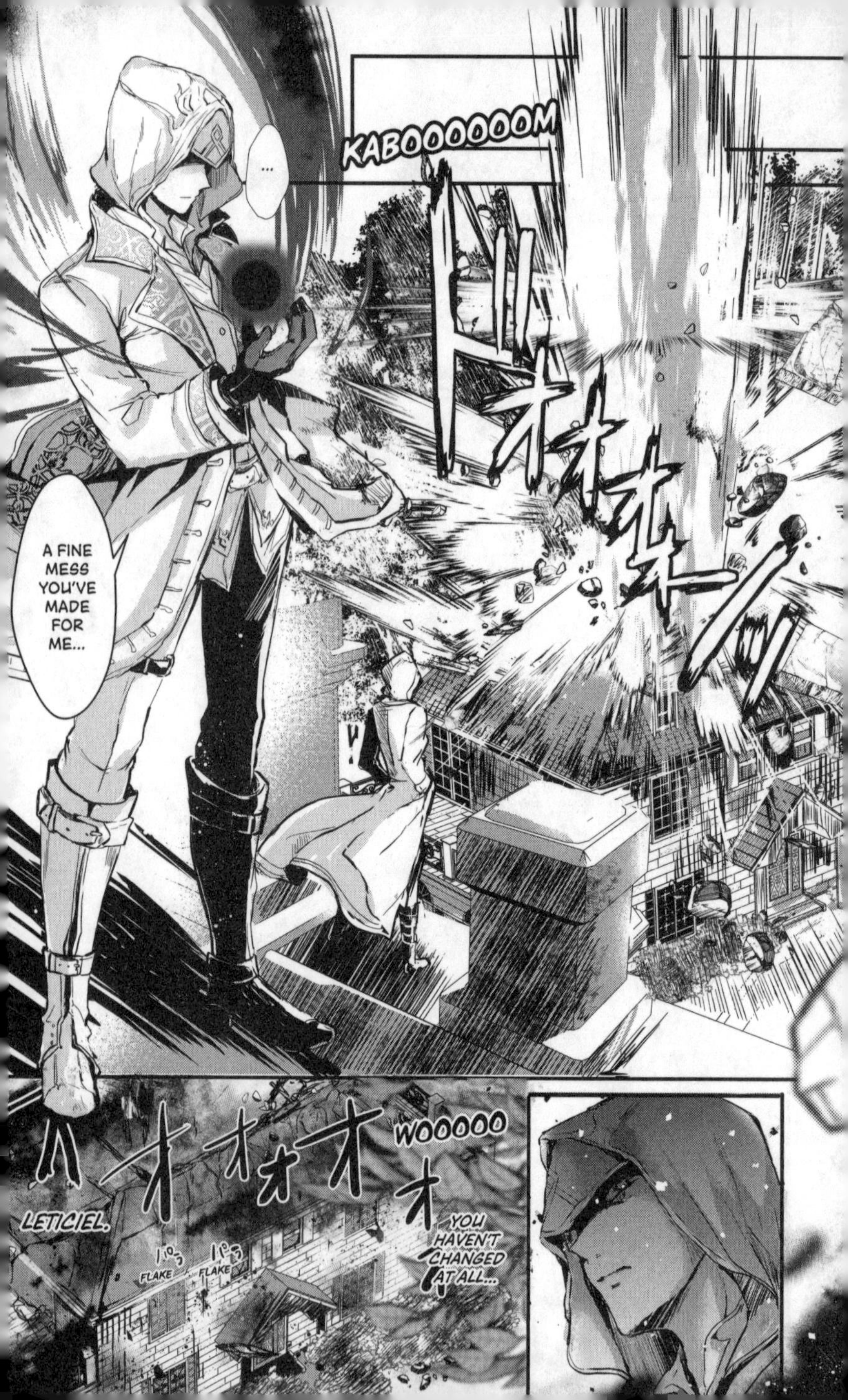
KABOOOOOOOM
...
A FINE MESS YOU'VE MADE FOR ME...
WOOOOO
YOU HAVEN'T CHANGED AT ALL...
LETICIEL.
FLAKE FLAKE

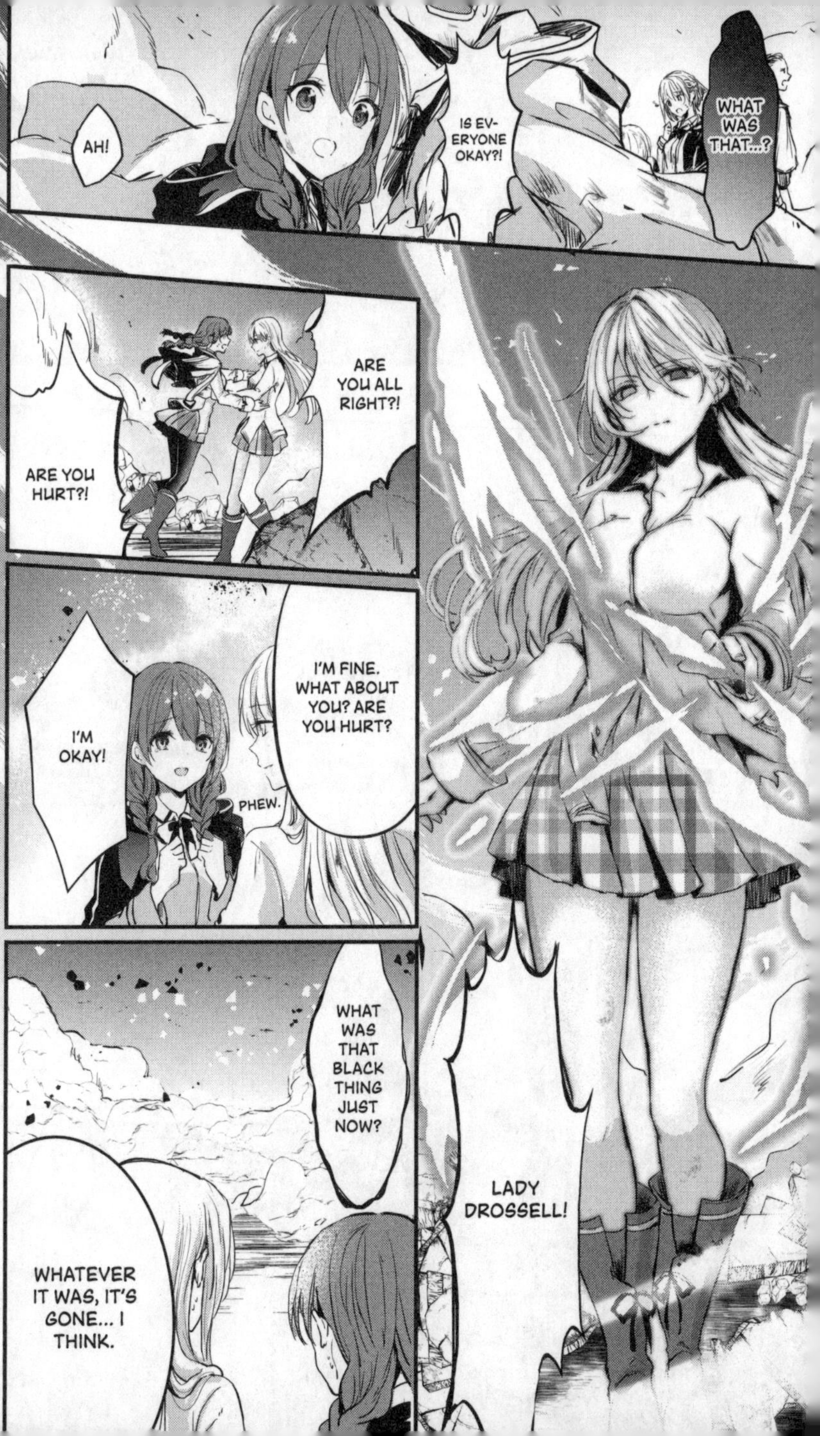
WHAT WAS THAT...?
IS EV-ERYONE OKAY?!
AH!
LADY DROSSELL!
ARE YOU ALL RIGHT?!
ARE YOU HURT?!
I'M FINE. WHAT ABOUT YOU? ARE YOU HURT?
PHEW.
I'M OKAY!
WHAT WAS THAT BLACK THING JUST NOW?
WHATEVER IT WAS, IT'S GONE... I THINK.

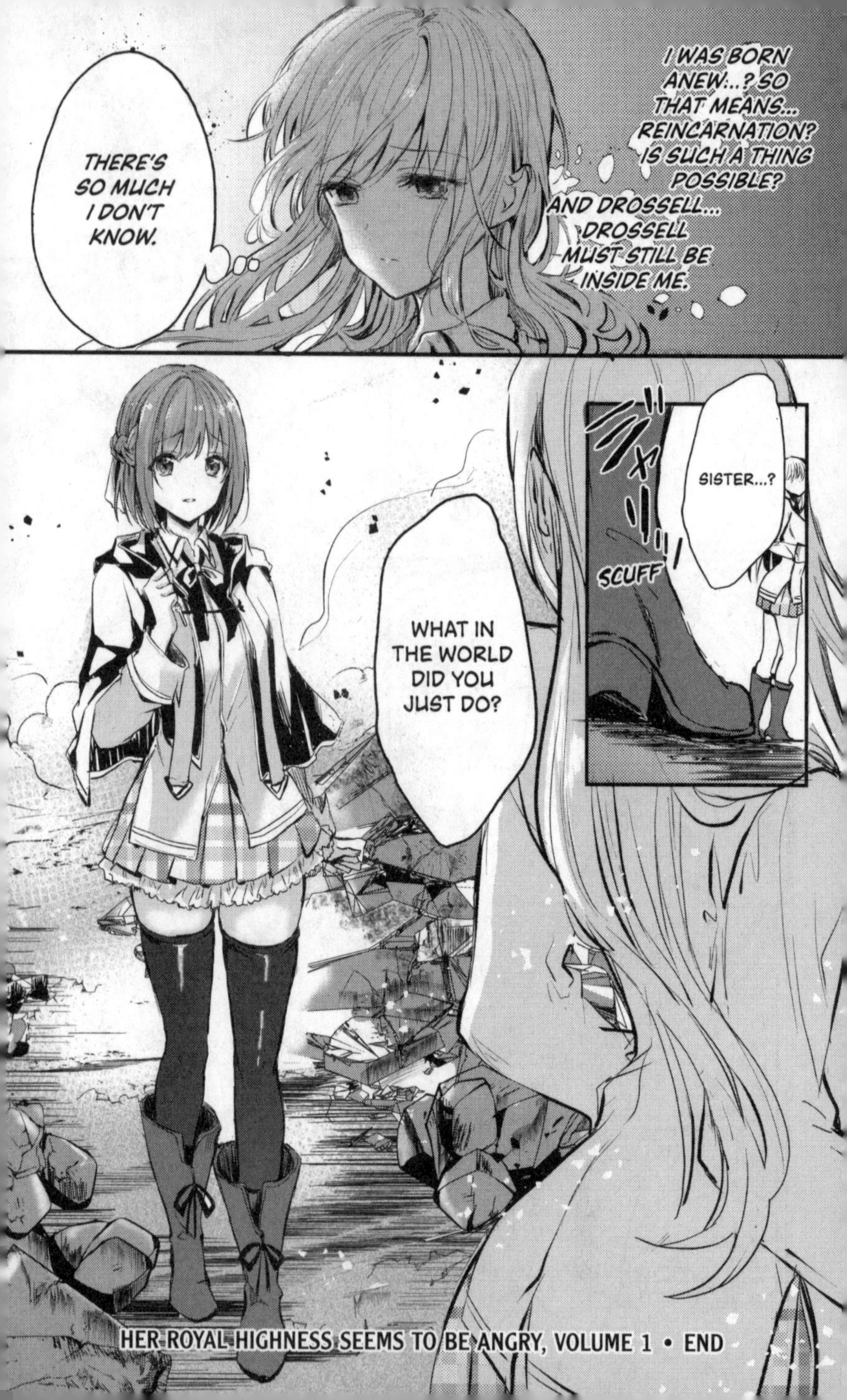
I WAS BORN ANEW...? SO THAT MEANS... REINCARNATION? IS SUCH A THING POSSIBLE?
AND DROSSELL... DROSSELL MUST STILL BE INSIDE ME.
THERE'S SO MUCH I DON'T KNOW.
SCUFF
SISTER...?
WHAT IN THE WORLD DID YOU JUST DO?
HER ROYAL HIGHNESS SEEMS TO BE ANGRY, VOLUME 1 • END

A Short Spell at Regenerose Castle

"I feel like there's been suspicious activity going on in the castle lately." It was late in the morning, and Leticiel was strolling the castle's inner court when she voiced her concern to her companion.

Nao's heart froze, but he endeavored not to let his disturbance show. Instead, he tried to put on an air of calm and replied, "Uh... W-what makes you think that?"

"I just mean that everyone in the castle seems so standoffish, and I've even ght glimpses of people sneaking around in the shadows."

"Y-you don't say. That is... well, certainly suspicious... I guess..."

Nao was a little worried that he was being too obvious, but Leticiel gave off no impression of paying his false tone of voice any mind.

"Could it be enemy spies from another country? If so, I must let my father know at once."

"Whoa, now! Whoa! Are you sure you're not just imagining things, Letty? After all, you've been staying up late researching these past few days, so maybe you're just tired."

"Hmmm. I just hope that's all it is..." Leticiel answered, but she didn't seem completely convinced.

DOOOOONG! DOOOOONG!

Just then, the bells rang throughout the castle. Checking the position of the sun, Leticiel turned back to Nao.

"There's the noonday bell. I'd better get back to my research. Thanks for hearing me out."

"Sure! No problem!"

And with that, Leticiel returned to her quarters. Once alone, Neo watched her departing figure, gave a small sigh of relief when she was gone, and then hurried away to come up to the door of a particular room.

"What is it? Don't tell me she's figured it out?" asked the man seated at the table at the far end of the room Nao had just entered.

The room was north-facing so even in the middle of the day, it was dark, and it was hard to make out the faces of the other people gathered inside.

"No, I don't think she's noticed anything, but she seems to be suspecting things of a completely different nature..."

"Hmm... It'll be tough work moving forward with this without risking her figuring out what we're up to."

"We'd better be even more cautious than ever. This is the one thing we cannot let her find out about."

For a while after that, the men put their foreheads together and continued to speak in whispers, but by and by the party dispersed, and in the end, the only ones left were Nao and the man who had first spoken.

"Nao. I don't think Leticiel will keep to herself before the date we have planned."

"I agree. She'll probably launch an investigation. And how we dodge that Sorcery will determine whether this plan is a success or not."

Nao got to thinking. Leticiel was a Sorcery prodigy. Not having the constitution to use Sorcery himself, there was nothing he could do, so rather than fight it and only make things worse, he decided to deepen her suspicions.

"Your Majesty... What do you think about this idea?"

After deliberating long and hard, Nao proposed his idea to his companion, albeit timidly.

Hearing what Nao had to say, the man — the Royal King of the Kingdom of Regenerose — smirked with amusement.

* * *

I knew it. Everyone in the castle really is acting peculiar, Leticiel thought to herself, furrowing her brow as she watched messengers and bureaucrats alike scurrying down the castle corridors.

She tried to take more breaks, thinking it was exhaustion, but she was still catching sight of suspicious figures. And what's more, she could've sworn it was happening even more frequently than before. It was enough to give her a headache.

"...!"

A shadow suddenly flashed to her left. Leticiel immediately turned in its direction and invoked an Inspection Sorcery. A triple-layered Spell manifested in the air, and wind blew about, centered around a blue circle in the middle, inspecting the Aether flow of the vicinity.

She didn't detect anyone, but there were traces of Sorcery having been employed. Expecting to have Inspection Sorcery used on them, whoever it was must've made themselves scarce with another Spell.

If I can't even track down one suspicious person, then I need to work on my Inspection Sorcery. First, I'll need to improve the abilities of the Inspection Spell, Leticiel decided, and threw herself into her research like never before, cooping herself up in her room morning, noon, and night.

And so Leticiel spent her days even more engrossed in her research than usual... until one night, when Nao suddenly showed up at her room without warning.

"There's a place I want to take you to."

Without any further explanation, Neo turned on his heel and started on his way. Though absolutely bewildered and having no idea what he was talking about, Leticiel hurried after him.

As they walked, Nao didn't say a word or even look at her. Eventually, he came to a stop outside the entrance to the soldiers' training grounds.

What business could he have here at this hour?

"Hey, Nao. What on earth are you—?"

But before she could finish, Neo opened the door leading to the soldiers' training grounds. On the other side of the door, the space was filled with unexpected bright lights, and without thinking Leticiel covered her eyes with both hands. As soon as they'd passed the lights...

"Surprise!! Happy Birthday, Your Highness!"

The space that spread before her was full of the sound of applause and congratulations, and the sight of smiling faces.

Under the night sky, the training field was filled with bonfires and rows of tables packed with various foods. There were so many people gathered, she could've sworn that everyone associated with the castle was present.

"...Wait, what?"

"Letty, today's your birthday, remember? So we all wanted to celebrate you.

"My birthday... Oh my goodness, you're right. I completely forgot."

"It was Sir Nao's idea. We would have never come up with it on our own, and we learned so much along the way! It was so fun and worth it!"

A soldier to her side struck a macho pose while he gushed excitedly at her. She recognized this soldier. He was the top apprentice Sorcery Soldier.

"I had no idea. Thank you, everyone!"

With the guest of honor having arrived, the festivities began. There was music and entertainment, and in no time at all, the soldiers' training grounds were enveloped in a lively air of celebration. In the middle of it all, Leticiel chatted with any and all who came to give their well wishes, accompanied by Nao as they made their way around the assembly.

"I really was surprised. Don't tell me all that suspicious behavior I was sensing in the castle lately was actually for this?"

"Yep. Everyone tried their hardest to keep you from finding out. If you'd caught wind of it, it'd have ruined the surprise, so I had a number of the soldiers apprenticing in Sorcery throw you off our trail with Sorcery of their own."

At that piece of information, Leticiel's eyes went wide. She thought back to the top apprentice Sorcery Soldier. He had said "we learned so much along the way." Could it be...?

"I proposed the idea to the king. You'd been saying for a while now that you thought the Sorcery Soldiers' level should be higher, so since it served as training for them too. I got to kill two birds with one stone. His Majesty was all for it."

Reflexively, Leticiel whipped around to look in her father the king's direction. He was surrounded by vassals and chatting pleasantly, and upon sensing his daughter's gaze, he gave a proud smile, as though to say *gotcha!*

"I do recall mentioning that to my father..."

That one smile said it all for Leticiel, and she puffed up her cheeks to show her displeasure before turning away. She wasn't sure whether to be glad that the soldiers had gotten stronger or angry that she had been so thoroughly duped.

"Still, this is nice too."

"What do you mean? The party?"

"No, I mean celebrating birthdays. In this day and age, when you never know when or where you might die, there's not much time to rejoice in life since we're already so busy dealing with the minutiae of survival and we know that death is inevitable... I thought there never was any point."

"Back when I was in my own country, I also thought that celebrating birthdays was pointless, but now I think of it as an opportunity for 'gratitude.'"

"Gratitude?"

"Sure, people can die at any time, but if they'd never been born in the first place, you wouldn't have the relationships or happiness you have now. So I think it's like thanking them for having been born and for meeting them. A celebration like that, I guess..." Nao felt more and more self-conscious as he went on, and he shifted his eyes in awkwardness as he scratched at his cheek.

"I see. I think that's a lovely custom."

"Yeah, me too."

"Then we'll have to celebrate yours. To make it even."

"Uh..."

All the more so since apparently celebrating a birthday expresses gratitude for that person's life, thought Leticiel. If Nao hadn't been born and she had never met him, Regenerose would have never changed the way it had.

But she was too embarrassed to say all that, so Leticiel just looked up and smiled at the night sky. The star-filled heavens twinkled as they presided over the small gathering.

I'm grateful with all my heart to have met you.

AFTERWORD

It's been an enormous honor to have Neko Yotsuba-sensei be in charge of the manga adaptation of my story. It makes me so happy to see the characters moving around within its pages as though they're alive, and I've learned a lot about layout and point of view and expressions that you can only get from a manga. In this volume, Leticiel and Nao's relationship was depicted so thoughtfully, and her encounter with Zeke was pulled off so dramatically. Getting to read the story like any other reader, I was excited for each and every chapter! Thank you so much for this wonderful manga.

Author of the Original Story: Kou Yatsuhashi

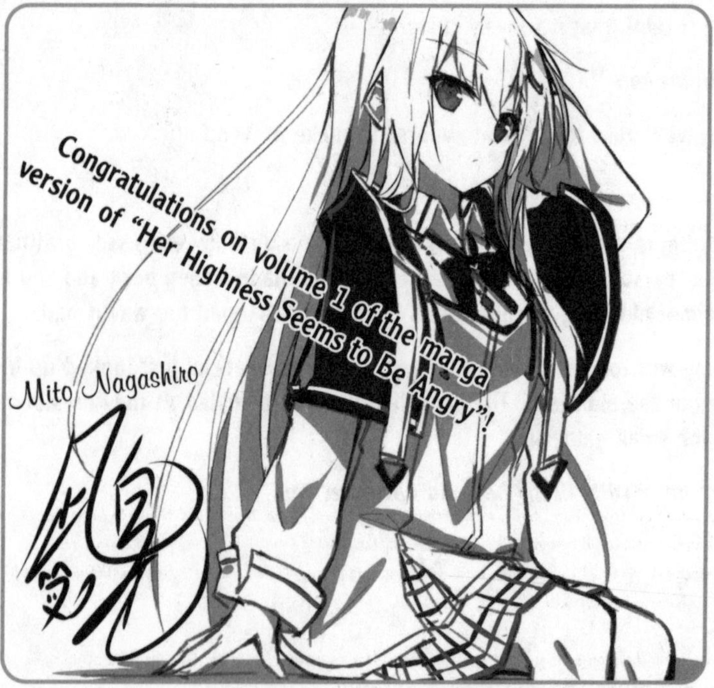
Congratulations on volume 1 of the manga version of "Her Highness Seems to Be Angry"!
Mito Nagashiro

Illustrator of the Novel: **Mito Nagashiro**

Nice to meet you. I'm Neko Yotsuba and I got to be in charge of the manga adaptation of "Her Highness Seems to Be Angry."

Since I received the offer to turn the story into a manga after having just read it online and already being obsessed with the prospect that it'd be adapted, I was super thrilled. The content differs between the published version and the online version, but in this comic version, I figured I'd weave in my favorite scenes from the online version. The second installment is beginning online, so as a fellow reader, I'm so stoked about it.

There were lots of issues surrounding the adaptation... but I managed to overcome them, if just barely, and though I know that I caused nothing but trouble for everyone along every step of the way, I hope I get to stay with the project. Besides all you wonderful readers, there were also lots of people who lent me their strength, and enabled this first volume to be published.

I'm going to keep giving it my best to make sure "Her Highness Seems to Be Angry" really shines, so I hope you'll continue to show me your support and kindness!

Neko Yotsuba

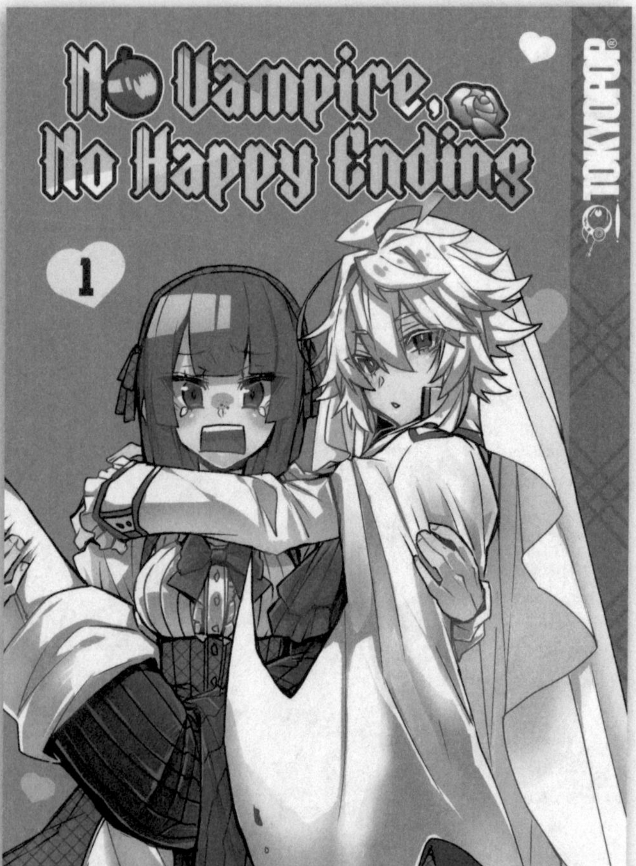
No Vampire, No Happy Ending
1
TOKYOPOP
SHINYA SHINYA

NO VAMPIRE, NO HAPPY ENDING, VOLUME 1

Shinya Shinya

LOVE-x-LOVE

Arika is what you could charitably call a vampire "enthusiast." When she stumbles across the beautiful and mysterious vampire Divo however, her excitement quickly turns to disappointment as she discovers he's not exactly like the seductive, manipulative villains in her stories. His looks win first place, but his head's a space case. Armed with her extensive knowledge of vampire lore, Arika downgrades Divo to a beta vampire and begins their long, long... long journey to educate him in the ways of the undead.

Fated to die as the villainess of an otome game, Mystia sets out to change her own unhappy ending!

Mystia Aren is the daughter of a noble family, and she just started high school. She's surrounded by a group of adoring classmates and her charming fiancé. Everything seems perfect.

Except that this world is actually a dating sim called Kyun-Love, and Mystia knows she's been reincarnated into the role of the main character's evil rival! Mystia is determined to do everything she can to avoid her fate, but it's not as easy as it sounds. Especially when all the boys keep falling in love with her!

A GENTLE NOBLE'S VACATION RECOMMENDATION, VOLUME 1

Misaki, Momochi & Sando

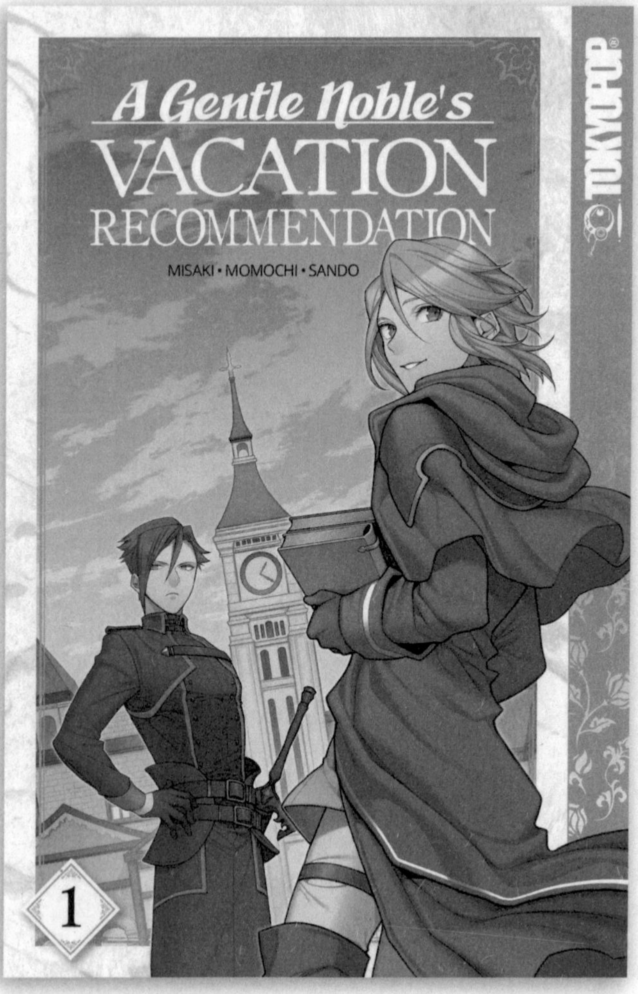
TOKYOPOP
A Gentle Noble's
VACATION
RECOMMENDATION
MISAKI • MOMOCHI • SANDO
1

ISEKAI

When Lizel mysteriously finds himself in a city that bears odd similarities to his own but clearly isn't, he quickly comes to terms with the unlikely truth: this is an entirely different world. Even so, laid-back Lizel isn't the type to panic. He immediately sets out to learn more about this strange place, and to help him do so, hires a seasoned adventurer named Gil as his tour guide and protector. Until he's able to find a way home, Lizel figures this is a perfect opportunity to explore a new way of life adventuring as part of a guild. After all, he's sure he'll go home eventually... might as well enjoy the otherworldly vacation for now!

THE TREASURE OF THE KING AND THE CAT

You Kajika

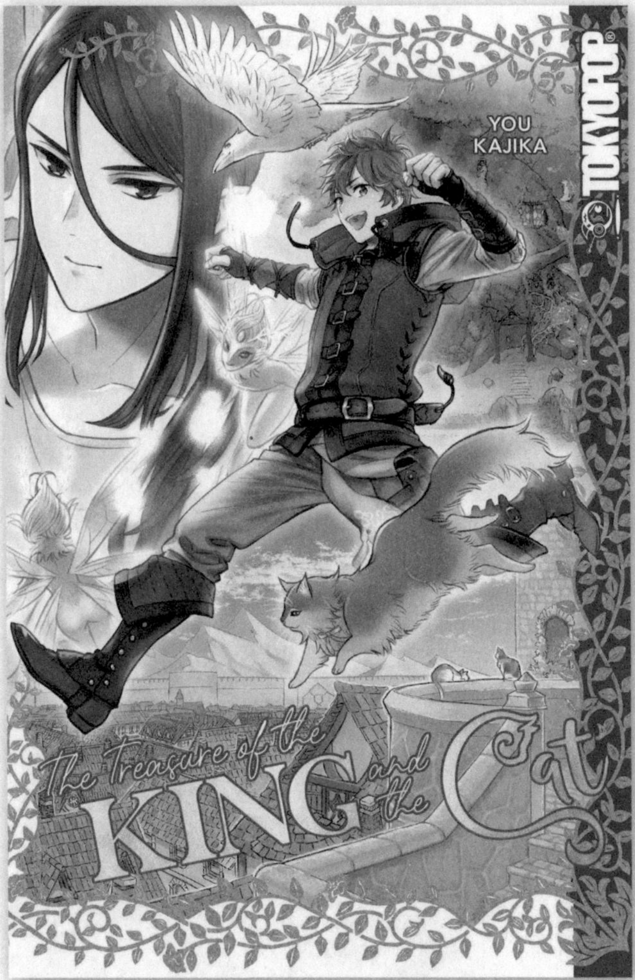
YOU KAJIKA
TOKYOPOP
The Treasure of the KING and the Cat

LOVE x LOVE

TOKYOPOP

One day, a large number of people suddenly disappeared in the royal capital. When young King Castio goes out to investigate this occurrence, he comes across the culprit... but the criminal puts a spell on him! To help him out, the king calls the wizard O'Feuille to his castle, along with Prince Volks and his loyal retainer Nios. Together, they're determined to solve this strange, fluffy mystery full of cats, swords and magic!

DEEP SCAR, VOLUME 1

Rossella Sergi

DEEP *Scar*

Rossella Sergi

1

♀LOVE-x-LOVE♂

Sofia is a quiet, shy young woman who's never been away from home for long. When she moves to Turin for school, it's her first time away from her family and her boyfriend Luca. But her new roommate, Veronica, leads a life very different from hers: she prefers evenings in the company of beautiful boys! Meanwhile, Luca dreads the influence of Veronica and her entourage on Sofia, and especially the presence of the enigmatic Lorenzo, who seems to be a little too interested in his girlfriend...

SCARLET SOUL, VOLUME 1

Kira Yukishiro

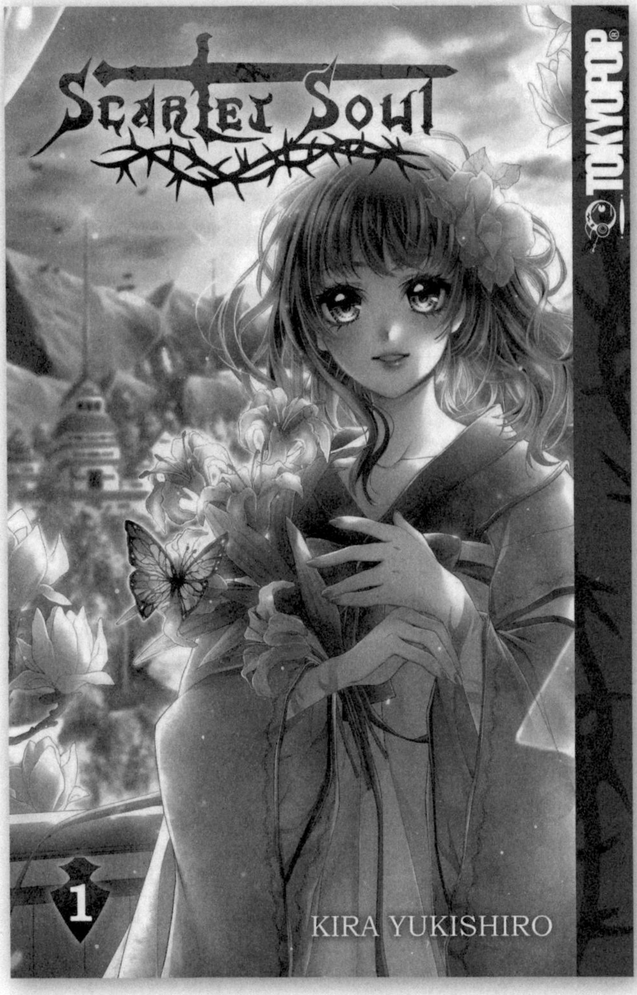

Scarlet Soul
TOKYOPOP
1
KIRA YUKISHIRO

LOVE-x-LOVE

Long ago, Eron Shirano used the sacred Sword of a Hundred Souls to seal away the demon underworld Ruhmon. Since then, the Kingdom of Nohmur has enjoyed peace and prosperity with the aid of his descendants, the exorcist clan that protects the barrier. Until one day, for unknown reasons, demons begin slipping through once more...

When Priestess Lys Shirano suddenly vanishes without a trace, it's up to her little sister Rin to take up the sword she left behind. Even though she's an outcast on friendly terms with the mysterious demon Aghyr, Rin sets out to find her missing sister... and try to restore balance to Nohmur before it's far too late.

TOKYOPOP

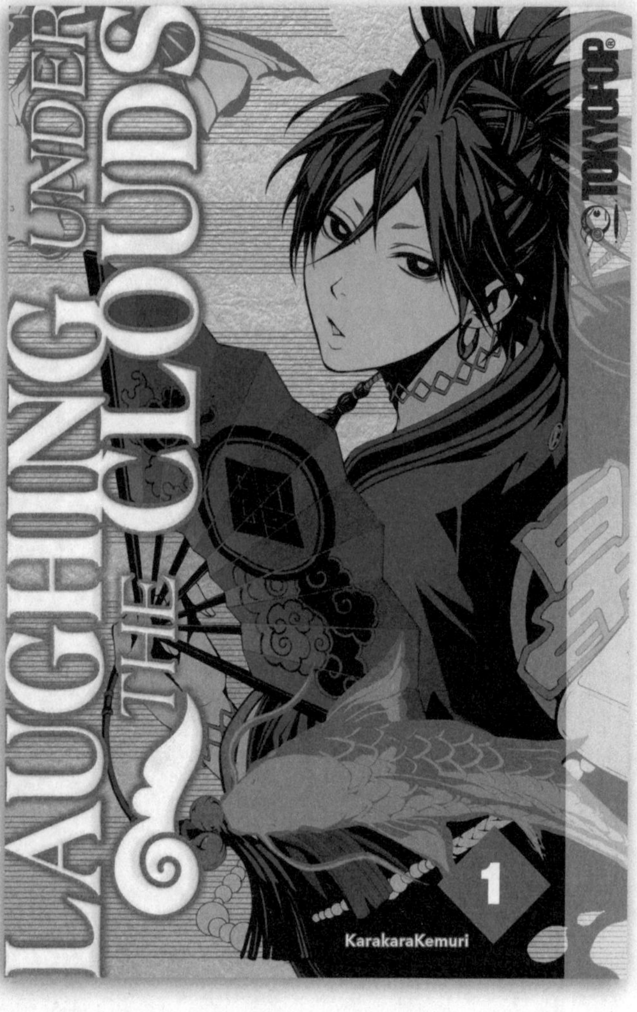
LAUGHING UNDER THE CLOUDS
TOKYOPOP
1
KarakaraKemuri

LAUGHING UNDER THE CLOUDS, VOLUME 1

KarakaraKemuri

FANTASY

Under the curse of Orochi, the great demon serpent reborn every 300 years, Japan has been shrouded in clouds for as long as anyone can remember... The era of the samurai is at an end, and carrying swords has been outlawed. To combat the rising crime rates, an inescapable prison was built in the middle of Lake Biwa. When brothers Tenka, Soramaru and Chutaro Kumo are hired to capture and transport offenders to their final lodgings in this prison, they unexpectedly find themselves faced with a greater destiny than any of them could have imagined.

TOKYOPOP

KONOHANA KITAN, VOLUME 1

Sakuya Amano

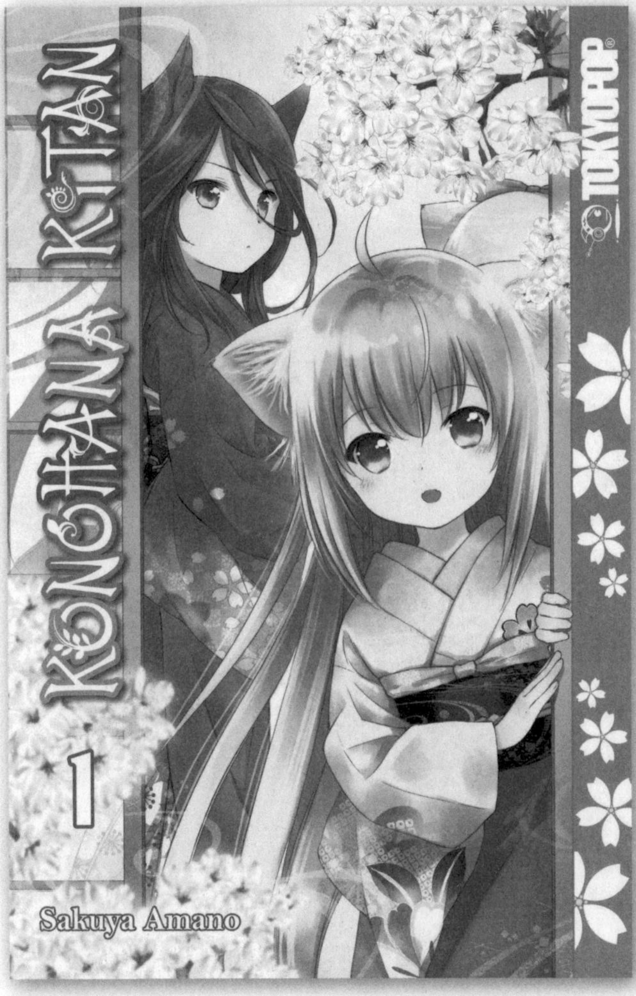
KONOHANA KITAN
1
Sakuya Amano
TOKYOPOP

FANTASY

Yuzu is a brand new employee at Konohanatei, the hot-springs inn that sits on the crossroads between worlds. A simple, clumsy but charmingly earnest girl, Yuzu must now figure out her new life working alongside all the other fox-spirits who run the inn under one cardinal rule - at Konohanatei, every guest is a god! Konohana Kitan follows Yuzu's day to day life working at the inn, meeting the other employees and ever-eclectic guests, and learning to appreciate the beauty of the world around her.

TOKYOPOP

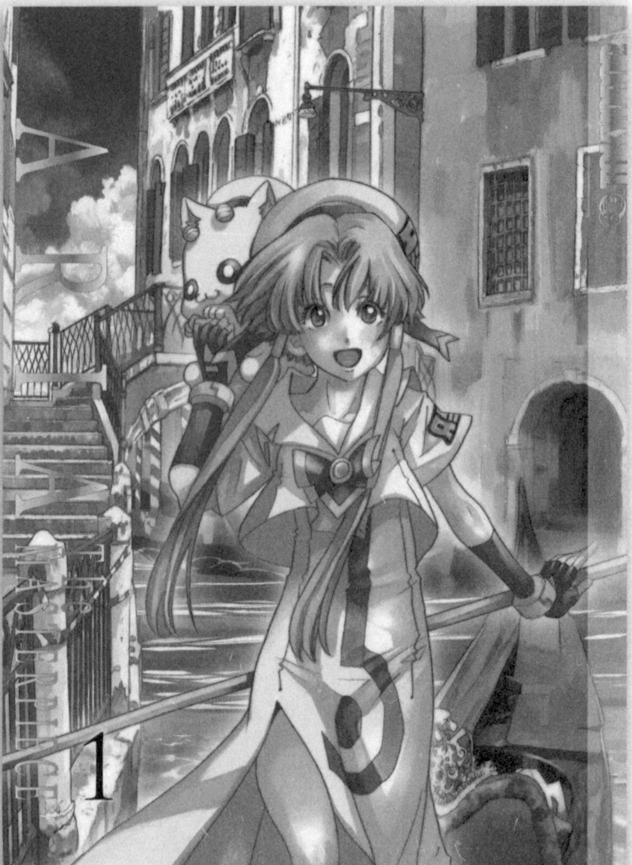
1
KOZUE AMANO

ARIA: THE MASTERPIECE, VOLUME 1

Kozue Amano

SCIENCE FICTION

On the planet Aqua, a world once known as Mars, Akari Mizunashi has just made her home in the town of Neo-Venezia, a futuristic imitation of the ancient city of Venice. In pursuit of her dream to become an Undine -- a gondolier who leads high-end tours around the city -- Akari joins as a trainee with the Aria Company, one of the three most prestigious water-guide companies in Neo-Venezia. There, she explores the beauty of the city and the world along with other trainees from Aria and rival companies, working hard for her dreams and making new friends along the way. Experience the world of Aqua like never before with Kozue Amano's gorgeously detailed illustrations and full-color spreads in this deluxe collector's edition!

TOKYOPOP

OCEAN OF SECRETS, VOLUME 1

Sophie-chan

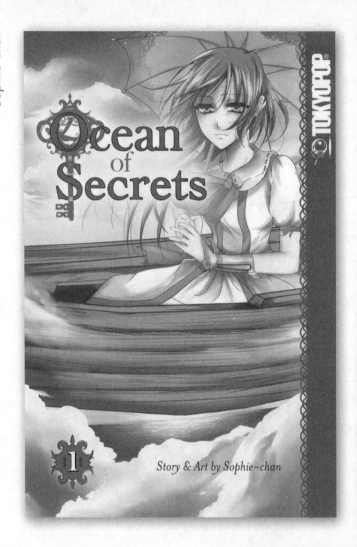

Ocean
of
Secrets

1

Story & Art by Sophie-chan

FANTASY

Lia, a 17-year old orphan living by the Atlantic is swept away by the ocean currents during a ruthless storm. She is then saved by Moria and Albert, a duo of illegal runaways on their magical ship! Her normal, mundane life suddenly becomes a supernatural adventure as she learns about the powers of their kind and their relations to the human world. But Lia soon discovers that there is a dark secret hidden in a mysterious kingdom. Join Lia as she unlocks the truth behind an Ocean of Secrets...

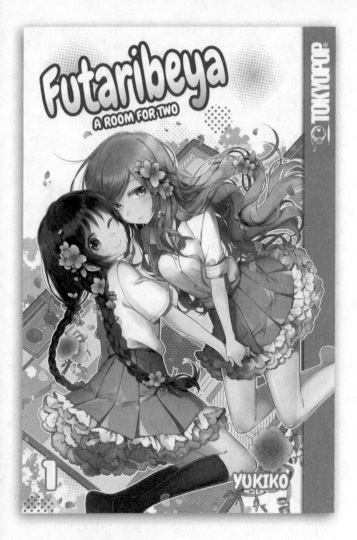

Yukiko

FUTARIBEYA: A ROOM FOR TWO, VOL. 1

♀LOVE-x-LOVE♀

As her exciting first year of high school begins, Sakurako Kawawa settles into her new lodgings. There, she meets her roommate — the stunningly beautiful Kasumi Yamabuki, who lives life at her own pace. From day one, responsible, level-headed Sakurako and lazy, easygoing Kasumi find themselves at odds with one another... But with their matching mugs and one bed to share, Sakurako and Kasumi's friendship is just beginning!

FUTARIBEYA: A ROOM FOR TWO, VOL 2

Yukiko

Futaribeya
A ROOM FOR TWO
TOKYOPOP
2
YUKIKO

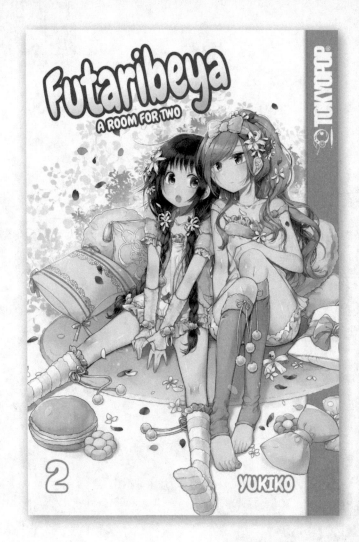

♀LOVE-x-LOVE♀

In terms of personality, Sakurako Kawawa couldn't be more at odds with her lackadaisical new roommate, Kasumi Yamabuki. But even though hardworking, friendly Sakurako might get top scores in class and do most of the cooking at home while Kasumi is constantly nodding off or snacking, these two roommates actually get along so well, you'll rarely see one without the other at her side. Whether they're just walking arm-in-arm to class, watching the cherry trees blossom, or sharing cotton candy at the summer festival, Sakurako and Kasumi are always having fun together!

TOKYOPOP

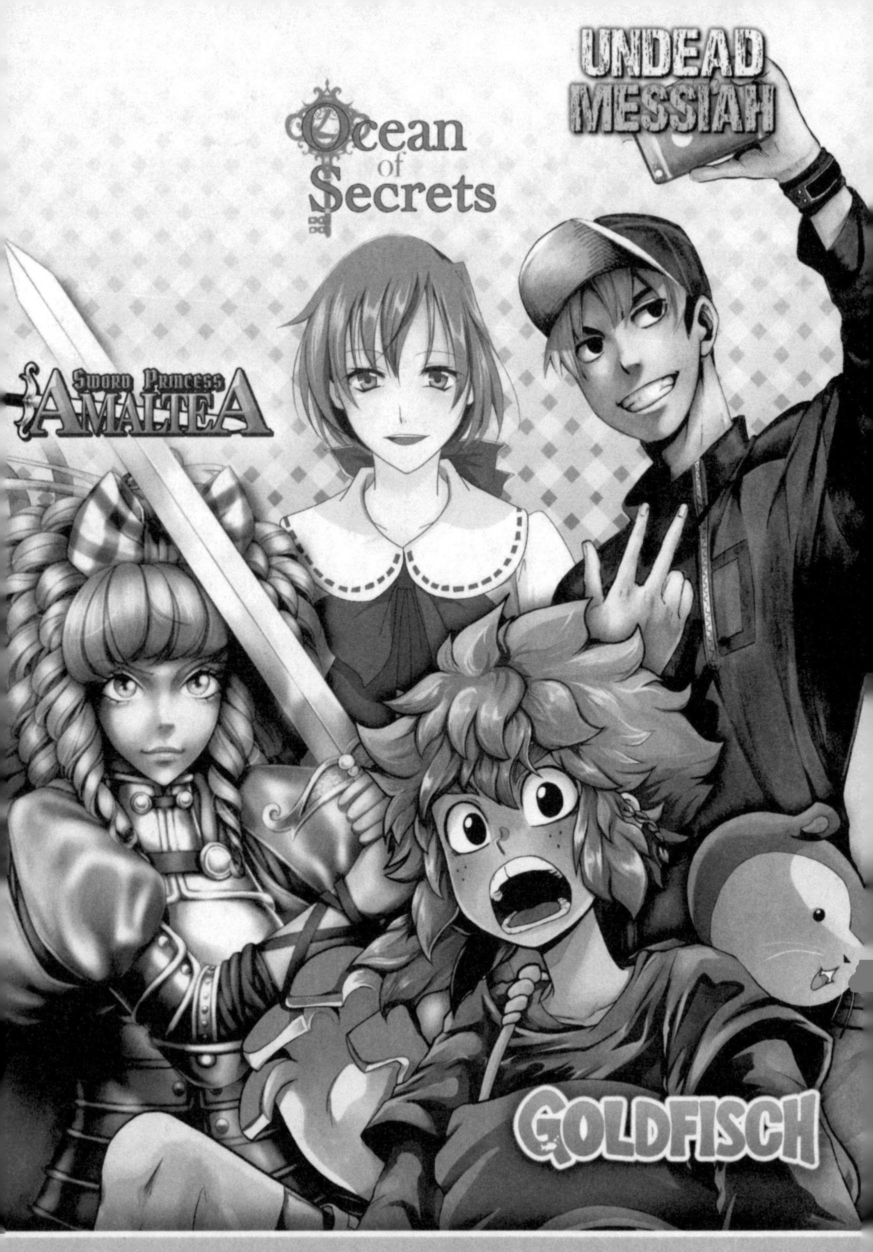
UNDEAD MESSIAH
Ocean of Secrets
SWORD PRINCESS AMALTEA
GOLDFISCH

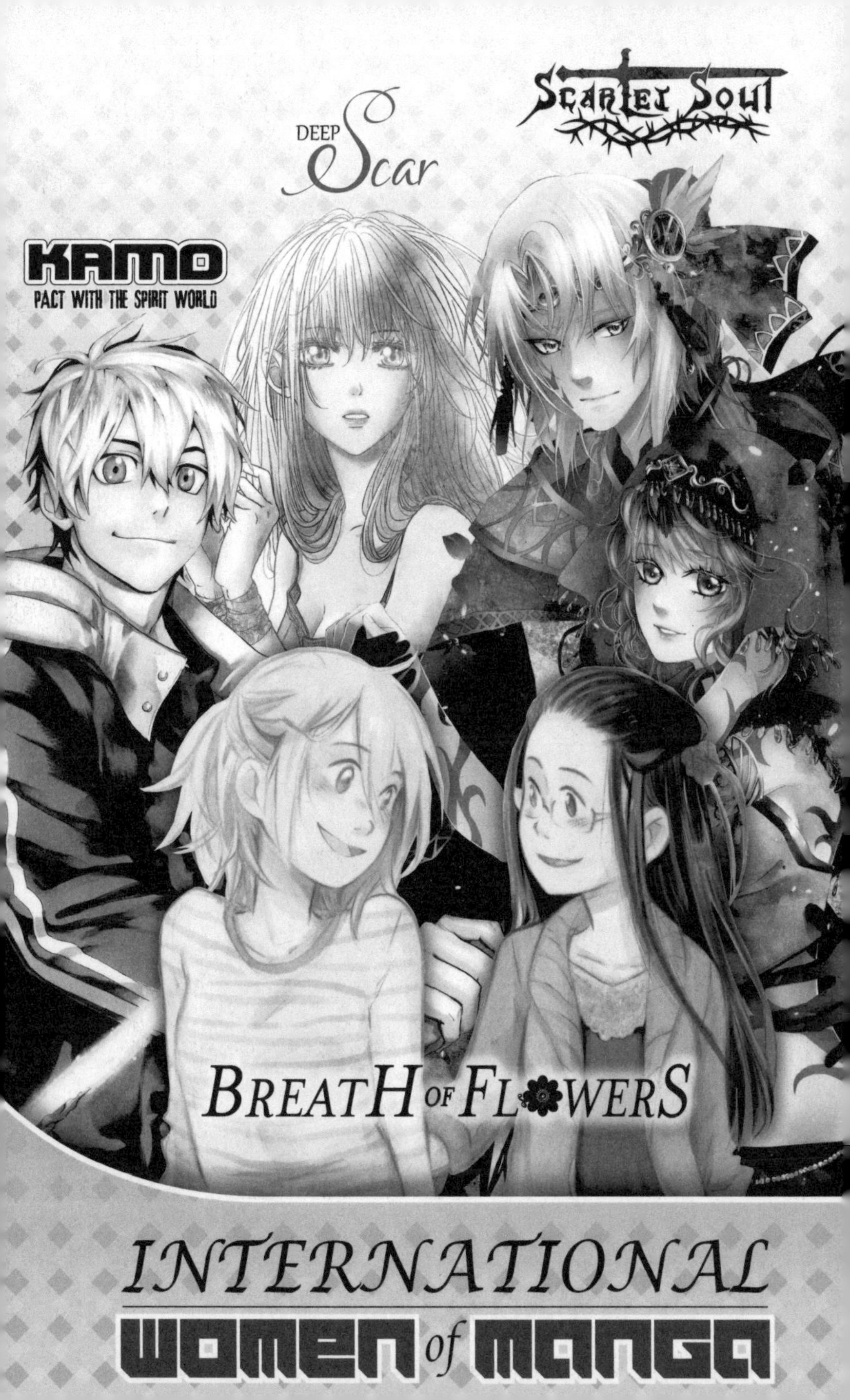
Scarlet Soul
DEEP Scar
KAMO
PACT WITH THE SPIRIT WORLD
BREATH OF FLOWERS
INTERNATIONAL
WOMEN of MANGA

Her Royal Highness Seems to Be Angry, Volume 1
Manga: Neko Yotsuba
Original Story: Kou Yatsuhashi
Character Design: Mito Nagashiro

Editor - Lena Atanassova
Marketing Associate - Kae Winters
Translator - Christine Dashiell
Copyeditor - M. Cara Carper
Designer - Sol DeLeo
Editorial Associate - Janae Young
Licensing Liaison - Arika Yanaka
Graphic Designer - Sol DeLeo
Retouching and Lettering - Vibrraant Publishing Studio
Editor-in-Chief & Publisher - Stu Levy

A  Manga

TOKYOPOP and 🐢 are trademarks or registered trademarks of TOKYOPOP Inc.

TOKYOPOP inc.
5200 W Century Blvd
Suite 705
Los Angeles, CA 90045 USA

E-mail: info@TOKYOPOP.com
Come visit us online at www.TOKYOPOP.com

f www.facebook.com/TOKYOPOP
🐦 www.twitter.com/TOKYOPOP
📌 www.pinterest.com/TOKYOPOP
📷 www.instagram.com/TOKYOPOP

ISBN: 978-1-4278-6791-9
First TOKYOPOP Printing: May 2021
10 9 8 7 6 5 4 3 2 1
Printed in CANADA

STOP

THIS IS THE BACK OF THE BOOK!

How do you read manga-style? It's simple! Let's practice -- just start in the top right panel and follow the numbers below!

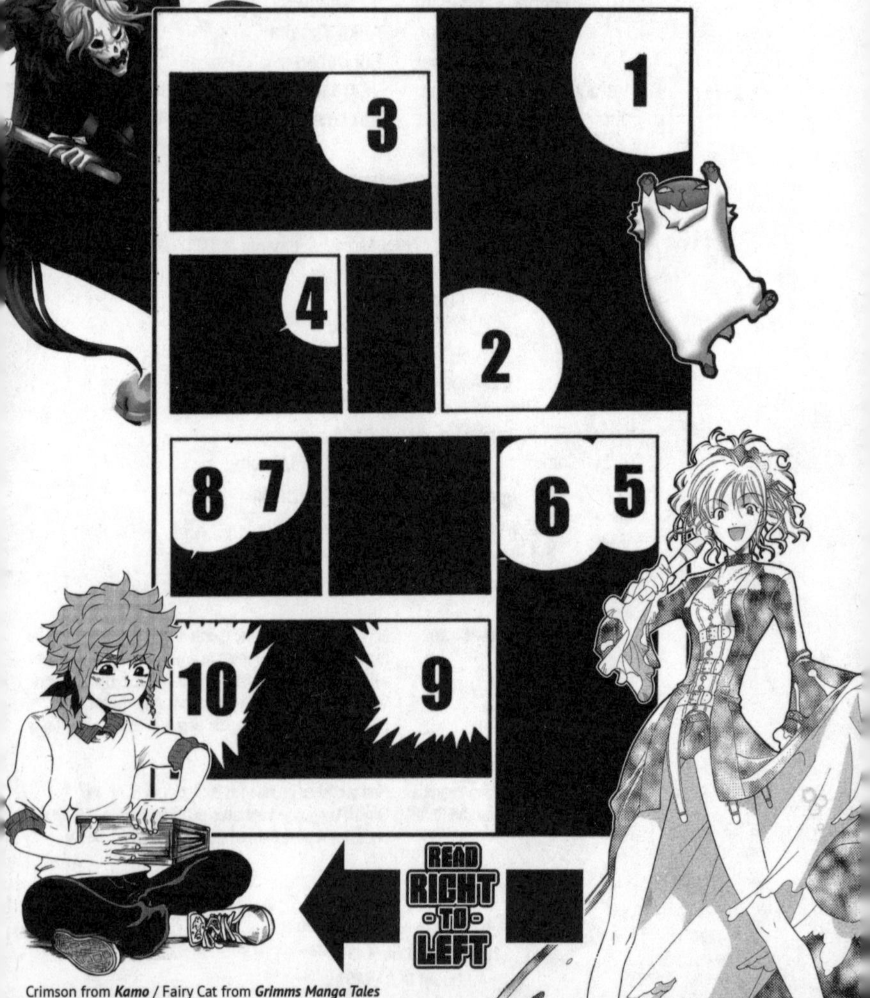
1
2
3
4
5
6
7
8
9
10
READ
RIGHT
-TO-
LEFT

Crimson from ***Kamo*** / Fairy Cat from ***Grimms Manga Tales***
Morrey from ***Goldfisch*** / Princess Ai from ***Princess Ai***